BURT FRANKLIN: RESEARCH & SOURCE WORKS SERIES 504
American Classics in History & Social Science 133

FRANCE IN THE
AMERICAN REVOLUTION

FRANCE IN THE
AMERICAN REVOLUTION

BY

JAMES BRECK PERKINS

BURT FRANKLIN
NEW YORK

Published by BURT FRANKLIN
235 East 44th St., New York, N.Y. 10017
Originally Published: 1911
Reprinted: 1970
Printed in the U.S.A.

S.B.N. 27257
Library of Congress Card Catalog No.: 78-122844
Burt Franklin: Research and Source Works Series 504
American Classics in History and Social Science 133

PREFACE

THIS book, the latest fruit of Mr. Perkins's long-continued devotion to studies in the history of France, was practically complete at the time of its author's death in March, 1910. In preparing the manuscript for the press Mrs. Perkins has been greatly assisted by Dr. John Franklin Jameson of the Carnegie Institution in Washington, who read the manuscript and made valuable suggestions; by Professor Charles Halstead Van Tyne of the University of Michigan, who has verified all the references and made other important suggestions; by Mr. George B. Ives of the Riverside Press, who has made the index; and by other gentlemen connected with that press, who have been most helpful in all stages of the publication of the work. To all these Mrs. Perkins desires to express thankful appreciation.

She finds great satisfaction in being able to give the book to the public substantially as Mr. Perkins left it. The work of final revision, which fell to her, has been done with that appreciation of the author's intention and with that understanding of his habits of thought and expression which no other editor could have brought to the task. To the wide circle of the author's personal and literary acquaintance, the editor has done great service with rare success.

RUSH RHEES.

THE UNIVERSITY OF ROCHESTER.

CONTENTS

INTRODUCTION

On Friday the 6th of February, 1778, plenipotentiaries met in Paris to sign a treaty for which there had been no precedent in history, and of which there has been no imitation since. Three of them represented a government that was independent only in its own estimation ; they were called Benjamin Franklin, Silas Deane, and Arthur Lee, and were delegates of the new-born " United States of North America"; the fourth represented the oldest monarchy in Europe, and was Conrad Gérard de Rayneval, destined to be later the first diplomat ever accredited to America.

Article II of the treaty provided that " the essential and direct end of the present defensive alliance is to maintain effectually the liberty, sovereignty and independence absolute and unlimited of the said United States." By other articles France pledged herself not to lay down her arms until this independence had been achieved, and, whatever be the delay, cost, or losses, to neither claim nor accept anything for the help thus provided. She even specifically consented that the harshest of the conditions of the 1763 treaty of peace with England be maintained : if conquests were made " in the northern part of America," the conquered land would be annexed to the United States, and not to the country which had settled Canada and possessed it until that peace.

A treaty of commerce had been signed on the same day, and in the same spirit, France reserving for herself no advantage but subscribing an agreement to which any nation, England included, would be welcome to be a party when it chose. France, wrote Franklin, has "taken no advantage of our present difficulties to exact terms which we would not willingly grant when established in prosperity and power." France, grumbled Mr. de Floridablanca, prime minister of Spain, when the treaties were read to him, "is acting like Don Quixote."

The treaties signed on the 6th of February, 1778, were certainly unprecedented. So much so that, in some minds, and for a long time (in that of John Adams, for example, to the last), doubts remained. Was that really possible? Were there no secret articles? No, there were none. Would France keep her word, and, if success was attained, reserve for herself nothing on a continent two thirds of which had been hers? She would, and did, keep her word. Even Washington had had his doubts and had wondered when, time and again, plans were submitted to him for an action in Canada, whether there was not in them "more than the disinterested zeal of allies" (Nov. 11, 1778). The event proved that such fears were groundless.

Extraordinary events have extraordinary causes. This was a unique one; how did it come about?

The answer will be found in the volume to which the finishing touches were being put by Mr. James Breck Perkins when death removed him from the place he so worthily filled among lovers of historical studies, and from Congress, where his sense, experience, and wisdom as chairman of the Committee on Foreign Affairs will long be remembered. There are in his book no better chapters than those in which he makes clear what took place and why.

Two principal motives explain what happened : a chief one which has usually been more or less neglected, and a secondary one to which historians usually give the foremost place.

The latter is the obvious one of France's animosity against her old enemy, Great Britain, the winner at the Plains of Abraham, the deviser of the harsh conditions of 1763. But because it is obvious and needs neither research nor even thought to be put forth, that has often been alleged as the chief, if not the unique, motive for what took place. Two distinct influences, in fact, acted together to bring about the alliance of France with the New Republic : that of statesmen and that of the nation. Among certain statesmen, as among many officers, the desire for reprisals was a potent factor, and the rebellion of the colonies was welcomed, chiefly because they rebelled against England. Among the French people at large it was quite otherwise : the rebellious colonies were popular, not especially because they wanted to throw off an English yoke, but because they wanted to throw off a yoke.

It must not be forgotten that the period of the War of Independence was not coincident with one of Anglophobia in France, but on the contrary with one of Anglomania. Everything English was admired, and, when possible, imitated : manners, literature, philosophy, sport, parliamentary institutions, and above all, writes one of the earliest French supporters of the colonists, Ségur, " the liberty, at once calm and lofty, enjoyed by the entire body of the citizens of Great Britain " ; Frenchmen " were crazy about the English institutions." It was the period when people would go to London in order to " learn how to become thinkers," and to learn also how the stiff rules of old should be discarded, whether the matter was of the laying out of a garden, of the government of empires, or the writing of a tragedy. The year of the Proclamation of Independence was also the one during which the complete works of Shakespeare, translated by Le Tourneur, took Paris by storm, and were published by subscription, the King and Queen heading the list. " All the youth of Paris is for Le Tourneur," wrote indignant Voltaire.

The anti-English sentiment existed indeed only within somewhat narrow limits. Even among military men that sentiment was not a universal one : examining the causes why so many young officers, and he himself among them, longed to play a part in the great struggle, Ségur enumerates the usual motives, such as a " desire of glory and of rank," the service due to the King and country, and concludes that, above all, they were impelled "by a yet more exalted principle, a sincere enthusiasm for the cause of American liberty." Of a desire to humble the old enemy not a word : people were rushing "to the field of battle," says he further, " in the name of philanthropy."

Liberty, philanthropy, natural rights, those were the magic words that were then stirring not only writers and thinkers, but the very masses in France. The day of unbending dogmatism and heavy yokes had passed ; privileges subsisted, but had scarcely any defenders left ; the aspirations were immense for a greater equality, more breathing space, simpler lives, more accessible knowledge, free discussion of common interests. Montesquieu, Rousseau, Voltaire, the encyclopedists, had said their say ; it had sunk deep into the nation's mind. Those who could read had read the books, the others had been talked to about them. The power of public opinion and of illiterate masses had wonderfully increased, more even perhaps than is shown in the present work. Peace had not yet been signed at Versailles when Necker published his epoch-making "Compte Rendu," enabling the whole nation to be judge of its own interests; peace had just been signed when he printed his "Administration des Finances de la France," of which, in spite of the opposition of his successors in office, eighty thousand copies were sold. The days indeed were not far off when the nation would show that it had ideas of its own, and would draw the famous *Cahiers* of 1789, some being compiled by mere peasants who offered excuses for their rough mountaineers' orthography.

Add to this that, while old ideas, old rules, the old Régime in its entirety, were losing ground, youthful enthusiasm and ardor pervaded the nation. Two years before American Independence was proclaimed, the correspondence of Grimm and Diderot tells us of the effect on the French public of "those general and ex- aggerated maxims that fire the enthusiasm of youths and would make them run to the world's end, and abandon father, mother, brother, to come to the as- sistance of an Esquimau or a Hottentot."

Now the time had come to run to the world's end and, like La Fayette, leave wife, child, and the pleas- ures of an easy life, for something greater indeed than the fate of any Hottentot. What was at stake was in fact what the French of the new generation held dear- est. All the reports that came concerning Americans showed them lovers of liberty, practisers of equality, accepting no privileges, tolerant of all creeds, leading honorable and simple lives, in their poetic solitudes.

Deane, Lee, and Franklin appear in Paris, and seem
" sages, contemporaries with Plato, or republicans of
the age of Cato and of Fabius " (Ségur). In the eyes
of Voltaire the insurgents are animated by the truest
philosophical principles, they fight for " reason and
liberty." The constitutions of the principal states are
translated into French a little later under the supervision of Franklin, and the admiration is unanimous
for those " charters of liberty." French officers leave
Versailles, the soldiers leave their villages and their
garrison towns : what they find on reaching America
fulfills, in most cases, their anticipation. They prove
friendly judges ; what they observed is thus described
by one of them : " Indigence and brutality were nowhere to be seen ; fertility, comfort and kindness were
everywhere to be found ; and every individual displayed the modest and tranquil pride of an independent man who feels that he has nothing above him
but the laws."

No wonder, when all this is considered, that French
public opinion was wrought up to the highest pitch
and that it played, as it did, a decisive part in the
grand drama. The animosity against England still
harbored by some statesmen and soldiers in this
period of Anglomania, would never have achieved the
momentous results that were at stake. The King hesitated, his ministers (Vergennes excepted) fell into
periodical doubts ; Necker, who held the purse-strings,
was a confirmed Anglophile ; official reports on America were not all as rose-colored as the private letters
of a La Fayette, a Ségur, or a Chastellux. But public
opinion never wavered. " During the five years that
the war continued," says Mr. Perkins, " the French
people remained constant in the cause." " On all sides,"

wrote that same good judge, Ségur, " public opinion urged a regal government to declare itself in favor of republican liberty, and even murmured at the irresolution and delay. The ministers gradually yielding to the torrent were, at the same time, alarmed at the prospect of a ruinous war."

Ruinous it was indeed, costing the French treasury seven hundred and seventy-two millions of dollars; [1] but public opinion remained faithful to the struggling states. The people groaned under the weight of taxation, but never grumbled at the expense for such a cause. Peace came, France kept her word; she did not try to recover any of her possessions on the American continent; she made a pro-American peace, not an anti-English one. Public opinion again was fully satisfied: what it wanted had been secured; there were no protests against the moderation shown towards the adversary; the joy was universal. Years after the war the same pro-American feelings which had apparently taken deep root still prevailed, as shown by the French National Assembly's adjourning at the news of the death of Franklin; the French army going into mourning at the death of Washington, and the glowing eulogies of the new republic still sent home by its French visitors. Talleyrand came to America in 1794, so as to become acquainted, he says, with " that great country whose history now begins." His impressions are most favorable to a people " that shall one day be a great people, the wisest and happiest on earth." He observes, it is true, in 1797, that the bulk of the trade goes to England, so that " Independence, far from having been hurtful, has proved, in many respects, helpful to that country." But he ob-

[1] See page 498.

serves this with perfect equanimity. "Americans,"
writes General Moreau, in 1806, from Philadelphia,
"are good people. . . . Their progress in trade and
navigation is truly wonderful. . . . One enjoys in their
country the most boundless liberty, and there is no
abuse. . . . Men who have lived under such a government will never allow themselves to be shackled
again."

On all this, the author of the present work has
much to say that should be remembered, and never,
perhaps, has the question of how and why what happened could take place, been so clearly put before the
American reader. The existence of an anti-English
feeling in certain French *milieus* is not denied and it
receives no less than its due in the first chapters. But
the other side of the question is then placed in such
full light that few readers will fail to agree with Mr.
Perkins's conclusion that "public opinion became, at
the last, the most potent factor in controlling the decision of the French government. . . . It was the
popular enthusiasm for American liberty which penetrated the council chamber and influenced the ministers in their decision, even if they failed to recognize
such a motive." [1]

Those views are the worthier of notice since Mr.
Perkins never allows himself to be led astray by enthusiasm or sentimentality. No excessive indulgence
marks his judgments on men or deeds, be they French
or American. This probity in his views is on a par
with the austerity of his style, an austerity which,
far from deadening, enhances, on the contrary, the
dramatic interest, and the romantic charm, not to say
the poetry of the events.

[1] Pages 205, 237.

Once more, under this trusty guide, the reader follows, scene by scene, the progress of the momentous
drama, with its alternatives of success and defeat,
fights by land and by sea, lucky or fruitless negotiations, fleets crossing and recrossing the ocean, cities
taken and lost, great New York impregnable with
its fortifications and its eleven thousand English and
Hessian regulars, the key, as it seemed, of a situation
that was in reality to be decided under the bastions
of a small borough along the Chesapeake. Before us
appear soldiers and sailors of fame : Wayne, Greene,
Rochambeau, d'Estaing, de Grasse, Paul Jones, La
Fayette, the grand image of Washington towering
above all the rest ; but room is found for many others
great and small, evoked before the reader in the clear
light of the author's lucid style : circumspect and
steady Vergennes, who favored the insurgents from
the first, and remained to the last " consistent and upright," Gérard and La Luzerne, my cool-headed predecessors, impetuous Beaumarchais, who has his statue
in Paris for that product of his brain, " Figaro," and
deserves a memorial in America too for that other product of his brain, " Hortalez and Co." The hard pil-
grimage is told us of American negotiators sent by an
optimistic congress " to various European courts, but
few of them were received," [1] and they secured, at best,
promise of friendship for the time when the danger
should be over. " The affairs of the colonies," wrote
Frederick II to one of his ministers, " are yet in too
great a crisis ; so long as their independence is not
more firmly established, all immediate commerce under
my flag seems to me too perilous and fraught with
too great inconveniences for me to run such risks."

[1] See page 221.

He thought however that the French would do well to run any risks, and, at the time when they had not yet taken sides, expressed himself as shocked at their " pusillanimity."

France and the States went their way, which led them to Yorktown and to one of the most honorable treaties of peace ever concluded : so honorable because it was so just and moderate.

In a sort of postscript Mr. Perkins carries the story down almost to our own days, recalling the difference of feeling toward America which, for well-known causes, existed in France, between the Imperial Government and the nation, at the time of the War of Secession. Once more on the eve of a transformation accompanied by terrible woes, the nation manifested how eagerly her wishes went to the maintenance of the then only great republic ; a popular subscription was opened (of two cents per head, so that the poorest might take part) for a medal to be struck in commemoration of the life and death of Lincoln, " honest man," as the inscription reads, " who abolished slavery, reestablished the Union, saved the Republic, without veiling the statue of Liberty."

In the midst of the conflicting judgments passed on the part played by France in the War of Independence, from that of Mr. de Floridablanca, who considered us quixotic, to those of Jay or Adams, who could never believe that we had no concealed plans, posterity will probably ratify the conclusions of Mr. Perkins's whole study, well condensed by him in the following admirable words : " The arguments on which statesmen based their action were not justified in the future. But the instincts of the French nation were right : they assisted a people to gain their free-

dom, they took part in one of the great crises of modern progress, they helped the world on its onward
march. . . . The reward is not to be found in more
vessels sailing laden with wares . . . but in the consciousness of the unselfish performance of good work,
of assistance rendered to the cause of freedom, and to
the improvement of man's lot on earth."

                              J. J. JUSSERAND.

WASHINGTON, *March*, 1911.

FRANCE IN THE
AMERICAN REVOLUTION

FRANCE IN THE
AMERICAN REVOLUTION

CHAPTER I

FRANCE AND THE NEW WORLD

WHETHER the American colonies would have succeeded in their struggle for independence if they had
not received aid in men and money from France, is
an interesting and not a simple question. A study of
the period impresses one with the difficulties under
which the colonists suffered, — difficulties which might
well have proved insurmountable, had the colonists
been left entirely to their own resources. Naturally we
assume that what did occur must have occurred, that
because the English did not succeed in reducing their
rebellious colonists to subjection, there was no possibility of their doing so. We can, indeed, be certain
that with the growth of population in this country, its
people, sooner or later, would have become independent of foreign rule; but it was entirely possible that
the struggle begun in 1775 should have ended in disaster, and the history and development of the United
States have been different.

The most important factor working for the colonists was the extraordinary incapacity manifested by
their opponents. Less than twenty years earlier, England had conducted a war against France, in which
her armies and navies had displayed skill, vigor, and
heroism to a degree exceeded in few great contests.

But the English government had sadly changed from the days in which Pitt was minister to those in which it was guided by North and controlled by George III. The Seven Years' War was one of the most glorious epochs in English history, the American Revolution was one of the most inglorious. A contest that had been precipitated by folly was conducted with stupidity; in seven years of fighting with their own colonists, not one English officer gained a first-class reputation; the movements of the English armies were sluggish, their generals were inefficient, golden opportunities were lost, great advantages were frittered away. Gérard, the French minister at Philadelphia, said with much truth: "If the English had shown themselves in America as we have seen them elsewhere, only too active, confident, and courageous, they would have met with little resistance." [1]

But if George III did not know how to select good generals or inspire vigorous action, he was resolute in his purpose. If he was not wise he was stubborn, and if the colonists did not encounter skillful opponents, they had to endure many years of fighting. A long contest our ancestors were in many respects unfitted to meet, and the reason for this unfitness was in their form of government. If the resources of three million people, fairly prosperous, intelligent, and courageous, could have been properly utilized, it would have been impossible for England to reduce them to subjection, though Chatham had commanded her councils, Marlborough her armies, and Nelson her fleets. But while a body with the limited powers of the Continental Con-

[1] Gérard to Vergennes; Doniol, iii, 319. Most of the citations from the French official correspondence are taken from the collection in Doniol's invaluable work, *La Participation de la France à l'Établissement des États Unis d'Amérique*, cited as "Doniol."

gress might suffice during a brief season of patriotic enthusiasm, enthusiasm will not take the place of an effective government. The character of the Congress deteriorated, and the helplessness into which that body was plunged rendered a seat in it unattractive to able men. Having no power to raise supplies or compel the formation of an army, it was at the mercy of the several states, and to expect vigorous action from thirteen different governments, was to show small knowledge of human nature. If the French King had not interfered, wrote his minister, "there is every reason to believe that the employment of the means of resistance would not have corresponded to the desire to maintain independence." This judgment may have been wrong, but as the war progressed the difficulties in raising, fitting, and equipping soldiers grew steadily greater, and a strong desire to be independent would not have secured independence if there had been no armies to fight for it.

The inherent weakness of the government hardly threatened greater danger to the patriot cause than the evils resulting from economic mistakes. If the blood circulating in the veins is corrupted, there can be no health in the body; when the financial system of the country was hopelessly diseased, the existence of the Republic was threatened. The issue of an irredeemable currency proved more dangerous to our country's liberties than the invasion of Burgoyne or the treason of Arnold. The land possessed resources, and there were plenty of men patriotic enough to be willing to use them; but in the financial confusion that prevailed when a continental bill for ten dollars was worth only ten cents, when a pair of boots cost one hundred dollars, and butter and sugar sold for three dollars a pound, when four months' pay of a private would not purchase a bushel of wheat and the pay of a colonel would not buy oats enough for his horse, when a wagon-load of money, as Washington wrote, would hardly purchase a wagon-load of provisions, it is not strange that the soldiers of Valley Forge walked barefooted in the snow, and the regiments of New Jersey and Pennsylvania deserted the colors under which they were starving.[1]

A currency that had no value and a government that had no head were the gravest perils to the success of the American Revolution. How serious they were may be judged from the writings of the most sagacious of American patriots, and the one who, from his position as commander-in-chief, had the fullest knowledge of the dangers of the situation. "Our affairs," Washington wrote in 1778, "are in a more distressed, ruinous, and deplorable condition than they have been since the commencement of the war . . . the common interests of America are mouldering and sinking into irretrievable ruin if a remedy is not soon applied."[2]

And a few months later, he wrote again: "The rapid decay of our currency, the extinction of public spirit, the increasing rapacity of the times, the want of harmony in our council, the declining zeal of the people, the discontents and distresses of the officers of the army, and, I may add, the prevailing security and insensibility to danger are symptoms, in my eye, of a most alarming nature. If the enemy have it in their power to press us hard this campaign, I know not what may be the consequence. Our army as it

[1] Hatch, *Administration of the American Revolutionary Army*, chap. 7.
[2] *Writings of Washington*, Sparks's edition, vi, 151.

now stands is but little more than the skeleton of an army." [1]

" I have never yet seen the time," he writes again in 1779, " in which our affairs, in my opinion, were at so low an ebb as at the present." [2]

Repeatedly in the long years of weakness and distress, Washington declared that unless aid came from France, the army would dissolve and resistance cease. "Unless a capital change takes place soon," he writes in 1781, " it will be impossible for me to maintain our posts and keep the army from dispersing." [3] With melancholy iteration came the statements of the difficulties in which the great patriot was involved, with a scanty army, that was often on the verge of dissolution, usually unpaid and sometimes unfed, with requests for recruits meeting a feeble response, and with a disordered currency, rendering the pay promised the men almost worthless, even if the promise had been kept.

Nor can we disregard the fact that a considerable portion of the people, a minority probably, but a minority prosperous and influential, had little sympathy with separation from the mother country, and that even among the " patriots " there could be no strong feeling for the newly created Republic. Their affections were for the states to which they belonged ; there was no united country for whose benefits they were grateful, to whose memories they clung, and of whose glories they were proud. A strong desire to be rid of the tyranny of George III was not an impulse so powerful as patriotic zeal for a beloved fatherland.

[1] *Writings of Washington*, Ford's edition, vii, 451, 452.
[2] *Writings of Washington*, Sparks's edition, vi, 252 (note).
[3] *Ibid.*, viii, 38, 39.

In our admiration for the great men of the Revolution, we are apt to overestimate the vigor of resistance
shown by the people of the thirteen colonies as a
whole. The history of the period is by no means one
of united zeal, or of strenuous self-sacrifice for the
common cause. It was natural that the French should
complain of allies whom they found less zealous than
they hoped, but their criticisms cannot be wholly disregarded. " I am beginning to have a poor opinion of
their firmness," Vergennes wrote of his new allies to
the French minister at Madrid, ". . . their Republic,
unless they correct its faults, . . . will never be more
than a feeble body capable of little activity. . . . I must
own that I have little confidence in the energy of the
United States." [1]

The people of the United States have displayed
energy, both in peace and war, to a degree never ex-
celled, but they have been formed and developed under
a more benign government than that the weakness
of which Washington as well as Vergennes deplored.
Prosperity not only brings happiness, but it develops
virtues. The unequalled readiness with which our
people in a later day responded to calls for the public
need, while largely due to the influence of a wisely
framed government, was in part the result of long
years of increasing wealth and well-being.

The French minister at Philadelphia was an intelligent, and not an unfriendly, observer of the people
among whom he was thrown ; and he owed to his superiors the duty of describing the condition of American affairs with accuracy. " Personal disinterestedness
and pecuniary probity," he writes, " do not illustrate
the birth of the American Republic. All the agents

[1] Vergennes to Montmorin, Nov. 27, 1778; Doniol, iii, 581.

have obtained exorbitant gains for their manufactures.
. . . The spirit of mercantile cupidity forms, perhaps,
one of the distinctive characteristics of the Americans,
especially those in the north, and doubtless this will
influence the future destinies of the Republic." [1]

Such criticisms might be disregarded as coming from
foreigners prone to judge harshly the conduct of another nation. To the unfavorable judgment of Gérard
we might oppose the fervent praise of La Fayette. If
the one reflected the ardent confidence of amiable
youth, the other savored of the suspicious apprehension
of cynical maturity. But Washington's opinions of the
situation were little more favorable than those of foreign observers. " Speculation," he wrote, " Peculation,
Engrossing, forestalling, with all their concomitants,
afford too many melancholy proofs of the decay of
public virtue." [2] Similar charges could be made in our
civil war, and perhaps in all wars of all nations, but
there is nothing to show that disinterestedness was
stronger in 1776 than in 1861, and much to show that
it was rarer.

There was less danger from gross cases of dishonesty than from the feeble response made to demands for money and troops. With much trouble
some troops were obtained ; and if these had been
properly fed and cared for, the supply of men might
have been sufficient; but without French aid it is hard
to see how they could have been furnished with guns
or clothing, with meat or bread. The length of the
contest increased the perils of the patriot cause. When
France made her treaty of alliance, the war had already lasted three years and the end was not in sight.

[1] Gérard to Vergennes, Aug. 12, 1778 ; Doniol, iii, 319.
[2] *Writings of Washington*, Ford's ed., vii, 388.

Hostilities were continued for four years more; weariness of the conflict was widespread when the alliance with France was made; it grew stronger each year that the conflict endured. Four years of warfare was a terrible tax upon a nation as rich and strong as our own in 1861; the burden of a much longer struggle upon a much poorer people might well have exhausted both their means and their zeal for resistance.

The hardships of Valley Forge might be endured by patriotic men for a winter, but soldiers cannot be kept together for years without food, or clothes, or money. Even with French aid Washington with difficulty maintained a small army of poorly equipped men; without that aid it is hard to see how he could have kept an army in the field at all. Such were the elements of weakness among the colonists, which might have proved fatal to success if they had received no assistance from abroad.

It is true that few of the victories won by the Americans were due to the direct assistance of the French army, or the French fleet. The capture of Yorktown was the only action of importance in which French and American soldiers fought side by side with success. The fleet which d'Estaing brought over in 1778 undertook no joint enterprise, save a futile movement against Newport, and from a military standpoint it was wholly unproductive. In the following year d'Estaing engaged in the siege of Savannah, but that resulted in a disastrous repulse. Not until 1781, the last year of actual warfare, did French and American armies again act together, but by their joint action the war was then brought to an end. The outcome of the American Revolution without French aid may be problematical, but it is certain that without that aid, the army under Cornwallis could not have been captured. The siege of Yorktown could not have been attempted without the coöperation of a fleet, and the Americans had no fleet; while of the forces which took part in the operations on land, one half were French.

It is hard, therefore, to see how the colonists, unaided, could have brought the struggle to a successful end, unless troops, money, and supplies had been furnished by the thirteen colonies on a far more liberal scale than was done during the last five years of the war. The colonies might indeed have united in a great and sufficient effort, but they might also have decided to accept some sort of decent terms from the mother country at the end of long years of exhausting warfare. At all events, at a time when our early history is studied from many standpoints, the part taken by France in the American Revolution, the aid she gave us, and its influence on the result of the contest, furnish profitable themes for investigation.

It is interesting to consider the effects of French assistance on the fortunes of the American Revolution. It is equally interesting to consider the effects of the action of the French government upon the French people themselves. How far did the increasing embarrassment of the French treasury, resulting from the cost of that war, hasten a financial crisis? Would the French Revolution have begun in 1789 had it not been for the impression produced on French thought by the successful revolution in America? Certainly the old régime could not have lasted much longer, but might not its overthrow have been delayed and the catastrophe have assumed a different shape?

The situation of our own country at the beginning

of our Revolution, and the causes which led to that event, are familiar to us all, but the social and political conditions in France which resulted in her intervention naturally are much less known. At first glance it might have seemed unlikely that France should lend her assistance to colonists across the Atlantic, who were seeking to shake off the home authority and establish a republic to be governed by its own citizens. Why should a Bourbon monarchy throw in its lot with a people in revolt against their King, who proclaimed the equal rights of men and denounced the evils of monarchical rule ? France had still many foreign possessions that were kept in close subjection by the home government. In France the right of self-rule was strictly denied. French statesmen had for centuries declared that on the absolute and untrammelled authority of the monarch rested the welfare and happiness of the nation. It seemed unlikely that the successor of Louis XIV, the grandson of Louis XV, would take up arms in behalf of the principles of the Declaration of Independence.

There were other reasons that might well have kept France from involving herself in a new war, of which the cost would be certain, and the results uncertain. The Seven Years' War had come to an end only twelve years before. It had been one of the most disastrous contests in French history, an almost unbroken chapter of defeat and disgrace. With disordered finances, with discontent among the people, with an increasing readiness to criticize the government and to question institutions that had once been regarded as sacred as Holy Writ, a judicious statesman might well have felt that a long period of peace, of financial recuperation, of internal improvement, would be best for the true interests of France. Such was the policy advocated by Turgot, the most sagacious French statesman of his generation, but it was advocated in vain.

In fact, the disasters of the Seven Years' War had created a desire in the French mind for a new war, in which old defeats might be avenged and old disgraces wiped out. The Treaty of Paris, in 1763, not only stripped France of a large part of her foreign possessions, but contained provisions that were specially ignominious. It ceded to England Canada and all the French possessions in North America except those transferred to Spain, various islands in the West Indies, and practically all of the great empire in India that Dupleix had sought to secure for France, while the conditions in reference to Dunkirk, which had been extorted from Louis XIV at the nadir of his fortunes, were reimposed. By the Treaty of Utrecht in 1713, the King had been obliged to agree that the fortifications of the French city of Dunkirk, which had been erected at great cost to protect that important harbor, should be demolished. It is rare that any nation will submit to the dictation of another power as to the use of its own territory; such terms might be imposed by Russia on Poland, but not, it would be thought, by England upon France.

Yet Louis XIV promised to destroy the fortifications of the city, to fill up the port, to ruin the locks and never to reëstablish them. When a new war broke out, naturally these agreements were no longer regarded. But in the Treaty of Paris, the French King again agreed that the fortifications of Dunkirk should be destroyed; and, as an aggravation of ignominy, the French consented that an English commissioner might reside in the city to see that they were not rebuilt.

It is hard to understand the wisdom of this provision ; it was a constant irritation to the French, it was of no great advantage to the English. The French were a proud people, and for many centuries their military record had been marked by much glory and little shame. The defeat of the Seven Years' War left a consciousness of disgrace in every patriotic Frenchman, and a strong desire for revenge. And the feeling was more bitter towards England than towards Prussia. Frederick had been fighting for his own existence, defending himself against enemies who proposed to dismember his kingdom. He had succeeded in keeping it intact, but he added nothing to it. No French territory had been wrested away by Prussia, no indemnity had been extorted as a punishment for defeat. But England had interfered in the contest, not to save herself, but to check the power of France. She had profited enormously from her success ; she had wrested from the French possessions far greater than France herself, and from them she might anticipate a vast increase in wealth and power. While there was not the yearning to recover these foreign possessions that the French afterward felt for the recovery of Alsace and Lorraine, the desire for revenge upon perfidious and triumphant Albion was quite as strong as the desire for revenge upon Prussia after the War of 1870.

At the same time the animosity felt against England was not accompanied by any love for England's colonists. The position of France, as the owner of vast territories in North America, had brought her into frequent conflict with the English-speaking settlers in that country. When war broke out between England

and France, the English colonies had taken an active
part with the mother country. And even when there
was peace between the home governments, there had
been frequent collisions between the representatives of
the two nations in North America. The jealousy and
the active opposition of the English-speaking colonies had done much to check French development
in the New World, and it was natural that French
statesmen should look upon our ancestors as an aggres-
sive, domineering, and disagreeable population. Certainly it was largely due to their action that the influence of France in North America, at the beginning
of the American Revolution, was far removed from
that position of ascendancy for which sagacious and
intrepid Frenchmen had hoped.

It once seemed possible that civilization in North
America might be as much French as English: the
territories which, nominally at least, were under the
control of France far exceeded those held by the English colonists in extent, and were not inferior to them
in fertility. At the beginning of the seventeenth century one might well anticipate that France would take
a leading part in the development of the New World.
French mariners had been among the early explorers
of North America. Only a few years after the landing
of Columbus in the West Indies, French fishing-boats
were found in large numbers off the coast of Newfoundland. The hardy mariners of Normandy and
Brittany sailed each year across the Atlantic in search
of fish, as their descendants do to this day.

In 1635 the settlement of Canada was begun by
Jacques Cartier, and that country became a French
province. French immigration was small, and the home
government did little to encourage the growth of a

prosperous colony; but French missionaries and explorers secured for their country claims of ownership over vast territories. The explorations of Joliet and La Salle carried the French lilies over the western prairies and the Valley of the Mississippi. La Salle established a station by the banks of the Illinois, and started an ill-fated settlement in Texas. It must be said that, save in Canada, there were no French colonies which could be compared with the English settlements along the Atlantic, and Canada itself, with its natural progress checked by the unwholesome restraint of the home government, ill-ruled, priest-ridden, sparsely populated, bore little resemblance to the prosperous communities of Massachusetts and Pennsylvania.

Yet French exploration spread over great territories. In the north and along the Mississippi Valley, scattered settlements, generally unprosperous, sometimes destroyed by plague, by famine, or by Indians, preserved the claim of French sovereignty over regions which now contain twenty great and populous states.

By the Treaty of Utrecht the Hudson Bay Territory, Newfoundland, and Acadia were ceded to England. But while these vast though barren territories were lost, France strengthened her claim over a great part of the fertile lands of North America. In the early part of the eighteenth century, the speculations of Law and the enterprises of the Mississippi Company gave a fresh impetus to French colonization. New Orleans was founded. The Company asserted its authority, not only over the Valley of the Mississippi, but over all North America west of the Alleghanies, except in the extreme north, and in the ill-defined territory over which the Spanish claimed a nominal sovereignty.

The efforts at colonization that were made under the auspices of Law's Company were often theatrical; some of them, it may be feared, were intended to influence the stock market rather than furnish Pilgrim Fathers to distant provinces. On one day one hundred and eighty girls and as many youths were married at Saint-Martin des Champs and embarked for Louisiana. Boats laden with women were sent out, to supply spouses for the unmarried settlers already there. They were eagerly sought for; but unfortunately the past lives of most had not fitted them to be wives of hardy pioneers, and the results of governmental matrimony, like those of many other governmental enterprises, were unsatisfactory. One body of adventurers penetrated into Arkansas in search of some fabled rocks of emerald. They did not find the emeralds and their settlement came to naught; but a colony of Germans sent over by Law, who were content to seek their fortunes in market-gardening near New Orleans, remained and prospered.

Some progress was thus made in strengthening the claims of France upon the Valley of the Mississippi, but a great and fertile territory could not be permanently held by a few forts over which floated the fleur-de-lis, or a few settlements in which French was spoken. The rich fields of the Valley of the Mississippi were in many respects more attractive for colonization than the fringe along the Atlantic in which the English-speaking colonists were found. The soil was more fertile, and the climate more agreeable; they were farther removed from the seashore, but this disadvantage was to some extent compensated by the proximity of the Great Lakes and by the great river flowing through to the Gulf. These possessions would surely attract the rising tide of English colonization, and this could be checked only by French settlement of sufficient dimensions to turn a nominal sovereignty into an actual occupation.

The failure of French colonization is often charged to defects in French character; it might more properly be attributed to mistaken theories in French government. English colonists were sometimes driven from the home country by persecution; but if they suffered injustice from the government at home, in their exile they received from it the greatest blessing it could bestow. To a large extent they were let alone and left to make their fortunes as best they could.

But a paternal government would not leave the French settler alone, though he had abandoned the banks of the Seine and the Loire for the shores of the St. Lawrence and the Saguenay. France sought to develop her foreign empire by granting monopolies and bounties, by every means except allowing the colonists to work out their own salvation. A little before the beginning of our Revolution it was figured that fifty-five great commercial companies, patronized by the French government and organized to trade in her foreign possessions, had come to ruin. They not only ruined themselves, but they deprived the settler of a fair chance to improve his lot; he was harassed by privileges and restrictions and monopolies in Canada and Louisiana as much as he would have been in Paris or Normandy. As a result few emigrated.

The French remained at home, not because they were necessarily averse to emigration, but because in the foreign possessions of their own country they saw small opportunity to better their condition. If the French government had furnished facilities for emigration, if it had encouraged its citizens in seeking new homes under the French flag, if it had even been content to let alone those who made the effort, the record of French colonization of North America would have been more creditable and more important. But as it was, the peasant of the province and the artisan of the city saw little reason for exposing themselves to the hardships of a new country, where they probably would fare no better than they did at home. As a consequence little attention was given to the question of American colonization by the French people, and still less by the French government.

There was one great opportunity for the development of French colonization, which was lost not so much by the inertness as by the bigotry of the home government. When the Revocation of the Edict of Nantes compelled large bodies of industrious Frenchmen to leave their own country, a considerable proportion of them, in all probability, would have preferred life in a French possession to life in a foreign land. Even though driven from the fatherland, they might still have lived under their own flag and listened to the speech of their own people. The French Huguenots would have made as hardy pioneers, they were as well fitted to be the founders of a new state, as the English Puritans, but this possibility was checked by the bigotry of Louis XIV and his successors. Neither the snows of Canada nor the prairies of the west could be profaned by the presence of heretics. The French government preferred that its American possessions should be occupied by Indians and wild beasts rather than by Huguenots.

Such were the conditions at the beginning of the Seven Years' War. That contest settled the question whether England or France should become the great colonial power of the world. Both in the east and in the west, France was forced to abandon her dreams of colonial empire. In India nothing remained to her but a few unimportant trading stations. Canada was ceded to England, the province of Louisiana, with its vague claims of empire in the west and southwest, was transferred to Spain as a consolation for her losses. The upper Mississippi was now regarded as a field for colonization by English colonists.

Yet the conquest of Canada by England prepared the way for the loss of her other American colonies. The colonists had needed her assistance against the dreaded power of France, and the constant peril of interference or invasion from the French in Canada. When this danger was removed, the usefulness of the mother country was much diminished, and the annoyance caused by injudicious restraints was no longer lessened by the feeling that a suzerainty which was often a burden was sometimes a blessing. Choiseul, with the sagacity that in him was strangely mingled with frivolity and poor judgment, early discerned this danger to England, and watched eagerly the growth of discontent among the colonists towards the home government, of whose aid they no longer had need.

CHAPTER II

THE terms of the Treaty of Paris were galling to French pride, and it was certain that French statesmen would seek revenge whenever there was reason to suppose that France had her old enemy at a disadvantage. There was no strong desire to win back the lost possessions in North America, especially in Canada. The Canadian colony had often been a thorn in the flesh, and the possible value of the great possessions held by France in America was not generally realized. Most persons regarded the West India Islands as worth more than the valleys of the St. Lawrence and the Mississippi. Voltaire had written of the acres of snow, in contending for which the government wasted more money than all Canada was worth; and he expressed the views of many Frenchmen.

But if there was no desire to recover Canada, there was a strong wish to humiliate England, and it was thought that the loss of her American colonies would be a ruinous blow to her prosperity. The gift of political prophecy is possessed by few. All then believed that the advantage of colonies to the home country consisted in holding a monopoly of colonial trade, and when this was lost, the commercial interests of the metropolis would necessarily suffer. No one foresaw that free trade with the new Republic would be better for England than forced trade with the colonists, or that the United States would add vastly more to English wealth than her American colonies had ever done. French statesmen, whose economic views were quite as antique as those of British merchants, felt a confident hope that American independence would insure England's decline, and they were eager for an opportunity to do England harm.

The Treaty of Paris was signed in 1763, and it is not surprising to find that in the following year the secret advisers of Louis XV were preparing plans for an invasion of England. These schemes were indeed of little importance. Designed by men of small judgment, approved by a king who regarded such intrigues as a relief from the ennui under which he suffered, they had no result except to furnish an unscrupulous adventurer with a pretext for extorting money from the French treasury, and to afford Beaumarchais employment which put him in the way of future dealings with America.

In 1758 the Duc de Choiseul became chief minister of France, and for twelve years he held that position with an influence such as had been exercised by no minister since Fleury. The obscure plots of the confidants of Louis XV in due time came to Choiseul's knowledge. These transactions throw a curious light on the French monarchy, when the power of the royal office was exercised by an infirm incumbent. Nominally, the king was supreme ; he could decide his own policy, select his own agents, and control his own councils. The theory had not been far from the reality when Louis XIV was king, except as the monarch was unconsciously guided by those skillful enough to make him believe that when he adopted their views he was announcing his own. But Louis XV left to his ministers the actual decision of questions of importance, and contented himself with obscure intrigues, carried on without the knowledge of his responsible advisers.

Such had been these schemes for a new war with England, and the King was now in terror lest his part in them should be known by his own chief minister. He was as unwilling to face Choiseul with a statement of what he had been doing as a school-boy is to acknowledge to his teacher the occupation of a truant afternoon. Choiseul soon discovered as much as he could wisely learn; he was too judicious a courtier to subject his master to open shame, and he knew that Louis was so alarmed by the prospect of exposure that he would willingly abandon his plans and sacrifice his confederates. But if Choiseul was unwilling that such schemes should be carried on by political opponents, he was eager for the day to arrive when plans of revenge against England could be put into execution, and in the mean time he occupied himself in preparing France for the contest.

The poor organization, the bad discipline, the scandalous abuses of the French army had much to do with the long list of defeats during the Seven Years' War. When Louvois was war minister, the armies of Louis XIV were the best in Europe, and French soldiers went forth to almost uninterrupted victory. Under Louis XV the soldiers were still brave; but inefficient generals, bad rations, and insufficient equipment involved the army in almost uniform defeat. The navy was no better, and when the English met the French on the sea, they were victorious as a matter of course.

Choiseul undertook a thorough reorganization of the army and of the navy. To improving the condition

of the navy he gave special attention; in ten years
its nominal strength was doubled and its efficiency
was probably increased four-fold. At the close of the
Seven Years' War the French navy consisted of forty-
four ships of the line and ten frigates, mostly in poor
condition.[1] In 1771 there were sixty-four men-of-war
and forty-five frigates, all in good condition.[2] France
was ready to meet England on the seas with some
chance of success.

It was important to strengthen the army and navy,
but it was still more important to foster the nation's
commerce, and increase the nation's wealth. Many
things assisted in bringing about this result, and the
minister was entitled to some of the credit. Methods
of taxation still remained bad, but there was some relaxation in laws which had done much to check the
nation's growth. New ports were opened to commerce,
the monopoly possessed by the East India Company
was abolished, trade with the West India colonies
greatly increased, restrictions on the movement of
grain from province to province and on its exporta-
tion from the country were relaxed, and agriculture
profited greatly. The doctrines of the physiocrats bore
fruit. The ancient laws, by which manufactures were
regulated and restricted, were in part repealed : a
woman could wear a cotton dress without being sent
to the pillory ; a merchant could make goods to suit
his customers without being put in jail. The business
of the country increased rapidly. Though the government was nearly bankrupt and the treasury was always
in distress, commerce flourished and the growth of
wealth in the community was apparent. In 1775,
France was much richer than when the Seven Years'

[1] Lavisse, *Histoire de France*, viii[2], 375.   [2] *Ibid.*

War ended : she had a better army, a stronger navy, a less prodigal king, and more sagacious ministers.

While Choiseul was endeavoring to prepare his country for a new war, he observed with watchful eye the possibilities of trouble in store for England. He was one of the first to suggest that the overthrow of French dominion in America would pave the way for a revolt of the English colonies. Naturally he viewed such a possibility with satisfaction, and it furnished him some consolation for the losses which France suffered as a result of the Seven Years' War. Any signs of discontent with English rule were closely watched, and the French minister did not have long to wait for their manifestation. Few statesmen on the continent paid any attention to the mutterings of war in scantily populated colonies three thousand miles away, but Choiseul observed them with close interest from their first beginning. He wished to be informed as to the sentiments and the resources of the colonists, and he was ready to incite them to resistance if the opportunity offered.

The American leaders did not need any stimulus from France to stir them into activity, but the reports made by Choiseul's representatives as to conditions in our country are not without interest. In 1764 M. de Pontleroy was despatched to America on a tour of observation, and full reports of his two years' wanderings were sent to the French minister.[1] He described the land as rich and prosperous, containing many hardy seamen and skillful ship-builders, who, in time of war, were well fitted to serve either on ships of war or on privateers. He declared that the colonists were beginning to feel their strength, and were too opulent

[1] Bancroft, *History of the United States* (ed. 1854), vi, 25.

to remain long dependent on any foreign power; he anticipated that they would not only shake off the rule of the mother country, but would invade the sugar islands of the West Indies and add them to their domain. A little later one of Choiseul's agents in London reported that only arms, a leader, and a feeling of self-reliance were required in order to secure the independence of the American colonies, and that it was the business of France and Spain to bring about that result.

In 1768 Choiseul wrote cheerfully that the quarrel would have no end, the colonists would soon do without the assistance of the mother country, England would be ruined, and her vast possessions in America prove a millstone around her neck.

So far as Choiseul was concerned it made little difference to him on which side of the ocean England became involved in trouble. Speaking of a report that there had been a riot in London and lives lost, he says, " I hardly dare hope that it is so. The English will never cut each other's throats to the extent that we desire."

In the mean time a new agent was selected to gather information, and one who was destined to play an important part in American affairs. Baron Kalb apparently took his title, not by hereditary right or ancestral claim, but because he thought that it would be an advantage in his career to be called a baron. Similar instances were common in that time, and are not unknown in our own. When there is no sovereign ready to bestow a title upon a man, his only remedy is to bestow one upon himself ; and if it is resolutely asserted, the owner's right is not often questioned.

At all events, Kalb, born near Bayreuth, of respect-

able but not of noble parentage, became while still a
young man a lieutenant in the French service. He
served with credit in the War of the Austrian Succession and in the Seven Years' War. After that he retired on a pension and married a rich wife, but he was
soon anxious to return to active service and sought
employment wherever there was opportunity. He first
desired a position in the Portuguese army, but after
two years of intriguing he failed to obtain it.

This disappointment resulted in his being assigned
to much more important work. Choiseul decided to
send a new agent to America. Kalb was strongly
recommended by Broglie and Soubise, under whom
he had served; he received a reappointment to the
French army and was ordered by Choiseul to go first
to Amsterdam and find out what he could about the
American colonies, and then sail for America.[1] There
he was to investigate the sentiments of the people, and
their ability to furnish munitions of war and competent
officers ; to ascertain how many troops they could raise,
the probability of a revolt against England, and of its
success if it were attempted. Kalb hesitated to undertake the mission, but Choiseul told him that, after
much deliberation, he had been selected for a difficult
task, and he must not decline it.

In October, 1767, Kalb sailed for America, and after
a voyage which lasted more than three months, in January, 1768, he reached Philadelphia. The reports he
sent back were not altogether calculated to encourage
the hopes of his superior. The discontents produced
by the Stamp Act and the duties on tea were still
active, so Kalb wrote ; even the women discarded tea
and sugar, and sought to do without silks and English

[1] Friedrich Kapp, *Life of Johann Kalb*, 1–46.

linen. "But," he added, "the question is how long they will adhere to this resolution." At present he did not think the colonies would be able to repel force by force, and said, what was undoubtedly true at that time, that at the bottom they were little inclined to shake off English supremacy, and especially with the aid of foreign powers. Yet he recognized the growing irritation produced by the policy of the British ministry, and he gave at much length the complaints which the Americans brought against the home government. All classes of people, he wrote later, were imbued with a spirit of independence, and if the provinces could be united, an independent state would soon be formed. "At all events," he adds, "it will certainly come forth in time." The country was becoming too powerful to be governed from London; the population was estimated at three millions, and was expected to double every thirty years. "It is not to be denied that children swarm everywhere like ants," he wrote. The size of the families of our ancestors impressed all foreign observers.[1]

In March Kalb writes from Boston: "I meet with the same opinions as in the provinces I had already visited, only expressed with greater violence and acrimony." But he added that in spite of this spirit, all, from the leaders down to the humblest citizens, cherished a strong affection for the mother country, and it would be difficult to induce them to accept assistance from other nations.

Kalb continued his journey to Canada, and his reports from there could not have been gratifying to the home government. Only a few years had elapsed since the Canadians had ceased to be French, but they

[1] Letter of Feb. 25, 1768; Kapp, *Life of Kalb*, 63.

had already discovered how much their lot was improved by becoming British subjects. They paid slight taxes, wrote Kalb, they enjoyed freedom of conscience, they took part in public affairs, and as a natural result of all this, their lands had increased in value.[1] The people of Canada, though they entertained a sentimental fondness for the land of their origin, had no desire to be again subjected to the evils of French colonial administration.

Kalb did not remain long in America. He gave as a reason for returning to France that he got no answers to his despatches, and feared they had not reached their destination ; but travel in this country was not then an alluring occupation. In January Kalb went from Philadelphia to New York. The weather was wintry, and when he endeavored to cross the Hudson, the boat was wrecked, the horses and luggage were lost, the passengers spent the night in a marsh without shelter of any sort, and two of them died from exposure. Kalb saved his life and his limbs, but he lost his baggage, the badge of his order, and several hundred louis d'or.

In June, 1768, he arrived again in Paris. In the mean time Choiseul's interest in American affairs had diminished. He was occupied with the annexation of Corsica, and there seemed no immediate prospect of any disturbance in America. When subscriptions were raised in England to assist the Corsicans, Choiseul said the French would retaliate by raising money to assist the Americans ; but he did not carry out his threat.[2]

Kalb waited long for an interview, and when at

[1] All the above reports are from Kapp, *Life of Kalb*, 53–70.
[2] Letter of Choiseul, Jan. 18, 1769 ; *Ibid.*, 72.

last one was granted, Choiseul brought it to a speedy
end. "You have returned too soon from America," he
said ; "you need not send me any more reports about
the country."

But if Choiseul, with characteristic fickleness, declined to bother himself further with American affairs,
the reports of his agents, the volumes of newspaper
articles and fugitive papers indicating discontent with
the mother country, which were carefully preserved
in the French archives, show how closely French
statesmen watched the possibility of trouble between
England and her American colonies. Even the sermons of discontented New England divines, who were
not afraid to preach politics to their flocks, found
their way to Versailles.[1]

If Choiseul's policy had been followed in another
matter, France might again have been involved in a
war with England, under circumstances much less
favorable than at the time of the American Revolution. Choiseul was bold and sometimes reckless in his
foreign policies; "unquiet, aspiring, and superficial,"
he was declared to be by Frederick II, the most aspiring, but also the most sagacious of European sovereigns. When the Comte de Broglie prepared plans for
an English invasion, and the half-crazy Eon was sent
as an agent to further them, Choiseul condemned such
follies. Yet he was quite ready to take the chances of
a new contest, if only he were the man to direct it,
and the compact with Spain, which had been renewed
by Choiseul, very nearly involved France in war with
England. In 1766 a small English settlement was
established on one of the Falkland Islands. These
islands were of little importance, and Spain's claim

[1] Kapp, *Life of Kalb*, 73.

upon them rested only on vague assertions of supremacy over the South Seas. The Spanish had taken
no steps to settle them, or make any practical use of
their asserted supremacy, but they were offended at
the action taken by England. In 1770 a Spanish
armament, sent out by the governor of Buenos Ayres,
landed on the islands, captured the English garrison,
and carried them away prisoners.

Though the territory in dispute was unimportant,
the English were justly outraged at the insolence of
this proceeding and they demanded that Charles III
should disavow the act of his governor and restore the
island. The Spanish were loath to do this, and yet
they recognized the madness of attempting to meet
England single-handed. But by the terms of the
Family Compact, France was bound to come to the
aid of Spain if she became involved in war, and accordingly the Spanish King declared that he would do
nothing that could infringe upon his honor, and intimated that he was ready for the contest.

There is no doubt that in this he was encouraged
by Choiseul, and that rash minister was ready to involve his country in a new war on a question of Spanish etiquette. He believed that France was prepared
for the contest, and he was ready to take the risk. If
he could avenge the defeats of the last war, he would
win great praise from his countrymen; and at any
rate, he believed that war would insure his continuance in office.[1]

The situation of affairs was changed by the interference of the King. It was not often that Louis XV
exercised any control over French policy; he was
quite right in saying that he had little influence with

[1] Mercy-Argenteau to Maria Theresa, Sept., 1770.

his own ministers. But he had had enough of fighting ; drawing plans for the invasion of England he regarded as an amusement, but when there was a possibility of actual hostilities, he was stirred from his ordinary apathy. He now intimated very decidedly that France would not go to war on any question of Spanish punctilio, and Choiseul's intrigues were brought to an abrupt close. In 1770 Louis XV dismissed him from the ministry, the Spanish at once abandoned their position, and the island was restored to England. There can be little doubt that if France had become involved in hostilities with England, instead of obtaining revenge for the calamities of the late war, she would have added to them. The French were not as well prepared as when they interfered in behalf of the Americans eight years later, and the English were in far better condition. Louis XV, who had plenty of intelligence when he wanted to use it, was quite right in saying, " War in our present condition would be a frightful evil for me and for my people." [1]

For a while, after the disgrace of Choiseul, American affairs received little attention in France. The whole of Louis XV's reign was ignominious, but its closing years were the worst. The old King was sunk in sensuality and vice ; Madame du Barry was at the height of her favor ; the ministers were men of small capacity ; sordid schemes and petty ambitions comprised the politics of the court. But on May 10, 1774, a loathsome disease ended Louis XV's unedifying life, and the face of French politics changed in a day. From his grandson, Louis XVI, who inherited the throne, a well-meaning youth of inferior intelligence

[1] Louis XV to Charles III, Dec. 21, 1770.

and narrow sympathies, nothing great could be expected; but he began his reign with a sincere resolve to do his duty, he desired to improve public conditions, he believed in morality and decency, and he sought the assistance of ministers who would aid him in his endeavors.

CHAPTER III

THE DIPLOMACY OF VERGENNES

THE young King received the popular favor which is readily bestowed on royalty combined with youth. Nothing could be worse than the old King, and the people looked with hope upon a new sovereign, who, though he had done little to arouse ardent anticipation, had done nothing to excite popular disapproval. It was natural that a new ruler should choose new ministers, and there was special reason for change. Those in office shared the discredit which attached to the closing years of Louis XV's reign, and in addition to this, they were regarded as the creatures of Madame du Barry.

Public opinion in France was not severe and was habituated to royal gallantries, but it had been outraged by the favor bestowed upon a woman like du Barry, and the ministers who had shared her power also shared her unpopularity. She was at once exiled from court, to the delight of all decent people, and the ministers of Louis XV were speedily removed.

It was believed by many that Choiseul would now return to power. He was the most prominent of French statesmen; if not the ablest, he was the most brilliant; he had been disliked by Madame du Barry, and his return to favor might naturally follow her overthrow. Such expectations were disappointed. Choiseul's brilliancy did not appeal to a slow-witted youth like Louis XVI, while many of the duke's qualities were distasteful to the King. Choiseul was a spend-thrift, his life was immoral, his tongue was bitter, and his criticisms had spared neither king nor courtier. Louis selected for the head of his Council the Comte de Maurepas, a man of seventy-three, who had been out of office for quarter of a century. He was well known as a wit, as a satirist, as a great nobleman who patronized literature and condescended to scholarship. He had held office almost from boyhood until middle age, and had then been driven from power by the hostility of Madame de Pompadour. That might perhaps have been to his credit; but as he had aroused her hostility by some very indecent verses he wrote concerning her, his overthrow excites less sympathy than if it had been due to the fearless performance of public duty. At all events, he was now recalled, and he remained in office until his death on November 21, 1781.

A man whom years of alternate favor and disgrace had left weary of the struggle was not likely, at seventy-three, to adopt new or vigorous measures, either in domestic or foreign policy; but the position of secretary of foreign affairs was filled by one who played a great part in the history of France and of our own country. For this office the King made choice of Charles Gravier, Comte de Vergennes, then stationed at the court of Sweden.

The selection of Vergennes was of much importance to the American colonists. It is indeed probable that France would ultimately have become our ally, no matter who was at the head of her foreign department. Yet Louis XVI was at no time eager to interfere in our affairs. His temperament was sluggish, and was not stirred by any love for adventure or for the hazard of war; his instincts were monarchical, and the pictures of republican virtue and democratic simplicity which charmed French society did not allure him. If he had been governed by the counsels of an adviser like Turgot, the colonies might have been left to fight out their own salvation.

Not only had Vergennes much to do with the momentous decision, but during five years of war he did his best for his allies. He did not respond to all their demands for money, but he gave liberally and steadily the pecuniary assistance without which the American armies might have dissolved from lack of clothes and food. He considered first the interests of his own country, as was his duty ; but never, during long years of indifferent success, did he waver in his resolution that peace should not be made until the independence of the United States was assured. For that object France had taken up arms, and until it was accomplished Vergennes would listen to no suggestion that she should lay them down. He was a cold man, but he was constant; his memory is not green in America like that of La Fayette; he had few of the endearing qualities and none of the ardent enthusiasm of the marquis; he felt for the American patriots little of the fervid admiration of some who fought for us and many who talked of us; but he did more than any other Frenchman to secure political independence for the American colonies.

Vergennes was fifty-seven years of age when Louis XVI selected him for secretary of state, and he had followed the profession of diplomacy during most of his active life. Almost quarter of a century earlier he had been minister at Trêves ; a few years later he represented France at a diplomatic congress at Hanover, and he was then sent as ambassador to the Porte, in which difficult position he conducted himself with judgment and sagacity. In 1771 he was intrusted with an important mission to Sweden, and it was there that a summons reached him to return to Paris and assume the office of secretary of state for foreign affairs.

He did not belong to the great nobility, he had little court influence, and he owed his appointment to the personal choice of the young sovereign. Vergennes was not a great man, but he was a sagacious and prudent statesman, and he devoted himself laboriously and intelligently to the service of his country. If he was not as brilliant as Choiseul, he was a much safer public servant. His industry was unwearied; he was often at his office at eight in the morning, he was not unfrequently there at ten at night, and to industry and intelligence he added, not perhaps unselfishness, but integrity. Making money out of official position, unless actual dishonesty was added to greed, was in that day regarded with no disapproval; the man who neglected such opportunities was thought to be a strange and not altogether an admirable creature. When Lord Stanhope declined the bribe of six hundred thousand livres which Dubois offered him, the abbé declared such conduct heroic. If not heroic it was unusual.

To the self-seeking politicians of England, the first Pitt seemed a marvel because he declined profits that he might have pocketed. Pecuniary standards were no higher in France. Vergennes was not a dishonest man, nor was he regarded as a greedy man. He did not accumulate great wealth out of his office as Richelieu and Mazarin had done, but it would have been thought absurd if he had not availed himself of what were deemed to be the legitimate gains of royal favor and important position. He left a fortune of about two million francs, an amount of which the purchasing power would be little short of two million dollars to-day. Such wealth did not indicate dishonesty, though probably the larger part of it represented the direct or indirect gains of holding office. Pecuniary disinterestedness in a public man was very nearly a thing unknown. We are disturbed when men in public life use their positions, not for actual corruption, but for greedy accumulation at the expense of those they represent. In the eighteenth century sentiment in Europe would not have been disturbed by such disclosures, and the number of offenders would have been very nearly measured by the number of those who had the opportunity. Few men got poor in politics a hundred and fifty years ago, except in a poor nation like ours, where there was little opportunity to make money. When Vergennes died, in 1787, Franklin, who knew him well, said that the taking away of so wise and good a man was a loss to mankind. He was surely a wise man and he was not a bad man, though both his political and his pecuniary standards were lower than those which public opinion now requires.

The King called to office a greater man than Vergennes. Those who recognized the necessity for a radical change in French administration might have felt ground for hope when Louis, in the summer of 1774, selected Turgot as his minister of finance. Turgot had neither a great family nor influential friends to help him into office, but he had shown his fitness for this position during his administration as intendant at Limoges. He was known as one of the few officials in France who improved the lot of those under them, as a disciple of legislative reform, identified with the economists and philanthropists. Turgot did away with the *corvée*, he reëstablished free commerce in grain within the kingdom, he abolished many iniquitous taxes, he checked many useless expenditures; his policy would have relieved the poor from much of the undue taxation which fell upon them and would have averted the bankruptcy to which the government was rapidly progressing. "It is only Turgot and I," said Louis of him, "who love the people." But if the King could recognize the wisdom of Turgot's plans and sympathize with his efforts to improve the condition of the people, he had not the firmness to support his minister against a host of enemies, exasperated by his reforms. Turgot's tenure of office was brief. The innumerable enemies excited by his efforts at reform were soon powerful enough to bring about his overthrow; if he had remained in office and been given a free hand, it is possible that the changes he would have carried into effect might have saved France from a revolution.

That he was opposed to an alliance with the colonists may forfeit his claim for gratitude upon Americans, but should increase their respect for his judgment as a French statesman. Turgot viewed the question from a financial aspect, and he was right in saying that such a war would complete the ruin of a financial situation already in desperate plight. Naturally, we admire the action of France in assisting our forefathers to achieve their national independence. If the policy of a nation is to be judged by its influence upon the world, the assistance France gave us was an act of high import to the interests of civiliza-

tion; but after all, it was the business of French statesmen, under the French monarchy, to preserve the system of which they were servants; to improve it
doubtless, to fit it for the future, but to save it from
destruction. The man who is willing to involve his
own country in ruin that he may assist other lands,
manifests a high degree of national altruism; but it
remains a question whether he is a useful citizen of
the country to which he owes his allegiance. If Louis
XVI had been governed by Turgot's counsel, the
monarchy would not only have escaped the dangers
threatened by a continuance of unbearable abuses,
but would have been saved from the perilous effect
on French thought produced by interference in behalf of a people who demanded political freedom. But
Turgot was a prophet without honor, and heads less
level and more visionary directed the destinies of
France.

Towards the last of July, 1774, Vergennes returned
from his mission in Stockholm to enter upon his duties as secretary of foreign affairs. The French were
already watching with attention the growing prospect
of revolt in the American colonies. Gérard de Rayneval, who was to take so active a part in the affairs
of America, was filling Vergennes's place in the
interim, and he wrote early in July to the chargé
d'affaires in London : "We are awaiting the moment
when the fate of the Bostonians will be decided. General Gage will need much talent and much sagacity
and patience to calm the spirit of insubordination
which has possessed almost all the English colonists." [1]
In September, after Vergennes had assumed the du-

[1] Gérard to Garnier, July 3, 1774; cited by Doniol, i, 12.

ties of his office, he wrote : "The quarrel between the colonies and the British government seems to become more serious every day. . . . It may prove the most fatal blow to the authority of the metropolis." [1]

The minister was right in saying that the quarrel constantly became more serious, and it was more closely watched in France than in any other part of the continent. Russia, Austria, and Prussia had no American colonies; they derived a mild pleasure from the complications in which England was involved, but they were little concerned by the progress of American discontent. Though Spain had great American possessions, her apathetic government exhibited no interest in anything, except the possibility of some immediate gain for Spain herself. But France could not be indifferent to the future of a continent in which for almost two centuries she had been largely interested, and her feeling of rivalry towards Great Britain was stronger than that of any other European state.

In time popular sympathy with the colonists became an important factor, but the probable results of American insurrection were considered by French statesmen long before they excited any interest in the French public. Vergennes and his associates believed that the loss of the colonies would prove fatal to England's commercial power. "If the resistance of the Americans is successful," wrote the French minister at London, "this memorable epoch will reduce England to a point where she will no longer cause disquietude to France, whose consideration on the Continent will increase in proportion to the enfeeblement of the British Empire." [2]

[1] Vergennes to Garnier, Sept. 11, 1774; Doniol, i, 13.
[2] Garnier to Vergennes, Aug. 16, 1776 ; Doniol, i, 585.

A similar belief was held in America, on the Continent, and in England herself. The feeling was widespread that if the American colonies achieved their independence, this would be a fatal blow to the power, the wealth, and the trade of England. The future was to show the fallacy of this belief, but it had a large influence in exciting the ardor of French statesmen for the American cause. Not only did they hope for harm to England, but for a great increase in French trade with the new republic, in return for assistance in her struggle. This hope, also, was disappointed. Trade between the United States and France increased as a result of the growth of the American people in numbers and wealth, but trade is governed by business conditions; the French who assisted the colonists gained no more than the Germans who furnished troops to King George ; French merchants would have sold as many pieces of silk and bottles of champagne to Americans if the United States had secured their independence without French aid. If gains in trade only were considered, France was poorly paid for the money she spent in assisting the American colonists.

In 1775 the first blood was shed, and the long dispute between the colonists and the motherland had at last resulted in actual war. The reports of these early events reached France for the most part through English channels. The letters of the French ambassador at London were filled with discussions as to the relations of the colonies with the mother country, and with surmises as to their future action and the plans of the British ministers. The French representative was active in procuring information, and he did not hesitate over the necessary means. No daily press then revealed to the world the debates of Parliament, but Garnier wrote that he had secured a member of Parliament who was to furnish full reports of the discussions for the guidance of the French minister. We may be sure that this member was liberally paid for his work. Parliamentary corruption was common, and selling reports of other men's speeches was not so bad as selling one's own vote.

Notwithstanding his efforts to get accurate information, the ambassador sent to Paris many statements which had small foundation in fact. He was very apprehensive that Russia might interfere in the conflict, and he transmitted various sinister rumors that Catherine had promised to furnish England with twenty thousand men with which to subdue her rebellious subjects.[1] Vergennes was not disturbed by this report. Catherine had many vices, but he knew that she was not a ruler of the type of the Elector of Hesse, and that she would not sell the blood of her subjects for the money of George III.[2]

Another rumor was more persistent and excited more alarm. The French ministers were haunted by the idea that England would seek relief from present troubles, or consolation for future losses, by declaring war on France and despoiling her of the scanty possessions she still held in the west; the recollection of the late war was fresh and excited apprehension for the future. When considering the complications of the American situation, nothing disturbed the French ministers so much as the possible return of Chatham to power. With him at the helm they thought that war

[1] Guines to Vergennes, Sept. 29, 1775 ; Doniol, i, 210.
[2] Doniol, i, 213.

with France was certain to come, and would probably
be disastrous.

In February, 1775, Garnier, chargé d'affaires, wrote
that only immediate success could prevent the fall of
the ministry, that the King would be forced to turn
to Chatham, who would make peace with the colonies
and find armies and navies ready at his hand. " It is
a naked sword in the hands of a madman," he added ;
and he then proceeded to show that Chatham's ambition would seek fresh fields of glory at the expense of
France.[1] " Lord Chatham will necessarily become the
conciliator and there is the man to dread," wrote
Guines in June; and he added : " What can be the
conditions of the conciliation? Conditions little honorable to England, and then an audacious minister,
accustomed to glory, will look upon our colonies as a
necessary compensation."

In reply Vergennes bade the ambassador to watch
the progress of the crisis with care, and especially to
ascertain what influence Chatham might obtain over
the King.[2] But there was no ground for fear. George
III was not the sovereign to be influenced by a man
like Lord Chatham, and no defeats in America could
induce him to turn to the great war minister for
aid.

Vergennes was uncertain as to his future policy ;
but he desired to be informed accurately as to the progress of events, and the prospects of the contest. In
July the ambassador at London wrote complaining of
the inaccuracy of the news from America, and he added,
" I think it might be advantageous to us, it would at
least satisfy the King's curiosity, to have among them

---

[1] Garnier to Vergennes, Feb. 20, 1775 ; Doniol, i, 69.
[2] Guines to Vergennes, June 16, 1775 ; Doniol, i, 81–83.

a capable man who could judge the situation from the political and the military standpoint, could foresee the course of events, and send on his reports by each merchant ship." [1]

This suggestion was received favorably, and a gentleman named Bonvouloir was sent as a secret agent to America; but Vergennes desired that the messenger should go without any trace of official character, so that his acts and words could in no way involve the French government. He could not even receive any written instructions, and lest his reports might fall into hostile hands, his letters nominally were to treat of commercial questions and be addressed to a correspondent at Antwerp, while the information he was sent to impart was to be written in some preparation of milk, which could be developed only when heated by a red-hot shovel. [2] With all these useless attempts at secrecy, Bonvouloir was assigned duties of some delicacy and importance. Not only was he to send home faithful accounts of all he saw and heard, but he was to insinuate into American ears suggestions of the desirability of France as an ally; he was to tell the colonists how the French people admired the grandeur and nobility of their efforts; and especially was he to impress upon their minds that under no circumstances would France seek to recover Canada. [3] Vergennes fully realized that nothing could be more distasteful to the English colonists, after half a century of conflict, than to see the French flag again floating at Quebec and Montreal. It would be idle to expect the permanent friendship of the new nation if

[1] Report, July 1, 1775; Doniol, i, 128.

[2] Doniol, i, 266.

[3] Vergennes to Guines, Aug. 7, 1775; Doniol, i, 155.

Canada were again French. Moreover, the French did not look with covetous eyes upon their lost Canadian possessions. Canada had been a source of anxiety and vexation of spirit to the home government. The colony had not increased in population as had its southern neighbors; it had not become an important factor in the trade of the home country; even at Versailles there was a dim consciousness that the colonial policy adopted for Canada had been a failure, and there was no desire to undertake the experiment again. No lust for the St. Lawrence or the Great Lakes interfered with the conviction that an attempt to regain Canada would surely excite the ill-will of the American colonists.

In addition to these instructions, Bonvouloir received the modest allowance of two hundred louis. "If nothing is accomplished," Guines wrote with praiseworthy frugality, "it is only a loss of two hundred louis." [1] Bonvouloir received his louis, and in September, 1775, he sailed for America. Though he had no official position, his expedition must be regarded as the first formal step towards action in behalf of America taken by France. Bonvouloir was not the man to take an important part in a crisis, but his reports may have tended to encourage the French minister in a policy of interference.

He reached America in December, after a stormy and dangerous passage. "I had a frightful passage," he writes. "I was one hundred days at sea, twenty times I thought I should perish; I was reduced to two biscuits a day, . . . a little salt beef and stale water." Having at last landed, he at once repaired to Philadelphia, and talked with the members of Con-

[1] Guines to Vergennes, Sept. 8, 1775; Doniol, i, 138.

gress gathered there; but the fear of exceeding his authority rendered him a timid negotiator. "I made them no offer," he writes, "absolutely none. . . . When asked if France would aid them, and at what price, I replied, . . . It is possible that she might, but I knew nothing about the terms, . . . and, in short, . . . all they could do was to submit their propositions to that country." [1]

But the secret committee insisted on regarding Bonvouloir as the representative of his country, and addressed him a set of written questions: Was the disposition of France favorable to their cause? Could they obtain from her two experienced engineers? Could they buy arms and munitions of war in exchange for American products? To this Bonvouloir replied that he was but a private citizen, he could only give his conjecture, but he believed that France wished them well, that she would furnish them two good engineers; and without making himself responsible for anything, he believed they might attempt an exchange of products at their own risk. [2]

Even these mild expressions disturbed him. He wrote for further instructions and said: "These affairs are so delicate that with all the good-will possible, I tremble as I advance." But still he drew a satisfaction from his exploits, which was not entirely justified. "No one will ever make such progress in their confidence as I," he writes, "nor manage them as I do. . . . I toil night and day, happy if I succeed. . . . I am learning to talk English very prettily."

Of more importance than these effusions of timidity and vanity, was the information he gave as to condi-

---

[1] Doniol, i, 267, 287-292.

[2] Bonvouloir to Guines, Sept. 28, 1775; Doniol, i, 368.

tions in America; it was not accurate, but it was of a character to encourage the plans of interference which the French ministry already entertained. "Every man here is a soldier," he writes, "the troops are well clothed, well paid and well commanded. They have about fifty thousand men under pay, and a still greater number of volunteers who wish no pay. Judge how this sort of men would fight." [1] This enthusiastic account was not correct, but it led Bonvouloir's superiors to overestimate the military strength of the colonists, and thus his lying was in a good cause. Indeed he seems to have believed his own statements, far as they were from the truth.

Bonvouloir remained for another year in America, but the results of his mission were not important. He had spent his money, and the Comte de Guines, who had selected him for the expedition, asked the minister to come to Bonvouloir's assistance.[2] Vergennes estimated the agent at about his real value : he said that Bonvouloir had failed to satisfy the curiosity which led them to authorize his journey, and the best thing he could do was to return as soon as possible. But Bonvouloir was at Philadelphia with his money all gone, and he could not return. At last Vergennes authorized Guines to send the unlucky envoy two hundred louis, and to send him at the same time instructions to return to France forthwith. Thus Bonvouloir faded out of the field of American politics and out of the attention of history.

It is difficult to decide how far, at this early stage, the French ministers had any definite thought of interfering in the American contest. The struggle had just begun, the resources of the colonists were un-

---

[1] Doniol, i, 289.   [2] Doniol, i, 510–513.

known, it was uncertain how stubborn a resistance they could make to the English armies. The situation was watched with no very strong sympathy for the insurgents, but with the lively desire that they should do England as much harm as possible.

In 1775 Vergennes was profuse in his assertions that France would take no part in the quarrel. And even if his asseverations were not entirely sincere, it seemed probable that he would keep his word. "You are right in explaining," he wrote the ambassador at London, "that . . . even if the interest of the King led him to stir up the flames of rebellion in America, justice would forbid it. And this is the most powerful consideration to his mind."[1] Far from seeking to profit by the embarrassment in which England finds herself on account of American affairs, wrote Vergennes in June, 1775, "we desire rather to aid her to escape from them. The spirit of revolt, wherever it appears, is always a dangerous example. With moral as with physical maladies, either can prove contagious." But it was in the American possessions of France that Vergennes foresaw the possibility of harm from the dangerous example of the American colonies; he did not foresee how potent was to be the influence of that example on France herself. In August he said that if the Americans asked help from France, it would be politely refused.

Lord Stormont was the English representative at Paris, a shrewd, hard-headed man, who afterwards proved a thorn in the flesh to Vergennes, when the latter was secretly assisting the Americans, and openly denying that he was doing so. .At this time Stormont believed there was no reason to fear unfriendly action

[1] Doniol, i, 149.

by France. He wrote on October 31, 1775, narrating a long interview with Vergennes in which the French minister had said that he regretted the troubles in America and declared that these were of advantage to no one; that if the Americans became an independent nation, sooner or later they would build up a great navy, seize the West Indies, extend their conquests over South America, and in time leave not a foot of earth on that hemisphere in the possession of any European power. "'You and I will not live to see these changes accomplished,' he added, 'but if these results are remote they are certain.' All this he said," wrote the experienced diplomat, "with the air of one who was expressing his own opinion." [1]

To this Vergennes added assurances which the future did not confirm. Instead of seeking to increase England's embarrassment, the French government, he said, viewed it with regret, and would prevent any assistance being given to the Americans. While they might not always be able to check private speculators, they would do their best to prevent any illegal commerce between France and the colonies. Maurepas, the chief minister, talked in the same way, and assured Stormont that France would never give any assistance to the insurgents, directly or indirectly.

These expressions were not wholly insincere. The French were very uncertain what action they would take in this crisis, and Vergennes was truthful in disclaiming any strong interest in the principles for which the colonists were contending; but if his statements were not altogether false at the moment, they were far from indicating a settled purpose to take no part in the contest between England and her colonies.

[1] Doniol, i, 200.

Whether these expressions were more or less sincere, the importance of the American contest was well understood. "This," wrote an officer in the West Indies, "marks a memorable epoch in the world's history. . . . The result will surely affect every commercial nation on either continent." [1] Vergennes frequently expressed the same idea. In July he wrote saying that England must either lose her colonies or destroy them in the effort to hold them, and in either event there would be the same loss of trade, the same decay in manufactures, and the same destruction of national credit. [2]

While Vergennes was giving fair words to the English ambassador, he wrote in a different strain to the Spanish minister, telling of England's crimes and suggesting that an opportunity now offered to obtain revenge for them. "That nation," he wrote, "is as depraved in its politics as in its morals. . . . England is the monster against which we should be always prepared." [3] They must not be deceived by any professions of friendliness on the part of England's ministers, he added; they could count on her only so long as her domestic embarrassments continued, while the great possessions of Spain in America would surely be a bait to English greed.

At so critical a period, the English ministers might well have avoided giving unnecessary offence to a powerful neighbor that bore England no love; but diplomatic adroitness has never been an English quality. They now pressed irritating inquiries as to Dunkirk, where a vigilant watch was constantly kept to see that the French King took no steps to fortify his own city.

[1] Doniol, i, 242.   [2] July 29, 1775; Doniol, i, 95.
[3] July 28, 1775; Doniol, i, 115.

" This question . . . has been threshed over a hundred times," wrote Vergennes in the summer of 1775; ". . . if we have no right to restore what was destroyed by virtue of the treaties, we have the right to maintain and preserve what was allowed to remain." But still, he added, the French officials would be strictly charged not to exceed the limits, because the King wished to preserve a good feeling between the nations, and not to profit by England's embarrassments.[1]

No important event marked the campaign in the autumn of 1775. It became evident to Vergennes that the uprising of the colonists was no brief or ill-considered movement, and yet he believed that unless they received foreign aid, the English would succeed at last in wearing out their means of resistance. Such a result would have been highly unsatisfactory to the French, and in December, 1775, Vergennes submitted to the King an elaborate statement of his views on the question.

There was little profession of interest in the future of the colonies, and this was natural. The relations between the French and the English colonists had been those of almost perpetual hostility; they had quarrelled and fought for generations. The principles which they advocated were soon to excite universal sympathy among the French people, but it would have been strange if ministers of Louis XVI had kindled into enthusiasm over declarations of popular rights and denunciations of the tyranny of kings.

The questions were discussed in cold blood; there was no altruism, no sympathy for a community struggling to be free. The minister sought to discover wherein lay the interest of France, and this perhaps

[1] Vergennes to Guines, July 22, 1775; Doniol, i, 93.

was the only concern of a French statesman. The
struggle between the colonies and England deserved
the attention of all the powers, he said, but France
and Spain had special reason to watch its progress.
Left alone, he believed that England would reduce
her rebellious subjects to submission; even if the endeavor cost her dear, she would still preserve the mercantile advantages which commerce with America had
secured to her. "England," he added, "is the natural
enemy of France, an enemy greedy, ambitious, unjust,
and false. The invariable and cherished object of her
policy is, if not the destruction of France, at least her
abasement, her humiliation, her ruin." [1]

Nor did he fear that the independence of the English colonies would foster other revolutions in the new
world. They would be fatigued by a long war, they
would adopt a republican form of government, and it
was admitted, he said, that republics rarely had the
spirit of conquest. The history of Greece, of Rome,
of Venice, might have thrown some doubt on this
aphorism, but Vergennes thought there was no reason
to suppose that the United States would become a
dangerous neighbor. Accordingly the minister advised
helping the colonists, so far as it could be done pru-
dently, and encouraging their efforts by the suggestion of still more active assistance; if at the end of
the next campaign the English had made no further
progress in reducing the colonies, France might then
decide to interfere openly and secure their triumph. [2]

Such was the policy which Vergennes advocated at
the close of 1775, and it was followed. France assisted
the colonists so far as she could without becoming

[1] Doniol, i, 244.
[2] Doniol, i, 243-249.

embroiled with England, but the course of events delayed actual interference until a later date than the
minister contemplated.

On February 27, 1776, the report of Bonvouloir
reached Paris. The rosy accounts which he gave of
the strength of the American army seemed to confirm
the reports which had already reached Vergennes by
way of London. In March the minister submitted to
the King another carefully prepared paper on the
American situation, and asked for the opinion of his
colleagues upon it. The minister now saw danger both
in the success and in the failure of England, and contemplated the possibility of a war against France
undertaken by Great Britain, either exultant over her
victory or seeking compensation for what she had lost
by defeat. "As to the possibility of an invasion," he
added, "which nothing had provoked, and which
would be contrary to good faith and the obligation of
treaties, he would be sadly mistaken who thought the
English would be restrained by such considerations.
They regard as just whatever they believe to be
advantageous." As a result of his arguments the minister decided that the continuance of the American
war would be advantageous to France, and that it
might offer an opportunity for action which would
reduce England to a second-class power, strip her of
the empire which she exercised with equal pride and
injustice, and deliver the universe from a greedy
tyrant which sought to absorb all power and all
wealth.

But neither France nor Spain was ready for open
hostilities, so the minister abandoned the alluring
dream of interference and recommended instead to
give the insurgents all the secret aid that was possi-

ble, without involving the country in actual war ; if, on the one hand, the English ministers could be persuaded that France and Spain desired peace, and, on the other hand, the courage of the colonists could be maintained and their resistance strengthened, this would be the best policy for the present, and future problems could be considered when they arose.[1]

Such a programme was in strict accord with the classic diplomacy, which indulged in no philanthropy and was much addicted to lying. At all events, it was favorably received by most of Vergennes's colleagues to whom it was submitted. The Comte de Saint-Germain was minister of war; his opinion was brief and did little more than echo the views which Vergennes had advanced. M. de Sartine, the secretary of the navy, was equally complacent. But Maurepas, whose influence was large with the young King, went somewhat further in his reply. While carefully guarded in expression, the programme advocated by Vergennes would ultimately result in war. Maurepas expressed the same purpose with less concealment ; he said that while forming these projects for the present, it must be remembered that there had never been a more favorable opportunity for reducing the dangerous power of England than when she was embarrassed and harassed, and when no continental power would interfere in her behalf. " From such considerations," he added, " it might be decided that a policy which would be actively offensive might be the true way to strengthen France, to weaken England, and to secure peace on the Continent, which was constantly disturbed by English intrigues and English money." [2]

[1] "Considérations "; Doniol, i, 273–278.   [2] Doniol, i, 285.

But the policy advocated by Vergennes met with no favorable response from the most sagacious of the advisers of Louis XVI. The young King displayed not only the desire to do right, which he always had, but an intelligence and independence which he rarely exhibited, when he selected Turgot as his minister of finance. Turgot returned this confidence by courage in action, and by wisdom in advice, which might have averted the dangers awaiting the King, but which resulted only in bringing about the speedy overthrow of the minister. On the American question, as on many others, Turgot made no effort to agree with the views of his colleagues, and he considered only the financial and internal condition of France.

For a month he meditated on Vergennes's proposition, and at last submitted a reply that was sagacious, lengthy, but more fitted to excite the ill-will of his colleagues than to control the conduct of the King. It would have been a better state paper if it had savored more of the politician and less of the professor of political economy. Turgot detailed with disagreeable accuracy the condition of the French treasury, the amount of the deficit, the impossibility of making ends meet except by a reduction of expenses. The King, he said, knew the state of his finances; that in spite of the economies already ·attempted there was a deficit of twenty millions, and this could be overcome only by the imposition of new taxes, by open bankruptcy, or by a further reduction of expenses. War, therefore, was the thing most to be avoided, because it would render impossible for a long period, and perhaps forever, the reforms necessary for the welfare of the state and the relief of the people.

Nor did he view the external situation with the

eyes of the majority. Colonies, he said, were of small
commercial value; it was the part of wisdom to
change them from subject dependencies to allied
provinces. "In view of this," he added, "what difference does it make to us whether England over-
comes her rebellious colonies or whether she does
not?" The loss of her colonies, he truly said, would
not injure England, and would be a great benefit to
the commerce of the world. He was less accurate in
forecasting the commercial policy of the new republic.
It must become, he declared, a nation of free traders,
which would throw open its ports to the world, and
prove to European nations that the colonial system of
restriction and monopoly was founded on delusion.[1]

Some of Turgot's theories have become common-
places of political economy, some of them are not yet
recognized, but in so far as his doctrines were correct
they were far in advance of the political thought of the
day, and the addition of unpleasant facts, disagreeably
told, rendered it still less likely that such revolutionary
views should make converts. Certain it is that they had
little effect upon the cabinet of Louis XVI, and Vergennes went on with his plan for aiding the colonies,
as if Turgot had never spoken.

In conformity with the principles of alliance between France and Spain, which still controlled the
French government, Vergennes submitted his arguments to Charles III as fully as to Louis XVI. They
met, however, with a cool reception. The Spanish
government was indifferent, if not inimical, to the
American colonists; if war was to be made upon
England, they desired that the conquest of Portugal

[1] "Mémoire sur la Manière dont la France," etc.; *Œuvres de Turgot*, ii, 551.

for Spain should be its object, and they advised an
attempt to free Ireland rather than the American
colonies from English rule. The dissensions between
the English and the Irish were notorious, the Spanish
ambassador wrote in February, 1776; with the help
of the Irish, who would be ready, Ireland could be
freed from tyranny and England would be no longer
a power to fear.[1]

This project was not favorably received at Versailles, and the Spanish returned to the American
proposition. It was not befitting the dignity of the
two nations, Charles III declared, to make common
cause with a people in revolt against their sovereign;
but it was for their interest to maintain the rebels in
their insurrection and furnish them secretly all they
needed in order to keep up the struggle.[2] His minister Grimaldi viewed the question from a standpoint
no more altruistic. "Certainly it is for our advantage," he wrote, "that the revolt of these people
should continue; we must wish that they and the
English should exhaust each other."[3]

As a result of these deliberations the two nations at
last decided upon the policy which, for the time being,
they would adopt in reference to the American colonies. The French government was not disturbed by
the idea of making common cause with a people in
insurrection, as were the ministers of Charles III; but
they contented themselves with giving aid which,
though secret, was none the less valuable. On May 2,
1776, Vergennes asked Louis XVI to authorize an
advance of a million livres, which was to be intrusted
to Beaumarchais for the use of the rebellious colonists,

---

[1] M. le Comte d'Aranda, Feb., 1776; Doniol, i, 352–358.
[2] April 1, 1776; Doniol, i, 342.   [3] Doniol, i, 370.

and this request was granted. It was the first direct aid given by France to our forefathers, and was the beginning of the interference of that country in the American Revolution, which at last led to an open alliance and war with England. Though such a result was contemplated as possible by Vergennes and his associates, no decision had yet been reached, and the French ministers were desirous to avoid doing anything which would necessarily involve their country in war. For this reason the action now taken was enveloped in mystery. Vergennes did not even venture to write the letter concerning the use of the money, nor intrust it to his secretary ; it was written by his son, a youth of only fifteen, in whose discretion, the father declared, absolute confidence could be placed.

The Spanish were asked to take similar action, and to this they agreed. Grimaldi sent to Paris a letter of credit for a million livres, to be used for the insurgents in the same manner as the million advanced by France.[1] This moderate sum represented almost the entire direct assistance which the Americans received from Spain, and it was not given in order to secure their success, but in the hope that the contest would be prolonged until both sides were exhausted. However, the guns and supplies bought with the money advanced by Spain were just as useful as if the motive of the giver had been more exalted.

France and Spain resolved on rendering this amount of assistance to the cause of the insurgents without any direct application from the thirteen colonies. It was decided to advance the money, in the hope that it would enable the rebellious colonists to prolong their resistance and make the situation more disagreeable

[1] Doniol, i, 485.

and more embarrassing for England. Indeed, the colonists had not thus far assumed the form of an independent government or formally renounced their allegiance to the mother country. The progress of events soon changed the situation, and the governments of France and the United States entered upon formal relations with each other.

CHAPTER IV

THUS far the colonists had no official representation at the court of France; their national existence had hardly assumed definite form; but in the summer of 1776 an envoy of the new republic arrived at Paris, commissioned to ask for the assistance of France.

When sporadic disturbances developed into actual war, the colonists at once considered the question of seeking aid from foreign powers. They believed, with good reason, that France would be the most likely of European nations to render assistance; she was powerful, she was rich, and she hated England. Yet it was not without some opposition that the colonists decided to ask succor from the French King. It was a break with all the traditions of the past; many who had been outspoken against England hesitated to seek the aid of a foreign nation against the mother country. Then, too, France and the French had been immemorial objects of dislike, sometimes ripening into hatred. The French had been the allies of bloodthirsty Indians, they had plotted against the peace of the English colonists, they had been bad neighbors, they were denounced as false in character and Papist in faith.

In September, 1775, a motion was made in Congress that envoys should be sent to France, and this received the active support of John Adams. But he was unable to persuade his associates; in his own phrase, "the resolution was murdered." The proposition, so Adams wrote, was too much for the nerves of Congress, "the grimaces, the agitations, the convulsions were very great."[1] Even Franklin thought that a virgin state should not go a-suitoring for alliances, an opinion which he found reason to change.

The progress of events soon did away with any such reluctance. A committee of foreign correspondence was appointed, of which Franklin was made a member, and the visit of Bonvouloir, notwithstanding the guarded expressions of that timid envoy, encouraged its members to believe that France was ready to come to our aid. Accordingly in March, 1776, it was decided to send Silas Deane to Paris to ask for clothes, arms, provisions, money, and any other assistance that a rich monarchy might extend to a needy republic. His qualifications for the position were of the slightest. He knew no French, he had no diplomatic experience, and in both respects he resembled almost all Americans. But he had some money and lived with a degree of style which, to his simple-minded countrymen, savored of the splendor of foreign courts. Unfortunately the social display in which Deane had indulged in Connecticut did not dazzle the courtiers of Versailles, and, with the best intentions, he succeeded in embarrassing his country and ruining himself.

His instructions regulated his conduct with much minuteness. He was to assume the character of a merchant, and might even pretend to be satisfying the curiosity which led so many to visit the renowned city of Paris.[2] But our forefathers did not intend that their agent should waste his time in such occupation.

[1] *Works of John Adams*, i, 199–201.   [2] *Deane Papers*, i, 123.

He was directed to see Vergennes as soon as possible, and the words he should use were almost put in his mouth. He was to suggest the advantages France might derive from furnishing assistance to the colonies, and he was to ask for aid on no modest scale; the envoy was to intimate that clothing and arms for twenty-five thousand men, one hundred cannon, and supplies of any sort would be welcome. To pay for these, the colonists would promise to send shiploads of American products, though the prospect of payment might have seemed doubtful even to the most sanguine speculator.

The inducements for French action were depicted in alluring terms : " If France will join us, in time," wrote the Secret Committee a little later, "there is no danger but America will soon be established as an Independent Empire, and France, drawing from her the principal part of those sources of wealth and power which formerly flowed into Great Britain, will immediately become the greatest power in Europe." [1]

If Vergennes should receive these demands coldly, Deane was bidden not to be discouraged : he must ask the minister to reflect further, inform him that the envoy could wait at Paris for a while to receive his orders, and endeavor to ascertain if France would make a formal alliance when the colonies were organized as an independent state. On the whole, in their first essay in diplomacy, our ancestors did not err in asking for too little, or in understating the advantages to the state that should come to their aid.

Thus instructed, Deane set out on his journey. In March, 1776, he sailed from America and, passing by

[1] *Deane Papers*, i, 298; letter from Secret Committee of Oct. 1, 1776.

the Bermudas on his voyage, landed in Spain. By this circuitous route he escaped the English cruisers; he then made his way over the Pyrenees, visited many French cities, and in July, 1776, arrived at Paris.

On July 17 he was presented to the French Minister of Foreign Affairs, and though the conversation had to be conducted by interpreters, as has been the case with so many American diplomatic representatives since Silas Deane, the interview was satisfactory to both sides. Deane asked the minister to pardon manners that perhaps were ill adapted to the usages of courts, and assured him the colonies would soon declare their independence and become a nation. Vergennes informed him, in words which certainly savored of superciliousness, "that the people and their cause were very respectable in the eyes of all disinterested persons." Our forefathers, at the beginning of the struggle, were glad if they and their cause could even be considered respectable.

In a conference of two hours, Deane presented the requests of the colonists, and these were received with as much favor as he could have hoped. Forgetting the assurance he had given Lord Stormont a few months earlier, Vergennes now said that while he could not openly permit the shipment of military supplies to the colonists, no obstacle should be put in the way. In conclusion he bade Deane confer in the future with his secretary, Gérard, who understood English and could converse with him with facility.[1] Vergennes did not understand English and Deane's French was very imperfect, even at a later period. "M. Deane," Beaumarchais wrote some time after this first interview, for fear of spies, "does not open his mouth before the

[1] Doniol, i, 494.

English-speaking people he meets. He must be the most silent man in France, for I defy him to say six consecutive words in French." [1]

Deane profited by his friendly reception, and devoted to the interests of his country an amount of zeal for which he received but scanty gratitude, either from his contemporaries or from posterity. His instructions were vague, but in a general way he was to incline the mind of the French ministers towards furnishing aid to the colonists. This task he performed with much earnestness, and his arguments may not have been wholly without influence. No one imagined at that time that, ere many generations had passed away, the American colonists would become a great commercial and manufacturing nation, and that Europe would find in them not only profitable customers but dangerous competitors. Every one over-estimated, also, the degree in which their trade would be governed by sentimental considerations, or by any considerations except those of advantage.

Great Britain, by means of the restrictive laws through which every nation then strove to monopolize trade with its own colonies, had controlled a large portion of the commerce with America. The future was to show that she would still control it, because her former colonists would find it to their advantage to trade with her. But both American representatives and French statesmen believed that, as a result of a political alliance between the two countries, a vast amount of trade which formerly belonged to England would in the future be carried on with France. The advantages of this Deane described in terms which were perhaps more glowing than accurate. He pictured an

[1] Beaumarchais to Vergennes, Aug. 13, 1776 ; Doniol, i, 501.

infinite number of customers who would, in the dim future, be crying out for French goods.

The families of Americans were larger then than they are now, and Deane prophesied an increase of population that would be in keeping with the increase in wealth. "American planters," he wrote, "who, from the early age at which their children marry, have generally the pleasure of seeing in their lifetime their descendants doubling their numbers in the third and fourth generations, have also the solid satisfaction of finding the produce of the world they were peopling increase in equal degree." [1]

This population, so vastly increased in the third and fourth generations, would still, Deane thought, be faithful in its love for the soil, a prophecy which has not been verified. "The production of necessary raw materials for the use of the manufactories and commerce of Europe, as well as the essential ones of bread and provisions for the support of mankind, will in all probability increase for a century to come, in nearly the same ratio as hitherto; and the aversion of the inhabitants of the United Colonies to the sedentary employments, joined with the charms found in the innocence and simplicity of agriculture in a new country, will coöperate with other motives to induce them to receive from abroad the manufactures of others for the produce of their country. It is impossible for any power to become eminent in commerce, without excelling in manufactures and navigation. America is capable of supporting and increasing both, by her supplies and consumption; attended with this peculiar circumstance, the United Colonies will never, let their increase of population be ever so great, interfere with

[1] *Deane Papers*, i, 186; Memoir of Aug. 15, 1776.

the powers of Europe, either in their manufactures or commerce, nor, from their situation and climate, can they ever become rivals with the colonies of those powers in America in their staple produce, but, on the contrary, they will (indulged with a free trade to the West India Islands) enable them to extend and enlarge the cultivation of sugar, cotton, coffee, and their other articles, the demand for which yearly increases in Europe, to the greatest possible degree."[1]

The development of the country soon proved Deane's arguments to be unfounded. But if Americans have not all been satisfied with the charms found in the innocence and simplicity of agriculture, if the United States have become rivals of the powers of Europe both in manufactures and commerce, Deane was no further wrong in his prophecies than men of greater sagacity who have tried to forecast the future.

In his early negotiations, Deane was more embarrassed by an excess of would-be friends of America than by any coldness of reception. When Franklin visited Paris some years before, he met a Dr. Dubourg and contracted a considerable intimacy with him. Dubourg translated some of Franklin's writings into French. He early manifested an active interest, not only in Franklin, but in the welfare of the revolted colonists, and sent long letters to Congress, in which, with much exuberance and a good deal of inaccuracy, he stated the readiness of France to assist them. Naturally enough, Deane was advised, when he should reach Paris as a stranger, to avail himself of the doctor's counsel in the intricacies of French diplomacy.

Dubourg was only too willing to give aid; he had already interested himself in obtaining supplies for

[1] *Deane Papers*, i, 192.

the colonists, he wished now to be the intermediary between Deane and the French ministry, and to be intrusted with the important operations that were to grow out of their relations. But, in truth, the doctor was a fussy and injudicious man, little trusted by Vergennes, and filled with an overweening desire to make himself prominent in the negotiations between France and the colonists. He was a most excellent person, but his bustling activity and exuberant vanity did not fit him for negotiations which require the faculty of working fast and lying freely.

When Deane arrived, he at once resorted to Dubourg for aid, and the doctor assumed to take charge of the American envoy and act as his representative with the French ministers; but, in his desire to appear as the best friend of the colonists, Dubourg courted a publicity which was distasteful to his superiors. He had already asked for aid from the French government for his American friends, for arms from the arsenals, and engineers from the army. Vergennes was willing enough to furnish both, but Dubourg proved a most indiscreet agent, so pleased with his activity that he wished all the world to know what he was doing. " One can wink at certain things," the minister wrote him, " but one cannot authorize them " ; and he bade the doctor pursue his course with greater discretion.

Vergennes decided, therefore, that Beaumarchais was better fitted for such enterprises, and he recommended Deane to confer with the house of Hortalez and Company, under which name Beaumarchais did business. It was in vain that Dubourg remonstrated against this decision. He accompanied Deane to the minister's, only to be treated with so little attention that the American envoy saw that he would be better off unaccompanied by his self-constituted adviser. Vergennes wished the part taken by the government to be carefully concealed, but the doctor kept talking of the plans for assisting America, and left his hearers in little doubt as to where the aid would come from. Beaumarchais was ready to point out the mistakes of his rival. "If, while we close the door on one side," he wrote Vergennes, "the window is opened on the other, surely the secret will escape." Silence must be imposed on these babblers, he added, who can do nothing themselves and who hinder those who can do something.[1]

Deane soon discovered that it was not through the doctor's agency that he could best reach the ear of the French minister. Dubourg, bitterly protesting, was no further heeded, and the task of obtaining and forwarding supplies to the colonists fell into the hands of Beaumarchais. The French minister was ready to furnish assistance to the colonists, but he desired to conceal such enterprises from the vigilant eye of the English ambassador. Deane was accordingly turned over to an intermediary who might pose as a speculator on his own account, but whose action would, in truth, be seconded by the government. We might expect that the man chosen for such an undertaking would be some great merchant or some bold speculator, but Beaumarchais was chiefly known as a famous writer of comedies. The part which he took in our war for independence was so important and so curious that it deserves a careful examination.

[1] Beaumarchais to Vergennes, Sept. 21, 1776; Doniol, i, 520.

CHAPTER V

The part taken by Beaumarchais in furnishing assistance to American patriots is a picturesque chapter in our early history, while the treatment he received from the people he befriended is not a thing of which we can be proud. There was little in Beaumarchais's career that was not picturesque; he was dramatic in life as in literature; whether he produced comedies or transacted affairs of state, he was always amusing, and not always high-minded. The morality of Figaro was very nearly the morality of the creator of Figaro.

It was by a devious route that Beaumarchais reached the position of a great contractor, the representative of the French government in giving aid to a struggling republic. His father was a respectable jeweller, by the name of Caron, who made watches and practised his trade with much credit and moderate pecuniary success. He seems to have been an intelligent man; in his letters he expresses himself with justness and sometimes with felicity. To his intellectual qualities the father joined an unusual virility; he married a second time at the ripe age of seventy-seven, and espoused his third wife when eighty-six.

The famous author was born in 1732 in his father's shop in the rue Saint-Denis. He learned the trade of a watchmaker, and learned it well. When only twenty years of age, he invented an improvement in escapements which brought him some prominence in his craft. Others sought to reap the benefit of the invention, but the young Caron early showed skill in litigation ; he prosecuted the offenders with success, and the Academy of Sciences declared that the invention belonged to him.[1]

Soon he made still more important progress, and succeeded in selling some of his watches to Louis XV and others of the court. Accordingly he styled himself " Watchmaker to the King," and in the strangely compounded assemblage at Versailles, where those of every rank and occupation often jostled one another, Caron had the entrée; he not only sold watches to courtiers, but he became in a certain way a member of the court, where his good looks and, still more, his agreeable conversation made him welcome. The ladies, we are told, were pleased, not only by his "lofty stature and his slender and elegant figure," but still more by the " ardor which he exhibited on their appearance." Versailles was in some of its features curiously democratic, and the young watchmaker, though he did not meet great officials and nobles of long descent as an equal, at least had an opportunity to meet them. Presently he found a way to render his position somewhat more assured, by buying one of the innumerable offices which, if they were of little worth otherwise, obtained for the holder the right to figure as a regular member of the court. Beaumarchais bought the office of controller of the pantry of the king's household ; in that capacity he marched with the procession that carried the meat to the royal table, had the honor of placing some of the dishes before the King with his own hands, and then stood watching the repast with sword at his side. If his

[1] Louis de Loménie, *Beaumarchais et son Temps*, i, 19.

duties were not weighty, at least they were as important as those of the Cravattier in ordinary, or the Captain of the Greyhounds of the Chamber.

The controller of the pantry made another step forward when he married a rich widow older than himself; and he took the name of Beaumarchais from a small fief belonging to his wife. M. Caron borrowed his name from one of his wives, wrote an enemy some years later. In 1761 M. de Beaumarchais, as he was now called, bought for eighty-five thousand francs the office of secretary to the king, which imposed no duties but conferred the rank of nobility.[1] When later he was taunted with being a plebeian, he replied that he could easily prove his nobility, he held the parchment which conferred it and a receipt for the money he had paid for it. No aristocratic prejudices kept the author of " Le Mariage de Figaro " from sympathizing with republicans across the Atlantic.

In his new surroundings Beaumarchais abandoned the humble trade of watchmaker, and his active mind led him into varied employments. He gave lessons on the harp to the daughters of Louis XV, four exemplary and somewhat insipid princesses, and organized concerts which were sometimes honored by the presence of the King himself. Such relations flattered his vanity, but did not fill his pocket, for he received no pay from these august pupils. But he had a taste for speculation, and Paris Duverney, the famous contractor, initiated him, said Beaumarchais, " into the secrets of finance." [2] Opportunities to get into enterprises "on the ground floor " could be found in the reign of Louis XV, as well as on Wall Street to-day.

---

[1] Loménie, *Beaumarchais et son Temps,* i, 91.
[2] *Ibid.,* 115.

Beaumarchais profited by such and made money; some of it he spent and some of it, like many a modern speculator, he lost in other ventures.

He continued his varied career, and burst into fame by a lawsuit with one of the judges of the new courts created by Chancellor Maupeou. It is not often that one gains literary distinction by legal pleadings, but Beaumarchais's pleas, which he prepared himself, were read all over Europe; they excited the admiration of Goethe and Voltaire, and by the time the lawsuit terminated in a judgment that deprived him of all political rights and declared him infamous, he had acquired an international reputation, and was one of the most popular men in France. " It is not enough to be declared infamous," said a friend, who feared Beaumarchais's head would be turned by flattery, " one must also be modest."

Beaumarchais's fame as a writer did not diminish his taste for speculation, nor his eagerness for work in connection with the court, and all these passions were gratified by the part he was allowed to take in the dealings with the United States. It was during a stay in England that he first became interested in American matters. His errand illustrated the carelessness and recklessness of the closing years of Louis XV's reign. The Treaty of Paris stripped France of a large part of her colonial empire, and it was not strange that patriotic Frenchmen should devise plans of revenge. Yet it was strange that such schemes should receive the written approval of the French King, and be placed in the hands of diplomatic agents as a guide for their conduct. Such, however, was the case. Louis XV was too indolent to attend to the active duties of his position, but he sought amuse-

ment in playing at politics. He had a little body of
secret advisers, and carried on, by their means, a
personal diplomacy, which had no practical effect except occasionally to embarrass the official representatives of the state.

One of these advisers was the Comte de Broglie,
and he prepared an elaborate plan for the invasion of
England. Officers were sent to England who investigated places of landing, means of subsistence, positions
for camps, and all the detail of an invasion, with as
much precision as if an army were ready to embark.
This might have been a harmless diversion, but the
plan was submitted to the King, who endorsed upon it
his written approval, with as little consideration as he
would have given to granting a pension to one of his
sultanas, and then intrusted it to the Chevalier d'Eon,
one of his agents in England.[1] Éon subsequently
gained extensive notoriety by the controversy excited
over the question whether he was a man or a woman.
This became a favorite subject of wagers with the fre-
quenters of White's, and enormous sums were staked
upon it. Eon himself declined to solve the problem,
and after wearing the garb and leading the life of a
man and an officer of dragoons for almost fifty years,
he donned petticoats and for twenty years passed as
a woman.

If it was uncertain whether the chevalier was a man,
there was no doubt that he was a rogue ; he quarrelled
with the French minister and was presently discharged from employment, very much out of pocket,
and the possessor of a document containing a plan
for the invasion of England and bearing the written
endorsement of the French King, which members of

[1] Duc de Broglie, *The King's Secret*, ii, 80–87.

the English opposition would gladly buy at any price. They had criticized the terms of peace made with France; they declared that the ministry had failed to profit by victories won on sea and land, had neglected to complete the work Pitt had begun and thus cripple for all time the dangerous power of France. What force would be added to such charges, if they could produce a plan for the invasion of England, formally approved by Louis XV, when the ink was hardly dry on the Treaty of Paris! Not perfidious Albion, but perfidious Gaul would be exposed to the contempt of mankind.

Having rashly intrusted so compromising a paper to a most untrustworthy agent, Louis was now in great distress lest the existence of this scheme should be disclosed, not only to the English, but to his own ministers. The King was somewhat afraid of the wrath of Chatham, and much more afraid of the rebuking look of Choiseul; and Eon knew the value of the document he held; he would not surrender it; he would not expose himself to the dangers of a return to France; he intimated that his needs were great and the project of an English invasion would not be surrendered at the French King's command, but only in exchange for the French King's money.

It was a delicate problem to deal with a rogue who was also half crazy, and the King's advisers in these foolish schemes now added to his alarm. "Is it not to be feared," wrote the Comte de Broglie,[1] speaking of the possibility of Eon revealing his secrets, "that the sacred person of your Majesty would be compromised, and that a declaration of war on the part of England would be the inevitable consequence?" After great

[1] Duc de Broglie, *The King's Secret*, ii, 137.

disquiet the King made his peace with his dangerous subordinate by promising him twelve thousand livres per year, and this payment was made with greater regularity than Louis observed in dealing with many more meritorious creditors.

Eon kept his peace during the remainder of Louis XV's life, but he did not surrender the compromising papers. While Louis XVI and his ministers were not responsible for these, they knew enough about them to be sure that their publication would cause disagreeable complications. It was decided to secure them if Eon would agree to any reasonable terms, and Beaumarchais was selected as the best man for this negotiation. He had already proved his fitness for such a task. In the days of Louis XV, he had been sent to London to negotiate for the purchase of all the copies of a book purporting to give a history of the early career of Madame du Barry. A large sum of money had to be paid in order to prevent the publication of anything that might cast a shadow on the fair fame of that lady, but Beaumarchais performed his errand in a manner that secured the good-will of his employer. He had again been employed in securing the suppression of a libel on Marie Antoinette, and he was now deemed well qualified to deal with a blackmailer of another sort. Beaumarchais was superior to Eon in adroitness and his equal in freedom from scruple, and he was sent to England to obtain the incriminating documents at the lowest possible figure.

Accordingly in 1775 he visited London and at last made terms with the culprit. Though the chevalier was as erratic as he was dishonest, his business qualities were well developed. Before turning over the documents which it was his duty to return, he demanded twelve thousand livres a year in *rentes*, and to this Beaumarchais agreed.[1] In addition, Eon received a liberal sum for the payment of his debts, but to the contract were annexed some singular stipulations. The chevalier agreed that as a condition of his return to France he would assume the dress of a woman, and continue to wear this for the remainder of his life.

Beaumarchais, with less acuteness than he usually displayed, was convinced that Eon was a woman. " I assured this lady," he writes Vergennes, " that if she were wise, modest, talked little, and bore herself properly, I could probably obtain some further advantages for her." Eon was wise enough to demand at once two thousand crowns to buy a lady's wardrobe, and this was granted. On the whole the chevalier got the best of the bargain, but still the incriminating papers were obtained, and the French government was glad to get them back at any price.

This curious errand, in its indirect results, exercised a large influence upon Beaumarchais's future career, and was not without importance to the thirteen colonies that were about to renounce their allegiance to the English King. Beaumarchais's visits to England led to his action in behalf of England's rebellious colonies. He met intimately some of the men prominent in the opposition to Lord North, and he heard their opinions on American questions ; naturally enough he formed views as to English sentiment that were not always accurate. He was also brought into relations with some of the colonists, who were intimate with his English friends. Wilkes, then Lord Mayor of London, was an ardent advocate of the American cause. Americans were welcome and fre-

[1] Loménie, *Beaumarchais et son Temps*, i, 419.

quent visitors at the lord mayor's, and among them
was a young man whose acquaintance Beaumarchais
was unlucky enough to make.[1]

Arthur Lee was a member of the famous Lee family of Virginia, and was then studying law in England. He possessed a restless desire for prominence,
and either from natural exuberance of imagination, or
from a willingness to pervert the facts to suit his
taste, he was reckless in his statements to an extraordinary degree. It is hard to say whether he lied intentionally or from mere inability to tell the truth,
but his looseness of statement made him a dangerous
associate. Beaumarchais was not the most cautious of
men in his talk; when he and Lee discussed the affairs
of their respective governments, probably each deceived the other, and from this intercourse sprang in
the future many serious complications. Beaumarchais
believed all of Lee's rosy statements as to the strength
of the insurgents, and Lee was persuaded that France
stood ready to assist their cause to the utmost of her
power.

Lee sent home a report that, as a result of his labors, he had an assurance that France would furnish
five million livres' worth of arms and ammunition as
a free gift to the United States.[2] Beaumarchais was a
fervent talker, but he could not have made such a
statement as this. Lee reported this fable, partly from
his eagerness to make himself prominent as one who
had extracted great promises of aid, and partly, doubtless, deceived by his own heated imagination.

At all events, Beaumarchais suggested to the French
government the advisability of lending aid to the col-

---

[1] Loménie, *Beaumarchais et son Temps,* ii, 113.
[2] *Ibid.,* ii, 115.

onies, and when Beaumarchais had undertaken a cause, he gave his whole soul to it. Even if he overestimated the strength of the insurgents and the weakness of England, he saw more clearly than many statesmen the opportunity which France had to injure her ancient rival, and he manifested an interest in the cause of America that was then felt by few Frenchmen. The creator of Figaro must be counted among the earliest friends of the American Republic, and the services he rendered were by no means inconsiderable.

The American cause excited in Beaumarchais a genuine enthusiasm, though doubtless his zeal for liberty was increased by his desire to take an active part in the relations between the French court and the patriots. His dealings with the Americans exhibited that mixture of motives which is found in the actions of most men. He was eager to take a part in politics, and he found pleasure in the intrigues and secrecy in which plans for assistance to the colonists were involved ; he did not disdain the possibility of pecuniary gain from his labors, but in addition to this he was sincerely eager for the success of the colonists, and one of the first to feel a strong sympathy with the young nation struggling for independence.

In September, 1775, having returned to Paris, he submitted to the King a formal memoir in which he predicted the triumph of the colonies. The Comte de Vergennes was inclined to favor the insurgents, but he hesitated before taking any overt action. Beaumarchais, therefore, devoted himself to arousing Louis XVI and his minister to activity; the task was not an easy one, but nothing discouraged his patriotic zeal. England, he wrote, was in such a state of disorder within and without, that her ruin was near at hand,

if her rivals would seize their opportunity. The resources and the virtues of the insurgents were then
depicted in a manner that the facts did not wholly
warrant. The Americans, wrote Beaumarchais, would
suffer all things rather than yield; they were not only
full of enthusiasm for liberty, but thirty-eight thousand men, resolute and well armed, were ready to defend the cause, without taking one workman from the
factory or one tiller from the soil. " Every fisherman,"
he continued, "reduced to poverty by the English,
has become a soldier and vows he will avenge the ruin
of his family and his country's liberty."

From this glowing picture, which was partly due to
Arthur Lee's heated imagination, Beaumarchais declared the Americans to be invincible, while so grievous was England's strait that the King was not sure
of his crown and the ministers were not sure of their
heads. "This poor English people," he writes, "with its
frantic liberty, inspires compassion in every reflecting
mind. Never has it known the pleasure of living tranquilly under a wise and virtuous king." [1] Beaumarchais's eloquence was rarely without some personal end.
He drew as a moral from the situation that the French
ministry was ill informed, that it was delaying important action, and that the services of an active, intelligent man were absolutely required in London.

Though Louis XVI was a wise and virtuous king,
his mind worked slowly, and all this eloquence did
not make him a convert to the American cause. Beaumarchais was not a man to brook delay. This letter
was written on September 21, and on the next day he
wrote again, complaining to Vergennes that the Coun-

[1] Memoir, Sept. 21, 1775; Loménie, *Beaumarchais et son Temps*, ii,
92–96.

cil had taken no action. "All the wisdom of the world," he wrote, "will not enable a man to decide on the policy he should pursue, if he receives no answers to his letters. . . . Am I an agent who may prove useful to his country, or am I a deaf and dumb traveller?"[1]

Beaumarchais's usefulness might be questioned, but it was certain that he would not remain a mute. Though he complained of delay and bewailed the loss of time, his suggestions were followed with considerable promptness, and on the following day, September 23, he was again on his way to London. His activity had already excited the suspicions of the English ministers, and he was now given the nominal errand of buying old Portuguese piastres, which were to be sent to some of the French islands and there used as currency. In fact, he was commissioned as an agent to investigate the condition of English feeling, to ascertain the strength of the American colonists, and to make suggestions that might be valuable to his government, but he was strictly warned that he must do and say nothing that could be embarrassing to the French King. "Let your Excellency be at ease," he wrote Vergennes; "it would be an unpardonable folly in such a matter to compromise the dignity of my master or his minister. . . . To do one's best is nothing in politics; it is by doing the best possible that one distinguishes one's self from the ordinary run of public servants."

In December, 1775, he addressed another long communication to the sovereign, who thus far had received his suggestions with silent disapproval. "There are plans of such importance," he now wrote, "that a zeal-

[1] Loménie, *Beaumarchais et son Temps*, ii, 98.

ous servant must present them more than once." His suggestions, so Vergennes informed him, had been rejected, " not because they possessed no utility, but from the delicate conscientiousness of the King."

Delicate scruples did not appeal to the creator of Figaro, nor, for that matter, to the diplomats of that age. Beaumarchais insisted that Louis must rise to the heights of political expediency, where the first law was to do the best for one's self, though this should, indeed, be accomplished with the least possible wrong to other governments. National policy, he declared, differed wholly from the civil morality which governed individuals. Starting with this moral principle, he reached the conclusion that Louis owed it to the French people, whose father he was, to weaken England, their eternal foe. "Such," he said, after expounding England's wickedness in the past, " is the audacious, unbridled, shameless people you will always have to deal with. . . . Have the usurpations and outrages of that people recognized any limit but their own strength? . . . The most solemn treaty of peace is to this usurping nation merely a truce demanded by an exhausted people; and yet your Majesty is so delicate and conscientious as to hesitate." Were men angels, he added, the devices of politics could be disdained, and earth would be a celestial abode; but while men were men, and the English were wicked, one must profit by their troubles. The English had chased the French from three quarters of the globe, they had seized the ships of the French King in time of peace and forced him to destroy his finest harbor, a humiliation which made the heart of every true Frenchman bleed; the King must not be deceived by the sophisms of a false sensibility, but must find in

England's necessity France's opportunity. "May the guardian angel of the state incline the heart and mind of your Majesty," was the pious sentiment with which Beaumarchais ended his long appeal, which was zealous almost to impertinence.[1]

Two months later the untiring agent sent another long communication, in which he again urged that aid be given to the Americans. The quarrel between America and England, he said, with just foresight, was to divide the world and change the system of Europe, and every person should consider how the impending separation would work to his own gain or loss. And then he proceeded to show that it was for the interest of France to aid the insurgents; that the Americans must be helped, was the proposition he sought to demonstrate.[2]

His letter discloses how far his mind was influenced by the exuberant promises of Arthur Lee, the man who was destined to be the cause of Beaumarchais's financial ruin in his dealings with the United States. "A secret representative of the colonies, in London," so he wrote, "discouraged by the failure of his efforts through me to obtain from the French minister supplies of powder and munitions of war, said to-day, 'Has France absolutely decided to refuse us all succor, and thus become the victim of England and the laughing-stock of Europe? . . . We offer France in return for secret assistance a treaty of commerce which will secure to her for a certain number of years after the peace all the benefits with which for a century we have enriched England.'"

If the ministers desired to avoid a war with Eng-

[1] Beaumarchais to Louis, Dec. 7, 1775; Doniol, i, 251.
[2] Same to Same, Feb. 29, 1776; Doniol, i, 403–407.

land, this could only be done, so Beaumarchais declared, by furnishing secret aid to the Americans
which would enable them to maintain the contest;
otherwise England, after subduing her colonists,
would send her victorious fleets to despoil France
of her remaining possessions in the West Indies.

To secure the advantages which the situation offered, Beaumarchais proposed a scheme which was
agreeable to himself. It was possible, he wrote, to
aid the colonists without involving France in war;
they might receive succor which could not be shown
to come from the French government; and he added:
" If your Majesty has not a fitter man to employ, I
will undertake the enterprise and no one shall be
compromised. My zeal will better supply my lack of
capacity, than the ability of another could replace my
zeal."

In May, 1776, Beaumarchais returned to Paris,
and on the day of his arrival he sent post-haste to
Vergennes to demand an audience. " At three o'clock
in the morning," he wrote, "my servant will be at
Versailles for your levee. He will return in time for
mine. I hope he will bring the tidings which I await
with the utmost impatience, and that is, permission
to go and assure you of my devotion." [1]

So eager an emissary could not long be delayed.
The plan of operations was acceptable to Vergennes,
and in May the minister wrote the French ambassador
at Madrid that, although the government was not
ready to make any combination with the Americans,
and that even to furnish them with arms and munitions of war might be proceeding too openly, yet the
King had decided to lend them a million livres with

[1] Doniol, i, 483.

which they could buy what they needed. All, he added, would be done in the name of a commercial firm which would color its zeal by the appearance of desiring to take a great part in American trade, when this should become possible.[1] The uncertainty of any repayment seems to have been recognized, for Vergennes adds that the company would furnish securities, "to tell the truth, not very binding." In this plan the Spanish King had agreed to join, and he was therefore to send a million livres to be used in the same way.

Beaumarchais had convinced Vergennes, if not the King, and he now formed the imaginary house of Roderigue Hortalez and Company, to carry into effect his scheme. The taste for Spanish literature which he showed in his plays appeared in the title which he selected for the mythical firm; it was Spanish, high-sounding, and fictitious. In the name of this house supplies were to be sent to the insurgents, the government furnishing as much money as it was willing to advance, and supplying munitions of war from the royal storehouses. How far the advances of the French King were to be repaid was left in obscurity. If Beaumarchais could obtain payment from the Americans, he was to do so; if he failed in this, it seems doubtful whether the French government intended to press its claim. It was evident that the enterprise would require considerable sums of money above any supplies furnished by the state, and to this extent, at least, Beaumarchais contemplated a speculation on his own account which might prove profitable, but was certain to be attended with risk; his ships might be captured by the English, or their

[1] Doniol, i, 375.

contents might never be paid for by the Americans; but he feared the danger of loss as little as he feared the judgment of a court.

On June 10, 1776, the French government made an advance of one million livres,[1] and Beaumarchais executed a receipt for the money, adding, " Of which I am to render an account to the said Sieur Comte de Vergennes." On August 11, 1776, the million livres arrived from Spain, and this also was given to Beaumarchais through the medium of the French government, and for this he executed a similar receipt, saying, " The use of which I am to account for to his Excellency M. le Comte de Vergennes." The second receipt did not figure in subsequent transactions, but a reference to the first advance of a million livres was subsequently made by the French government in stating the moneys it had furnished to the colonies, and caused Beaumarchais untold woe. Whether any of this money was ever repaid does not appear, but we can safely assume that it was not. Doubtless Beaumarchais used the two millions in the purchase of supplies for the Americans, and in the course of his transactions with them. For that purpose the money was given him, and Vergennes never found any fault with his administration of the fund.

In the mean time a new actor appeared on the scene. In July, 1776, Silas Deane arrived in Paris with a commission from Congress to purchase supplies, which were to be paid for by the proceeds of cargoes of produce shipped from this country. Vergennes was ready to assist the colonists if he could do so without being found out, and he suggested to Deane that he had best apply to Beaumarchais, who was prepared to deal with

[1] Loménie, *Beaumarchais et son Temps*, i, 439.

such matters on a large scale. Beaumarchais met these overtures with alacrity, and at once offered to ship merchandise on the credit of Congress, to the amount of three million livres.[1] The American representative felt, however, a certain distrust of Beaumarchais's ability to perform this agreement, he being known, so says the report, "as a man of more genius than property"; but Vergennes replied there need be no fear. "That a man," Deane writes to the Secret Committee, "should, but a few months since, confine himself from his creditors, and now on this occasion be able to advance half a million, is so extraordinary that it ceases to be a mystery"; and the explanation was, as Deane adds, that "everything he says, writes or does, is in reality the action of the ministry." [2]

Beaumarchais admitted that his resources for aiding the colonists were by no means as great as he desired, and, therefore, he must have prompt returns in order to continue his advances; but, he adds, " I desire to serve your country as if it were my own, and I hope to find in the friendship of a generous people the true reward of a labor that I consecrate to them." [3]

A contract was promptly entered into, which was plainly within the authority Deane had received from Congress, and Vergennes gave his assurance that Beaumarchais would be properly supported, and be able to fill his engagements on the most advantageous terms. By this contract Beaumarchais was authorized to procure the supplies desired and ship them to America, and these were to be paid for by the proceeds of tobacco and other articles, which would be shipped by Congress as fast as vessels could be pro-

---

[1] B. F. Stevens, *Facsimiles of Manuscripts in European Archives relating to America*, no. 890.

[2] *Deane Papers*, i, 183, 217.   [3] July 22, 1776; *Ibid.*, 158.

vided. Twelve months, it was said, would be the long-
est credit required, and it was hoped that considerable remittances would be made within six months.[1]

The fact that these supplies were to be paid for was
specified with frequency and clearness in the contract
with Deane, and Congress hardly seems justified in
assuming later that they were not to be paid for,
merely because Arthur Lee said so. In the instructions given to Silas Deane, requesting him to obtain
clothing and arms for twenty-five thousand men, the
Committee said: "We mean to pay for the same by
remittances to France"; while as to linens, woollens,
etc., they were to be settled for at once and no credit
asked.[2] In conformity with these instructions Deane
promised prompt payment to Beaumarchais's house,
and reported to Congress the purchase of the goods,
and also that he had certified to the merchants "that
the Congress would pay for whatever stores they would
credit them with." He adds further on that he is
negotiating for purchases from Beaumarchais on a
credit of eight months from the time of delivery. "If
I effect this, as I undoubtedly shall, I must rely on the
remittances being made this fall and winter without
fail, or the credit of the Colonies must suffer."[3]

Beaumarchais himself was equally explicit, when
he reported this transaction to the Secret Committee.
He speaks of the cargoes that were to be sent in return and says, "I request you, gentlemen, to send me
next spring, if it is possible for you, ten or twelve
thousand hogsheads, or more if you can, of tobacco
from Virginia, of the best quality."[4] It should be

[1] *Deane Papers*, i, 153.

[2] *Revolutionary Diplomatic Correspondence of the United States,*
Francis Wharton, editor, ii, 79. Cited hereafter as "Wharton."

[3] Wharton, ii, 113-120.   [4] Wharton, ii, 129.

said that the Secret Committee never sent a reply to any letters of Roderigue Hortalez and Company; but that unlucky firm could hardly regard this as signifying that their offer of supplies was accepted, while their request for payment was declined.

It was agreed that two hundred brass cannon and arms and clothing for twenty-five thousand men should be provided, and more if they could be procured. If Beaumarchais's anticipations had been verified, very much larger quantities would have been supplied. In February he had submitted a further letter to the King, by which he showed that if money to the amount of a million livres could be furnished Hortalez and Company, and tobacco be promptly received in payment and sold at the satisfactory figures that Beaumarchais anticipated, by the time the King had invested for the second time the profits of the operation, the Americans would receive two millions in gold and seven millions in powder, and this would continue to increase in geometrical progression, using three as a multiple: " If the first million produced three, these three employed in further operations, on the same theory, ought to produce nine, and these nine, twenty-seven, etc., as I think I have sufficiently demonstrated." [1] Unfortunately, the demonstration of Beaumarchais was not realized, any more than that of Deane showing the immense return the French would enjoy from America's commercial favor.

All shipments were to be made in the name of the mythical house of Roderigue Hortalez and Company. The French King could do nothing himself towards providing the insurgents with contraband of war, but it was correctly assumed that his officials would wink

[1] *Deane Papers*, i, 110–115.

very hard when Beaumarchais was smuggling such articles out of the country to be sent to America.

The task of furnishing these supplies was beset by difficulties of every kind, and had it not been for Beaumarchais's indefatigable zeal, it is doubtful whether the much-needed powder, guns, and clothing would ever have reached the American army The first embarrassment arose from the jealousy of those who wished to take part in the work and found themselves superseded. Dr. Dubourg regarded himself as the unofficial representative of the colonies, and was greatly displeased when he found that Beaumarchais had been selected as the person to furnish them aid. His vanity was injured, and probably he honestly believed that a man of Beaumarchais's erratic character was ill adapted to the business of obtaining coats, powder, and second-hand guns, and shipping them over to America. Accordingly he wrote Vergennes, protesting against this selection. " He likes splendor," said the doctor; " it is asserted that he maintains young ladies at his expense ; in short he passes for a prodigal; in France there is no merchant . . . who would not hesitate very much to transact business with him." [1]

This accusation, it is feared, amused Vergennes, instead of alarming him, and he forthwith transmitted it to the culprit. Beaumarchais at once sent a characteristic reply. " How does it affect our business, if I like pomp and splendor, and maintain young ladies in my house ? The ladies . . . are your very humble servants. There were five, four sisters and a niece. . . . Two of the girls have died, to my great sorrow. I now keep there only two sisters and a niece. . . . But what

[1] Loménie, *Beaumarchais et son Temps*, ii, 120.

would you think of it, if . . . you had been aware
that I carry the scandal so far as to support . . . two
young and pretty nephews, and even the miserable
father who brought such a scandalous person into the
world? As to my splendor, it is still worse. . . . The
best black cloth is not too good for me, sometimes
I even push my recklessness so far as to wear silk
when it is very warm, but I supplicate you not to report these things to the Comte de Vergennes. You
would entirely destroy me in his opinion." [1] " Deliver
us," he writes again, " from this blundering and fatal
agent, this cruel babbler, this doting doctor."

Having made his contract, Beaumarchais undertook its execution with characteristic ardor. He rented
in the Faubourg du Temple an enormous house known
as the Hôtel de Hollande, in which the Dutch ambassadors had formerly dwelt; there a great force of
clerks and employees were installed, and there the
famous author was himself to be found early and
late, overseeing the operations of the house of Hortalez and Company with an energy that, to some extent, compensated for deficiencies in business methods
and ignorance of commercial affairs. Undeterred by
opposition, Beaumarchais proceeded to fulfil his part
of the agreement with zeal, though not always with
discretion. He announced his purpose to the Secret
Committee of Congress in the extraordinary language
which the imaginary Hortalez generally used in his
business correspondence. " The respectful esteem
which I have toward that brave people who so well
defend liberty under your guidance, has induced me
to form a plan of concurring in the great work by
establishing an extensive commercial house solely for

[1] Loménie, *Beaumarchais et son Temps*, ii, 120–125.

the purpose of serving you in Europe and supplying
you with necessaries of every kind. . . . Your deputies, gentlemen, can find in me a sure friend, an
asylum in my house, money in my coffers, and every
means of facilitating their operations." The King of
France, he said, and his ministers, must manifest opposition to anything that carried the appearance of
violating treaties with foreign powers. "But," he
added, "I promise you, gentlemen, that my indefatigable zeal shall never be wanting to clear up difficulties, soften prohibitions, and facilitate the operations of a commerce which your advantage, more than
my own, has made me undertake." [1]

It must be said that his performance very nearly
equalled his promise. He ransacked the government
storehouses in order to obtain arms; he purchased
clothes and chartered vessels. A fevered activity pervaded the Hôtel de Hollande, where tranquil Dutch
ambassadors had formerly smoked and dozed. Complications constantly arose from the desire of the
French government to avoid any responsibility for
what Beaumarchais was doing. There was an abundance of brass cannon in the armories, but the arms
of France were stamped on them; if any of these
were captured by the English it would be apparent
that they had been furnished by the French King. In
view of this, Vergennes said the arms must be erased,
if it could be done without weakening the cannon too
much, and if this was not possible, then new guns
must be cast.[2] But Beaumarchais obtained, mostly
from the French arsenals, over two hundred cannon,
twenty-five thousand guns, two hundred thousand

[1] Wharton, ii, 129.
[2] Narrative of Bancroft; *Deane Papers*, i, 182.

pounds of powder, twenty or thirty brass mortars, and clothing and tents for twenty-five thousand men, and these he loaded on boats which he himself provided.

The work was necessarily attended with much publicity, and the report of it soon came to the ears of the English ambassador. At this period Lord Stormont haunted Vergennes's chamber with complaints, almost always well founded, of the assistance France was giving the rebels, in violation of all principles of neutrality, and he now protested with special vigor against allowing these ships to sail, laden with contraband of war for the use of the American insurgents.

Vergennes maintained the farce of neutrality, and directed them to be stopped. He was perhaps the more ready to do this because the affairs of the colonists were at this time in very unpromising condition and it seemed probable that their struggle for independence would result in entire failure.

Beaumarchais was indefatigable in his efforts to get the boats off, but was not always equally judicious. He went to Havre on this errand, and Kalb, with good reason, complained of his conduct. It was important that his presence should not be known, and he accordingly assumed the name of Durant. But, wrote Kalb, there was little gain in that, when he occupied any leisure hours in superintending the representation of one of his comedies, and drilling the actors at the rehearsal.[1] There were inconveniences in purchasing powder and clothing from a man of genius.

At last, however, in December, 1776, the Amphitrite, one of Beaumarchais's boats, actually set sail.

[1] *Deane Papers*, i, 433.

But the exultation over its departure was soon turned
to sorrow. There sailed on it an officer named du
Coudray, one of the numerous French volunteers
whom Deane employed in the service of the United
States, and whose misdeeds had much to do with the
ill-favor into which he later fell in his own country.
Du Coudray insisted that his services would be invaluable to the colonies, and Deane took him at his own
estimate. By the contract made with him, he was to
be a major-general and command the engineer corps,
with power to fill all vacancies. He was to have
horses and carriages, at the expense of the colonists,
in going from one place to another, and at the end of
his service he was to be retired on an " honorable
annual stipend."

The employment of this man was an instance of
the lamentable lack of judgment which finally involved Deane, a well-meaning and, at the beginning,
an honest man, in utter ruin. He wrote of du Coudray
that he was "a plain, modest, active, sensible man."[1]
Of all the undesirable foreign recruits who sought
their own advantage under the guise of coming to our
assistance, du Coudray was perhaps the least entitled
to be designated by any of those adjectives. He soon
showed the manner of man he was. The accommodations on the Amphitrite were not to his taste, and
he accordingly ordered her to return, and in January
the boat sailed back into port.

Both Deane and Beaumarchais were in despair.[2]
"The devil is in our affairs," wrote Beaumarchais,
and with good reason he poured reproaches on du
Coudray, and directed him to turn over the command
to another officer. Two other boats were ready to sail,

[1] Wharton, ii, 124; *Deane Papers*, i, 229.   [2] Wharton, ii, 252.

and Beaumarchais gave Vergennes no rest until the prohibition upon their departure was revoked. If this was not done openly, it was done secretly; and, at last, thanks to the connivance of the French government, the three boats set sail for America, carrying much-desired provisions and a considerable number of officers. Some of these proved less valuable than the powder and cannon, but among them was Steuben, and his virtues atoned for the deficiencies of many others.

Beaumarchais was indefatigable as a correspondent, and embellished the details of warfare with the flowers of rhetoric. He sent over a recommendation of Steuben in which he wrote: "The art of making war with success being the fruit of courage combined with prudence, intelligence and experience, a companion in arms of the great Frederick, who was with him during twenty-two years, seemed to us all a man most fit to assist Monsieur Washington."

Beaumarchais's ships escaped the perils of the sea and the vigilance of British cruisers. They reached Portsmouth and landed greatly needed supplies in time to be used against Burgoyne. Many a soldier who marched in that campaign wore shoes on his feet, a coat on his back, and carried a gun on his shoulder, which came from the magazines of Louis XVI, and had been procured and furnished by the author of the "Barbier de Seville." Several more ships, loaded by Beaumarchais, were allowed to sail from France and in due time reached their destination. By September, 1777, he had shipped munitions of war to the value of five million livres.

But the shiploads of tobacco and American produce, the proceeds of which were to pay for all this, did not make their appearance; he did not even get a letter acknowledging the arrival of the boats and the receipt of the supplies. In October, he wrote in characteristic tone: "There is no news from America, and no tobacco either. This is depressing, but depression is a long way from discouragement." [1]

His troubles grew largely out of the indefatigable and pernicious activity of Arthur Lee. Lee was one of the most suspicious, the most atrabilious, and the most cantankerous persons whom the Revolution produced, and he excited in those with whom he had to deal a degree of irritation difficult to describe. He was eager to take a prominent part, and jealous of those who were preferred to him; believing all men to be liars except himself and possibly John Adams, with an extraordinary power of hating, an endless fund of acrimony, and an exhaustless capacity for lying, he did an amount of evil out of all proportion to his very moderate ability. When he found that Beaumarchais was dealing with Deane instead of with him, he took steps which proved very disastrous to the creator of Figaro.

Lee wrote Congress that these munitions of war were not to be paid for, but were the free gift of the French King. "M. de Vergennes," he said, "has repeatedly assured us that no return was expected for the cargoes sent by Beaumarchais. This gentleman is not a merchant, he is known to be a political agent employed by the Court of France." If the latter assertion was true, the former was the reverse of the truth. Vergennes had said nothing of the sort, and Lee's statement was an unblushing lie. The French court had furnished Beaumarchais with one million

[1] *Deane Papers*, i, 318.

livres, and Spain as much more, and while he was instructed to get pay for all the supplies, it is not probable that the advance of the two millions was regarded as a business transaction. But the material furnished by Beaumarchais absorbed much more than the two millions, and for all over that amount he had advanced his own money and that of his associates, or pledged their credit. He now asked for payment as agreed. Lee said nothing was to be paid, and intimated that the demand was in fraud of the French government, and intended to fill the pockets of Beaumarchais and Deane with illegal gains. Congress knew not what to do, and in its perplexity was inclined to do nothing. When it was difficult to pay debts of unquestioned legality, it was easy to delay payment of claims which perhaps were not debts at all.

So no tobacco was sent, and the enterprising firm of Hortalez and Company soon found itself in financial distress. Beaumarchais applied to Vergennes for relief, and succeeded in extracting another million to help him out, but there still remained a large balance. He repeatedly asked for payment. Lee as repeatedly assured Congress that these demands were either part of a commercial comedy and not intended to be answered, or rascally attempts to cheat Congress and defeat the liberal purposes of the French King.[1] It was in vain that Beaumarchais wrote that he had exhausted his money and his credit. Congress insisted upon regarding him as a generous benefactor, who, representing the French King, was sending goods from love and asking pay for amusement.

At last one small cargo of rice and indigo reached France, and even this the American envoys said be-

[1] Wharton, i, 402, 494.

longed to them. Beaumarchais got possession of the cargo, but it was worth only one hundred and fifty thousand livres. "You will see," he wrote his agent in America, "that there is a great difference between this drop of water and the ocean of my debts. . . . I am contending with obstacles of every nature, but I struggle with all my might, and I hope to conquer with patience, credit and money. The enormous losses to which all this puts me appear to affect no one; the minister is inflexible, even the deputies at Passy claim the honor of annoying me, — me, the best friend of their country."[1]

All this seems to be strictly correct, and it is sad to know that the ships laden with tobacco, in visions of which Beaumarchais indulged in this letter, never appeared on the horizon. Yet it is not remarkable that Congress thought him a merchant of so strange a type that it could hardly be believed he was selling them goods in the expectation of payment; for, after lamenting his woes, he continued in his letter: "Through all these annoyances, the news from America overwhelms me with joy. Brave, brave people, their warlike conduct justifies my esteem and the noble enthusiasm felt for them in France. Finally, my friend, I only wish some return from them in order to meet my engagements, and be able to serve them anew."

His relations with the colonies still rested upon the agreement signed by Deane. He had delivered large quantities of supplies and received small remittances in return, and he therefore sent one Francy to the United States, to see if he could not obtain some settlement of past accounts, and make satisfactory ar-

[1] Beaumarchais to Francy, Dec. 20, 1777; Loménie, *Beaumarchais et son Temps*, ii, 147.

rangements for the future. " Be like me," he writes his agent, in a tone that certainly is not often assumed by merchants, "despise small considerations, . . . and small resentments. I have enlisted you in a magnificent cause. You are the agent of a man who is generous and just. Remember that success is due to fortune, that the money owing me is at the hazard of a great combination of events, but that my reputation is my own, and that you to-day are the artisan of your own good name. Let it be always good and all will not be lost, whatever may happen to the rest."[1] " After what I have done," he added, "I hope that Congress will not doubt that the most zealous partisan of the Republic in France is your friend Roderigue Hortalez and Company."

It seems immaterial whether or not Deane had authority to contract with Hortalez and Company: the guns and powder, the coats and shoes had been shipped, they had been received and used by American soldiers. But any further transactions were put upon a still surer basis, as a result of Francy's negotiations. In April, 1778, a contract was executed between the commissioners of Congress and the adventurous house of Hortalez and Company. It recited that the house had already shipped considerable quantities of arms, ammunition, and clothing, which had been received by the agents of the United States, and that they were willing to continue furnishing supplies if satisfactory assurance were given for payment at a just price. It was therefore agreed that the cost of the shipments already made should be fairly stated at current prices ; that orders thereafter given should be filled at not

[1] Beaumarchais to Francy, Dec. 20, 1777; Loménie, *Beaumarchais et son Temps*, ii, 147.

higher figures, adding only the usual mercantile charges at the places whence they were exported; that the agents of Congress should be allowed to inspect all goods, and reject those which they should judge too dear or unfit for use. It was further agreed that bills might be drawn on the house of Hortalez and Company for the accommodation of Congress, to the amount of twenty-four millions of livres, payable during the ensuing year. In consideration of this the committee promised that cargoes of merchandise should be shipped to Hortalez and Company, who would credit our government with the proceeds of the sales; that they should be allowed 6 per cent interest on advance, together with a commission of $2\frac{1}{2}$ per cent on the amount of invoices, freight, and moneys paid and disbursed by them for the account of the United States; and that remittances should be made to them from time to time in produce or money until the entire indebtedness should be discharged. This agreement was signed by Ellery, Forbes, Drayton, and Duer as the committee of the American Congress.[1]

Notwithstanding this formal contract, the accounts of the firm remained unliquidated, and Arthur Lee still insisted that most, if not all, of the supplies furnished were the free gift of the French government, for which there could be no liability. Congress decided that the only way to solve this dispute was to ascertain the facts from the French government itself. Accordingly the American commissioners at Paris were instructed to seek information from Vergennes, and to inquire how far these supplies were the free gift of the French King, and how far they were property furnished by

[1] April, 1778. John Durand, *New Materials for the History of the American Revolution, from Documents in the French Archives*, 119–126.

Hortalez and Company for which payment should be made. "You will observe," so ran the instructions, "that their accounts are to be fairly settled, and what is justly due paid for, as, on the one hand, Congress would be unwilling to evidence a disregard for, and contemptuous refusal of, the spontaneous friendship of his Most Christian Majesty, so, on the other, they are unwilling to put into the private pockets of individuals what was graciously designed for the public benefit. You will be pleased to have their accounts liquidated, and direct, in the liquidation thereof, that particular care be taken to distinguish the property of the crown of France from the private property of Hortalez and Company, and transmit to us the accounts so stated and distinguished. This will also be accompanied by an invoice of articles to be imported from France, and resolves of Congress relative thereto. You will appoint, if you should judge proper, an agent or agents to inspect the quality of such goods as you may apply for to the house of Roderigue Hortalez and Company, before they are shipped, to prevent any impositions."[1]

The commissioners submitted these instructions to Vergennes, and then proceeded with their inquiries. "We are under the necessity of applying to your Excellency upon this occasion," so they wrote, "and of requesting your advice. With regard to what is passed, we know not who the persons are who constitute the house of Roderigue Hortalez and Company; but we have understood, and Congress has ever understood, and so have the people in America in general, that they were under obligations to his Majesty's good will for the greatest part of the merchandise and

[1] Letter of Sept. 10, 1778; Durand, *New Materials*, etc., 127–131.

warlike stores heretofore furnished under the firm name of Roderigue Hortalez and Company. We cannot discover that any written contract was ever made between Congress or any agent of theirs and the house of Roderigue Hortalez and Company; nor do we know of any living witness, or any other evidence, whose testimony can ascertain for us who the persons are that constitute the house of Roderigue Hortalez and Company, or what were the terms upon which the merchandise and munitions of war were supplied, neither as to the price, nor the time or condition of payment. As we said before, we apprehend that the United States hold themselves under obligations to his Majesty for all those supplies, and we are sure it is their wish and their determination to discharge the obligations to his Majesty as soon as Providence shall put it in their power. In the mean time we are ready to settle and liquidate the accounts according to our instructions, at any time, and in any manner which his Majesty and your Excellency shall point out to us." [1]

Nothing could seem fairer than this letter, but its promises were not fulfilled in the subsequent conduct of the American Congress. Vergennes did not answer directly, nor could he. He could not acknowledge any responsibility for the doings of Hortalez and Company, whose action in furnishing supplies to the Americans when France and England were at peace was, nominally at least, without the knowledge or sanction of the French government. He wrote the newly appointed French minister to the United States, and said:—

"M. Franklin and his colleagues would like to know what articles have been supplied by the King, and those that have been supplied by M. de Beau-

[1] Durand, *New Materials*, etc., 129–131.

marchais on his own account, and they insinuate that Congress is persuaded that all, or at least a large portion, of what has been sent, is on account of his Majesty. I am about to reply that the King has not furnished anything; that he has simply allowed M. de Beaumarchais to provide himself with what he wanted in the arsenals, on condition of replacing what he took; and that, for the rest, I will gladly interpose in order that they may not be pressed for the payment of the military supplies."

Apparently this statement was regarded as satisfactory, and in January of 1779 Congress extended its formal thanks to Beaumarchais for his efforts in behalf of the colonies. Nothing could have been handsomer than their expression of regard.

Sir: The Congress of the United States, sensible of your exertions in their favor, present you with their thanks and assure you of their regard.

They lament the inconvenience you have suffered by the great advances made in support of these States. Circumstances have prevented a compliance with their wishes; but they will take the most effectual measures in their power to discharge the debt due you.

The liberal sentiments and extensive views which could alone dictate a conduct like yours are conspicuous in your actions and adorn your character. While with great talents you served your Prince, you have gained the esteem of this infant Republic and will receive the united applause of the New World.

JOHN JAY,
President.[1]

---

[1] Durand, *New Materials*, etc., 134.

Doubtless this gave great pleasure to its recipient, who cared more for public applause, not to say public notoriety, than ever he did for money. But this expression of gratitude was neither accompanied nor followed by any remittances on account. Arthur Lee had been recalled from Paris, and his activity with members of Congress was quite sufficient to prevent any settlement of the claim. It may be said that Congress was in such pecuniary straits that it was prone to seize any excuse for postponing the claim of a creditor, but it must also be said that it showed no eagerness to pay for supplies which were certainly of great value. The fact is that our country at that time was in the condition of a needy personage constantly asking and frequently receiving the bounty of those better off in the world. The receipt of pecuniary assistance is apt to be demoralizing. When much is given, the recipient naturally thinks that all should be given ; the desire to pay to every one his legal dues is apt to be blunted in those who are in a condition of chronic impecuniosity. The members of Congress were evidently little distressed by the possibility that their country owed Beaumarchais not only thanks but cash.

Probably Beaumarchais hoped for gain as well as glory from his dealings with the Americans. It is quite possible that in his accounts he neglected to credit the sums which had been advanced him from the French and Spanish treasuries, and of which, apparently, no repayment was expected by those governments ; but certainly he was interested in the cause, and continued to furnish supplies when a prudent merchant would have delayed further shipments until he had been settled with to date. Not only had he received practically nothing on his great advances in excess of the money furnished by the French King, but war was now declared between France and England, and fresh perils awaited any ships which hazarded the long journey across the Atlantic.

Beaumarchais was undeterred by the danger that his merchandise would never reach the other side, or by the still more serious danger that even if it were received, it would never be paid for. In December, 1778, he despatched a new fleet laden with arms and supplies. The vessels sailed at his own risk, and this was certainly serious in time of war, when the ocean was patrolled by English cruisers. He writes: " Congress will not be obliged to pay for cargoes it does not receive, which may have been lost on the passage from Europe." His zeal for the cause was unabated by past troubles, though the remissness of Congress might well have discouraged a less enthusiastic friend. He treated the United States as he did others whom he assisted.

In the same letter he writes: " Remember me often and kindly to Baron Steuben. According to. what I hear from him I congratulate myself on having sent so fine an officer to my friends the free men, and for having compelled him, in a certain way, to enter upon such a noble career. I am not at all uneasy about the money I lent him for an outfit. Never have I made a more satisfactory use of money, for I have placed a man of honor where he ought to be. I learn that he is inspector-general of all the American forces! Tell him that his fame pays the interest of his debt, and that I have no doubt of its payment in this way at usurious rates." [1]

[1] Durand, *New Materials*, etc., 140.

This was apparently the only payment ever made, for at the inventory taken of Beaumarchais's assets after his death in 1799 there appears an advance made to Steuben and his nephews in order that they might go to America. The claim is entered with the accuracy with which Beaumarchais kept his accounts, and which contrasted with the liberality with which he advanced his money and the carelessness with which he allowed it to remain unpaid. 5995 frs. 2 sols 7 deniers was the amount of the advances to Steuben, as they appear in Beaumarchais's books, and if the interest on the debt was paid by Steuben's fame, the principal remained wholly unliquidated.

Beaumarchais not only equipped ten merchant ships, but he fitted out at his own expense a man-of-war named the Fier Roderigue, and sent it forth to guard the merchantmen. The result of this enterprise was gratifying to his pride and costly to his purse. The little fleet came sailing along, when d'Estaing was about to engage Admiral Byron. Discovering that the man-of-war belonged to Beaumarchais, d'Estaing compelled the Fier Roderigue to join his fleet and take part in the battle. She acquitted herself with great credit, but the captain was killed, and the ship suffered more severely than any other of d'Estaing's command.[1] She had to be refitted at great expense, and the convoy came to grief. Beaumarchais suffered ruinous losses, though he finally obtained two million livres as indemnity. Even this payment was so delayed that he received the last installment seven years later, on leaving the prison in which he had been thrown for using impertinent language.

The United States at last made some payment on

[1] Loménie, *Beaumarchais et son Temps*, ii, 164.

account, but with hardly less deliberation. They did not send cargoes of tobacco, which could at once have been turned into money, but remitted two million and a half livres, in bills payable three years in the future. Such obligations of a government whose existence was still at stake could not be discounted on favorable terms, and even when the time for payment came round, Robert Morris suggested to Franklin that they might as well be left unpaid. But Franklin said they were in the hands of the bankers and must be met for the country's credit, and paid they accordingly were.

Beaumarchais not only furnished supplies to the United States, but he undertook similar operations with Virginia and South Carolina. These were no more successful than his dealings with the general government. He sent to these states two cargoes of supplies, and received his pay in paper money which was worth little or nothing by the time it reached him.

It illustrates the character of the man, that, undisturbed by all these embarrassments and undeterred by all these losses, he entered on various other commercial speculations in the West India Islands. Loménie, who went over Beaumarchais's accounts from 1776 to 1783, the period of his commercial career, says that they disclosed expenditures of twenty-one million livres, and receipts exceeding this great amount by only the beggarly sum of forty-eight thousand livres.[1] It is safe to say that when all the accounts were in, the balance was on the other side. What Beaumarchais wrote his confidential agent Francy about his private expenses, was true as to his great commercial operations. "When I try to arrange my expenses in

[1] Loménie, *Beaumarchais et son Temps*, ii, 204-205.

part, I am mortified to hear that every one about me is wasting my money. . . . Live simply and do without the things that are unnecessary. . . . I am robbed on every side on account of the lack of order by which they all profit. . . . I have three coachmen who are leagued together to pillage me. . . . Where is confusion, there is robbery. I wish in the future to live in the greatest simplicity."

There was equal confusion and probably much more robbery in the affairs of the great house of Hortalez and Company, and when we add the fact that its chief debtor declined to settle, the financial distresses of the great dramatist are easily understood.

At last, even Beaumarchais's zeal failed, or, what is more probable, his finances were exhausted. He had obtained assistance from various persons; the names of some great nobles are found in the list of those who took a share in his ventures; but if his statement can be credited, they were less indulgent towards their creditor than he was with his American friends. At all events, he decided to send no more supplies until he could obtain a settlement for what he had already furnished. It is unpleasant to reflect that the difficulties he had met with and overcome in obtaining and shipping supplies to the United States, were much less than the difficulties which he was unable to overcome in getting his pay. The adjustment of Beaumarchais's claims extended over a period of almost half a century.

In 1781 Silas Deane undertook the settlement of Beaumarchais's accounts. He had made the original contract, and he was more familiar with this intricate affair than any other representative of the United States. Notwithstanding all the slanders poured upon him by his enemies, there is nothing to show that in his relations with Beaumarchais he acted corruptly, or even negligently. Deane had always insisted that Beaumarchais was to be paid for the supplies he furnished. Such had been the express wording of the contract which Deane executed, and he constantly bore witness to Beaumarchais's activity and good faith. In November, 1776, he wrote Congress: "I should have never completed what I have, but for the generous, the indefatigable and spirited exertions of Monsieur Beaumarchais, to whom the United States are on every account greatly indebted ; more so than to any other person on this side of the water; he is greatly in advance of stores, clothing, and the like, and therefore I am confident you will make him the earliest and most ample remittances." [1]

Deane now went over the accounts and found there was a balance due Beaumarchais of three million six hundred thousand livres. But in the mean time Deane's own affairs were involved in hopeless complications. Not only Lee, but Paine and many other rancorous opponents, pronounced him a monster of corruption. Adams and his associates looked upon Deane with distrust and dislike. His conduct had been indiscreet, Congress was mistrustful of him, and his adjustment of Beaumarchais's accounts was formally declared to be without authority.

In 1783 Mr. Barclay, then consul-general at Paris, undertook a new examination of the records. Beaumarchais declared his accounts had already been settled. Barclay said that Congress would not pay him a cent unless they were again examined. The unlucky creditor was forced to submit; but before any

[1] *Deane Papers*, i, 378.

decision could be reached a new incident added new confusion, and resulted in the postponement of any settlement until many years after Beaumarchais had been in his grave.

In 1783 a memorandum had been signed between Franklin and Vergennes as to the advances made by the French government to the United States. In this it was stated that three million livres had been given to our government prior to the treaty of alliance in 1778. At the time no question was raised as to this figure. But three years later Franklin, for the first time, seems to have awakened to the fact that he had only received two million livres in money from the French government prior to the treaty. In addition to this he had received a million as an advance from the French farmers-general, which was to be repaid in produce, though our government, dealing with the farmers-general much as it did with Beaumarchais, had sent them tobacco to the value of only one hundred and fifty-three thousand livres. With a business-like spirit that, though doubtless commendable, was certainly unusual when proceeding from a nation that had been the recipient of boundless charity, it was now suggested to the French government that perhaps the three millions included the money supposed to be advanced by the farmers-general, and if so, the farmers-general must at once pay for the tobacco they had received. It might have been suggested that if the French government had not furnished the million which the farmers-general advanced eight years before, it might be well for the United States to think about paying the eight hundred and fifty thousand livres which they still owed. No such suggestion, however, was ever made.

The question put to Vergennes was very embarrassing. It was doubtless by inadvertence that the amount given the United States was stated at three million instead of two million livres, for the other million had been turned over to Beaumarchais, and for it he was to account. Vergennes was reluctant to admit publicly that he had given Beaumarchais money to buy military supplies while France was still at peace with England, for he had often assured the English that he was doing nothing of the sort. He was unwilling also further to embarrass Beaumarchais, who had already been for years trying to get a settlement of his accounts with the United States. At all events, the Americans were informed that the French King had nothing to do with the advances made by the farmers-general, and that this million was paid from the treasury in June, 1776. Grand, acting for the United States, asked for a copy of the receipt, but the French government declined to furnish it.

From all this the American Congress decided that Beaumarchais had received the million, in which they were entirely right; that he ought to turn this million over, in which they were wrong; and that they would pay him nothing until the matter was cleared up. Vergennes had repeatedly declared that the French King had nothing to do with the supplies furnished by Beaumarchais, and if his word were to be credited, Beaumarchais was entitled to be paid. If Beaumarchais had had dealings with the French government, manifestly, in view of the position taken by that government, it was for us to settle with our creditor, and for him to settle with his creditor. If a portion of his claim represented supplies furnished by France, there was no reason that the United States should insist this was intended as a gift, in the face of the declaration of the French minister that it was not a gift. Presumably, if Beaumarchais had received supplies from France and was paid for them by the United States, he would pay to the French government whatever was its due ; and even assuming that he had omitted to credit the money advanced, and that it was a just credit, there still remained a large balance due to Hortalez and Company. But Congress would do nothing and would pay nothing until the mystery of the million was cleared up.

In 1787, when the account was now ten years old, even Beaumarchais's good-nature failed him, and he wrote the President of Congress : " What do you suppose is the general opinion here of the vicious circle in which you have involved me ? We will not reimburse M. de Beaumarchais until his accounts are adjusted by us, and we will not adjust his accounts, so as not to pay them ! With a nation that has become a powerful sovereign, gratitude may be a simple virtue unworthy of its policy; but no government can be relieved from doing justice and from discharging its debts. I venture to hope, sir, that, impressed by the importance of this matter and the soundness of my reasoning, you will oblige me with an official reply stating what decision the honorable Congress will come to, either promptly to adjust my accounts and settle them, like any equitable sovereign, or to submit the points in dispute to arbiters in Europe with regard to insurances and commissions, as M. Barclay had the honor of proposing to you in 1785, or, finally, to let me know without further shift that American sovereigns, unmindful of past services, deny me justice. I shall then adopt such measures as seem best for my despised interests and my wounded honor, without lacking in the profound respect with which I am, sir, the very humble servant of the general Congress and yourself." [1]

A creditor who during ten years had been in vain asking for a settlement of his accounts could hardly be charged with any impropriety in thus presenting his claim, but Congress regarded this language as impertinent and unseemly and resolved to discipline the offender. Accordingly it voted to adjust Beaumarchais's account and referred it to Arthur Lee to settle the amount due. This was equivalent to saying that it would pay nothing. Lee was Beaumarchais's bitter enemy. He insisted that all articles furnished by Hortalez and Company were gifts from the French government, and that the entire claim was a fraud. He now promptly reported, not only that the United States owed nothing to Beaumarchais, but that Beaumarchais owed the United States almost two million francs. How this result was reached does not appear. Probably Lee's process was a simple one. All the supplies furnished by Hortalez and Company were gifts from the French government; any shipments of produce from this country, which by any possibility came into the hands of that firm, were charged against them. In other words, Beaumarchais's account contained no credits, and consisted solely of debit items.

Thus the matter remained for five years longer, until, in 1793, Congress ordered a new examination to be made by Alexander Hamilton. The financial ability of the investigator, his integrity and his standing, made it certain that his report would be just to all parties. It seemed also that a statement by Hamilton of

[1] Loménie, *Beaumarchais et son Temps*, ii, 192.

the amount due should carry conviction to Congress, and that if Beaumarchais could obtain an award at his hands, his troubles would be over. This was far from being the case. Hamilton examined the claim, decided that Lee's decision was wrong, and fixed the sum justly due from the United States to Beaumarchais at two million two hundred and eighty thousand francs. The question of the million he left open, saying that further inquiry should be made by the French government, and if it appeared that the United States was entitled to the credit, that sum should be deducted. It is probable that this decision came as near the truth as it was possible to reach in this intricate matter. It was, however, of no benefit to Beaumarchais. Congress declined to pay the award of its own arbitrator. It still insisted that the million furnished by the French government should be applied on the debt, and decided that, as it was uncertain how much ought to be paid, the safest way was to pay nothing.

In the mean time the French Revolution involved Beaumarchais in financial ruin. He fled from France and sought refuge in Hamburg, where he lived in great poverty in a garret. Not long before his death in 1795, he prepared a memorial in behalf of his daughter. The style is flowery and effusive, but it is not a paper that any American can read with pleasure. Whatever were Beaumarchais's faults, he had given useful aid to a country struggling for existence. Even if the exact amount due him was uncertain, it was certain that the sum was large. The struggling republic had now become, not perhaps a rich and powerful nation, but prosperous, fully able to pay its debts, and with infinite possibilities before it. The creditor who had waited for twenty years was old, poor, sick, broken in health and fortune. Thus he writes : —

"Americans, I served you with untiring zeal. I have thus far received no return for this but vexation and disappointment, and I die your creditor. On leaving this world, I must ask you to give what you owe me to my daughter as a dowry. When I am gone she will, perhaps, have nothing, on account of other wrongs against which I can no longer contend. Through your delay in discharging my claims Providence may have intended to provide her with a resource against utter destitution. Adopt her after my death as a worthy child of the country! Her mother and my widow, equally unfortunate, will conduct her to you. Regard her as a daughter of a citizen . . . Americans, . . . be charitable to your friend, to one whose accumulated services have been recompensed in no other way! *Date obolum Belisario*." [1] To this appeal no answer was given.

Beaumarchais died unpaid, and thirty-six years passed before his heirs obtained a settlement. Various French ministers interested themselves in behalf of Beaumarchais's family, but their efforts were in vain. Talleyrand did not put the case unfairly in his letter to the French minister at Washington. "Opposition is made to M. de Beaumarchais's heirs on account of a receipt he gave June 10, 1776, for one million francs, paid to him by order of M. de Vergennes, and it is pretended that this sum should be credited on the supplies which he furnished to the United States. As the payment and purpose of this million related to a meas-

[1] Durand, *New Materials*, etc., 154; Loménie, *Beaumarchais et son Temps*, ii, 196.

ure of secret political service ordered by the King,
and immediately executed, it does not seem either just
or proper to confound this with mercantile operations,
later in date, carried on between Congress and a private individual. . . . A French citizen who hazarded
his entire fortune to help the Americans, and whose
zeal and activity were so essentially useful during the
war which gave them their liberty and their rank
among nations, might unquestionably pretend to some
favor; in any event he should be listened to when he
asks nothing but good faith and justice." [1]

Many years later the American government again
asked the question which it had been putting from
time to time for over thirty years: Would the French
government say that the million given Beaumarchais
had nothing to do with the supplies which Beaumarchais had furnished the United States? The Duc de
Richelieu was then minister of foreign affairs, and
he promptly made the required statement. [2] In one
sense it was untrue, for the money had been used by
Beaumarchais to buy supplies. In another sense it was
true, for Beaumarchais was accountable for this sum
to the French government alone, and it was none of
our business. But at all events, having asked the question of the French government, it would have been
courteous to accept its answer as true. Nothing of the
sort was done. Beaumarchais had now been dead for
almost twenty years, and his heirs still continued their
efforts to obtain a settlement of the claim. Opinions
sustaining its justice were obtained from American
lawyers, but they availed nothing.

In 1822 Beaumarchais's daughter, then his only sur-
viving heir, once more submitted her case to Congress,

[1] Loménie, *Beaumarchais et son Temps*, ii, 198.   [2] *Ibid.*, 200.

and truly said that all she asked was justice. Among other authorities to support the claim were the opinions of the two attorneys-general, Rodney and Pinkney, and the daughter adds: "After having paid some attention to the aforesaid documents, you will wonder, no doubt, that justice has been asked for without success so many years. Will it be refused to me again? As a reward for the devotion of Beaumarchais to your cause, shall his daughter be deprived of her fortune, and finish her life in vain and cruel expectation, as her father did, whose existence was shortened by troubles and sorrow? Till the last moment of his life he begged you to decide upon his claim. He said to you: 'My proceedings towards you were zealous and pure; my letters, my commercial conventions attest it; they are in your hands; they have been thoroughly examined: examine them again.' The proofs which those frequent examinations have established are warranted by illustrations and unexceptionable testimonies, among which I find, with pride, those of some of your countrymen: their veracity could not be questioned. Decide, in your own cause, with equity and impartiality! Or, at least, be pleased to appoint special commissioners to settle that discussion, to end the unequal struggle, and I will accept them from you with confidence as my judges: but I beg that a speedy decision may take place." [1]

In 1824 she came to Washington and solicited payment of the claim in person. Eleven years more passed before the matter was closed. In 1835 the heirs were at last informed that they could have eight hundred thousand francs, if they would execute a receipt in full. Fifty-seven years had passed since the claim ac-

[1] Durand, *New Materials*, etc., 267.

crued. With interest at three per cent the settlement represented an original indebtedness of three hundred thousand francs. This was not one seventh of the amount which Alexander Hamilton had decided was due, not one fourth of the amount which he reported should be paid, even after deducting the million francs advanced by France, for which it was insisted Beaumarchais was not entitled to payment. It was a settlement at twenty-five cents on the dollar, after a delay of half a century, made by a rich and prosperous nation, with the heirs of a man who had furnished our ancestors with assistance when our national existence was in doubt, who had lost much by the perils of war and had risked losing all if we had failed to achieve our independence. It cannot be regarded as a liberal settlement, but after fifty years of hope deferred, the claimants were not inclined to wait longer ; they took what was offered, but they had no reasons to feel any gratitude.[1]

[1] The history of Beaumarchais's relations with the United States is very fully and very fairly related in Loménie's valuable and agreeable work, *Beaumarchais et son Temps.*

CHAPTER VI

IN relating the part taken by Beaumarchais in behalf of the United States, and the disasters in which
his zeal involved him, we have been carried beyond
the time when Deane appeared as the representative
of the colonists at the French court. It was through
the medium of Beaumarchais, either acting for himself or as agent for the government, that military
supplies were first sent to America in any large
quantities. But he was not the only French merchant
who engaged in these enterprises, though no one else
conducted them on so large a scale. The others employed in this contraband trade seem to have obtained
the connivance of the government, but not its active
assistance. Among those who took part in such ventures was Dubourg, who thus sought to console himself for his disappointment that Beaumarchais was
preferred to him as agent of the government. He was
unfortunate in this undertaking also; he loaded a
ship at his own expense, which was captured by the
English, and the doctor, like his successful rival, was
a pecuniary loser by his efforts to aid the cause of
American liberty.

Having started to furnish military supplies to the
United States, the French government was soon on
the point of actual interference. Had it not been for
the ill-success of the American army, France would
have acknowledged our independence not long after

we ourselves proclaimed it. A little over a month after Deane's arrival at Paris came the news that the United States had renounced allegiance to the British crown, and this intelligence was received with great satisfaction in France. There had been a constant fear that the colonists would agree on terms and make peace with the mother country; this seemed less probable when by solemn resolution they had abjured their allegiance to the British King. The English had declared that vigorous measures would soon bring to their senses unruly demagogues and their deluded followers. But the armies that had been sent over to repress insurrection by force had not yet succeeded, and at the end of a year the rebels, neither disheartened nor alarmed, had declared themselves an independent people.

Moreover, the sounding phrases of the Declaration aroused enthusiasm, not among politicians like Vergennes, but in social and philosophic circles. It is curious to contrast the responses which the sentiments of the document met in France and in England. It was natural that English political leaders should declare this matter of small importance; but while the Declaration asserted principles dear to most Englishmen, it aroused little interest even among those who were friendly to the colonists. It seems to have been regarded as a highly impudent and not very important act.

The French attributed to it far greater weight, and in this, history has shown they were right, even if they were not correct in some of their anticipations. When the chargé d'affaires at London reported this momentous act, he added, "If the resistance of the Americans is victorious, this ever memorable epoch will reduce England to a point where she will no longer be a subject of disquiet to France, whose influence on the Continent must increase in proportion to the diminution of the British empire." [1] The sentiments of the Declaration of Independence were welcomed, not only among the disciples of Rousseau, but in the large class which admired the principles of liberty and democracy, when applied anywhere except to the government of France. The Declaration excited a degree of enthusiasm among the French people which had been aroused by no other public document, and feeling grew constantly stronger in favor of extending the aid of France to the American patriots.

This decisive step also strengthened Vergennes's inclination to interfere actively in behalf of the colonists. Popular sympathy with their cause had become outspoken, the English had made small progress in their military efforts, and the time seemed ripe to take part in a controversy in which the French government would receive the approval of its own people and might hope for speedy and decisive success. It was about the middle of August, 1776, that the news of the Declaration of Independence reached Paris, and on the thirty-first the Council met to consider the questions which now arose. The King was present and with him were Maurepas, the prime minister, St. Germain and Sartine, the ministers of war and of the marine, and the secretary of foreign affairs, Vergennes, who presented a report which apparently received the approval of all his auditors.

It began with a discussion of general principles, a manner of arguing which so often distinguishes

[1] Garnier to Vergennes, Aug. 16, 1776; Doniol, i, 585.

French from English political documents. An English cabinet considering practical questions would not indulge in any debate on the principles of government, but Vergennes sought to place his argument upon a philosophical basis. The purpose of all social institutions, he said, was their own advantage and preservation; on that basis societies had been established, and only when governed by that consideration could they maintain themselves and prosper. Thus the object of every administration should be to secure whatever advantages it could for the country committed to its charge.

After some further discussion of the evils of war and the wickedness of England, Vergennes at last reached the practical question, Should France interfere actively in behalf of the American colonists? His report was an elaborate and powerful argument in favor of interference, and immediate interference. Now, he said, there was a unique opportunity for France to avenge herself for all the perfidies and outrages committed by England in the past, and to render it impossible for her to repeat them for a long time to come. England was the hereditary enemy of France, jealous of her greatness, envious of her rich soil and her advantages of situation, using all her power to attack France, or to band Europe against her. Now there was an opportunity, which might not recur for ages, to abate England's pride and lessen her influence. If one should balance the advantages and disadvantages of a war against England in the present juncture, the advantages would be incomparably greater; not only was it possible to visit that country with just punishment and weaken her dangerous power, but much could be hoped from the friendship of the new re-

public. A union between France and the United
States was not one of those casual combinations that
would cease when the need of the moment was over.
" No interest," he said, " can divide two peoples connected only over vast tracts of sea ; the relations of
commerce will form a chain which, if not eternal, will
be of long duration." [1]

Vergennes called attention also to the European
situation, which was singularly favorable for any such
action. The affairs of this world are closely linked
together, and the condition in which Europe was left
after the Seven Years' War rendered possible the
interference of France, and the establishment of
American independence. If France became involved
in war, this often excited the activity of rivals who
dreaded her preëminence on the Continent and were
eager for any opportunity to check her power. But
the Seven Years' War had changed the position of
that country in Europe ; her prestige had been lessened, and, as some compensation for this, her neighbors watched her with less apprehensive eyes. Austria
was not an ally, and the relations between the countries were fairly cordial. Frederick II was always a
man to be closely watched, but he had no desire for
more warfare, and he took a malicious interest in any
misfortunes that might befall England ; he had never
forgiven her desertion in his own hour of peril, and
his representative at Paris repeatedly assured the
French minister that if France were to interfere in
the American contest, she need fear nothing from
Prussia. " I protest to you," he wrote his minister in
London, " that it is more possible that a good Chris-

[1] Doniol, i, 567–577. Read to the King and a Committee of the
Council, Aug. 31, 1776.

tian should form an alliance with the devil than I with England." Russia was far distant, and Catherine had no desire for war.

To all these favorable conditions Vergennes called attention, and he concluded by saying: "It is certain that if his Majesty seizes this unique opportunity, which perhaps the ages will never again present, we can deal England a blow that would abate her pride and place her power within just bounds, . . . and he would have the glory, so dear to his heart, of being the benefactor not only of his own people but of all nations." [1]

As a result of these lengthy reasonings, Vergennes was in favor of enlisting in the cause of the American colonists without further delay. Apparently his views met the approval of his associates, and were not disapproved by the King. Louis had little sympathy with the colonists, and no taste for war, but he was a dull, inert youth, and if his ministers were resolved on their policy, he was not likely long to resist them. An American who could have known the secrets of the royal councils would have thought that the hour of deliverance for his country was near at hand.

The only delay in deciding on immediate action seems to have come from a desire to communicate this resolution to Spain and ask her to join. Vergennes held closely to the traditions of the Family Compact, and on September 7 a report of his argument, which had received the approval of his colleagues, was sent to Madrid, and the coöperation of the Spanish King was asked.[2]

The Spanish were not averse to war with England, but they had no thought of undertaking it except upon

[1] Doniol, i, 567–576.   [2] Doniol, i, 578.

the promise of large reward. "One does not make war," said the Spanish minister, "except to preserve one's own possessions or to acquire those of others." Having thus disavowed any altruistic motive, he declared that the recovery of Portugal would be especially advantageous to Spain and would also redound to the advantage of the entire Bourbon family. It was more than one hundred and thirty years since Portugal had freed itself from a foreign yoke, but the Spanish people clung with Spanish tenacity to the hope of recovering this lost possession. The French were willing that Spain should reconquer Portugal if she could, but they had no thought of undertaking a war against England for that purpose. Such a result would not benefit France, nor would it seriously injure England.

Before the letter which stated the price Spain would charge for her aid could reach Paris, the aspect of affairs had changed, and the purposes of the French minister had changed with it. Vague rumors of the progress of arms in America had reached France, full of the inaccuracies that might be expected in reports that had crossed three thousand miles of water. Howe, it was said, had met with disaster in his expedition against New York, and had been forced to reëmbark his troops. It was reported, so Vergennes wrote his representative in London, that there had been a bloody engagement on August 12 or 13, on Long Island. Ten or twelve thousand men had been killed on the two sides, and the English troops had been forced to reembark.[1]

These illusions were soon dispelled. On October 16 an authentic report reached Paris, which announced that the American army had been defeated on Long

[1] Letter of Sept. 28, 1776; Doniol, i, 613.

Island, and that New York would soon be in the hands of the English. The Americans had been defeated, so Garnier wrote from London, with a loss of thirty-three hundred men, while the English loss did not exceed four hundred; the intrenchments of the Americans had been ill made and worse defended, and the supporters of the government in London declared that the rebels could now make no effective resistance and must speedily submit.[1]

These unfavorable predictions were not accepted by the French ministers, but their zeal for immediate interference was checked. The disaster of Long Island delayed for almost two years the French alliance, and the war which, with the active aid of France, might perhaps have been brought to a speedy close, now became a long and weary struggle.

The demand of Spain that Portugal should be reconquered as the price of her assistance furnished an excuse for a different tone in the negotiations with that country. This suggestion was not favorably regarded by French statesmen; they were unwilling to involve France in a war which must continue until Portugal should become the prize of Spain, and if they had been ready for immediate action, they would have sought some modification of these demands. As it was, they treated the entire question as one that might be considered at leisure. "There is no pressing haste," Vergennes said to the King. "All that circumstances now require from your Majesty and the Catholic King," wrote the minister, "is to see that the Americans do not succumb for lack of means of resistance."[2]

A long despatch was sent to Spain, filled with the

---

[1] Letter of Oct. 11, 1776; Doniol, i, 615.
[2] Oct. 26, 1776; Doniol, i, 620.

terms of affection which should be expected between near kinsmen, but indicating with clearness that France was no longer eager for speedy action, and that the price demanded for Spanish assistance was not acceptable. "The French King will always view without jealousy," said Vergennes, "the aggrandizement of the Spanish monarchy, but he cannot conceal from the King his uncle that the conquest of Portugal would be alarming to all rulers interested in preserving a just balance, and they would not view with tranquillity the power of the House of Bourbon increased by the reunion of the rest of the Spanish peninsula. . . . If M. Grimaldi was right, that one makes war only to make gains, . . . they should regard it as a great gain to lower the power of England. Let us secure the separation of her colonies in North America, and her diminished commerce, her burdened finances, will render that power less unquiet and less haughty."[1]

To this sentiment Vergennes remained constant. When the war came he sought for France no acquisition of territory, no gain except the injury to England that would result from the loss of her American colonies. Whatever degree of disinterestedness this represented, France and her minister are entitled to be credited with. And so these negotiations terminated by the resolution on the part of France that the fire already kindled should not be extinguished; that means should be provided by which the colonists could obtain the succor necessary to enable them to continue the contest, but that neither France nor Spain would at present enlist openly in the war. If the English had failed in the endeavor to capture New York, possibly the colonists might have been successful with-

[1] Despatch of Nov. 5, 1776; Doniol, i, 686.

out an alliance with any foreign power; but it is quite certain that France would speedily have made a treaty with the United States and taken an active part in the war had it not been for the disasters which befell our army. She was anxious to prevent the collapse of the American cause, but did not wish to embroil herself with England if the failure of the colonies was assured. No matter how desperate the condition of the colonists might seem, the French ministers were ready to render all the assistance they could give without becoming involved in war with England. They were quite willing to take part in the contest if they could insure the independence of the thirteen colonies, and thus deal, as they hoped and believed, a fatal blow to the power of their great adversary; but they did not wish to expose France to an expensive war with a powerful state if the probable result was that the American colonists, even with French aid, would be unable to secure their independence. For a long period little favorable news came from across the Atlantic, and the French ministers doubted if there were any possibility of success for the American insurgents. As they doubted so they delayed, giving to the colonists, indeed, much valuable aid, but hesitating to acknowledge the new nation and declare themselves its ally. In the mean time the Continental Congress decided to take more active measures to obtain the assistance of France.

CHAPTER VII

DEANE had gone to Paris in search of assistance, with no official position. But immediately after the Declaration of Independence it was decided to send accredited representatives of the new government to France, and in September, 1776, Franklin, Jefferson, and Deane were chosen by Congress as commissioners. Jefferson declined the mission, and in an evil day Arthur Lee was selected in his place. Franklin was unanimously elected on the first ballot. He was by far the most prominent of the commissioners, and was in France the best-known American; his experience and character peculiarly fitted him for the position, and Congress would have acted wisely if he had been sent over as its sole representative. When the vote was announced, he turned to one near and said: "I am old and good for nothing, but, as the storekeepers say of their remnants of cloth, 'I am but a fag end, you may have me for what you please.'" So far as the welfare of the United States was concerned, the most valuable part of Franklin's life was still before him. The results of his mission in France could have been accomplished by no one else, and without them it is by no means certain that American independence would have been achieved until many years later.

A proposed treaty was drafted by Congress, which the commissioners were authorized to sign, with such changes as might be required. It was nothing more than a commercial agreement, but it was hoped that the French government would go further and form an alliance with the new republic. Not only were the commissioners to negotiate for a treaty, but they were to obtain supplies of arms and ammunition, for which Congress would make payment. It was especially important to secure munitions of war, for the colonists were almost entirely unprovided, and there were practically no facilities for manufacturing guns or powder in this country. The guns with which the American soldiers had thus far been furnished were of every variety, and few of them were fit for service. Agents had gone from house to house to obtain muskets, and these were largely old weapons which had been rejected by the inspectors of the English army and had drifted into the hands of the colonists. There was no manufactory where guns could be made in any quantity, and the authorities met with almost insurmountable difficulties in obtaining powder. When the battle of Lexington was fought, it was said there was not enough powder in the thirteen colonies to last for a week's fighting, and that English troops could have marched from Boston to Savannah almost without resistance, because the colonists could not have obtained enough powder for serious opposition.

In July, 1775, the Committee of Safety in New York wrote: " We have no arms, we have no powder, we have no blankets." [1] This was still the condition in every part of the United States, and it was for this reason that the necessity was so great of obtaining supplies abroad. The quality of the stores sent from France was occasionally criticized; doubtless some of

---

[1] W. G. Sumner, *The Financier and the Finances of the American Revolution,* i, 107.

the powder was poor and some of the guns were defective, but they were vastly superior to anything that could be had on this side of the water.

On October 26, 1776, Franklin sailed for France on the sloop of war Reprisal. The boat was several times chased by English cruisers; she not only escaped capture, but as she neared the other side made two prizes, with which in tow she sailed into Quiberon Bay after a voyage of thirty days. The weather was rough, Franklin had a small and uncomfortable cabin, the fowls were too tough for his teeth, and he lived chiefly on salt beef; between stormy weather and poor nourishment, he was in a very reduced condition when he finally reached land.[1]

On December 3, he landed at Auray, and from there he proceeded to Nantes. Travel in those days was not luxurious. The carriage, the doctor writes, was uncomfortable and the horses tired; they met few persons, and their spirits were not raised when the driver told them that two weeks before a gang of robbers had plundered and murdered some travellers on the road. But the doctor's party made the journey safely, and at Nantes he was hospitably received. The citizens thronged to see him, he was given a great dinner, and after waiting a few days to recruit, he went to Paris.

The news that Franklin had arrived in France excited widespread interest. He had become an object of special dislike in England, except among those who sympathized with the colonists, and his journey across the Atlantic loosened the tongues of his adversaries. It was currently reported that, foreseeing the ruin of the insurgent cause, he had abandoned his country,

---

[1] E. E. Hale, *Franklin in France*, 49.

like a rat leaving a sinking ship; that he had fled like
a poltroon from the ruin he had helped to create. The
accusation was so often repeated that it moved Burke
to say he could not believe that Franklin would close
a life "which has brightened every hour it continued
with so foul and dishonorable a flight." "I have just
seen," writes Franklin, "seven paragraphs in the English papers about me, of which six were lies."

Franklin's arrival was especially distasteful to the
British ambassador, and Stormont poured out the
vials of his wrath. "It is generally believed here," he
writes, "that he comes in the double capacity of a
negotiator and a fugitive; this suspicion, joined to the
knowledge of his former character, and to that reputation of duplicity which he has so justly acquired,
will, I hope, throw many difficulties in his way." [1]
"He will lie, he will promise, and he will flatter, with
all the insinuation and subtlety that are natural to
him," Stormont writes again.

But it was not alone to the English minister that
Franklin's arrival furnished a theme for thought.
"His arrival," writes Deane, "is the common topic
for conversation, and has given birth to a thousand
conjectures." When the doctor had reached his destination, the interest increased instead of diminishing.
"The celebrated Franklin arrived in Paris the 21st
of December," writes one, "and has fixed the eyes of
everyone upon his slightest proceeding." Probably in
the whole world there was not another man so fitted
for the work he had to do as Franklin. His scientific
discoveries, his reputation as a philosopher and a sage,
the simplicity of his dress, the shrewdness of his talk,

[1] Charlemagne Tower, *The Marquis de Lafayette in the American
Revolution*, i, 164.

the dignity of his expression, all helped to give him in France a position such as had been held by few Frenchmen and by no foreigner.

The Comte de Ségur has told us of the reception which the representatives of the thirteen colonies met with in France. "It would be difficult to describe the eagerness and delight with which . . . these agents of a people in a state of insurrection against their monarch were received in France, in the bosom of an ancient monarchy. Nothing could be more striking than the contrast between the luxury of our capital, the elegance of our fashions, the magnificence of Versailles, the still brilliant remains of the monarchical pride of Louis XIV, and the polished and superb dignity of our nobility, . . . and the almost rustic apparel, the unpowdered hair, the plain but firm demeanor, the free and direct language of the envoys, whose antique simplicity of dress and appearance seemed to have introduced within our walls, in the midst of the effeminate and servile refinement of the eighteenth century, sages contemporary with Plato, or republicans of the age of Cato and of Fabius. This unexpected spectacle produced upon us a greater effect in consequence of its novelty, and because it occurred precisely at the period when literature and philosophy had spread amongst us all an unusual desire for reforms, a disposition to encourage innovations, and the seeds of an ardent attachment to liberty." [1]

"Men imagined," writes another, "they saw in Franklin a sage of antiquity, come back to give austere lessons and generous examples to the moderns. They personified in him the republic, of which he was

[1] James Parton, *Life of Franklin*, ii, 211; Ségur, *Mémoires*, i, 109.

the representative and the legislator. They regarded his virtues as those of his countrymen, and even judged of their physiognomy by the imposing and serene traits of his own." [1]

The French police authorities gave full reports of the distinguished visitor : " Dr. Franklin . . . is very much run after, and fêted, not only by the savants, his confrères, but by all people who can get hold of him. . . . This Quaker wears the full costume of his sect. He has an agreeable physiognomy. Spectacles always on his eyes ; but little hair, — a fur cap is always on his head. He wears no powder, but a neat air, linen very white, a brown coat." [2] When he was presented to Louis XV, his chestnut-colored coat was replaced by black velvet ; but while he was not in all respects dressed like the ambassador from Austria, no one would have suspected that he was a peasant come to court.

When Franklin arrived at Paris, he first took lodgings at the Hôtel de Hamburg on the rue de l'Université ; but a residence in the centre of the city he found inconvenient and disagreeable. Le Ray de Chaumont, a wealthy Frenchman and an ardent friend of the colonists, offered him a more retired abode in the spacious Hôtel de Valentinois in Passy. With the enthusiasm displayed by so many Frenchmen for the American cause, Chaumont gave the use of the house free of charge, saying only that when American independence had been established, Congress, if it saw fit, could compensate him with a grant of American land.

This offer was in every way acceptable. Passy was

[1] Parton, *Life of Franklin*, ii, 211.
[2] Hale, *Franklin in France*, 90.

then a pretty village on the outskirts of Paris, about half a mile from the limits and two miles from the centre of the city, conveniently removed from the confusion and bustle of the capital. It was an advantage to Franklin to have a residence so far removed as to lessen somewhat the crowd of visitors that sought him, and this choice was also agreeable to the French ministers. They did not care to have the representative of the rebellious colonies too conspicuously in view. Lord Stormont might find less opportunity to complain if Franklin was somewhat obscurely lodged in a quiet suburb than if he were within a stone's throw of the Louvre. What perhaps was of no less importance, in such a spot 'it was more easy for the French ministers to have communication with the American representative, and yet escape the vigilant observation of the English ambassador.

The Hôtel de Valentinois had recently been purchased by Chaumont. It had had many distinguished owners. In the early part of the century the Duchesse d'Aumont had occupied it as a country residence. It was afterwards owned by the Duc de Valentinois, and in 1776 it was purchased by Chaumont, who was a gentleman of large wealth. The property consisted of two dwellings, and it was the smaller of the two, known as the *petit hôtel*, which Franklin occupied.

A portion of the house still stands in what is now a thickly populated part of the city, and an inscription on the façade informs passers-by that this was the home of Franklin. Chaumont offered the use of the property rent-free, though the arrangement was so convenient for the French ministers, and Chaumont's relations with them were so intimate, that it has been suspected that the French government, rather than this liberal gentleman, was really the benevolent landlord.

However this may be, it was occupied by Franklin for nine years. Any house in which Franklin dwelt was sure to bear his mark, and upon this he placed a lightning rod, which was said to be the first ever put up in France. There the negotiations between the colonies and France, and subsequently between the colonies and England, were carried on ; there he exercised an extensive hospitality, and was visited by great numbers of people. Franklin liked society and he had full opportunity to gratify his taste. Six days in the week he dined out, meeting almost every one who was prominent in political, literary, or social life. This was not the least arduous nor the least useful part of his career as an ambassador. He spoke French, not with entire correctness, but with fluency and wit. Never did he weary his auditors by talking too much of America, and never did he lose the opportunity, by fit and felicitous reference, to interest them in the American cause. Every entertainment which he accepted, said one of his listeners, gained him admirers, who became partisans of the American Revolution. Every dinner-party at which the wise doctor was present was a diplomatic success, and aided the cause which he represented. Sundays he stayed at home, and his Sunday dinners were attended by a large number of Americans, as well as by some of his French friends. His doors were open to all Americans, even those who bore him little love. Lee and his followers were often there. Franklin tried, so he said, to bring them all together and compel them, if possible, to forget their animosities. In this endeavor he was not successful, and at last the virulent abuse which Izard poured out upon him disturbed even the doctor's tranquillity, and he refused to receive him further at his house.

While Adams was a joint commissioner, he occupied the same hôtel, but Arthur Lee was of too irritable a temperament to be willing to sleep under the same roof with Franklin. The doctor's social life was little to Adams's taste, and the terms on which the American representatives were occupying the house were also distasteful to this practical Yankee. In 1778 he wrote Chaumont, begging as a favor that he would state what rent should be paid for the house and furniture, both for the past and future. "It is not reasonable," he said, "that the United States should be under so great obligation to a private gentleman, as that two of their representatives should occupy for so long a time so elegant a seat with so much furniture and such fine accommodations, without any compensation."

The enthusiastic Chaumont would not accede to Adams's views. "When I consecrated my house to Dr. Franklin," he wrote, "and his associates who might live with him, I made it fully understood that I should expect no compensation. . . . It is so much the worse for those who would not do the same, if they had the opportunity, and so much the better for me to have immortalized my house by receiving into it Dr. Franklin and his associates." [1]

As Adams's letter by inference suggested that Dr. Franklin was remiss in living in this house for two years, undisturbed by the fact that his occupation was rent-free, so Chaumont, in his reply, delicately intimated that it was the name of Franklin and not

[1] John Bigelow, editor; *The Life of Benjamin Franklin, written by himself*, ii, 429–430.

that of Adams which would immortalize the Hôtel de Valentinois.

Chaumont's dealings with the United States were by no means confined to furnishing a residence for their commissioners. He took an active part in sending supplies to the colonies, and his experience was hardly more fortunate than that of Beaumarchais. It is sad to reflect that almost every one who attempted business relations with our country, at the time of the Revolution, ended in bankruptcy. Chaumont often acted for the French ministers in obtaining supplies and equipping ships for the colonists, and he also furnished them on his own account. Soon after the beginning of the war he sent a shipload of powder to Boston, with instructions to his agent not to insist on repayment unless the Americans were successful in their struggle for independence. The colonies succeeded in their struggle, but they do not seem to have paid Chaumont for the powder and supplies which he furnished them.

Partly as a result of this, though chiefly from a loose administration of his business matters, of which his dealings with the United States were a fair sample, Chaumont became embarrassed before the outbreak of the French Revolution, and he was forced to make an assignment soon after that. In 1785 his son visited this country and endeavored to obtain a settlement of the father's claim. His father was, so Franklin wrote Washington, "the first in France who gave us credit, and before the Court showed us any countenance, trusted us with two thousand barrels of gunpowder, and from time to time afterwards exerted himself to furnish the Congress with supplies of various kinds, which, for want of due returns, they being of great

amount, has finally much distressed him in his circumstances."[1] Notwithstanding this, the son stayed here
many years without obtaining either money or settlement, and finally, like many other creditors of the
Confederacy, abandoned the claim as hopeless. He
remained in this country and entered into a great land
speculation in the interior of New York State. Among
the shareholders of his company were many illustrious
names, — Caulaincourt, Grouchy, Necker, and Joseph
Bonaparte. But he fared no better than his father in
American speculations; he finally became bankrupt
and returned to France to die.

In the Hôtel de Valentinois Franklin lived in comfort, and even with a certain amount of luxury, which
disturbed the prudent soul of John Adams, but was
appropriate and useful in the position which the
doctor held. Though he led an existence that could
fairly be called strenuous, yet he preserved in his country home a certain official semi-obscurity which was
agreeable to the French government. Vergennes declared that the laws of hospitality forbade refusing a
home in Paris to Americans who wished to stay there,
but he did not wish to have the fact that the rebellious colonists were officially represented obtrusively
paraded before the English minister. The police reported that Franklin was difficult of approach and
lived with a reserve that was supposed to be directed
by his government. He had no such orders and
needed none: his own tact enabled him to adopt the
most judicious procedure for the accomplishment of
his ends.

If he avoided any unnecessary prominence as a representative of the American government, he attracted

[1] Bigelow, *Franklin*, iii, 437.

personally an amount of attention that would have satisfied the most insatiate lover of publicity. There were no great newspapers that could daily report his sayings and doings; but Franklin, his appearance, his opinions, his modes of life, were known to all Paris. Franklin's reputation, says John Adams, " was more universal than that of Leibnitz or Newton, Frederick or Voltaire ; and his character more beloved and esteemed than any or all of them. . . . His name was familiar to government and people, to kings, courtiers, nobility, clergy, and philosophers, as well as plebeians, to such a degree that there was scarcely a peasant or a citizen, a *valet-de-chambre*, coachman or footman, a lady's chambermaid or a scullion in a kitchen, who was not familiar with it, and who did not consider him as a friend to human kind. . . . If a collection could be made of all the Gazettes of Europe, for the latter half of the eighteenth century, a greater number of panegyrical paragraphs upon ' *le grand Franklin* ' would appear, it is believed, than upon any other man that ever lived." [1]

It was as a man of science and by his discoveries in electricity that Franklin was best known in France. Scientific studies then excited widespread interest, and this republican sage had made valuable researches. The zeal for such studies was not confined to scholars, but extended through the community. Franklin had been elected a member of the Academy of Sciences, and he attended its meetings with great regularity. The sage who had already snatched lightning from the sky, aroused an admiring sympathy when he was engaged in wresting the sceptre from tyrants.

The writings of Franklin were widely known in

[1] *Works of John Adams,* etc., i, 660.

France and exceedingly popular. The neatness of his expression, the delicate humor of his style, was peculiarly fitted for French taste, and so also was the philosophy which he taught. It was not abstruse, it was not metaphysical, it was not, perhaps, very elevated, but it inculcated virtues that were dear to the French heart. The apothegms of Poor Richard were almost as familiar to the French as to Americans. They had been often translated; bishops and priests advised their flocks to profit by their study. Poor Richard taught no exalted philosophy, but he preached practical wisdom, and he constantly praised the quality of thrift. No virtue is dearer to the average Frenchman; no one appreciates better than he the wisdom and the delights of a careful economy. When Poor Richard told them that industry pays debts, and if you kept your shop, your shop would keep you; when he bade his readers think of saving as well as of getting, to beware of little expenses, and remember that silks and satins put out the kitchen fire, his words were dear to the industrious, thrifty, penny-saving bourgeois of France.

It is not strange that representations of the wise doctor were multiplied indefinitely, — medallions, busts, medals of every kind and size. He writes his daughter, in reference to medallions, with the smiling, half-contemptuous vanity that was characteristic of him: "A variety of impressions have been made of different sizes; some large enough to be set in the lids of snuff-boxes; some so small as to be worn in rings; and the numbers sold are incredible. These, with the pictures, busts, and printings (of which copies upon copies are spread everywhere), have made your father's face as well known as that of the moon."

It was the fashion for every one to have an engraving of M. Franklin on the mantelpiece, writes a contemporary.

Franklin was fond of women; the homage paid to him by a great circle of ladies was agreeable to the philosopher, and was by no means without value in the work he was sent to do. Petticoats and alcoves still held their place in French political life. There were many Frenchwomen who possessed and liked to exercise an influence in politics, and there were few of these who were not ready to say a good word for the cause which their dear Dr. Franklin advocated. Madame Helvetius was one of those with whom the doctor was most intimate, and if her appearance shocked the New England mind of Mrs. Adams, she was not a useless friend to the American minister. Mrs. Adams has recorded her impressions, which certainly were less favorable than those of the doctor: —

"Her hair was frizzled; over it she had a small straw hat, with a dirty gauze half-handkerchief round it, and a bit of dirtier gauze than ever my maids wore was bowed on behind. She had a black gauze scarf thrown over her shoulders. She ran out of the room; when she returned, the Doctor entered at one door, she at the other; upon which she ran forward to him, caught him by the hand, — 'Hélas! Franklin'; then gave him a double kiss, one upon each cheek, and another upon his forehead. . . . I should have been greatly astonished at this conduct, if the good Doctor had not told me that in this lady I should see a genuine Frenchwoman, wholly free from affectation or stiffness of behavior, and one of the best women in the world. For this I must take the Doctor's word; but I should have set her down for a very bad one, although sixty years of age, and a widow."

The well-known Comtesse d'Houdetot was one of Franklin's ardent admirers, and long accounts are given of the great fête which she gave in his honor at her château. When it was known the doctor was approaching, the whole company set off on foot and met him half a mile from the château. Then they walked by his carriage as an escort, and the countess handed him from the carriage, when they had arrived. "The venerable sage," says the French chronicler of the fête, " with his gray hairs flowing down upon his shoulders, his staff in his hand, the spectacles of wisdom on his nose, was the perfect picture of true philosophy and virtue."

In the year following Franklin's arrival at Paris, Voltaire reached that city after twenty-eight years of absence. The orders which forbade his return had never been rescinded, but no one thought of enforcing them. When the officers at the city gates asked if the carriage contained anything dutiable or forbidden, the poet replied that there was nothing contraband except himself, and the exclusion of that prohibited article was not insisted upon. The enthusiastic Parisians could not be content until the great American had met the great Frenchman. In April, 1778, they were both at the Academy of Sciences, and the audience cried out that they should be presented to each other. They rose and bowed, they grasped each other's hands, but it was not enough; the clamor continued until the two philosophers threw their arms about each other and kissed each other's ancient cheeks. Then the French heart was content: Solon and Sophocles

[1] *Letters of Mrs. Adams* (2d ed.), ii, 55, 56.

had embraced, and the requirements of the situation were satisfied.[1]

Immediately after the arrival of Franklin the commissioners entered upon the important duties with which they had been intrusted. Deane was already at Paris, Lee came over from England and joined his associates, whose existence he was to do so much to render miserable. He was already unfriendly to Deane because the latter had supplanted him in the confidence of Beaumarchais. It was with Deane that Hortalez and Company were arranging for the supplies they were to send to America, while Lee had expected that he would be the intermediary to take charge of this important business. Therefore he looked upon Deane with disfavor, and the person whom Lee disliked he was sure to regard as a rogue, and to impress upon others his opinion. He soon came to dislike Franklin even more than Deane, and if he did not accuse the doctor of dishonesty, he found in him other faults which he declared were quite as grievous.

For a time, however, while the three commissioners did not regard each other with great cordiality, they at least observed the forms of united action. They were sent over to obtain the aid, and, if possible, the alliance of France, and they at once sought an opportunity to present their case to Vergennes; but the reception of envoys from a government which was not recognized and whose existence was not yet established, presented many difficulties. On December 23, 1776, the American representatives sent a formal letter to Vergennes asking for an audience. Congress, so they wrote, was ready to negotiate a treaty of amity

[1] *Works of John Adams*, etc., iii, 147.

and commerce and turned first to France. "We
flatter ourselves," they added, "that the propositions
we are instructed to make are such as will not be
found unacceptable." On December 28 they were received at Versailles, but the French minister sought
to escape further complaints from Stormont, of which
he had already heard so many, and the interview was
accordingly secret; it was, however, none the less cordial.

The business was veiled in such mystery that Lord
Stormont was kept in torment in his endeavors to discover the facts. On December 18 he wrote Lord
Weymouth that half Paris believed Franklin had
been twice at Versailles, but really he had not yet
arrived. On the 23d he was certain that Franklin
had arrived and had had an interview with Vergennes,
but he was consoled by trustworthy information that
Franklin pressed for an interview with the King and
was refused, so he went away in a bad humor. Two
days later Stormont sent reports of another interview
which was also imaginary. Finally on January 1 he
reported that Franklin had had a conference with
Vergennes, which was true; but he consoled himself
by the rumor that the doctor came away from Versailles dissatisfied, which was untrue. "I continue to
watch Franklin's motions as narrowly as I can," he
writes later, and this he certainly did, though not always with good success.[1]

At the interview, the details of which the English
were so anxious to know, the American commissioners
obtained no formal promise of aid, but they were received with courtesy, and they could expect no more
at the beginning of their negotiations. Their demands

[1] Letters to Weymouth; Hale, *Franklin in France*, ii, 419-426.

were simple. A treaty of commerce was submitted to Vergennes; but the commissioners did not even suggest an alliance, nor did they present any request for aid. Begging, unfortunately, was to be an important part of the duties of our representatives in Europe, still at their first interview the commissioners did not ask for money. The moderation of their requests surprised Vergennes. " Whether it is modesty," he wrote, " or fear, . . . such sentiments are very praiseworthy." [1]

The Americans were content to be received unofficially at first, but Franklin intended that they should soon be placed on the same footing as the representatives of other nations. A formal audience was requested for January 5. The request was not promptly acceded to, and thereupon Franklin prepared a letter and submitted it without more ado. Such a procedure was not conventional, but the doctor was ready to disregard the rules of diplomatic procedure, if he saw any advantage in so doing. Even in the detail of dress he adopted a style not so removed from ordinary usage as to seem uncouth, but which showed that when he found a fashion distasteful he did not fear to disregard it. He was sufficiently conventional to be decorous, and sufficiently unconventional to be unique. He did not attend the royal levee in the Quaker garb appropriate for Philadelphia, and when he was received by Louis XV he was dressed in black velvet, with white silk stockings and silver buckles, but he thought a wig uncomfortable and did not wear one. All the court knew that the man with the scanty unpowdered locks was the American philosopher and sage.

[1] Doniol, ii, 120.

In his diplomatic conduct, while always courteous, he was rigorous in preserving the dignity of his position and yielded to no conventional requirements which he thought might lessen it. If the representatives of ancient monarchies greeted with informality the envoy of a new and small republic, Franklin, with perfect amiability, treated them quite as unceremoniously in return. When Vergennes hesitated to grant a public reception, the doctor sent him a letter, as he might have done to a merchant from whom he wished to purchase a ship. In this communication the commissioners asked for thirty thousand guns, for which Congress would make payment. If the English declared war, the colonies agreed to coöperate with France and Spain in an effort to secure for them the West India Islands belonging to England. North America, they wrote, now offered to those countries her friendship and her commerce.

The arguments presented by the commissioners were made in good faith and in a good cause, but they have not all been realized. Trade with the colonists, so said their memoir, must be very advantageous, as it would consist in an exchange of the products of the soil and raw material for manufactured goods. The colonies, in offering their commerce to France, offered what had been the principal source of England's wealth. Of this France would now reap all the benefits, without any of the burdens of sovereignty. If still attached to Great Britain, the colonists might aid her to conquer other territories; returned to her allegiance, they would threaten the safety of any nation which had possessions in America. But separated from her, their interest and their inclination would lead them to pursue a pacific policy towards all the

world for many generations; by reason of their customs and the immense expanse of their territory, they
would long give their exclusive attention to agriculture, which was, they added in a phrase inspired by
Rousseau, "the most natural, the most interesting and
the most innocent of all human occupations." Nor
would they ever, even when they had acquired sufficient strength, become embroiled with European states
holding possessions in America, nor invade their territory. Few have the gift of prophecy. No Monroe
Doctrine, no Mexican nor Cuban war loomed up before
the imagination of our first representatives in Europe.
Nor did they foresee any more accurately the future
of England. Not for six months, they declared, would
her finances allow her to carry on war with France.
The loss of her commerce with America would soon
render it impossible for her to borrow a shilling.[1]

But the French ministers were not certain that
American friendship would compensate for the dangers of a war with England. "We know," Vergennes
wrote the Spanish minister, "that republics are less
sensible than monarchies to the requirements of honor,
and that they regard fidelity to their engagements
only as a means to advance their interests, by which
alone their action is determined."[2] The request for
ships was declined, but the King promised to show his
good-will by furnishing secret succor to the colonists,
and making them a gift of two million livres.[3] This
advance enabled the commissioners to proceed with
the purchase of greatly needed supplies, and was the
first of many gifts and loans which went far towards

[1] Memoir of Dec. 31, 1776; *Deane Papers*, i, 434–442.
[2] Vergennes to Ossun, Jan. 12, 1777; Doniol, ii, 123.
[3] Doniol, ii, 121.

preventing the collapse of the American Revolution from lack of funds.

The French hesitated at the prospect of war with England, yet the American commissioners had every reason to believe that sooner or later such a contest must come. Vergennes and his associates realized indeed how serious this might be. The arguments which Turgot had used against interference in the American quarrel were as forcible now as when they were advanced a year earlier. It is doubtful if Louis XVI at any time really desired an alliance with the colonies. His timidity and his common sense were affected by Turgot's arguments, his monarchical instincts were offended by republicans rebelling against their king. The enthusiasm for the Americans, which pervaded French society and literature, found no echo in his dull mind.

But the King was not an important factor in the administration; it was not he who decided whether France should make war in behalf of American independence, and his ministers were agitated by conflicting hopes and fears. The Americans suggested the evils that might come to France and Spain if the colonists should be forced to submit to Great Britain; that country could then turn her aims to driving her rivals from America. It was of such a result, of some reconciliation by which the rebellious colonists should again become loyal Englishmen and seek consolation for their defeat by laying violent hands on the French and Spanish West Indies, that Vergennes and his associates lived in constant dread. The evils of war with Great Britain were admitted; but it was declared that a worse evil would be the submission of the colonists to the dangerous power of England, which would then be strengthened by the profits of American trade and by the arms of her American subjects.

To these apprehensions was added a strong suspicion that England would declare war on France, without waiting for that country to form an alliance with the colonists. It was known that France was giving to the colonists all the aid she dared to give, without incurring a certain rupture; she lent them money, she furnished them arms, she received their envoys, she violated all principles of international law in the manner in which American cruisers were allowed to seek a refuge for themselves and a market for their prizes in French ports.

Lord Stormont complained with good cause, and threatened war with much justification. Vergennes met his reproaches with entire disingenuousness and small regard for truth. " Franklin," wrote Vergennes, when the English minister complained of the encouragement given that fugitive rebel, — " I don't know what Dr. Franklin has come to do among us. At first one might suppose he had some important commissions, and then suddenly he shut himself up with the philosophers, and if he is engaged in any political intrigues, it is not with the ministers of the King." [1]

The English were not deceived by such assurances; if the objects of Franklin's mission were unknown to Vergennes, they were well known to the British ministers; the French, so they complained, were furnishing the insurgents with succor of every kind; Franklin and Deane held frequent conferences with the ministers of the Most Christian King; ships loaded with money and clothing for the rebels had already left the ports, and if the voice was that of Beaumar-

[1] Vergennes to Noailles, Feb. 22, 1777; Doniol, ii, 326, 327.

chais, the hand was believed to be that of Vergennes.[1]
If such action led the English to declare war upon
a power whose conduct was so inconsistent with its
professions, naturally the American representatives
would have viewed the result without regret.

[1] Report, March 7, 1777.

CHAPTER VIII

IT was not only by assisting the enterprising house of Roderigue Hortalez and Company that the French government sought to help the colonists: it rendered aid quite as important to the Americans, and quite as inconsistent with the neutrality towards England which was steadfastly proclaimed, in furnishing refuge and shelter to American privateers. The treatment of American privateers in France excited the just complaints of the English, and Americans can excuse it only by the reflection that it was for their benefit. International law was indeed in a very primitive condition, and England had been so persistent a violator of all principles of neutrality, that her complaints came with a poor grace when she was herself a sufferer from their infraction.

No sooner had war broken out, than the equipment of privateers became a favorite industry in the colonies. The hardy New England sailors were admirably fitted for such work; and privateering not only inflicted great injury on English commerce, but furnished the foundation of many a snug American fortune. The industry had much fascination; there was the possibility of greater gain than in whaling, and not much more danger; a good prize might turn the captain into a well-to-do man, and furnish the sailor with the wherewithal for a month's steady debauch when he landed at Newport or Boston. There was less everyday hardship than on a merchantman or a fishing boat, more leisure, and better food. The bill of fare as given in the log of one of these privateers is not unattractive. Breakfast was served at eight and dinner at noon. Each man had six pounds of bread per week, butter for breakfast, a pound of beef at dinner three days in the week, and on the other three a pound of pork with pulse, while on Sunday there was rice and molasses for breakfast, and bread and beef for dinner. When to this was added a half pint of rum per day, the sailor should have been contented with his lot, though his grog was stopped for wrangling, quarrelling, or getting drunk. Of course, supplies sometimes failed on a long cruise. " I am afraid I shall be obliged to get a puncheon of rum, although dear," writes a captain to the owner; " there is no doing without it. We were once entirely out for eight days, but, to do our people justice, I never heard the least murmur on that account, as they knew it could not be had."

While the exploits of these cruisers were confined to our side of the Atlantic, their prizes could be taken into American ports, and there was no fear of international complications; but they soon extended their field of operations to the English Channel and the Irish Sea. It was impracticable to sail across the Atlantic with their prizes, and they sought shelter in the friendly ports of France. The American navy came into existence as a result of these enterprises, and it then consisted of a few ships commanded by enterprising and daring captains, who devoted themselves to the capture of English merchantmen. They probably did more harm to the enemy than a larger and more formidable fleet, which would have occupied its energies in fighting men-of-war. John Paul Jones was the best known of those freebooters, but the names of Wickes and Nicholson and Conyngham were almost as much dreaded by the British merchant and shipper.

The field of operations furnished rich profits. Here is the record of Captain Wickes, who brought Franklin to France, and then turned his energies to cruising along the British coast. It reads like the record of Don Juan's triumphs when sung by Leporello: —

"June 19, when we took two brigs and two sloops; . . . 20th, took the sloop Jassans from White Haven; . . . 21st, took Scotch ship from Prussia . . . loaded with wheat; took a small Scotch smuggler and sunk her; 22nd, took the John and Thomas from Norway . . . loaded with deals, the brig Jenny and Sallie from Glasgow . . . in ballast; . . . 22nd, took à brig from Dublin . . . sunk her. Took three large brigs loaded with coals . . . bound for Dublin, sunk them in sight of that port. . . . Took the brig Crawford from Glasgow, . . . in ballast; 23rd, took the ship Grace from Jamaica . . . loaded with sugar, rum, cotton, and tobacco, and the brig Peggy from Cork . . . loaded with butter and hides . . .; 25th, took the sloop John and Peter from Havre de Grace . . .; 26th . . . took a skow . . . from Gibraltar . . . loaded with cork."

After so active a cruise, it is not strange that the captain went to St. Malo to refit, and he was certainly justified in asking Franklin for a credit of money as soon as possible.[1]

When Paul Jones became famous, France was the ally of the United States, there was war with England, the French ports stood open for American ships of

[1] Wickes to the Commissioners, June 28, 1777; Hale, *Franklin in France*, i, 122.

war with their prizes, as did those of their own land. But the hardy pirates who carried devastation to British commerce, while France still professed to be at peace with England, found some embarrassment in the successful prosecution of their trade. They recognized the principles of international law only when they could be applied in their own behalf. It is pleasant to note the rigid views of Captain Wickes in this respect, for when returning from his cruise, he fell in with an English ship of war, and forthwith ran for St. Malo in order to find a safe harbor. The English ship chased him all day; he escaped, but he says indignantly: "They pay very little regard to the laws of neutrality, as they chased me and fired as long as they dared stand in for fear of running ashore." [1] If the English men-of-war did not regard the laws of neutrality when pursuing these piratical craft, the French observed them no more when the privateers had escaped into port. The Americans expected the same facilities which they would have found at Gloucester or Boston, opportunities to refit their ships, to buy ammunition and supplies, and sell their prizes, and they received very nearly what they desired.

It was plainly the duty of the French to refuse these cruisers any shelter, except in stress of weather or urgent need. Apart from the general principles of international law, the Treaty of Utrecht between France and England provided that privateers should not fit out their ships nor sell their prizes in ports of either country, nor even purchase victuals except such as would enable them to get "to the next port of the Prince from whom they have their commission."

[1] Hale, *Franklin in France*, i, 124.

The French were willing to see any harm done to England, but they did not wish to be forced into a war. Therefore they closed their eyes to infractions of neutrality until a complaint was lodged, and then made much ado, with the purpose of accomplishing the smallest possible result. But even Vergennes dared not violate all laws of propriety, and the conduct of these freebooters was so shameless that at times he took, or at least threatened, sharp action.

In addition to his other duties, Franklin was practically secretary for the incipient American navy; he had to do with the purchasing of boats, the payment of men, and the complications which constantly resulted from the actions of these buccaneers. It was his own theory that all privateering should be abolished. He urged not only that free ships should make free goods, but that unarmed trading vessels should be undisturbed in time of war, and an article to that effect he endeavored, without success, to have inserted in the treaty of peace between England and the United States. But no such principles had been adopted, and the doctor's abstract views did not prevent his assisting the American cruisers to do the greatest possible harm to English commerce. He had constantly to make excuses of questionable truth, and more questionable validity, for the conduct of American ships that were refitting in French ports. Such action was forbidden, the ships were sometimes seized, and the officers imprisoned; but these troubles were sure to be adjusted, and in due time the cruiser, again in good order, with a fresh supply of powder and her money-bags well filled from the sale of prizes, sailed out from a French port to carry destruction to English shipping.

The English, in justifying their conduct during our Civil War in reference to the Florida and the Alabama, could have found precedents in the action of France in the time of our Revolution. Their attempts to prevent Confederate cruisers sailing from English ports were marked by the utmost good faith, when compared with the procedure of France at that period; if there had then been a Geneva Commission, acting on the principles established at the Alabama Arbitration, France would have been unanimously condemned to pay many millions of indemnity for damages to English commerce, caused by a reckless disregard of the obligations of international law.

Franklin came over in the Reprisal, commanded by Captain Wickes. So well was the time employed during the voyage, that the captain sailed into the harbor at Nantes, carrying not only the American minister, but two prizes in tow. These he proposed to sell in order to equip his boat for a protracted cruise of privateering, but the English officials stoutly remonstrated. Vergennes replied in the tone which must have become very wearisome to the English before open war was at last declared two years later. " Though a faithful execution of the treaties," he wrote, " was strictly commanded, infractions would occur. If prizes taken by the Reprisal had been sold, and French merchants had purchased them, nothing could be more irregular, but he felt sure that the owners would find redress if they brought action in the courts." [1]

In the mean time, Wickes peacefully pursued his illegal courses, and made strenuous protest when he was disturbed. " I have this day," he writes, " very extraordinary orders from the intendant of this port,

[1] Doniol, ii, 334.

demanding me to leave the port in twenty-four hours.
. . . I shall run into Nantes and there enter a protest, . . . though I am ordered not to go into any port
in France. These are very extraordinary orders, such
as I little expected to receive in France." [1] Three
weeks later, writing from the same place, having remained there notwithstanding all orders to quit, he
complains: the commissary of the port "still continues to threaten to drive me out immediately. . . . It
vexes me very much to be treated in this manner, and
I would not submit to it elsewhere." [2]

A few months later, having returned from a successful cruise and taken refuge in St. Malo, he
writes in great distress that the authorities there would
not allow him to take on board cannon, powder or
military stores. "I am told they have wrote [*sic*] to
the minister informing of my having taken my cannon
on board clandestinely at the night. . . . If so,"
says the captain, and doubtless with truth, "you may
safely deny the charge, as I took them on board at
noonday publickly." [3]

In fact, these freebooters made no concealment, and
when upon complaint of the British minister an order
came down from Paris stopping their proceedings,
they wrote to Franklin and he, in due time, got the
order modified, or else the local authorities decided
that they could safely wink at its infraction. Even
this was very galling to men like Captain Wickes.
"I am heartily tired of France," he writes. " I can
only say I am sorry our situation is such as puts us

---

[1] Wickes to the Commissioners, Feb. 26, 1777; Hale, *Franklin in France*, i, 115.

[2] Same to Same, March 15, 1777; *Ibid.*, 119.

[3] Same to Same, Aug. 12, 1777; *Ibid.*, 126.

under the disagreeable necessity of submitting to such
indignities as are exercised over us in the ports of
France." [1]

Franklin did all he could to assist the success of
these enterprises, although he deemed them so reprehensible. He wrote a French merchant, who doubtless
wished to pick up some of the good bargains furnished
by the sale of these prizes : " The prize cannot, as you
observe, be sold and delivered in your port, it being
contrary to treaties. . . . But I suppose it may be
done in the road without the port, or in some convenient place on the coast where the business may be
transacted and conducted with discretion, so as to
occasion no trouble to the ministers by applications
from the English Ambassador. . . . But a formal
order from the minister to permit such a sale and
delivery in any port of France is not to be expected
while the peace continues." [2]

Some of the documents in the French Foreign Office
read curiously like those of the English law officers,
when our minister was endeavoring to stop the Alabama. " We must admit," wrote Maurepas, speaking
of the complaints of selling prizes in French ports,
" that means have been found to avoid the prohibitions, . . . but it is necessary to apply to the Admir-
alty to obtain legal proof and we will not fail to send
them there." [3] If Wickes was disturbed by orders that
wounded his feelings but did not hinder his enterprise,
Lord Stormont, with better reason, was angered
because the American cruisers sold their prizes and
refitted their ships with almost as much impunity as

[1] Wickes to the Commissioners, Aug. 12, 1777; Hale, *Franklin in France*, i, 128.
[2] *Ibid.*, 134.　　　　　　　　　　[3] Doniol, ii, 335.

if they were in their own land, instead of in a country which professed to be at peace with England.

Vergennes wrote in July, 1777, that Lord Stormont had called, complaining of the action of the three American cruisers, Reprisal, Lexington, and Dolphin, that were then ravaging the British coast. " I will not endeavor," says the minister, " to report to you the warmth of his expressions. It was extreme." [1] To such complaints Vergennes replied, complaining of the heat of his adversary's remarks : " We do not use a tone of arrogance," he wrote; " our style is simple, honest, and firm. The King does not seek to justify wrongs ; he fears the less to do justice because that is in his character, and he regards the exercise of this as one of the fairest jewels of his crown, one of the most sacred duties of his office." [2] After this outburst of eloquence, he continues : " The position we take of holding these corsairs until we can have security that they will return to their own country without again infesting the waters of Europe, is all the satisfaction we can give."

To the American commissioners he wrote at the same time : " I call your attention to the article of the treaty which forbids our allowing privateers free access into our ports, unless through pressing necessity. . . . You promised, gentlemen, to conform thereto." And he then related the trials he had experienced from the conduct of Captain Wickes and his consorts. " You are too well informed, gentlemen, and too acute not to see how far such conduct affects the dignity of the King, my master, and at the same time violates the neutrality which his Majesty professes. I expect,

---

[1] Vergennes to Noailles, July 19, 1777 ; Doniol, ii, 514.

[2] Doniol, ii, 515.

therefore, from your sense of justice, that you will be
the first to condemn conduct so contrary to the laws
of hospitality and of propriety." [1] The cruisers must,
accordingly, said Vergennes, give bonds for their immediate return to their own country.

In reply, the commissioners said that as soon as the
ships had taken in sufficient provisions, they would
sail for America, eschewing all privateering on the
British coast. Nothing of the sort was done, nor was
it probably expected or really desired on either side
that any such thing should be done, but the official
representatives of the two nations at least observed
the proprieties.

Sometimes the indignation of Vergennes, as well
as of Stormont, was excited by the boundless audacity
of the American freebooters. In the spring of 1777
a privateer was fitted out in the port of Dunkirk,
Deane, then one of our representatives, taking an active part in the enterprise. The cruiser set sail, under
the command of Captain Conyngham, and at once
captured the Harwich packet-boat, plying between
England and Holland, and sailed back in triumph,
bringing her prize, with all on board, into Dunkirk.
But this was too flagrant an infraction of the law
of decency as well as neutrality. The capture of the
packet created a panic in England ; rates of insurance
went up, boats running between Dover and Calais had
to pay ten per cent, travellers were afraid to go to sea.
The English minister remonstrated with his usual vehe-
mence, and even Vergennes was angry. The cruiser
was seized, and Captain Conyngham, who seems to
have expected a triumphant reception after his successful trip, was thrown into jail; the packet, and a

[1] Vergennes to the Commissioners, July 16, 1777; Doniol, ii, 521.

brig that Conyngham had also captured, were returned to the English, much to the chagrin of the captors.

Deane, who had taken an active part in this pirat-ical enterprise, remarked sadly that this gave the English a temporary triumph. Their triumph was only temporary. A new and better ship was bought for Conyngham and equipped with thirty-six guns. The release of the captain and crew was obtained on the agreement that they would sail at once for Amer-ica, and Mr. Hodge, who apparently was a partner in the enterprise, signed a bond to that effect. Conyng-ham then sailed out from Dunkirk, ostensibly on a trading expedition, and as soon as he was out of sight of land, began to pursue every English boat he saw, and captured all he could; he even endeavored to burn a few towns along the English coast. On hearing of this violation of the agreement, Vergennes had Hodge arrested and put in the Bastille, but the American commissioners applied for his release, pro-testing that they could not believe a man of Hodge's standing capable of any willful offence against the laws of the nation. Upon this certificate of character, Hodge was released from prison, and Conyngham proceeded on his privateering cruise along the English coast.[1]

A few months later, Captain Conyngham was un-lucky enough to be made a prisoner, and the English proposed to hang him as both a rebel and a pirate. The specific act charged against him was capturing the Harwich packet, having, as was alleged, no com-mission from the United States government. Conyng-ham averred that he held a commission, which was probably true, but, unfortunately, this he had lost at

[1] *Deane Papers*, ii, 108, 109.

the time the French government shut him up in jail
at Dunkirk. Thus the capture of the packet, which
had disturbed all England, very nearly cost the captain his neck. But Franklin and others asserted that
he was a regularly commissioned officer, and the possibility of retaliation, more than any belief in the regularity of Conyngham's status, saved his life. Congress held three English officers in close confinement,
to abide the decision as to Conyngham's fate. At
last he made his escape from prison, and he wrote
Franklin, dwelling upon his sufferings. " Irons, dun-
geons, hunger, the hangman's cart, I have experienced.
. . . Sir George Collier ordered irons on my legs,
with a sentry on board the ship. Mr. Collier, going
on an expedition, ordered me to jaole, there put me
into the condemned room. The first night a cold
plank my bed, a stone for a pillow. . . . Then, not
contented, they manacled my hands with a new-fash-
ioned pair of ruffels fitted very tite." [1] As Franklin
said when Conyngham was captured, " He has done so
much harm to the enemy that he can expect no mercy
at their hands."

Early in 1778 France signed an alliance with the
United States, and the English declared war. American cruisers enjoyed hardly more privileges in French
ports after this than they had when France was at
peace, but no one could longer complain that the
hospitality thus extended was contrary to the laws of
nations and the principles of neutrality.

[1] Hale, *Franklin in France*, i, 347, 349.]

CHAPTER IX

APART from the aid surreptitiously given by the French government, and the supplies sent over by Beaumarchais and other friends and speculators, there were numerous offers from a class who made arms their profession and who wished to enter the American army. Many of these, it is to be feared, were actuated by the hope of personal gain rather than by any zeal for the cause of American liberty. They were well-bred adventurers who had little to furnish except valor, and for this they demanded a high price. When their own country was at peace, they were ready to bear arms in America, and they would have been equally ready to enlist under the flag of the Great Turk if he had been in need of troops. The field in America seemed to present special attractions. Among a new and little-known people they could entertain hopes of gaining wealth and promotion that would have seemed absurd in Europe. In most continental wars the countries involved possessed a sufficient number of trained officers, and were not eager for foreign volunteers. Frederick declined the services of the young English noblemen who wished to serve under his flag during the Seven Years' War, because he thought they would be an embarrassment rather than an assistance.

But the American colonists, it was felt, must be ignorant of anything deserving to be called the art of war; they had no body of trained officers; they had little experience in fighting except with Indians, and the conflicts in which they had taken part bore no resemblance to scientific warfare. The selectman of the town, or the keeper of the country store, must, it was argued, be unfit to act as a captain or a colonel; and yet from them, and those like them, the officers in the new army were selected. That men with some knowledge of wilderness life, who had hunted wild animals and been hunted by wild Indians in the primeval forests, were better fitted for conditions in America than an officer who could manœuvre a regiment with the utmost precision on the plains of Germany or France, was not understood in the military circles of Europe.

But it was not the love of adventure and the hope of reward alone, that led so great a body of young Frenchmen to seek out Deane and Franklin and tender their services. The American cause was truly popular, and young nobles who sighed for the excitement of war felt also a sincere sympathy for the principles for which the American colonists had taken up arms. Inspired by philosophers who predicted a new era of felicity, by politicians who declared the time was ripe for new forms of government, by nobles who discovered a new interest in the welfare of the people, many a young soldier, with a genuine enthusiasm for the cause, wished to help the American patriots in their efforts to throw off kingly misrule.

Whatever their motives, the number and the urgency of those who sought positions in the American army soon became embarrassing. Deane wrote in November, 1776: " The rage, as I may say, for entering into the American service increases and the consequence is that I am crowded with offers and proposals, many of them from persons in the first rank and eminence." [1] He writes a little later: "I am well-nigh harassed to death with applications of officers to go out for America"; and he added, with a confidence that unfortunately was not well founded, "Those I have engaged are, I trust, in general of the best character." [2]

In the following March the commissioners wrote: "The desire that military officers here of all ranks have of going into the service of the United States is so general and so strong as to be quite amazing. We are hourly fatigued with their applications and offers, which we are obliged to refuse, and with hundreds of letters which we cannot possibly answer to their satisfaction." [3]

When Franklin arrived, the pressure to enter the American service was no less, but he was more cautious than Deane in giving employment. He wrote that many had been previously engaged by Deane, who could not resist the applications made him, but that he gave all the discouragement in his power, and he adds: "You can have no conception of the arts and interest made use of to recommend, and engage us to recommend very indifferent persons. The importunity is boundless. The numbers we refuse incredible." [4] All these officers, so Franklin wrote, were reported to be full of courage and zeal, in short, "were Cæsars." Some offered aid more valuable than

[1] Deane to Committee, Nov. 6, 1776; *Deane Papers*, i, 342.

[2] Same to Same, Nov. 28, 1776; *Ibid.*, 375.

[3] Commissioners to Committee, March 12, 1777; *Diplomatic Correspondence*, Sparks's ed., i, 202.

[4] Franklin to Lovell, Oct. 7, 1777; *Writings of Franklin*, Albert H. Smyth, editor, vii, 66.

carrying a musket, and he notes an offer from a priest who wrote that if Franklin would pay his gaming debts, he would pray for the success of the American cause.[1]

Notwithstanding Deane's confidence that he had selected only those of the best character, he was induced to send many who would have been of little value to any cause, and in addition to this, he sent over many more than were needed, even if they had been officers of the highest merit. He dealt with this matter with his usual indiscretion, and enrolled many volunteers, under liberal promises of rank and pay which Congress was unwilling to fulfil. It was not possible, so the committee of Congress reported, to provide for these gentlemen in the manner they wished, and many at once returned to France. "We have done all in our power to prevent discontent," they said; but these efforts in many cases were unsuccessful. Congress had asked only for four engineers; it received a host of volunteers, of whom there was no need, and for whom there was no place. American officers naturally were not willing to step aside for some foreigner who could not even give orders in a language which the men could understand, and the most of those whom Deane sent over were unfit for such service as was required in America. To command a company of French soldiers in a campaign in the Low Countries was a very different thing from having charge of a body of Americans, fresh from the plough or the shop, amid the privations that awaited them in New Jersey or Virginia.

One of the most troublesome of those chosen by Deane was du Coudray, who had so disturbed Beaumarchais by ordering back the ship on which he em-

[1] Hale, *Franklin in France*, i, 79.

barked. Du Coudray was one of the first of the foreign officers who arrived in America, and he did much to insure a cold reception for those who followed him. Deane had written Congress that the character and extraordinary exertions of du Coudray entitled him to much, and he hoped that the sum stipulated for him would not be considered extravagant. Relying on Deane's agreement, du Coudray at once asked for a commission as major-general, and to be put in command of the artillery and engineer corps. He was a soldier of some experience, and the American officers were probably less versed in the art of engineering or the use of artillery, but they had no thought of yielding the chief command to an unknown foreigner.

General Knox was in command of the artillery at this time ; if we can believe Steuben, he had no idea of the use of cannon either in attack or retreat, but he had no desire to be superseded or taught by a foreigner. It was reported that du Coudray's demand had been acceded to, and thereupon Generals Knox, Greene, and Sullivan sent their resignations to Congress. For this act they were properly reprimanded, but Congress declined to recognize Deane's agreement, and created for du Coudray the position of inspector of artillery with the rank of major-general.

Du Coudray had a high sense of his own importance and a strong desire for his own advancement ; he insisted that he would have everything or nothing and would suffer no abatement in his demands. He sent memoirs to Congress, magnifying his own services and belittling anything done by Beaumarchais or others; he refused the commission offered him and said that he would enter the army merely as a volunteer, with the rank of captain. This act of magnanimity was only to prepare for further intrigues; but fortunately, on September 16, 1777, when crossing the Schuylkill, he was drowned, and his career came to an end. Even the charitable La Fayette writes that du Coudray's death was perhaps a happy accident. After his death, most of those who came over with him returned to France, having found neither gain nor glory in their American expedition.

Yet among these volunteers were some whose services exceeded any promise of reward they received from Deane. La Fayette, Kalb, Steuben, and Pulaski were among these early recruits, and when France became our ally they were followed by many others who did good service in the cause of American liberty.

The name of La Fayette is more familiar to the American people than that of any other actor in the Revolution, with the exception of Washington. When very young he gained an extended fame which has not waned with the progress of time. He was not a man of unusual intellectual powers, nor of uncommon ability as a soldier, but he possessed courage, enthusiasm, and an amiable character, he threw himself with zeal into a great cause, and he attained the fame which he so eagerly desired.

The Marquis de La Fayette belonged to an ancient and illustrious house. They traced their lineage back beyond the year 1000, and had no need of the ingenuity of genealogists to prove the antiquity of their race. Members of the family served in the Crusades, one of them fell at the battle of Poitiers, another was marshal of France in the days of Charles VII, and many won distinction in their country's wars during the centuries that followed. If the men were renowned for their bravery, some of the women were equally noted for their charms. The beautiful Mademoiselle de La Fayette, who excited the chaste affection of Louis XIII, and Madame de La Fayette, the author of several novels and tales, of which the "Princesse de Cleves," the most famous, has still many readers, — these were among the celebrated members of the La Fayette family.

The grandmother of our hero was a Chavagniac, and was married at the early age of twelve. She was a woman of good judgment and strong character. Her grandson writes that she was respected in all the province, and persons came from twenty leagues around to consult her on questions of importance. His mother was a daughter of the Marquis de la Rivière; she possessed virtue, piety, and illustrious pedigree and very little money. The father of La Fayette, like almost all of his ancestors, served in the army, and in July, 1757, he was killed at the battle of Hastenbeck. It was a tradition that the La Fayettes fell on the field of battle, and that they met their fate when young; the father was killed at twenty-five, his only brother had already fallen in Italy, a young man of twenty-three.

On the 6th of September, 1757, the famous Marquis de La Fayette was born, a posthumous child. He lived for some years with his mother and grandmother in the Château Chavagniac, in what is now the department of the Haute-Loire. It was an ancient and massive building, erected in the fourteenth century for purposes of defence, strongly fortified and flanked by towers, and from it one had an extended though somewhat austere view. It still stands with its heavy and severe lines, little changed in appearance since the days when La Fayette was a child.

In his early years the family was poor. His father and uncle left small estates; the lands about Chavagniac were not fertile, the climate was cold, and the revenues were small. The lad led an active and hardy life, taking much exercise and growing up stout in body and courageous in mind. The wolf of Gévaudan, whose real or imaginary misdeeds made it famous all over France, committed its ravages in this part of the country, and La Fayette tells us that when only eight his walks were animated by the hope that he might encounter this extraordinary beast and become famous by killing it.[1] He never met the wolf, and he owed his fame to other exploits.

When still a youth La Fayette inherited from an uncle of his mother a great estate. He was taken to Paris and received into the ranks of the highest nobility. Though not brilliant, he was pleasing, amiable, rich, and young, and he was everywhere made welcome. Early marriages were the custom of the time in the circle to which La Fayette belonged. When only fourteen he was proposed as a husband for one of the five daughters of the Duc d'Ayen, who was afterwards Duc de Noailles. It seems to have been a matter of indifference which of the five should be agreed upon, and the father selected the second. But the mother hesitated about consenting to the match.

We are apt to regard French society at this period as frivolous and corrupt. Of corruption and frivolity there was certainly enough, but there were in the highest classes, as well as among the bourgeoisie, many families in which piety ruled and every virtue was found. The women of the Noailles and La Fay-

[1] *Mémoires, Correspondance et Manuscrits du Général Lafayette, publiés par sa famille*, i, 20.

ette families were examples of purity of life and elevation of character; we hear less of such than of the Montespans and the Pompadours, but they were always numerous, and without them French society would have ceased to exist. The Duchesse d'Ayen was one of these women. She was educated in a convent, filled with a sincere piety, entirely devoted to her husband and her children, and she trained the latter to follow the same paths she had herself pursued. Like other women of her class, she was scrupulous, we may think over scrupulous, in the performance of religious duties. Though fond of chess, she would not play on Saturdays because she found that recollections of the game sometimes distracted her thoughts at mass on the following morning. Such things savor of a narrow devotion; but narrowness should not be charged against a woman who trained five children to lead pure lives, and who herself met death on the scaffold during the Terror with the courage of a soldier and the tranquillity of a saint.

Such a mother was not ready to consent to the proposed marriage of her daughter to La Fayette merely because he had wealth and rank. The future bride writes that the extreme youth of the proposed husband, the loneliness of his situation, having lost all his near relatives, and his great fortune, which her mother regarded as a danger rather than an advantage, decided her to refuse her consent.[1] In this she persisted for several months; but the father manifested still greater pertinacity, the alliance was finally agreed upon, and in 1774, when La Fayette was sixteen and his bride not yet fifteen, the marriage was celebrated.

[1] Mme. Adrienne de La Fayette, *Notice sur Madame la Duchesse d'Ayen.*

Though married, the parties were little more than children and they were treated accordingly. The marquis continued his military education at the Academy of Versailles and seems to have been regarded by the family of which he was now a member as an amiable child.

His own rank and the position of his wife's family secured him admission everywhere, but the youth seems to have had by nature little taste for courts. He was, so he tells us, awkward in his manners, a small and by no means a brilliant talker, and little fitted to shine in society. His father-in-law wished to secure him a position at court; but La Fayette, from chance or design, advanced some views that were distasteful to the future Louis XVIII, and the place was refused. The young nobility of this period found court life less attractive than had their sires. His companion, the Comte de Ségur, rejected a similar position, and speaks of it as a gilded slavery.

La Fayette, so Ségur tells us, was cold and even dull in appearance, but he concealed a firm character and an ardent spirit. In 1775 the marquis, then eighteen years of age, was performing duty at Metz. It was there, according to his statement, that his interest was first excited in the affairs of the American colonists. At a dinner given by the Comte de Broglie, the Duke of Gloucester, a brother of George III, was present. The brothers and sons of the House of Hanover were usually at loggerheads, and the duke was quite ready to criticize his brother's policy; he told of the treatment the American colonists had received, and spoke warmly of these patriots struggling for their liberties. Every word met with a ready response from La Fayette, who was young and ardent, and filled with that vague enthusiasm for popular rights which had begun to show itself in the highest circles of the French aristocracy. He tells us that he then decided to enlist in the cause of American freedom, and there is no reason to question his word. Doubtless he was influenced by the taste for military life, and by the desire for military glory that was common among young French nobles. But in addition to this, he was actuated by a strong and genuine interest in those whom he believed to be oppressed, and he was eager to have a hand in the establishment of a free government on the other side of the water.

La Fayette's youthful enthusiasm was accompanied by a pertinacity and steadfastness of purpose unusual in men of any age. It was an easy thing to sympathize with the American patriots, but for a youth like La Fayette to leave his country and enter the insurgent army was a difficult enterprise. He was young, rich, highly placed, newly married. Naturally all of his family were aghast at the suggestion that he should desert his home and take part in a war waged in a land which seemed more remote from France than Abyssinia now seems from New York.

The very prominence of his position made it more difficult for him to go. An obscure young man could have taken ship to Boston and joined the army under Washington, and the French government would have disquieted itself very little. But the Marquis de La Fayette could not lightly be allowed to take such a step. The English might insist that such a man would not have enlisted in the American cause except with the tacit approval of his own government. The American insurgents would believe the same thing, and expect that the adhesion of La Fayette would be the first step toward an alliance with the French King.

Two other young nobles, hardly inferior to La Fayette in position, the Vicomte de Noailles, his bro-ther-in-law, and the Comte de Ségur, who afterwards married another kinswoman, endeavored to embark with him in the American cause. All three applied to Deane, and he naturally was anxious to secure the support of such notable recruits. French opinion was already favorable to the Americans, and it would surely assist in obtaining the open support of the French government if representatives of the great French families were fighting for the patriot cause. But the prominence of the new recruits stood in the way of the accomplishment of their plan. Such a step was distasteful to the government and it was promptly forbidden.

Noailles and Ségur sighed and obeyed, but La Fayette was made of more stubborn material. His family were incensed at his project and were equally surprised. La Fayette's reserved character and his slowness of speech were in marked contrast with the brilliant youths of his own class, and had created the impression that, if worthy, he was also dull. His father-in-law desired the Comte de Ségur to breathe some of his own fire into La Fayette's sluggish tem-perament, and he was amazed when this silent youth of nineteen announced his decision to sail across the Atlantic and hazard his life in a land and for a people of which even educated Frenchmen had the vaguest notions. Surprise at this action was accom-panied by prompt resolve that it should be prevented. Even if the officers of the government had been will-ing to connive at La Fayette's escape, his father-in-law was persistent in demanding that, if necessary, the youth should be put under arrest to keep him from deserting his country and his family on a fool's errand.

With the stubbornness which was a marked feature in his character, La Fayette persisted in his purpose, in defiance of the wishes of his family and the orders of his government. He applied for assistance to the Comte de Broglie, who, like any sensible man, advised him to abandon the project. "I saw your uncle die in the war in Italy," he said, "I was present at the death of your father at the battle of Minden.[1] I do not wish to contribute to the ruin of the sole remaining branch of the family." But the count at last was overcome by La Fayette's persistence, and agreed to assist him so far as he could.

Baron Kalb had already decided to volunteer for the American service, and was Broglie's representative in the scheme to make the count commander-in-chief of the American forces. By Kalb, La Fayette was, in 1776, presented to Deane, who had to deal with the numerous recruits who were eager to enlist in the American cause. Most of these volunteers set a value on their services that was justified neither by their past nor by their future performances. It was different with La Fayette — he had much to give and asked little in return. He had indeed no military record behind him, but he had a great name and large wealth; he only asked the opportunity to serve, and wished no pay for his service. How valuable this service was to be, no one could foresee, and La Fayette tells us that " in presenting my nineteen-year-old face

---

[1] The count was mistaken in his recollection; La Fayette's father was killed at Hastenbeck. Tower, *The Marquis de Lafayette*, etc., i, 21.

to M. Deane, I spoke more of my zeal than of my experience, but I made him realize the little éclat that would result from my departure, and he signed the contract."

A paper was drawn promising to La Fayette the rank of major-general in the American army, and positions for the various subordinates by whom he was to be attended. The rank of major-general was a high one for a young man of nineteen who had seen no service in war, but Deane justly thought it was not too high for a recruit who bore the name of La Fayette. "I have thought that I could not better serve my country, . . ." Deane wrote, "than by granting to him, in the name of the very honorable Congress, the rank of major-general, which I beg the States to confirm to him. . . . His high birth, his alliances, the great dignities which his family hold at this Court, his considerable estates in this realm, his personal merit, his reputation, his disinterestedness, and, above all, his zeal for the liberty of our provinces, are such as to induce me to promise him the rank of major-general in the name of the United States." [1]

Deane made some foolish contracts for the employment of foreign officers in the American service, but the wisdom of this engagement should atone for many mistakes. The manner in which La Fayette accepted the offer shows how far he was removed from the greedy adventurers who were pressing for high rank and high pay in the American cause. "I offer myself," he wrote, ". . . to serve the United States with all possible zeal, without any pension or allowance." And he added the unnecessary clause that he reserved for himself the liberty of returning to Eu-

[1] Tower, *The Marquis de Lafayette*, etc., i, 35.

rope whenever his family or his King should recall him. Neither his King nor his family wished him to go, but he persisted in his purpose, and had no thought of abandoning the American cause at the bidding of any one. The news from the other side was unfavorable, and even the American commissioners advised La Fayette to postpone his undertaking, but he paid as little attention to their advice as to the orders of his own government. " We must show our confidence," he said to Deane; " it is in time of trouble that I wish to share your fortune." [1]

The plans for furnishing him transportation failed, and thereupon he resolved to buy a ship for himself. In order to get the ship he was obliged to purchase the cargo, and he bought from some merchants in Bordeaux, for 112,000 francs, a vessel that was to sail in March, 1777. In the mean time, perhaps in order to avert suspicion, he amused himself by a trip to England, where he was presented to George III.

Though La Fayette was resolved to go to America, he was anxious to obtain the consent of his government, expressed or implied; as an officer of the King he did not wish to desert his colors, and embark in a foreign service, without the permission of his superiors. From London he sent a letter to his father-in-law, stating that he was now a general officer in the army of the United States, and was about to start for that country. " I am filled with joy," he writes, " at having found so good an opportunity to increase my experience and to do something in the world. . . . This voyage is not a long one; people go farther every day for the sole purpose of travelling, and, be-

---

[1] Lafayette, "Mémoires de ma Main," in *Mémoires, Correspondance et Manuscrits du Général Lafayette* (ed. 1837), i, 12.

sides, I hope I shall return from it better deserving
the esteem of everybody who is kind enough to miss
me. . . . Good-bye, my dear father, I hope to see you
soon again. Do not withdraw your affections from
me." [1]

This letter carried consternation to La Fayette's
family; his wife was plunged in tears, and his father-
in-law was plunged in rage. The expressions of affection with which the epistle was filled did not soften
the duke's heart; he went at once to the ministers
and demanded of them to arrest the youth and compel
him to return to his duties. It is doubtful if this demand was altogether agreeable: the ministers were
quite content that La Fayette should try his fortunes
in the New World, if only the English could be made
to believe that he had gone without the knowledge or
authority of his own government.

In the mean time La Fayette left London and
made his way to Paris. He did not wish his arrival
to be known, and for three days he remained concealed in the residence of Baron Kalb at Chaillot. On
March 16, in company with the baron, he set out for
Bordeaux. There they arrived on the 19th, and on the
25th of March, 1777, they sailed from that port on
the ship Victory, which La Fayette had purchased.[2]
The forms of secrecy were still preserved. In the
registry of passengers La Fayette inscribed himself
as the Sieur Gilbert du Mottie, Chevalier de Cha-
vaillac, aged twenty years, height tall, hair blond,
about to sail to the Cape, on matters of business.[3]

[1] Letter of March 19, 1777; Tower, *The Marquis de Lafayette*, etc.,
i, 37.
[2] Kalb's letters of March 24 and April 1; Kapp, *Life of Kalb*, 104.
[3] Doniol, ii, 384.

"We are weighing anchor in the most glorious weather," Kalb wrote his wife. "I shall write you once more before my arrival in America, because we shall touch at a European port."

There was no reason why, once having set sail, the Victory should not have proceeded directly to America. But La Fayette was anxious to receive the consent of his government, and still indulged the hope that his letters would soften the hearts both of his father-in-law and of the minister of foreign affairs. Accordingly he sent a courier to Paris to obtain the desired permission. This was exactly what the minister was loath to give, and what the Duc d'Ayen was resolved should not be given. The Victory stopped at Los Pasajes, a small Spanish harbor on the Bay of Biscay, a few miles from the French frontier, and there the marquis received some correspondence that was little to his taste. A *lettre de cachet*, forbidding his departure, had been sent to Bordeaux, and followed him to Los Pasajes. Accompanying this were letters from his family, which he informs us were terrible. He was directed to abandon his enterprise, to meet his family at Marseilles, and to accompany them on a long trip to Italy.

La Fayette's matters had now become generally known, and excited the interest of every salon and every café in Paris. The sympathy of the public was with the young adventurer. His youth, his zeal, his willingness to leave wealth and station in order to share the fortunes of the American insurgents, aroused universal enthusiasm. Public feeling was already friendly to the Americans, and this was strengthened by La Fayette's resolution to join their cause. On the other hand, the conduct of his father-in-law and of the government excited much animadversion. The duke, said one enthusiastic lady, if he treated an estimable son-in-law like La Fayette in this manner, could not expect any one to marry his other daughters.

La Fayette, however, was loath to continue his journey in defiance of the express orders he had received, and accordingly he returned to Bordeaux. His companion, Kalb, viewed this performance with great disfavor. He was anxious to sail for America as soon as possible, and he now regarded La Fayette's expedition as practically abandoned. " I do not believe he will rejoin me," Kalb wrote his wife, "and have advised him to settle with the owner of the ship at a sacrifice of twenty or twenty-five thousand francs." [1]

Kalb's letters to his wife disclose other anxieties which beset these volunteers in the cause of American liberty. The baron thought that La Fayette would return to Paris, and he intrusted to his wife the adjustment of some pecuniary matters with the marquis. Evidently the young hero had spent money with a free hand on his trip to Bordeaux, and had failed to settle accounts with his older companion. If the marquis received back some part of the money which he had advanced for the ship, so Kalb wrote his wife, she might choose that moment to speak of a note La Fayette had given for 13,500 livres, not indeed to ask payment before it was due, but to suggest that he leave orders for its payment on the 20th of May; and then the baron adds, "perhaps he will pay you at once." There was, moreover, a further account between the associates. Kalb had bought the horses at Paris, La Fayette had paid the expenses of the

[1] Letter of April 1, 1777; Kapp, *Life of Kalb*, 105.

journey to Bordeaux, and the fear that the marquis expected him to pay part of these disturbed the baron. La Fayette had expended at the inn at Bordeaux 408 livres from Wednesday evening to Friday, because he gave many dinners and suppers which did not concern Kalb. " I think, therefore," he added, " you should delay to say anything of the expenses at Bordeaux, but say simply, ' Here, monsieur le marquis, is the account my husband has sent me of what he advanced for you, and he says he owes you two-fifths of the expenses to Bordeaux,' and see what he answers. I flatter myself it is his intention to repay part of my advances and perhaps all." [1]

In another letter, Kalb says, " It is certain that his foolish enterprise will cost him dear. I call the enterprise foolish, from the moment that he dared not execute his project, and bid defiance to threats." But Kalb did not fully understand the stubborn resolution of his companion in arms. La Fayette returned to Bordeaux and there despatched letters to the ministers defending his conduct, and asking that he be allowed to continue his enterprise.

The reports which he received from Paris held out little hope that either his family or his government would consent to his departure, and thereupon he resolved to go without their consent. He notified the commanding officer at Bordeaux that he was about to start for Marseilles, in conformity with the royal order. Having done this, he took a carriage and set out in company with his friend, Vicomte Mauroy. As soon as they were fairly out of the city limits, they left the Marseilles road and turned their faces towards the Spanish frontier. Mauroy rode in the chaise,

[1] Doniol, iii, 208.

while La Fayette went along on horseback disguised
as a postboy.

At Bayonne, while Mauroy attended to some necessary business, La Fayette remained concealed in a
stable. At St.-Jean-de-Luz, La Fayette had to ask
for fresh horses, and he was recognized by the inn-
keeper's daughter as the gentleman who had been
there a few days before on the road to Bordeaux.
But she did not betray his incognito, and when some
officials turned up in pursuit she sent them off on the
wrong road.

Thus befriended, on the 17th of April, La Fayette again reached Los Pasajes, and he was hindered no further by his government. Only the zeal
of the Duc d'Ayen had incited measures so active
as those that were taken. The young marquis was
now again safely in Spain, popular sympathy was on
his side, the fashionable world in Paris praised his
bravery and condemned the conduct of those who
sought to keep him from winning name and fame.
The ministers were secretly willing that he should
start on his expedition, and they gave him no more
trouble.

La Fayette's efforts to enlist as a defender of
American liberty blew into flame the interest in that
cause already kindled in France. "All Europe is for
us," wrote Silas Deane exultantly on March 12;
". . . the prospect of an asylum in America for
those who love liberty gives general joy, and our
cause is esteemed the cause of all mankind." [1] "La
Fayette," wrote Deane and Franklin a little later, "is
exceedingly beloved and everybody's good wishes
attend him. . . . Those who censure it [his expedi-

[1] Wharton, ii, 287.

tion] as imprudent in him, do, nevertheless, applaud his spirit." [1]

On Sunday, the 20th of April, 1777, La Fayette rejoined his ship, and, accompanied by Baron Kalb and twelve French officers whom he took as his staff, he àt last set sail for the coast of America.

La Fayette always insisted that he had the consent of the government for his departure. A formal consent certainly he did not have, but it is quite possible that intimations reached him that, though he could expect no authorization of his enterprise, yet his future fortune at court would not be imperilled if he persisted in it. He himself wrote to Maurepas that, as he had received no answer to his letters, and the government had not refused to remove its interdict, he should interpret this silence as signifying consent. This he probably regarded as a pleasantry, and apparently the ministers did the same; at least they expressed no serious indignation.

The Marquis de Noailles, then ambassador at London, was disturbed that his young kinsman, after being presented to the English King, should at once start to join the insurgents against that King's authority. But Maurepas quieted his apprehensions. "Your family," he wrote, "has nothing with which to reproach itself, and the King will not bear you any ill favor for the action of a young man whose head has been turned." [2] Vergennes wrote, "Lord Stormont seems to be in a very bad humor over this. He has the talent of attaching much importance to very small things." [3]

[1] Letter of May 25, 1777; Tower, *The Marquis de Lafayette*, etc., i, 59.

[2] Doniol, ii, 410.   [3] See letter of May 2, 1777; Doniol, ii, 411.

The forms of propriety were still maintained. An order was issued, forbidding any French officer to enter the service of the colonies, and enjoining those who should arrive in the West India Islands, and especially the Marquis de La Fayette, to return to France forthwith. This was sent to the Minister of the Marine to forward; but his clerical force seems to have been insufficient, for he returned the order for copies to be made that he might have one to send to each of the islands. It does not appear that copies were sent to any of them, and the matter apparently was intentionally neglected.[1]

In the mean time the Victory was peacefully pursuing her way to the New World. The young hero suffered from seasickness as well as homesickness. " I was very ill during the first part of the voyage," he writes his wife, " but I had the consolation of the wicked, that I suffered with many others." [2] The weather was unfavorable, but they were lucky enough to avoid any English cruisers, and after a journey of fifty-four days they landed near Georgetown, South Carolina.

The defenders of our country met at first with a cold reception. La Fayette and some of his officers rowed to the shore and proceeded to a house near by. It was now dark; they were met by the howling of the dogs, and the people within prepared to repel them as a band of marauders. Fortunately Kalb knew

[1] The authorities for La Fayette's expedition are found in: his own *Mémoires;* Doniol, volumes i and ii ; the account given by La Fayette to Sparks and contained in the latter's *Writings of Washington,* volume v, Appendix 1 ; *Mémoires de Ségur;* and the correspondence of La Fayette. A full account is given by Tower in his *Marquis de Lafayette in the American Revolution,* volume i.

[2] Lafayette, *Mémoires,* etc., i, 112.

some English, and when it was discovered who the
strangers were, they were received with great hospitality. La Fayette was charmed with all he saw; even
the mosquito curtains around the bed interested him
with their novelty and filled him with delight. He
went to Charleston, and from there sent home enthusiastic accounts of the new people among whom he
found himself. They were, he wrote, all his fancy had
painted them; simplicity of manners, love of country,
and a delightful equality prevailed everywhere; the
worthiest and the poorest were on a level; though
there were some large fortunes, he discovered no distinction in the manners of different classes towards
each other. The city of Charleston he found one of
the handsomest and best built he had ever seen, and
its inhabitants among the most agreeable people. The
women were pretty, simple in their manners, and
neater even than their English sisters. Even the inns
were charming, and the inn-keepers did not charge
too much. Yet there were some trials in this paradise. The heat, he wrote, was dreadful, he had discovered the sinister meaning of mosquito-nets, and
was devoured by the insects.[1]

His companion was less enthusiastic. "I have arrived here," Kalb wrote his wife from Charleston,
"after many toils and pains, and in an unsupport-
able heat. . . . Everything is exorbitantly dear; a
shirt for the marquis's servant cost fifty livres. At
Paris it would have cost four and a half at most, and
everything else is in proportion, provisions, lodging,
horses." [2]

From Charleston, La Fayette and his officers made

---

[1] See letters to his wife; Lafayette, *Mémoires*, etc., i, 124.
[2] Letter of June 18, 1777; Doniol, iii, 213.

their way to Philadelphia. The era of enthusiasm
over natural beauty had arrived in France, and La
Fayette wrote of his delight in the vast forests and
the immense rivers which he traversed, the freshness
and the majesty of the country through which he trav-
elled.

But the journey was a hard one, and his associates
were more impressed by the difficulties of the way
than by the beauties of the forests. Their carriages
broke down and they suffered from heat and hunger.
" We made a great part of the journey on foot," one
of them writes, " often sleeping in the woods, dying
of hunger, overcome by heat, several of us sick of
fever and dysentery. . . . There is no campaign in
Europe harder than this journey. There the hardships
are not continual, and are compensated by many
pleasures, while in this journey our evils grew greater
every day, and we had no solace except at last to
arrive in Philadelphia." [1] That city they reached after
thirty-two days of toil and trouble.

The American Congress was already beginning to
weary of the host of adventurers whom Deane was
sending over, and to whom, in his indiscretion, he
had promised rank and pay out of all proportion to
the value of their services. The committee received
this new arrival of recruits with a chilliness that was
very distasteful to them. " We were received in the
street by a member," writes one of the French officers. " When he left us, after having treated us, in
plain words, like adventurers, he finished by saying,
' You have papers from M. Deane. We authorized
him to employ four French engineers. He sent us

[1] Mémoire d'un des Officiers français [Chevalier du Buysson]
passés en Amérique avec le Marquis de La Fayette; Doniol, iii, 217.

M. du Coudray, with some pretended engineers who are not such, and some artillerymen who have never served. . . . The French officers come to serve us without our asking for them.' " [1]

The unlucky volunteers were stupefied by their reception, but they finally admitted that the conduct of du Coudray and his associates had justly prejudiced the Americans against all foreign recruits. On the whole, they took their repulse with philosophy, were paid their expenses, after some delay and difficulty, and the most of them returned to France wiser if sadder men. They had no opportunity for distinction, nor did any period of cordial reception and social excitement atone for their disappointment. " For two months," writes the secretary of the expedition, " Baron Kalb and myself were reduced to two shirts and one suit, badly torn ; but despite my ill fortune I am glad to have made the voyage. My constant ill luck has accustomed me to suffer patiently, and to find moments of pleasure in the midst of trial and misfortune." [2]

La Fayette brought special recommendations, and when he stated that the two favors he asked in return for his sacrifices were to serve at his own expense and to begin his service as a volunteer, the members of Congress found they were dealing with a recruit of a new order. On the 31st of July Congress passed a resolution in which they declared that inasmuch as the Marquis of La Fayette, by reason of his zeal for the cause of liberty, had left his family and was willing to expose his life without asking pay or indemnity, it was resolved that his services should be accepted and he should receive the rank of major-general. He

[1] Mém. d'un des Officiers, etc.; Doniol, iii, 218.   [2] Doniol, iii, 221.

was presented to Washington, who at once received
him into his favor. "I came to learn and not to
teach," said La Fayette,— a tone different from that
of most of the foreign officers who expected to show
the Americans how to fight.

The arrival of a young man of twenty, untried
either in warfare or in public affairs, might not seem
of great importance. But the services of La Fayette
were of inestimable value to the American cause; not
only did he prove himself a good officer and an exceedingly discreet adviser, but he was a connecting
link between the Americans and the French government; the influence of his counsels, the enthusiasm
incited by his conduct, were of considerable weight
in bringing the French authorities to espouse openly
the American cause.

His enthusiasm had a quality of Gallic effusion
that was not always found among the Americans,
even when fighting in their own behalf. He writes his
wife soon after he reached here: "Defender of that
liberty which I adore, . . . I bring only my frankness and my good-will. . . . In toiling for my glory
I work for their happiness. . . . The happiness of
America is linked to the happiness of all humanity;
she will become the sure asylum of virtue, honesty,
tolerance, equality and a peaceful liberty." [1]

Amid the dissatisfaction so common among the foreign volunteers, La Fayette's zeal and amiability stood
out in pleasing contrast. Kalb writes his wife in January, 1778, complaining of the various annoyances he
met. "One," he said, "is the mutual jealousy of almost all the French officers, particularly against those
of higher rank than the rest. These people think of

[1] Letters to his wife, June 7, 1777 ; Lafayette, *Mémoires*, etc., i, 115.

nothing but their incessant intrigues and back-biting.
. . . La Fayette is the sole exception. . . . La Fay-
ette is much liked, he is on the best of terms with
Washington." [1]

Washington at once appreciated the character of
his new assistant, and reposed in him a confidence
that was not misplaced.

The sights which met the new arrival must have
seemed strange to one accustomed to the armies of
Europe, but he was discouraged by nothing. In August, 1777, he joined the army in which he was now a
volunteer, and comments upon the appearance of the
soldiers. He found some eleven thousand men, poorly
armed and worse clad; the best garments were a sort
of hunting shirts, or loose jackets made of linen, while,
as he says, the varieties of nakedness equalled the
varieties of clothes, and the tactics were as primitive
as the uniforms. In spite of these disadvantages, he
recognized the fact that the men not only had in them
the making of good soldiers, but were already well
fitted for the requirements of an American campaign,
and that bravery with them took the place of science. [2]

La Fayette soon had an opportunity to show his
qualities as a soldier. He served as a volunteer at
Brandywine with great courage, and received a bullet
in his leg which laid him up for a few weeks. He was
cared for by the Moravians, and they, like every one
else, were impressed by his amiability; in a diary of
one of them is an entry recording that "the French
Marquis, whom we have found to be a very intelligent
and pleasant young man, came to bid us adieu."

With all of La Fayette's zeal and amiability, he

[1] Kapp, *Life of Kalb*, 143.
[2] Tower, *The Marquis de Lafayette*, etc., i, 217.

was ambitious for distinction, and while serving cheerfully as a volunteer was desirous of a more important
command. Washington befriended him, and wrote
the President of Congress in his behalf, stating the
qualifications of the young volunteer with his usual
justness of expression. "He is sensible, discreet in his
manners, has made great proficiency in our language,
and . . . possesses a large share of bravery and military ardor." [1] La Fayette's wish was gratified, and he
was given the command of a division. So friendly
was the feeling towards him, that this selection was
criticized by none. He wrote his father-in-law: "I am
cautious not to talk much, lest I should say some foolish thing; I am still more cautious in my actions, lest
I should do some foolish thing, for I do not want to
disappoint the confidence that the Americans have so
kindly placed in me." [2]

His judgment was soon put to a severe test, for
the cabal sought to avail themselves of La Fayette's
popularity and win him away from Washington, by obtaining for him the command of an army that was to
conduct a campaign in Canada. Naturally he was gratified by so flattering a selection, but he soon discovered the ill-will of the cabal to Washington, and no
flatteries from them could affect his loyalty to the
commander-in-chief. He writes to Washington of
Conway: "I found that he was an ambitious and dangerous man; he has done all in his power by cunning
manœuvres to take off my confidence and affection for
you. . . . I am now fixed to your fate, and I shall
follow it and sustain it as well by my sword as by all
means in my power." [3]

[1] *Writings of Washington*, Sparks's ed., v, 129.
[2] Tower, *The Marquis de Lafayette*, etc., i, 256. [3] *Ibid.*, 262.

The young marquis not only detected the plans of his new associates and declined to join in them, but he soon found that the expedition against Canada was little more than a farce. He reported at Albany, in compliance with instructions received from Gates, who was then president of the Board of War, but he found the northern army a myth. He met General Stark at Albany, who told him he had never heard of the undertaking, and he soon discovered that the whole scheme was an impossibility. The disappointment was bitter, but he accepted it with his usual amiability. The Canadian expedition was abandoned and La Fayette returned to Valley Forge, and in the following summer took an honorable part in the battle of Monmouth.

In the mean time, France had become the ally of the United States; La Fayette was no longer nominally a fugitive from his own country, acting in disobedience to the orders of his sovereign; he could now serve with his own countrymen in the cause in which his country had enlisted, a result which was to some extent due to the interest and admiration which his own example had excited.

CHAPTER X

OF the French who wished to enlist in the American cause La Fayette proved the most useful friend, and was among the most illustrious in rank. But there were others whose military reputation far exceeded his, and who had already won name and fame in the world. The Comte de Broglie was perhaps the most conspicuous of these would-be recruits, and the intrigues by which he sought to obtain high employment in this country possess a curious interest. To us it seems like a crazy dream to suppose that a foreign adventurer would be chosen to replace Washington as commander-in-chief of the American armies, that the American patriots would ask a French nobleman to become the dictator of the new republic. But to us the history of the war is known, and the record of the men who took part in it; all this was veiled in mystery when Broglie cherished his ambitions; the capacity of Washington for a great place in the world was still to be demonstrated, his fame was still to be won.

The Comte de Broglie himself was a very considerable person, and a member of a distinguished family. Though it was little over a hundred years since his ancestors had left Piedmont to push their fortunes in France, they had already furnished two marshals to the French army,[1] they had filled important positions

---

[1] Duc de Broglie, *The King's Secret*, i, 23.

under the government, and enjoyed the most intimate relations with the sovereign, and this great prosperity had been justified by uncommon ability. The count himself was a typical member of this active and pushing family. He was an experienced soldier and a lifelong intriguer. He was a very small man, but his head was as erect as a bantam cock, said one contemporary; his sparkling eyes, when he was excited, made him resemble a volcano in eruption, said another. When a young man, he was sent as ambassador to Poland, and afterwards he returned to his occupation as a soldier and served in the Seven Years' War. After that, he had been associated with Louis XV in that secret diplomacy with which the King sought to dispel his ennui, but only succeeded in annoying his ministers.

But while the count had gained a certain amount of prominence, his ambition was far from gratified. He was, moreover, regarded with ill-favor at the court of Louis XVI; the ministers were not willing to excuse the part he had taken in some of Louis XV's unlucky intrigues, and he was looked upon as an injudicious and dangerous man. This inclined him to turn his attention to a remote field of action. Its very distance lent enchantment, and made it easy to hope that vague dreams of ambition might there be realized. He knew the actual conditions in France and Germany, and he had little reason to expect any great advancement in those countries. But on a field of action over three thousand miles removed, among a people new in the politics of the world, there might be opportunities that it was idle to anticipate in settled governments, amid experienced and sagacious competitors for favor and fame.

It shows how little was known as to the character of the American people, that any one could believe they would accept a foreign nobleman as a practical dictator. Information as to the colonists was naturally very scanty. The French people knew that the English colonies in America had white men as well as red men for their occupants, but their knowledge did not extend much further. That there could be found in those remote parts of the world men really competent to govern a state seemed to them improbable ; and especially was this true at the beginning of the war, before it became the fashion to regard America as the home of virtue and wisdom. The colonial leaders were unknown on the continent, and many intelligent Frenchmen might think it doubtful if among them was a man fit to command armies and lead a revolt against Great Britain ; they deemed it unlikely that in remote and semi-civilized colonies a leader could be found to compare with a nobleman who had learned generalship in campaigns against Frederick, and had studied politics in the chambers of Versailles.

There is to us a mild amusement in reading suggestions that our forefathers might fail under the leadership of Washington, but could insure success by taking a second-rate French general as their commander, and yet the arguments suggested in Comte de Broglie's behalf seemed plausible to many. It was in his interest that Kalb was led to volunteer for the American service. He went over as an advance agent, to suggest, if the opportunity seemed favorable, that the struggling patriots might wisely avail themselves of the sagacity and military prowess of the count, a man versed in warfare and accustomed to deal with the great questions of the world, and that, if the colonists should ask him to come to their aid, upon fitting terms he would be willing to comply.

In 1776 Kalb submitted to Deane a curious paper in which he stated the hopes of his patron. The very title of the communication suggested its great import: " A project of which the execution would perhaps decide the success of the cause of liberty in the United States." "Congress," so Kalb declared, "should ask of the King of France some one who would become their civil and military chief, the temporary generalissimo of the new republic." The course which had been so beneficial to the Dutch provinces, when suffering from the tyranny of Spain, would be equally advantageous in the present case. " It was necessary to furnish the infant states with foreign troops, and especially with a chief of great reputation, whose military capacity would fit him to command an army against Prince Ferdinand of Brunswick or the King of Prussia himself; who would join to a name made illustrious by many heroes great experience in war and all the qualities necessary to conduct such an enterprise with prudence, integrity, and economy. . . . Numerous armies and courage," Kalb wrote, "are not sufficient to obtain success, if they are not sustained by ability and experience. (In speaking thus I have no intention to reflect on the glory, the conduct, or the achievements of the officers who are actually in command; on the contrary I think they acted very well and bravely on all occasions, especially General Washington. But my plan is to have a man whose name and reputation alone would discourage the enemy.) . . . Many young noblemen would follow him as volunteers, for the sake of serving and distinguishing themselves under his eyes. That nobility, by its

interest at court, by its own credit, or the management of its friends and kinsmen, could decide the
King in favour of a war with England. . . . Such
a leader," he declared with enthusiasm, "with the
assistants he would choose, would be worth twenty
thousand men, and would double the value of the
American troops. . . . This man may be found, I
think that I have found him, and I am sure that once
he is known he will unite the suffrages of the public,
of all sensible men, of all military men, and I venture
to say, of all Europe. The question is to obtain his
acceptance, which, as I think, can only be accomplished by loading him with sufficient honours to satisfy his ambition, as by naming him field-marshal
generalissimo, and giving him a considerable sum of
ready money for his numerous children, the care of
whom he would have to forego for some time during
his sojourn beyond the seas, to be equivalent to them
in case of the loss of their father, and by giving him
all the powers necessary for the good of the service." [1]

If it was suggested that the generalissimo might
make himself a king or a tyrant, Kalb declared that
such a thought would never enter Broglie's generous
heart, and that the title of duke in France would be
more acceptable than that of king in America.

This document Kalb asked Deane to submit to
Franklin, who had just arrived in Paris. It is doubtful if the doctor ever saw it, and it is certain that
such a project would have been condemned by his
common sense. But Deane seems to have been influenced by Kalb's arguments; he was acting with much
zeal and little wisdom in enrolling foreign officers for
the American service, and the idea of furnishing

[1] Kalb to Deane, Dec., 1776; translated in *Deane Papers*, i, 427.

not only colonels and major-generals, but a general-in-chief, was calculated to allure a man of not very sound judgment.

On December 6, 1776, he wrote the secret committee of Congress : " I submit one thought to you ; whether, if you could engage a great general of the highest character in Europe, such, for instance, as Prince Ferdinand, Marshal Broglie, or others of equal rank, to take the lead of your armies, whether such a step would not be politic, as it would give a character and credit to your military, and strike perhaps a greater panic in our enemies." [1]

In the mean time Kalb had enlisted in the American service and received from Deane a promise of the rank of major-general, together with twelve thousand livres, for expenses and as an advance upon his appointment. No less than fifteen other officers were also engaged by the eager Deane, with rank ranging from major-general down and with money paid in advance for some. Nearly all of them, curiously, were adherents of Broglie; they might advance his interest in the colonies, and be trusty members of his staff, when the count assumed his duties as general-in-chief of the American army. [2]

Broglie had remained quietly at his country seat at Ruffec while his friends were pushing his interests with the American representatives, but it was now supposed that Kalb would shortly sail for America on his mission, and on December 11, 1776, the count wrote, explaining fully his views. A certain reserve kept him from using his own name, but he described

---

[1] Deane confounds the Comte de Broglie with his brother, the marshal and duke. *Deane Papers*, i, 404.

[2] Kapp, *Life of Kalb*, 320; Doniol, ii, 50–84.

himself with entire clearness and without any undue modesty. " I am sure," he wrote, " that you approve the plan which M. Dubois has communicated to you." There was needed in America a military and political leader who would unite all parties, and attract to himself brave and efficient followers. Kalb's mission was to convince the colonists of the necessity of having such a man, one of elevated rank and large experience. " When you propose the man," said the wily count, " you must act as if you were ignorant whether he desired such a position, and you will make it understood that he will only consent to make the supposed sacrifices if he is granted extraordinary advantages." He then suggested what these advantages should be : the rank of generalissimo ; supreme authority over the army ; and he adds, " Great pecuniary advantages and a large pension for life, though the amount of these would be reimbursed a hundred-fold by the value of his services." Finally the envoy was instructed to report the actual condition of feeling, and the possibility of success. If all went well, Congress was at once to send full powers to Deane to engage the future commander. "I leave this unsigned," adds the count at the end. " You know who I am." [1]

Such were the ambitions and the selfish desires of the man who thought he was better fitted than George Washington to serve the cause of American liberty. His agent was quite right in saying that Broglie had no thought of making himself a king or permanent dictator in America. He hoped to be well paid for his services, but what he most desired was that the distinction he might win there would assist him to at-

[1] Doniol, ii, 70–73.

tain the rank of duke and marshal when he returned to France.

Kalb was long delayed in embarking for America. He expected to sail on the Amphitrite in December, but at the last moment the government forbade its departure, and some of the officers associated with him were discouraged by the delay and abandoned the project. At last, in the spring of 1777, he embarked with La Fayette on the Victory. La Fayette had seen much of Broglie, and had been assisted by him in his efforts to join the American cause. Kalb presented La Fayette to Deane, and sailed with him for America. It would seem probable that the marquis heard something of these plans, but he took no part in them, nor in his memoirs does he disclose any knowledge of them. Certainly he went to America to gratify his own desire, and not to further the ambition of any one else. He fought for his own hand.

Kalb also desired to become himself an actor in the western war; but he was ready to further Broglie's project, if it were at all feasible, and he hoped to create a feeling that might lead Congress to turn to the count as a protector and a savior. But he was a sensible man and soon discovered that the American Congress had small need of foreign volunteers, even of less rank than a generalissimo. It needed but a brief sojourn for him to see how chimerical were Broglie's schemes. Like an honest man, he at once sought to undeceive his patron, and in September, 1777, he wrote: "If I return to Europe it is largely on account of the impossibility of succeeding in the great project with which I occupied myself with so much pleasure. M. de Valfort will tell you that the proposition is impracticable. It would be regarded as a crying injustice against Washington, and an affront to the honor of the country." [1]

The desires of Broglie to play a great part were not gratified either in America or in Europe. There was no more talk of choosing him as generalissimo of the American armies; even the count realized that this ambition had been only a day-dream, and he was no more successful in his efforts to obtain important employment from Versailles. He submitted to the King an elaborate plan for the invasion of England, and called attention to the confidence with which Louis XV had honored him during twenty-three years. This did not secure him the confidence of Louis XV's successor, his memoir received no attention, and he had no opportunity to show his skill as a general either in Europe or in America.

It is interesting to watch the change in Kalb's opinion of the American general-in-chief. Though he was free from the excessive self-assertion of many of the foreign volunteers, yet he arrived here with the prejudices of a soldier who had seen long and important service in great European wars, and with a readiness, that was neither unnatural nor blameworthy, to criticize those who, in military experience, were far his inferiors. Washington had won no brilliant victories, and while his campaigns had been marked by some degree of success, they had also been attended by some serious disasters. Kalb writes of Washington in September, 1777, soon after his arrival : " He is the most amiable, kind-hearted, and upright of men, but as a general he is slow and even indolent, much too weak and not without vanity and

[1] Letter of Sept. 24, 1777 ; Doniol, iii, 227. Translated by Kapp, *Life of Kalb*, 127.

presumption. In my opinion, if he achieves some important successes, it will be due more to fortune and the faults of his adversaries, than to his own capacity." [1] A little later his judgment is somewhat more favorable. " It is unfortunate that Washington is so easily led. He is the bravest and truest of men, and has the best intentions and a sound judgment. I am convinced that he would accomplish some great results if he would only act more upon his own responsibility, but it is a pity that he is so weak and has the worst of advisers in the men who enjoy his confidence."

A letter written still later from Valley Forge shows that Kalb was slowly coming to appreciate the greatness of the man. " He will rather suffer in the opinion of the world than hurt his country in making appear how far he is from having so considerable an army as all Europe and great part of America believe he has. This would show that he did, and does every day, more than could be expected from any general in the world in the same circumstances, and that I think him the only proper person (nobody actually being or serving in America excepted), by his natural and acquired capacity, his bravery, good-sense, uprightness and honesty, to keep up the spirits of the army and people, and that I look upon him as the sole defender of his country's cause." [2] " Washington's integrity, humanity, and love for the just cause of his country, as well as his other virtues, receive and merit the veneration of all men," Kalb wrote in 1778, and this judgment he never found occasion to modify. [3]

[1] Doniol, iii, 226–227. [2] Kapp, *Life of Kalb*, 137, 145.
[3] Kalb to his wife, May 12, 1778; *Ibid.*, 159.

Some account has been given of the long negotiations which at last resulted in France espousing the cause of the new republic. In the lengthy memoirs of Vergennes there is abundant statement of the reasons which led him at last to advocate such action, and in the French ministry his influence on this question certainly was of the greatest.

But a review of the diplomatic relations, an examination of the memoirs prepared by ministers, and a study of the minutes which described the acts of the Council do not tell the entire story. The assistance given by France was so important to the United States that it is worth while to trace the varied causes which at last resulted in that assistance being given. I have already said that it seemed unlikely that the ancient monarchy of France should assist rebels against their king. It is interesting to consider why interference in behalf of the colonists, which certainly would not have been attempted by France if our Revolution had occurred in the early years of the reign of Louis XV, was enthusiastically decided upon in the early years of the reign of Louis XVI.

CHAPTER XI

AMERICA AND THE FRENCH PEOPLE

MANY reasons united in leading France to espouse the cause of the American colonists. Hatred of England and a desire to lessen her power and obtain revenge for the calamities of the Seven Years' War, worked powerfully on the French mind. The hope of gaining commercial advantages from the gratitude of the new republic allured French statesmen. All these considerations had their weight in the deliberations of the French ministers, in whose hands were the issues of peace or war.

And yet there was an influence more potent than any of these considerations of policy, of national advantage and national dislike. If the American cause had not excited strong enthusiasm among the French people, unless interference in behalf of our forefathers had been not only approved but demanded by the representatives of French thought, it is doubtful if the government of Louis XVI would have taken up arms in behalf of American independence. The American Revolution occurred at a most opportune time. If the struggle for independence had begun fifty years or even twenty-five years earlier, France would have been as unlikely to interfere in our behalf as Spain or Austria. But the principles for which our ancestors contended, the political and social ideals which they represented, touched a sympathetic chord in the France of Louis XVI. Our Revolution found a welcome in the ferment of French thought that had begun. It was for this reason that Franklin's influence was of such value to the people he represented. At any time his talents and his wit would have insured him a hospitable reception among the French people. But when changes in scientific beliefs, in political faiths, in social aspirations, were preparing the way for a political and social revolution in France, Franklin was to an extraordinary extent able to appeal to the people, and to arouse among them enthusiasm for the nation and the cause of which he stood as the exponent. Public opinion became at the last the most potent factor in controlling the decision of the French government.

The problem of the American colonies attracted the attention of French statesmen when French society hardly distinguished Virginia from Massachusetts Bay ; but in the rapid changes of French thought, the public in 1778 exceeded the King's counsellors in eagerness for interference in the cause of American liberty. We are apt to think that public opinion has become an element to be reckoned with only in these later days, and that, in the time of an absolute monarchy, it could be safely disregarded. Such a belief is far from correct. The influence of public thought was as potent perhaps in the reign of Louis XVI as it is in France to-day. It was indeed exercised by a much smaller body. The mass of the population were too ignorant to hold any views on public questions, except as these were brought home to them by the burden of taxation or by a dull perception that others further up in the social scale enjoyed unfair advantages. But if the body that formed public opinion was small, it was exceedingly active. There had never been a

time when, among the nobility, the scholars and philosophers, the prosperous bourgeois, discussion had
been so alert and so free. No subject was deemed too
sacred to be talked about, no institution was too venerable to be questioned.

To such expressions, which found utterance in literature and in the journals of the day, in the talk of
the court and of the salon, the ministers of the King
could not turn a deaf ear. Necker, who became minister of finance only a few months after the Declaration of Independence, recognized to the fullest extent
the influence of public opinion upon the administration in France. "Favored by various causes," he says,
"it is constantly increasing. It controls all spirits, and
princes themselves respect it. . . . Most strangers can
hardly form a just idea of the authority which it
exercises in France. They comprehend with difficulty
that invisible power which, without treasure, without guards, and without arms, imposes its laws on
the city, on the court, and even in the palaces of
kings."

It might have been supposed that neither the principles nor the characters of our ancestors would have
aroused sympathy in French salons or among the
French people. Certainly this would have been true
a century earlier, and that it was not so now showed
how rapidly French thought was drifting from its ancient bearings. The rebellion of 1640 in England
excited no approval in France. The adherents of the
Parliament were regarded by the French as men
actuated by pernicious principles, who murdered their
King, and illustrated the evils of an unbridled and
lawless liberty. Nor were the strict morals, the long
faces, the formal dress of the Puritans any more pop-

ular than their politics among the nobles and courtiers of Versailles or the wits and poets of Paris.

A little more than a century had passed, and the descendants of the Puritans of 1640 were rebels against their King, and were proclaiming theories of government that would have seemed advanced to their ancestors. The social life, the religious beliefs of the American colonists were not altogether those of the soldiers of Cromwell, but they were quite as far removed from those of Paris. In their rigorous theology, in their strict and often tedious modes of life, there was apparently little to attract a French noble or a French philosopher. A people leading a provincial existence, very strict in its religious observances, very loose in its political orthodoxy, among whom a French philosopher would have found few listeners, and a courtier from Versailles would have died of ennui, seemed ill fitted to excite enthusiasm among the French people. And yet new political aspirations and discontent with existing social conditions led the French people to sympathize with the American colonists in their struggle for independence.

At the close of the reign of Louis XV, one who possessed the rare power of forecasting the future might have anticipated a revolution in France, quite as much as in America. The causes which at last resulted in the great upheaval in France had long existed. The expressions of discontent and of a desire for change had become so frequent that no one could disregard them, though few realized their significance.

If one had contrasted the lot of the people in France and in the American colonies, he might have anticipated that in the one country revolution would result in a violent social upheaval, while in the other it would only modify political relations and leave the beliefs and condition of the people little changed. Great wealth was rare in the thirteen colonies, but their people as a whole enjoyed a prosperity which was not exceeded in any other land. Nowhere else in the world, probably, were there so few in actual need of the necessities of life, were beggars so rare, was the number so small of those who went hungry to bed. In France very different conditions prevailed. The lot of the peasantry in that fertile land was not worse than in most of Europe, but great was the contrast between the peasant of Brittany or Auvergne and the farmer of Kent or the colonist of Massachusetts.

No more accurate picture has been given of a people than Arthur Young drew when he visited France not long before the outbreak of the Revolution. In Salogne, he says, " the fields are scenes of pitiable management, as the houses are of misery " ; in Brittany " the country has a savage aspect, husbandry not much further advanced, at least in skill, than among the Hurons, . . . the people almost as wild as their country." From Montauban he writes, " one third of what I have seen of this province seems uncultivated, and nearly all of it in misery." And thus he described the condition of a large part of the French people, and their deplorable lot he justly attributed to bad government and feudal exactions; he found only privileges and poverty.[1]

" The people of our country," wrote the Bishop of Clermont-Ferrand, " live in frightful misery, without beds, without furniture, . . . obliged to snatch bread

[1] Young, *Travels in France*, 19, 123, 125.

from their own mouths and their children's to pay the taxes. . . . The negroes of our islands are infinitely more happy." [1] Poorly fed, dressed in rags, living in a hut, with half his scanty earnings absorbed by taxes and feudal dues, the lot of the French peasant was a melancholy contrast to that of the American farmer.

The privileges of the aristocracy had become grievous. The peasant looked with anger on the game which fed on his crop and which he dared not kill; he paid with bitterness the feudal dues that were still enforced; he sullenly performed the corvées to which he was still subjected. The prosperous bourgeois, the wealthy farmer-general, better educated and better mannered than their ancestors, and eager for a social equality to which their great-grandfathers had not aspired, found in some artificial distinction, some high-bred sneer or snub, a sting more bitter and more irritating than the serious grievances of the peasant. The rise of a country in which equality prevailed, where the merchant and the lawyer held their recognized position in the best society, where farmers were prosperous, and dingy huts and hungry children were unknown, helped to strengthen resentments that were already strong.

To those who claimed for the people a voice in their own government, to those who pointed out the abuses of the old régime, the American Republic appeared as the ideal state of which they had declaimed. It has been said that the Orleans family committed a grave political error when they allowed the bones of Napoleon to be placed in a tomb in France, on which the Napoleonic legend might grow anew. The Bour-

[1] Clermont-Ferrand, *Résumé de l'Histoire d'Auvergne*, 313.

bon dynasty and the old régime made a like error when they assisted in holding up to the French people the spectacle of a newly created republic, inhabited by a prosperous and contented people, proclaiming the doctrines of popular sovereignty and the equality of all men before the law. At almost any other period the Declaration of Independence would have wakened few echoes in France. But French philosophy and French literature had prepared society to receive with enthusiasm the political doctrines and the pictures of social life which came from across the Atlantic. The desire to injure England, and the hope of profiting by the trade she might lose, had more influence on Vergennes and the advisers of Louis XVI than any sympathy with American colonists. But if these motives had most weight with the politicians, they did not account for the popular enthusiasm with which French society embraced the American cause.

It was not among the peasantry, always ignorant and usually miserable, that sympathy was felt for the American colonists; to most of them the existence of America was hardly known. But the condition of the common people now received from those better provided with this world's goods a degree of attention unthought of in the past. It was the time, as has been said, when a man about to sup suddenly reflected that there were those who had not yet dined. When a new interest was felt in the lot of the masses, when plans were rife for improving agriculture, for relieving poverty, for lessening the burden of taxation, society was ready to espouse a popular cause on the other side of the Atlantic.

The seventeenth century was one of the great eras of French literature, but few indeed were the French

books which treated of political theories or political
questions. Of criticism of a man who held prominent
position there was somewhat; the administration of
Mazarin and the troubles of the Fronde created a
copious literature of pamphlets and Mazarinades, but
these discussed personal animosities rather than political principles. In all the picturesque chapters of
the Fronde there is little to be found except personal
politics ; whether insurrections were led by princes of
the blood or judges of the courts, they had for their
object changes in the persons who should possess
power, rather than changes in the system by which the
state was to be administered.

The influence of the salon was considerable in
France long before the days of Louis XVI; but until
well into the eighteenth century, while the salons were
centres of social and at times of literary action, in
politics they took little part. The appointment of a
minister, the granting of a pension, most of all, the
selection by the sovereign of a new mistress, were indeed eagerly discussed; but the principles of government were not much more debated in the salon of
Madame de Sévigné or the palace of the Prince de
Conti than they were in the home of some bourgeois
of Tours or the hut of some peasant in the Cévennes.

Under Louis XIV the burden of taxation fell
heavily upon many, the lot of large portions of the
population was hard, yet there came no demand for
change ; conditions were unfavorable, but they were
regarded as being as much a result of unchangeable laws
as the devastating blasts that came from the mountains
or the drought that destroyed the crops. In the reign
of his successor, the situation was greatly altered. The
sanctity that hedges round a king had been dispelled,

criticism was outspoken, a desire for change was widespread. This was not due to the fact that conditions
had become worse, that poverty was more general or
distress more common. The contrary was the case.
The latter part of Louis XV's reign witnessed a
marked improvement in the economic condition of
France. Business was more active, the accumulation
of wealth was more rapid ; bad as was the condition
of the peasantry, it was better than it had been in
the reign of the Grand Monarque. Agriculture was
still backward, and yet during the thirty years preceding the Revolution it probably made more progress
than it had in three centuries before. The rapid
growth of Paris excited the dismay of those who regarded this as a portentous omen, while Bordeaux,
Marseilles, and other cities doubled in population during the century.

The voice of complaint, the disposition to blame
the government for unfavorable conditions, became
more pronounced when these conditions tended to improve. Nor is this strange. When a man's lot seems
hopelessly bad, he submits to it in dull despair ; when
a measure of improvement suggests the possibility of
still further gain, his discontent becomes more active
and the demand for change more articulate.

The demand for change had become not only aud-
ible but insistent before Louis XV closed his career
of shame. The nation, wrote the Austrian ambassador, not long before Louis's death, "pours out sedi-
tious words and indecent writings, in which the person
of the monarch is not spared."[1] Kings are for the
people and not the people for the king, declared a
document issued by a body of lawyers, usually the

[1] Mercy-Argenteau to Maria Theresa, April 16, 1771.

most conservative class in the community. A profession of atheism would not have seemed a more monstrous sentiment to Louis XIV. " The cause of the people, by whom and for whom you reign," said a remonstrance addressed to Louis XV; and with similar declarations in pamphlets and official documents, in the writings of philosophers, and from the mouths of the rich and the noble, from lawyers and littérateurs, one could have filled volumes.

At no era has conversation been more brilliant or the charm of social influence more alluring, and at few periods has there been greater freedom of discussion. Subjects which a century before would, in France, no more have been brought into controversy than would the inspiration of the Scriptures at a conventicle presided over by John Knox, were now discussed by all the world. There was no phase of religious belief, no form of human government, hardly any institution of social life, that was not considered as freely as the state of the weather or the prospect of the crops.

The customs of the times made it possible for social intercourse to be more attractive and more important than in our era of pressing business and brief conversation. Only those who lived before the Revolution, said Talleyrand, knew the charm of life. Neither the nobles nor the philosophers who met for constant discussion were pressed for time; the exchange of thought was not a diversion but an occupation. At Baron Holbach's, says an inmate of that salon, the conversation was the most animated and the most instructive that it was possible to hear; the guests met at two, they dined and talked until seven, often to meet again in the evening, unwearied of discussions which never grew dull.

Few took an active interest in the affairs of state under Louis XIV; their curiosity was satisfied when they were told of the latest victory of the Grand Monarque or of the last fête at Versailles. There was no such indifference under Louis XV. Thirty years ago, wrote Argenson, "the public was not curious about the news of the state, now every one reads the Gazette de France."[1] The Gazette de France did not furnish as much information as a great daily of London or New York does now, but its readers gained some knowledge as to the affairs of their own country, while of transient publications, that discussed every act of government and often with great freedom, there was an unfailing supply. Words that had been little used in talk or literature now became common speech. An acute observer remarked that the word "nation," hardly pronounced under Louis XIV, was now on every tongue. An enemy of the new philosophy wrote: "This word 'liberty,' which is familiar in these days, is very dangerous."

The influence exerted by the talk of the salon was less than that of the newspapers of to-day, but never has there been a time when literature so controlled public opinion. The great writers of the age had done much of their work before the troubles of American colonists were discussed in French salons. Voltaire had long been at the height of his fame, Rousseau had written his "Social Contract," Holbach's "System of Nature" had appeared, the publication of the Encyclopædia, extending over years, had been brought to an end. The popularity of these works was unabated. Discussions of government and society, of religion and science, found a widely extended audience.

[1] *Mémoires d'Argenson*, 1754; Miss Wormeley's translation, chap. x.

The more vigorously did they attack the beliefs of the past, the more eagerly were they received; boldness in thought, as well as skill in expression, characterized the literature of the day, and however revolutionary the theories advanced, they circulated in France, practically, with the same freedom as in England. There was indeed, nominally, a government censorship of the press; only books which it authorized could be sold and read, and on the circulation of those under its ban ruinous penalties were imposed; but this censorship was little more than a farce. The governmental supervision of literature in France in the latter half of the eighteenth century furnishes another illustration of the impossibility of enforcing laws which no longer find a support in public feeling. Many of the famous writers under Louis XV spent brief terms in Vincennes or the Bastille; they emerged from a mild confinement into a blaze of glory. Many a book was burned by the public executioner; it was sold and read all the more. If a writer could be sentenced to imprisonment and his books be condemned to the flames, he might regard his literary fortune as made. And thus a great mass of subversive and revolutionary matter was circulated in France, among a public ready to receive it; the seed was cast upon a soil in which it speedily fructified. A society that a hundred years before would have regarded our ancestors as rebels against the just authority of the King, now saw in them the representatives of public liberties and political reforms, which Frenchmen advocated with all the more vigor because very often they did not understand them.

Activity in scientific research is apt to be the precursor of change in political as well as in religious beliefs. The scientific discoveries of the eighteenth century excited great interest in France, and Frenchmen took an important part in them. " More new truths concerning the external world," says Buckle, " were discovered in France during the latter part of the eighteenth century than during all the previous periods put together." In geology and natural history, in anatomy and chemistry, in electricity and the laws of heat and light, French students did pioneer work. Interest in scientific questions was not confined to those who studied them, but extended to the great numbers who wished to hear of them. The lecture-rooms of well-known professors of chemistry and anatomy were almost as crowded as the theatres, and more crowded than the churches. The work done by Franklin in electricity had much to do with the reception he received in France when he first visited that country. Fame in scientific discovery secured for him a more prompt and cordial greeting than if he had been known only in literature or politics. The experiments with the kite excited in France a degree of interest which was not exceeded, even if it was equalled, in his own country.

It was not only religious thought that was affected by these new phases of intellectual activity; but a community which was interested in discussing the laws of the universe and the anatomy of man soon began to consider the laws of government and the anatomy of the state. A desire for change, new conceptions of government, a willingness to be done with the institutions of the past, an infinite confidence in the promise of the future, had taken possession of French literature and French society.

An era of boundless hope preceded the French

Revolution, and it has been well portrayed by one of the young nobles who crossed the Atlantic to fight for liberty in America. Describing this idyllic period, at the close of a long and active life in which he had seen the overthrow of an ancient monarchy, had been imprisoned in the Terror, had served under Napoleon at the height of his glory, and had witnessed the downfall of the Emperor and the dismemberment of his empire, the Comte de Ségur says : " Without regret for the past, without anxiety for the future, we walked gaily on a carpet of flowers that concealed an abyss. . . . All that was ancient seemed to us wearisome and ridiculous. The gravity of old doctrines oppressed us. The laughing philosophy of Voltaire amused and bewitched us. . . . We were ready to follow with enthusiasm the philosophical doctrines advanced by bold and brilliant leaders. Voltaire appealed to our intelligence, Rousseau touched our hearts." [1] Naturally they praised the heroes of Greece and Rome and read the republican literature of Switzerland and Holland ; at the theatre the praise of liberty and the abuse of tyrants met with thunders of applause, " at the court they lauded the republican maxims of Brutus, we talked of independence in the camps, of democracy among the nobles, of philosophy at balls, and of morality in boudoirs." [2] " Every one believed that he was marching to perfection, without being embarrassed by obstacles and without fearing them. We were proud of being French and still more proud of being French of the eighteenth century, which we regarded as the golden age brought upon earth by the new philosophy." [3]

It was natural that in this condition of idyllic

[1] Ségur, *Mémoires* (2d ed.), i, 27, 41.   [2] *Ibid.*, 82.   [3] *Ibid.*, 257.

hopefulness in the future progress of society, the principles declared by American colonists should captivate men who looked with distrust on all that was old and turned with eagerness to all that was new. Wearied with artificial modes of life, French aristocrats discovered what they believed to be their ideals among the American folk; they were charmed by the simple, earnest life of New England farmers, and discovered the virtues of Roman worthies in American statesmen. The Continental Congress seemed the image of the Roman Senate, and its cause the cause of progress and liberty. The first cannon fired in the New World to defend the standard of liberty, says Ségur, resounded in all Europe. Even at the watering-places the seekers for amusement made of America a fashion, and invented a game at cards which they styled Boston.[1]

Thus it was that popular sentiment exercised its influence in the councils of the King and that an alliance with the United States and war with England not only received the approval of statesmen, but excited the enthusiasm of the nation. During the five years that the war continued, the French people remained constant in the cause. Doubtless some of those who were most eager would have stood aghast if they had realized that the part taken by France in the American Revolution was to have its influence in preparing the way for the French Revolution. The very causes, the conditions of thought, the relaxation of ancient beliefs, the confidence in advantages that would result from future change, distrust of the past, and hope for the future, which were preparing the French for their own revolution, made them enthusiastic in their efforts to assist their American allies.

[1] Ségur, *Mémoires*, i, 81.

CHAPTER XII

FRANKLIN'S presence gave to the negotiations for French support an importance they had not possessed when Deane, with an ill-defined errand, had been the sole representative of the States. And though Lord Stormont affected to regard Franklin as a fugitive seeking safety in a foreign land, he at once recognized the assistance which the party in France eager for an American alliance derived from the presence of the famous philosopher. "If reports are true," writes Stormont of Franklin, "he has already abused their ignorance . . . concerning the Americans so far as to proclaim roundly . . . that the affairs of the rebels are in a flourishing condition, while ours are desperate. When I hear such talk I make no reply. I leave that to General Howe, and I am sure that sooner or later it will be as good a reply as ever has been made." [1]

The alliance with France and the fate of the American colonies depended on the reply that Howe should make. Our ancestors were fond of using Roman names in their letters to newspapers, and Roman anathemas in their bursts of eloquence. If they had shared in Roman superstitions, they might have anticipated with confidence the enormous prosperity in store for the government they sought to establish. The old Romans found in lucky incidents at the beginning of any great

[1] Doniol, ii, 103.

undertaking the assurance of its happy accomplishment. No nation in the throes of birth was ever more favored in the character of its enemies than the American Republic. The stupidity of kings and ministers, the inefficiency of generals and admirals, permitted a rebellion to succeed which, with vigor, energy, and intelligence, could have been suppressed before the French made up their minds whether it was wise to assist the rebels.

Stormont left General Howe to make response to Franklin's prophecies of American success, but the expected response did not come. The prospect was indeed sufficiently unfavorable to delay the French in interfering in behalf of the colonists, but the procrastination and bad judgment of English generals gave Franklin plenty of time in which to obtain the assistance of a people already inclined to grant it. When he sailed from America in October, 1776, the opportunity to capture the American army on Long Island and win an advantage that would have crippled the insurgent cause beyond the power of resuscitation had been neglected by Howe. This crowning mercy was not, however, followed by any special prosperity for the colonists. While Franklin was on the sea, Fort Washington was captured with three thousand troops. The news followed him to France, and this calamity was succeeded by a long season of misfortune. The army under Washington was fast disintegrating, and only his wisdom and fortitude kept together a few thousand ill-fed, ill-clothed, and ill-armed men. The indignation excited by the brutalities of the Hessians, and Howe's failure to destroy the remnants of Washington's army, were all that the colonists could count in their favor, and the French ministers hesitated to declare in behalf of a rebellion which seemed to be in its last gasp.

Amid such discouragements, Franklin and his associates continued their efforts to obtain French aid, receiving all that the ministers dared grant without coming to an open breach with England, but failing to make of a secret friend an open ally. Not only the ill-success of the American armies, but the unfortunate character of some of the American envoys, added to the difficulties of the situation.

The American representatives at Paris were, as has been shown, far from harmonious; their relations were always unfriendly, and at times became almost a public scandal. The blame for this did not rest upon Dr. Franklin, who at Paris, as elsewhere, was one of the most affable and politic of men. But his associates had been selected with less judgment, and the character of many of our representatives in Europe during the Revolutionary War was not all that could be desired. Congress had sent over envoys and ambassadors accredited to various European courts, but few of them were received, and at Paris most of them made their headquarters. The finances of the United States were in great confusion, and as a result its representatives abroad were often put in embarrassing positions. Their pay was uncertain, their duties were ill defined, and most of them were ill fitted for any duties they had to perform.

Franklin, Deane, and Lee constituted the commission to France. Of Deane's embarrassments and misfortunes we have already spoken, but Arthur Lee did most to involve his associates in constant trouble. He came over to Paris filled with a sense of his own importance, and ready to regard his fellows with jeal-

ousy and ill-will. He soon decided that Deane was
surely dishonest, Franklin was perhaps dishonest and
surely incompetent. Lee was unquestionably an honest man himself, but he believed that no one else possessed that virtue. His scheme for the proper arrangement of American affairs on the Continent he stated
to his brother. Dr. Franklin, he thought, should be
sent to Vienna, a respectable, quiet place, and Deane
to Holland. "France remains the centre of political
activity, and here, therefore, I should choose to be
employed."

Even the affability of Franklin could not soothe
Lee's vanity nor allay his irritation. He sent constant
complaints to Congress, and not only abused his associates behind their backs, but quarrelled with them
to their faces. There prevailed at headquarters, so he
wrote, " a spirit of neglect, abuse, plunder, and intrigue
in the public business, which it has been impossible
for me to prevent or correct. . . . Things are going
on worse and worse every day among ourselves. . . .
I see in every department neglect, dissipation, and
private schemes. . . . There is but one way of re-
dressing this and remedying the public evil," and that
was to send Franklin to Vienna, and leave Lee at
Paris.[1]

Lee found a fit associate in Ralph Izard, who was
sent over as envoy to the Grand Duke of Tuscany.
Izard made no attempt to visit the court to which he
was accredited, but remained at Paris, demanding
from Franklin large amounts of money, and pouring
out the most virulent abuse when he did not get it.
He received from Franklin two thousand guineas,
and a few months later asked for five hundred more.

[1] Wharton, i, 499.

Franklin refused to honor the draft, calling attention to the fact that Izard had not incurred the
expense of going to Tuscany. " You are a gentleman
of fortune," Franklin added. " You did not come to
France with any dependence on being maintained
here with your family at the expense of the United
States in the time of their distress, and without rendering them the equivalent service they expected."
That Izard should reimburse his country for what it
had already spent on his fruitless mission, was Franklin's final suggestion.

If Lee regarded himself as a proper representative
of the United States to France, that belief was not
shared by the ministers of the French government.
Nominally Franklin was one of three commissioners;
practically he was treated as the sole representative,
and a position of inferiority was irksome to Lee's
jealous vanity. He resolved to seek other fields for
his activity, a course which was agreeable to his associates and authorized by his instructions. In the
minute prepared in October, 1776, Congress had said
that the commissioners at Paris would doubtless
have opportunities for conversing with the representatives of other European princes, and had added :
" You shall endeavor, when you find occasion fit and
convenient, to obtain from them a Recognition of our
Independency and to conclude Treaties of Peace,
Amity and Commerce between their Princes or
States and us."

The representative of Spain at Paris was the Conde
de Aranda, who exceeded Vergennes in his zeal for
immediate action in behalf of the American colonies.
The ardent minister and the ardent commissioner
conferred together, troubled only by the necessity of

having an interpreter. " English," wrote Aranda, " is the only language that Lee knows."[1] Encouraged by the zeal of the count, which unfortunately was not shared by the government he represented, Lee resolved to start for Madrid, in the sanguine hope of obtaining from that country a treaty of alliance before Franklin could overcome the cautious resistance of the French ministry.

The announcement of Lee's purpose created violent commotion at the Spanish court. He was indeed to preserve the strictest incognito, to pass for a merchant attending to his affairs, furnished with a passport which described him as an Englishman. But this did not reconcile the Spanish to his visit. " This intelligence," writes the prime minister, " has been very disagreeable to the King. . . . It would be most unfortunate to have Lee at Madrid." He adds : " There was no necessity for the voyage." He would be discovered, and the English ministers would complain. " And still we don't want in any way to disgust or irritate these colonists."[2]

To avoid such embarrassment, the Spanish minister adopted an expedient that was simple and effective. He sent an emissary to meet Lee at Vittoria, who was to keep him there in genteel confinement and prevent his penetrating to Madrid. Even Lee was obliged to yield to so firm a refusal to receive him. At Vittoria he remained, offering to conquer Pensacola and other possessions in return for Spanish aid, obtaining some promises and a little money. " A virgin state," Franklin said to him, using a metaphor of which he was fond, " should preserve the virgin character, and . . .

---

[1] Letter of Jan. 31, 1777; Doniol, ii, 197.
[2] Letter of Feb. 17, 1777; Doniol, ii, 196.

wait with decent dignity for the application of others.
. . . While we are asking aid it is necessary to . . .
comply with the humors of those we apply to." [1]
There is no doubt that the virgin state, when coun-
selled by so astute a politician as Franklin, showed
much readiness to meet the peculiarities, not of those
who pursued her, but of those whom she pursued.

After these vain efforts to penetrate the recesses of
Spain, Lee turned to another country, where in some
respects he met with better fortune. No one could be
more indifferent than Frederick II to the fate of the
American colonies, but no fear of English complaints
would make him arrest an American envoy at the
Prussian frontier. If he wasted no more affection on
the Americans than on any other foreign people, he
had some vigorous animosities that would be gratified by American success. Though Frederick was not
willing to spend the money or the blood of his own
people, even for so desirable an end, he was not only
willing but very desirous that the French King should
do so. A war that might cripple England, and would
perhaps weaken France besides, was certainly a pleasing prospect. Frederick was constant in his efforts
to incite the French to take up arms for the colonies,
and indirectly he gave valuable aid to the American
cause by his assurances that while France was thus
engaged he would not stir up any continental question that would require her attention.

It would not cost Frederick one groat to allow an
American representative to visit Berlin, and accordingly Lee made his way undisturbed to the Prussian
capital. But there he met with small success. Lee
had already sent a request that American ships be

[1] Franklin to Lee, March 21, 1777; Wharton, ii, 298.

allowed to enter any Prussian port, but this Frederick politely evaded, not willing, as he wrote his minister, to irritate the colonists by an absolute refusal.[1] Arriving at Berlin, Lee asked that some port be indicated where American privateers could sell their prizes, and he sought to form a treaty of commerce with Prussia. These suggestions were unfavorably received by the Prussian monarch. Until the independence of the colonists was more firmly established, he states in another letter, any commerce with them would be perilous and not worth the risk; and as for a treaty, he was in no humor to embarrass himself by complications with England in order to favor the Americans.[2]

A new interest was given to the situation by an extraordinary incident. Elliot was the English ambassador at Berlin, and, proceeding with a degree of vigor that modern diplomacy would not approve, he had some one force his way into Lee's chamber and steal his papers. This high-handed act enraged Frederick, though it also answered his purpose, for it furnished him abundant excuse for showing some attention, even to an unofficial representative of an unacknowledged state, who had been so indecently treated by the English ambassador. But the prudent King had no thought of spending a florin of his own in assisting American rebels, and no emissary could have been less to his taste than a vain and injudicious intriguer like Arthur Lee. The British government made due apologies, Lee soon left Berlin for Paris, and employed himself in sending home lies about Franklin.

Though the American commissioners were constantly wrangling among themselves, they united in

[1] Doniol, ii, 345.   [2] Doniol, ii, 557.

efforts to obtain further assistance from the French government. Their first requests for assistance were moderate, but in March, 1777, they submitted a more ambitious proposition in which they offered to form an alliance with France and proceed to the conquest of Canada, Newfoundland, and the West India islands. Of these spoils Canada and Newfoundland should be the share of the colonists, and the British West Indies should become the property of France.

While the French ministers were not specially allured by this project, they were rapidly reaching the point where they were ready to exchange the pretence of neutrality for the reality of an alliance. In April, 1777, Vergennes declared that, having done so much for the colonists, they must now do more. " We cannot expect," he wrote, " that what we have thus far done for the United Colonies is enough to secure their gratitude, and if they unite their forces with those the English already have in the New World, we should have small means with which to resist." [1]

While the French minister constantly asserted that his government was giving no heed to the demands of American representatives, the English ambassador was not deceived. In March he writes : " That M. de Vergennes is hostile to us in his heart, and anxious for the success of the Rebels, I have not a shadow of doubt," and he adds : " The provocation they give us is great, and there is nothing that would please me so much as to unmask their artifice and confound their duplicity and fraud ; but that must not be attempted until the day of retribution comes." [2]

[1] Letter, April 7, 1777 ; Doniol, ii, 341.
[2] Stormont to Weymouth, March 26, 1777 ; Hale, *Franklin in France*, ii, 430.

It was because Vergennes had so bad a conscience, and knew full well that the assistance he was secretly giving the Americans would justify the English government in declaring war on France, if a favorable opportunity should offer, that he was in constant fear of such action, and was the more inclined to begin a contest that he believed was inevitable. But still he did not wish to act without the coöperation of Spain, and his arguments were insufficient to induce that timid and uncertain power to undertake war in behalf of American independence.

The Spanish minister went so far as to promise aid to the Americans, but his assurance was marked by commendable thrift. He wished to give "a little so as to nourish their hopes." Even this promise was not kept, for some Spanish ships were captured by American captains, who, unfortunately, were not well read in Pufendorf and Grotius. By such an act Spanish dignity was offended, and it at once assumed its sternest aspect. Some French ships also were captured, but Vergennes accepted the situation philosophically, and sought to avert such evils in the future. This was not the policy of the Pardo; the ministers stormed and the King stopped the promised payments; luckily for the Americans, the promised payments were small. The American commissioners expressed their regrets and reproached the injudicious corsairs, but this did not smooth the ruffled feathers of Spanish diplomacy.

Undisturbed by such incidents, the French would probably have formed an alliance with the colonists during the summer following Franklin's arrival, had it not been for the ill-success of the American arms. During the weary months of 1777, when the commissioners at Paris fluctuated between the joyful belief that France would at once take up arms in behalf of the colonists, and the disappointment caused by constant delay, the reports from America for the most part brought tidings of disaster, and it seemed that the colonists would be forced to succumb before their possible allies could decide upon assuring their salvation. In July Ticonderoga was captured, and this success was regarded as of far more importance than it really was. George III declared that the Americans were now surely beaten, and Vergennes was afraid that such was the case. " It is a problem," he wrote, after the news of the abandonment of Ticonderoga reached France, " whether they can preserve the liberty for which they have taken up arms; attacked in the rear by the English army of Canada, while General Howe assails them in front. Have they the force, the unity, the leadership, to resist this storm ? " [1]

Another note states some of the embarrassments which hindered any decisive action: the divisions among leading men, it declared, the intrigues of the Tories, the inaction of the Quakers, or some untoward event might overthrow the edifice so hastily erected, and the powers that espoused the American cause would find themselves exposed to danger without being of any assistance to their allies. [2]

But if these disasters chilled Vergennes's ardor, his delay aroused a storm of criticism that was valuable to the colonists. French public sentiment had long favored interference; the philosophers and littérateurs lauded the principles professed by the American patriots; ladies and gentlemen of fashion sang the praises of Franklin and Washington and their asso-

[1] Sept. 19, 1777 ; Doniol, ii, 572.   [2] Doniol, ii, 628.

ciates; young men of gallantry and ambition, like La Fayette, were embarking in the American cause. The disasters of the year were now charged by the French people to the remissness of the French government; they had delayed too long, they had let the critical and auspicious moment go by. The enemies of Vergennes filled the King's ears with complaints of the inert and unwise conduct of the minister. Even Frederick II declared that France had allowed the opportune moment for her interference to pass.

Vergennes was disturbed by these criticisms, and in November, 1777, he sent a M. Holker to visit the United States and ascertain the disposition of Congress, the resources of the people, what they were ready to do for a nation that would embark in their cause, and the actual condition of the English army.[1]

Holker's mission was not important, for the die was cast long before he could make his investigations and send his report. On October 31, 1777, at ten o'clock on a fine morning, the brigantine Perch sailed from the Long Wharf in Boston, carrying Jonathan Loring Austin of that city, with messages from the Massachusetts Council announcing the surrender of Burgoyne and the capture of his army of six thousand men. Saratoga is justly reckoned by Creasy among the fifteen decisive battles of the world. If Burgoyne's expedition had been successful, it is doubtful if France would have interfered in the American cause, and still more doubtful if the colonists, without such assistance, could have achieved their independence.

The Perch was favored by remarkably fine weather, and in thirty days reached the French coast. On

[1] Doniol, ii, 615.

November 30, writes Austin, he first announced the news in France, and it was received with manifest joy by French as well as Americans. Leaving Nantes in a chaise drawn by three horses abreast, he made his way to Versailles, and from there to Passy. As he drove into the courtyard of the Hôtel de Valentinois, he was met by Franklin.

" Sir, is Philadelphia taken ? " asked the doctor.

" It is," replied the messenger ; " but, sir, I have greater news than that. General Burgoyne and his whole army are prisoners." [1]

Beaumarchais was then visiting the commissioners at Passy. He started to carry the news to Paris in such hot haste that his carriage tipped over and he nearly broke his neck. Such casualties seemed unimportant to so eager and impetuous a friend of the American cause. " My right arm is cut," he writes, " the bones of my neck were nearly crushed, . . . but the charming news from America is a balm to my wounds." [2] It is sad that the American Congress, in settling Beaumarchais's accounts, showed so little of the alacrity with which he carried to the French court the good news of American success.

Upon receiving the intelligence of Burgoyne's surrender, the French government decided to espouse the cause of the American insurgents. They had long hesitated, and during the disasters of the summer, critics had declared that the ministers had hesitated too long: the golden moment had passed and the Americans, aided by no helping hand, had been overpowered by the British. It was then thought that France had delayed until the ruin of the colonies had

---

[1] Hale, *Franklin in France,* i, 159.

[2] Beaumarchais to Vergennes, Dec. 5, 1777 ; Doniol, ii, 682.

been consummated: it was now feared that she had waited until the victory of the colonists would force England to grant acceptable terms, and the opportunity to gain the friendship of the new republic would be lost.

Vergennes had always been haunted by a vision of some sort of reconciliation between England and her colonies, and of their united arms turned to despoil France of her American possessions. He had feared this when it seemed that the cause of the colonists was hopeless; he now feared it when he thought the victory of the colonists was assured. The English, he said, were irritated because France had given so much aid to the colonists; the colonists were irritated because she had given so little.

"If the English learned wisdom from their misfortunes," wrote Vergennes as soon as he heard of Burgoyne's surrender, . . . "and made terms of peace, what could France do to prevent a reconciliation?" And he continued with inaccurate prophecy: "The power which first recognizes American independence will gather all the fruits of this war."[1] "France must anticipate such action on England's part," he wrote again, "by greater speed in making the colonists our friends. . . . My reflections are not agreeable," he said, "as I see the fatal period approach which I have always regarded as the most critical."[2] In his uncertainty he did not derive the amusement which otherwise would have been furnished him when Lord Stormont had to announce the tidings from Saratoga. "He should have blushed," wrote Vergennes, "if he had recalled the audacious statements he had lately made about those cowardly insurgents, . . . but the

[1] Doniol, ii, 632.   [2] Doniol, ii, 622, 623.

present crisis demands something more than pleasant-
ries." [1]

The American commissioners at once renewed their
demands, with the confident expectation that a favorable answer would not be long deferred. It was a
year, wrote Franklin to his associates, since they had
proposed to France a treaty of commerce and alliance. Their overtures had remained without definite
reply, but now a favorable response would establish
the credit of the United States and discourage their
enemies. Thanking the King for his gracious gift of
three million livres, they pressed for a further answer,
desiring, next to the liberty of their own land, a firm
and everlasting union between the two nations. [2]

To these suggestions a reply was soon made. The
long months of delay and uncertainty were at last
a thing of the past. Vergennes at once prepared a
paper in which he outlined the policy required by the
new condition of affairs. At heart he had long been
ready for an alliance with the United States and its
necessary result, a war with England, but the ill-success of the colonists and the unwillingness of Spain
to coöperate had prevented any final decision. Now
he felt that the time for action had surely come, and
there must be no more delay. He therefore prepared
for the King's approval a paper in which he advised
that a treaty of alliance be forthwith made with the
United States.

His arguments were submitted to Maurepas, the
chief minister, and by him they were presented for
the consideration of the King. Maurepas fell ill of
the gout, Louis visited him for further consultation,
and the whole matter was gone over again. Ver-

[1] Doniol, ii, 704. [2] Letter of Dec. 8, 1777; Wharton, ii, 445.

gennes's decision was made, at last the entire Council agreed, and the resolution to form an alliance with the United States was unanimous.

At an earlier period Louis XVI had regarded interference as unwise; he had believed with Turgot that French finance would not stand the strain of war; he felt that good faith to England and a just regard for the cause of kings forbade his espousing the cause of rebellious subjects. But now, if we may credit the statements of his ministers, the King was convinced of the wisdom of action, and ready to meet the risk of war. Louis XVI's judgment was indeed largely formed by the opinion of those around him; he had not an intelligence sufficiently active to form his own conclusions and control the action of his ministers by his own will. With different advisers he could probably have been persuaded that it was the part of wisdom for France to leave England and her colonies to fight out their own battles. On the other hand, so strong was the pressure of public opinion, so universal was the enthusiasm for the American cause, that any other ministers would probably have reached the same conclusion as Vergennes and his associates.

It was certainly a critical moment, and the deliberations between the King and his ministers were of an importance that it is hard to overestimate. The history of the war makes it seem at least probable that the colonists, left to themselves, would have failed in their effort to throw off British rule. Notwithstanding the judgment and patriotism of Washington and the fortitude of the men who bore patiently the sufferings of Valley Forge, exhaustion, the lack of arms, the lack of money, might at last have reduced the colonists to submission. After three years more of war, with the benefit of French assistance, the result still seemed doubtful, until the capture of Yorktown secured a successful termination. Without French aid, the capture of Yorktown and of Cornwallis's army would have been impossible. The United States might have won their liberty after a longer struggle ; they might have failed, and at some later period have become an independent state ; they might have obtained practical independence and still remained a portion of a greater England.

Nor were the results of the alliance of much less importance to France. They modified her political development, and had a large influence on the events that were soon to change the form of French government, to lead to the reign of the greatest conqueror of modern times, and at last to leave France a republic instead of a monarchy. These issues were considered by men who were sagacious but not great, and who did not realize the importance of the questions they had to decide. But the same thing can be said of most statesmen in great crises. The gift of prescience is given to few, and the most far-sighted can penetrate but little into the infinite complexity of future events.

If the motives which actuated the French ministers in their decision were not wholly philanthropic, they were neither petty nor sordid. The advantages for herself which France could hope for, and the only ones for which she asked when peace was made, were not, as Vergennes justly said, of sufficient importance to justify an appeal to arms : release from the ignominious conditions at Dunkirk imposed by the Treaty of Utrecht, some increase in fishery rights on the coast of Newfoundland, and the recovery of some petty islands in the West Indies. These were of small importance.

To separate the United States from England and weaken the insolent enemy of the House of Bourbon was the object and the justification of the war.[1]

In all these long diplomatic papers we find no discussion of wrongs suffered by the American colonists, of rights to be protected, or liberties to be assured. Vergennes thought that France should interfere in behalf of the colonies because thereby she could humble a rival and avenge past defeats. But though he was not moved by altruistic motives, the assistance was none the less valuable. Moreover, the spirit which led La Fayette to risk his life in aid of a people struggling to be free, represented the feelings of the French people better than the arguments of a minister who saw in this war only an opportunity for selfish advantage. Among the French people, the desire to assist the colonists in their struggle for independence was as unselfish as it was universal. The Americans loomed up before enthusiastic French eyes as heroes possessing the virtues of antiquity, and struggling for the freedom which had been dear to patriots of old. The subjects of an absolute monarchy sang the praises of liberty, and were enthusiastic for the success of its cause across the ocean. The popular feeling was strong and generous, based upon no selfish considerations of state, but upon genuine sympathy for fellow men.

Such sentiments were less potent among the statesmen in whose hands rested the final decision. It was their duty to consider the interests of their own land, and not to enter into war without proper regard for the welfare of the people whose servants they were. And yet, though the reasons for helping the Americans

[1] Doniol, ii, 781–788.

were discussed in grave official papers, with as little pretence of philanthropy as if it had been a question of the balance of power in Europe, it was the popular enthusiasm for American liberty which penetrated the council chamber and influenced the ministers in their decision, even if they failed to recognize such a motive.

As is often the case, the generous intuitions of the people were truer guides than the selfish counsels of statesmen. The advantages, so carefully considered by Vergennes and his associates, were realized in small degree. For some years a strong feeling of gratitude and kindliness toward France was cherished by our ancestors. This was agreeable to the French, but it was of small practical value. France did not obtain the chief share of American trade; that went to England, which had more to sell us, and was ready to buy more from us. The decline of English power, which Vergennes so confidently anticipated, he was not destined to behold. English merchants made more money out of the people of the United States than they had ever made from the American colonists; the power of England was greater under Pitt, when the people of the United States were independent, than it had been under North, when they were grumbling and discontented subjects. Nor is there any reason to believe that if peace had been made between England and the colonists before France interfered, they would have joined arms in order to strip the French of their possessions in the West Indies. Thus the arguments on which statesmen based their action were not justified in the future. But the instincts of the French nation were right: they assisted a people to gain their freedom, they took part in one of the great crises of modern progress, they helped the world in its onward march. For nations, as for individuals, that is the greatest work. The reward is not to be found in more vessels sailing, laden with wares, nor in more dollars gained and deposited in banks, but in the consciousness of the unselfish performance of good work, of assistance rendered to the cause of freedom, and to the improvement of man's lot on earth.

On the 17th of December, 1777, Gérard went to the house of Franklin and his associates at Passy, and imparted to them the momentous intelligence that Louis XVI had decided to recognize the independence of the United States, and to make with them a treaty of commerce and friendship. A ship was to sail forthwith that would carry the news to America, and the commissioners had the pleasure of reporting to Congress the resolution of the French King. The news of the surrender of Burgoyne, they wrote, had been received by the French with as universal joy as if it had been a victory won by their own troops over their own enemies. This joy had soon ripened into action. Gérard yesterday, they said, informed them that the King was ready to acknowledge our independence and make a treaty. " In this treaty no advantage would be taken of our present situation to obtain terms from us, which otherwise would not be convenient for us to agree to, his Majesty desiring that the treaty once made should be durable and our amity subsist forever." [1]

As the representatives of France were ready to agree to the terms which the American commissioners proposed, there was little delay in the negotiations. On February 6, 1778, treaties of alliance between the

[1] Letter of Dec. 18, 1777; Wharton, ii, 452.

King of France and the United States were signed
by the French ministers in behalf of Louis XVI, and
by Franklin, Deane, and Arthur Lee for this country.
The commissioners reported that in the negotiations
the promise to make no effort to take advantage of
present difficulties in order to obtain disadvantageous
conditions was fulfilled. The states were in great
need and France could have driven a hard bargain in
return for her aid, but the treaty was drawn as if the
two powers had been of equal strength and equally in
need of the alliance. Such had been the King's goodness, reported the commissioners, that nothing had
been proposed which they could not well have accepted in a condition of complete prosperity and recognized power. Equality and perfect reciprocity had
alone been desired, commercial privileges had been
mutual, and nothing had been granted that could not
be accorded to any other nation. Having reason to be
satisfied with the good-will of the court and of the
French nation, they hoped that Congress would adopt
every means that could render the alliance lasting.[1]

Vergennes, in reporting the treaty to the French
ambassador at London, took the same view of it as
the American envoys. " We have not wished to procure," he said, "commercial advantages which could
make any other nation jealous, and which the Americans would regret in the future that they had granted
us." [2]

Two treaties were executed : one of commerce, and
the other providing for mutual defence and alliance.
The terms of the treaty of commerce conformed largely
to the proposals which Congress had intrusted to the

[1] Letter of Feb. 8, 1778; Wharton, ii, 490.
[2] Vergennes to Noailles, March 10, 1778 ; Doniol, ii, 822.

commissioners. Each party was placed on the footing of the most favored nation. The French King promised his good offices with the Emperor of Morocco and the rulers of Algiers and Tunis, that those much-dreaded pirates might leave the ships and citizens of the United States in peace. Our own privateers and their prizes were granted free access to French ports, but they obtained few advantages by treaty which they had not already been allowed by favor. How remote were the two sides of the Atlantic was shown by the provision in reference to the carriage of goods belonging to citizens of a power with which either of the contracting parties might in the future be at war. Two months were granted to ascertain the fact that such a war had begun. At the expiration of that period it was to be presumed that the news would have crossed the Atlantic, and penetrated into the ports of seafaring men.

Of greater importance was the second treaty, by which France agreed to come to the aid of the thirteen states. The only condition that France imposed upon her American allies was that they should make no peace until their independence was recognized, and that the allies should unite in any treaty. This surely was not a grievous condition. France guaranteed to the United States her independence, and in turn our country guaranteed to France her possessions in the West Indies. It must be confessed that at that period the French guarantee would have been regarded as of higher value. By secret agreement it was provided that Spain might join in the alliance, but of this privilege she never availed herself.

The American commissioners at once reported to Congress the great intelligence, with a pardonable pride in the result of their negotiations. It was with good cause that they congratulated their fellow citizens on an event destined to thwart the desires of their enemies and fortify the hopes of their friends. To this they added fervent expressions of gratitude to France, and of admiration of the upright and disinterested conduct of Louis XVI.[1]

Vergennes endeavored, but in vain, to have Spain join France in an alliance with the American colonies. When it had been finally resolved that a treaty should be made with the United States, the Spanish King was at once notified of the decision reached by his nephew in France. The critical moment had at last arrived, he was told, and the French King could no longer remain inactive. "Providence has marked this epoch," it was said, "for the humiliation of a power, greedy and unjust, which has never known any other law than its own interest"; and the letter proceeded with a statement of the somewhat dubious political morality which then prevailed in every European monarchy. "Kings, when the welfare of their people is concerned, are not perhaps subjected to the rules of as rigid a morality as binds private persons in their actions."

Yet without any necessity of appealing to such a principle, there were many reasons which made an immediate war with England entirely just. Such a contest was certain sooner or later; the question was whether it was better to meet it with America as a friend, or with America again united to England. "Shall we sleep in false security, and lose the one chance which may offer itself for centuries to reduce England to her true position? . . . Never was such

[1] Wharton, ii, 490.

an opportunity furnished the House of Bourbon " to lower the pride of her enemy, and to form with the United States an alliance of which the benefits should be incalculable.[1]

But Spain could not be moved to sudden action by any arguments. The French ambassador visited the Spanish minister and debated the matter with him for five hours, but neither hours of argument nor reams of correspondence could induce the Spanish government to reach a decision. There was no haste, said Florida Blanca, and he submitted a letter containing not less than sixteen elaborate questions, to which answers must be given before any decision could be made. Vergennes sent the answers, but he did not wait for the close of a debate which would surely occupy many months. It was most painful to the King, he wrote the French ambassador at Madrid, to make this decision alone, but the interests of the two monarchies would not permit his Majesty to remain in a state of inactivity which might be fatal to both.[2]

Though with much reluctance, Louis XVI signed the treaty of alliance with the United States without waiting for his Spanish kinsman. The Spanish were neither ready for action nor pleased that the French should act without them. While unwilling to reach a conclusion himself, the Catholic King manifested considerable annoyance because his Most Christian nephew had decided to help the Americans without waiting for the coöperation of Spain. As they disapproved of any treaty, naturally they were ready to criticize the terms of the one made, and declared them absurdly liberal. The Spanish minister com-

[1] Doniol, ii, 627, 664.   [2] Jan. 8, 1778; Doniol, ii, 730.

pared the American commissioners to the Roman consuls whose aid eastern kings had begged, and said that the treaty, on the part of France, was quixotic in its liberality.[1]

Now that the French King had formally recognized the new republic and had entered into treaty with it, the position of the American commissioners was altered. They had been kept in obscurity, had negotiated in stealth, and been received by under-secretaries or at private interviews. This was now changed. On March 16 Stormont left Paris for London, and on the 20th the American commissioners were formally presented to Louis XVI by Vergennes. They were not, indeed, received with all the ceremonial of accredited ambassadors, but their interview was as agreeable as if every detail of diplomatic etiquette had been complied with, and the presentation excited a degree of attention which was rarely given when the representatives of powerful governments and ancient monarchies were received at Versailles.

It was indeed a notable event in Franklin's extraordinary career. His government had been acknowledged by a great European power, and a treaty made that insured the liberties of his nation, and this was, in large degree, the fruit of his own labors. His admirers recognized how great was the triumph. As he proceeded to the interview he was greeted by applause, not only in the streets of the city, but in the sacred precincts of the palace. The King was less enthusiastic, but he was civil, and all went well. The impressions produced upon Franklin himself, as he has recorded them, are characteristic of the man. He was little affected by the splendors of Versailles, but the

[1] Doniol, iii, 23.

fact that the palace was ill kept, that sweeping and other sanitary provisions were neglected, impressed his practical and somewhat prosaic mind.[1]

After the reception was over the commissioners called to pay their respects to Madame de La Fayette, who was then at Versailles, and assured her of their gratitude for her husband's efforts; and they then dined with the Secretary of Foreign Affairs.

These formalities had been preceded by another ceremonial still more interesting. Paul Jones was then commanding the Ranger, from the mast of which floated the flag of the new republic. The hardy corsair, who now found himself the officer of a recognized government, wrote to Deane telling him of the first salutes exchanged between the flag of liberty and that of the ancient monarchy of France. On arriving at Nantes, Jones inquired if the French admiral would return his salute, and was informed that, as a senior officer of the American navy now in Europe, he would be given the salute authorized for an admiral of Holland. A little after sunset on March 14, the Ranger discharged thirteen guns in honor of the French admiral, and in reply nine guns saluted the flag of the United States. Jones would have preferred equal honors, but the difference between an ancient monarchy and a new republic had to be recognized. French officers visited the Ranger and delighted Jones's heart by declaring her a "perfect gem."[2] It was fitting that the founder of the American navy should receive the first honors rendered to the American flag.

In April the news of the French alliance reached

---

[1] Sparks, *Diplomatic Correspondence*, i, 374.
[2] Translation of intercepted letter; Doniol, iii, 3.

America and was welcomed with an enthusiasm befitting its importance. In Congress a resolution was passed expressing its high " sense of the magnanimity and wisdom of his most Christian majesty," and presenting " grateful acknowledgments " for the " generous and disinterested treaties." It sincerely wished that the friendship so happily commenced might be perpetual.

The treaty excited no less enthusiasm in the army, and no one appreciated its importance better than the commanding general. No one recognized more clearly than he the defects in our military and financial system and the importance of an alliance with a great military power. In an order issued by Washington at Valley Forge on May 6, he declared that it had pleased the Almighty Ruler of the universe to raise up for us in our need a powerful friend among the princes of the earth. In recognition of this the brigades were to meet at nine the next morning, when the chaplains would communicate the intelligence, offer up thanksgiving, and pronounce discourses suitable to the occasion. The men were then to be inspected, amid discharges of cannon, and at a given signal the whole army should huzza " Long live the King of France," and this should be followed by a huzza for the American states.

Our ancestors celebrated the alliance in a manner befitting good Puritans by listening to lengthy sermons, but they indulged also in other festivities. The sermon was followed by a great dinner, a somewhat rare occurrence at headquarters, where supplies were often scanty. It was attended by the officers and their wives and many distinguished personages. Washington, Greene, and many other generals were present;

conspicuous among them all was the youthful La Fayette, who had done so much to excite among the French people an interest in the American cause. Mrs. Washington, Lady Sterling, and other ladies were among the guests.

Similar celebrations occurred in many places. Ministers preached and cannon roared in honor of the great event. Yet, while the intelligence of the alliance was hailed by all earnest patriots as the guarantee of ultimate success, the old distrust of France appeared in the outcry with which some greeted the treaty. Dancing-masters, said the critics, would now instruct the Puritans in manners, and priests would save their souls; Americans had left a loving though severe mother for a treacherous step-mother, and the French alliance would bring to the American cause inevitable ruin. Such were the predictions made by the Tories, but they were not to be verified in the future.[1]

[1] C. H. Van Tyne, *The Loyalists in the American Revolution*, 152–156.

CHAPTER XIII

THE new republic was now a recognized ally of the ancient monarchy, and this recognition was at once followed by sending to the states an accredited diplomatic representative. For some years Franklin and his associates had represented the United States at Paris, but France had sent to America only unofficial agents, whose duty was to spy out the land. The position of minister to this new and unimportant republic was not regarded like the great ambassadorships, to Vienna, London, and Rome, and it was rendered less attractive by the perils and discomforts of the long voyage across the water. Furthermore, life at Philadelphia among a strange people, with different manners and customs, possessed no charm for a diplomat used to the society of the large cities of Europe. Yet, with the certainty of war with England, it was important to have a representative who could judge accurately of conditions among the new allies and stimulate them to zealous action in the common cause.

The choice fell on a man who did not belong to the great nobility, to which the most important diplomatic posts were usually assigned, but who was peculiarly fitted for this position. Conrad Gérard de Rayneval had been Vergennes's first assistant, and was familiar with all the negotiations which led to the alliance with the United States. To long experience he added a qualification less common among

French diplomats, a good knowledge of English. Partly for this reason the negotiations with the American colonies had been largely committed to his charge. When Franklin first arrived and Vergennes wished neither to repel the Americans nor to excite the wrath of the English ambassador by treating with them too publicly, it was easy to refer them to Gérard, who could talk their language, and was therefore a fit person to conduct the negotiations. Gérard entertained the American representatives at his house, and was the mouthpiece of the ministry, before the French government decided on open action in behalf of the colonies; when this resolution had at last been reached, Gérard was intrusted with the agreeable duty of visiting the American commissioners at Franklin's house in Passy, and informing them that Louis XVI was ready to form an alliance with the new republic. Gérard's name was signed to the treaties, and it was natural that he should be chosen as the minister from France to the Republic of the United States; there was no Frenchman more familiar with the conditions to be encountered in America or better fitted to deal with them. He was the first of a long line of distinguished representatives.

The instructions given Gérard disclosed the hopes and the fears of the French government. He was to guard against the possibility of Congress making a separate peace with Great Britain, and to assure that body in the most positive terms that Louis XVI would listen to no propositions from the enemy, and would not lay down arms until the absolute independence of the thirteen states had been recognized by England.

The relations of France with Spain now, as during

all the progress of the war, were a source of embarrassment. While Spain had made no treaty with the
United States, France was bound to act in their interest and to secure for them Florida and a possible
share in the Newfoundland fisheries. Gérard, therefore, was to dissuade Congress from any plan that
might include the acquisition of the Floridas. Nor did
France desire that Canada should be added to the thirteen states, for reasons which the instructions stated
with unaltruistic clearness : the retention of Canada
by England would make the Americans feel their
need of the friendship of France.

Gérard's skill was sufficient to secure these objects,
but the final instruction which he received was beyond
his power to accomplish. " It is probable," said the
document, " that Congress will show a desire for subsidies from France." Such requests Gérard was to
check, by explaining that the efforts which France
must make in the common cause would involve great
expense and render it impossible for her to furnish
pecuniary aid ; he must convince the Americans that
the French fleet was worth more to them than French
money. " His Majesty was persuaded," so the document ran, " that Congress would easily yield assent to
such conclusive reasons." [1]

If the King was thus persuaded, he was much mistaken. In part, perhaps, influenced by Gérard's advice, Congress displayed no covetous desire for Florida and made no vigorous effort to conquer Canada,
but nothing could keep it from demanding subsidies ;
fortunately for the interests of the states, the French
King was not persuaded by his own arguments, and
gave to repeated requests repeated satisfaction.

[1] Instructions to Gérard, March 29, 1778; Doniol, iii, 153.

It was thought desirable that Gérard should conceal his departure, and on April 11 he sailed from Toulon, ostensibly for Antibes; but when off Hyères he embarked on the Languedoc, one of d'Estaing's fleet, bound for the United States. After a journey of ninety-one days he reached his destination and was landed a few miles from Philadelphia.

There was no lack of interest in the reception of the representative of our powerful ally. A delegation from Congress met him, and he drove to Philadelphia in Hancock's carriage. Soldiers were drawn up in the streets to greet his entrance, and salutes were fired. The importance of the event was not underestimated. "I had the honor of being present the last Sabbath," writes Henry Marchant, a member of Congress from Rhode Island, "at the most interesting interview that ever took place in America, or perhaps in the world, between Monsieur Gérard, the plenipotentiary of France, and the President of Congress. . . . This interview was most cordial, generous, and noble." [1]

No permanent residence had yet been selected, and Gérard was entertained temporarily by Benedict Arnold, who was then commander at Philadelphia. Although arrangements were not yet made for his formal reception, the house overflowed with visitors; most of the members of Congress and the principal officers of the city, "even the most phlegmatic," we are told, hastened to pay their respects. Representatives of the English King had lately visited Philadelphia in the hope of recalling the colonists to their allegiance by the offer of liberal terms. The news of the alliance with France destroyed even the remote possibility of

[1] William Read Staples, *Rhode Island in the Continental Congress*, 191.

success in such an effort. The English, it was charged, were provided not only with arguments, but with money, with which to persuade the members of the Continental Congress. None of the money seems to have been used, but presents which indicated good fellowship had been scattered about. These were now put to a use which would have been distasteful to the donors. A grand dinner was given Gérard, and he wrote home that the guests feasted on turtle and wine that had been sent members of Congress by the English commissioners.[1]

The members of Congress were most pleased to have a representative of France accredited to them, but they were somewhat uncertain as to the proper manner of receiving him. So embarrassing was the question that a special committee was appointed, which investigated the reception of foreign representatives with great care. They found that the proper form when an ambassador arrived was to have three members "wait upon him in a coach belonging to the states" and that "the person first named of the three shall return with the ambassador and his secretary in the coach"; and on reaching the chamber of Congress he should be seated on a chair raised eighteen inches above the floor. Since Gérard was only a minister, he must be content to be waited on by two members and was not entitled to have his chair raised from the floor at all.[2]

Not until August 3 did Lee and Samuel Adams, as commissioners of Congress, formally notify Gérard that on the 6th, at noon, Congress would give him audience. On the morning of that day Lee and Adams

[1] Doniol, iii, 270.
[2] Journals of Congress, Ford's ed., July 17, 1778; Doniol, iii, 302.

called on him, and mounted in a carriage, drawn by six horses, they proceeded to the hall of Congress.

There the minister was placed in a chair opposite the president. The thirty-two members of Congress were arranged in a half-circle around the room; we are told that the chairs of the president and the minister were large and of equal size, while those of the other members of Congress were of modest proportions. Gérard presented his letters, which were first read in French, and the thirty-two members listened attentively, though few understood them. Afterwards an English translation was read. The minister was then formally presented and delivered his address standing; the president made his reply, also standing; the minister saluted Congress and Congress saluted the minister, and the function was closed.[1]

As we have seen, if Gérard had been an ambassador instead of minister plenipotentiary, etiquette would have required a larger delegation for his escort, and that he should have read his address sitting. "Congress has somewhat confused notions," wrote Gérard, "concerning the dignity and etiquette befitting a sovereign state, but they desire no unnecessary ostentation and pomp."

Marchant writes of the reception: " It was an important day, . . . and I hope replete with lasting advantages to the United States in general and to the State of Rhode Island in particular. . . . I think the

[1] A doggerel verse ran : —

> "From Lewis M. Gérard came
> To Congress in this town, sir ;
> They bowed to him and he to them,
> And then they all sat down, sir."

Rivington's Gazette, Oct. 3, 1778. — See Frank Moore, *Diary of the American Revolution,* 607; Journals of Congress, Ford's ed., Aug. 6, 1778; Doniol, iii, 311–318.

connection brought about by the hand of Heaven, and that thereupon it promises to be lasting." [1]

A great dinner at the city tavern ended the day. Twenty-one patriotic toasts were drunk, to the booming of cannon and to the reasonable exhilaration of those who joined in all of them.

Gérard proved himself a useful representative for his government. He was judicious, discreet, and avoided any diplomatic entanglements. His reports on the country to which he was sent were not always laudatory, but they were reasonably accurate. He was in sympathy with Vergennes's resolve that no peace should be made until the independence of the United States was acknowledged, and to that end he was always loyal. When the question of the western boundaries arose later, though Gérard was guilty of no unfairness to the Americans, his sympathies were more with Spain. He wrote Vergennes, advising him to encourage Spain to get possession of whatever posts she could in the Mississippi Valley. He had told Congress that its persistence in an effort to establish its power on the Ohio, and the Illinois, and at Natchez would show an unfair spirit of conquest, that such an acquisition was absolutely foreign to the principles of the French and American alliance. He declared "that his King would not prolong the war one single day to secure to the United States the possessions which they coveted. . . . Besides the extent of their territory already rendered a good administration difficult, and so enormous an increase would cause their immense empire to crumble under its own weight." [2]

Nor was his sympathy any stronger for our fore-

[1] Staples, *Rhode Island in the Continental Congress*, 193.
[2] Doniol, iv, 72–75.

fathers on the question of the fisheries. He was indeed content that the Americans should get what they could, but he did not feel that France was bound to prolong the war in order to gain for its allies advantages which were not stipulated in the original treaty. But in this there was no cause for complaint. Gérard was the representative of France and not of the United States. His career was marked by courtesy, by regard for the obligations which France had undertaken, and by a sincere desire to assist the allies of France to bring their struggle for independence to a successful termination.[1]

In September, 1779, Gérard was relieved from his position as minister to the United States, and returned to the French Department of State. He carried with him the good-will of those to whom he was accredited. Congress asked that his portrait might be placed in its halls, so that it should recall how much his constancy and zeal had contributed to the consolidation of the alliance and the prosperity of the two nations. The merchants of Philadelphia presented him an address. All joined in wishing him godspeed, and to this friendly greeting he was fairly entitled.[2] He had done his work satisfactorily to his own government and with reasonable regard to the interests of the people of the United States. The most important part of the work was now accomplished. He was glad to return to his own land, while La Luzerne assumed the position of French minister at Philadelphia.

César Anne de La Luzerne arrived in Philadelphia September 21, 1779, but did not have his first audience with Congress until the 17th of November. From that time until the end of the war he performed his

[1] Doniol, iv, chap. 3.　　[2] Doniol, iv, 209, 210.

official duties faithfully, winning the esteem of the American people by the suavity of his manners and the discretion of his conduct. He tried to carry out the spirit of the alliance on principles of equity and reciprocal interests. He remained in the United States for five years, and was succeeded by Barbé-Marbois.[1]

[1] Wharton, i, 423.

CHAPTER XIV

THE French ministers had anticipated that a treaty with England's rebellious colonies would be followed by war with England, and in this expectation they were not disappointed. There was little delay in announcing that France had thrown in her lot with the colonists; indeed, it was impossible that such an alliance could long be kept secret; the news had been officially communicated to Congress, and would soon return from across the Atlantic, even if any effort at concealment were made in Europe. Lord Stormont had been insistent in his inquiries as to the negotiations between France and the American commissioners, and though he had always received untruthful answers, he had not been deceived.

The treaty had now been made, and Vergennes was willing that it should be known to all the world. On the 13th of March, the Marquis de Noailles, the ambassador at London, received an order to convey to the English minister the important tidings. He performed his errand with alacrity. At four o'clock of the same day he waited upon Lord Weymouth, and read the official announcement of the treaty. The statement that his Majesty made public this act in pursuance of his resolution to cultivate good intelligence between France and England, and in the hope that the British sovereign would avoid anything that might disturb this harmony, could hardly have been regarded as sincere. A private letter to the ambassador expressed the more reasonable expectation that the declaration would excite not only surprise but effervescence.[1]

The effervescence was for the time repressed. Though Weymouth could have been little surprised at this declaration, yet, if we may trust the account of the French minister, he was almost moved to tears of wrath in listening to it.[2] But he contented himself with saying he could make no reply until he had received the instructions of the King, his master.

The instructions were brief and to the point. On March 14 a courier crossed the channel in hot haste, passed from Dover to Calais in less than three hours, with orders for Lord Stormont to demand his passport at once, without the formality of paying any farewell visits. On the 16th he left Paris; he had issued invitations for a dinner on the following Thursday, but the guests were notified that their host could not have the pleasure of receiving them. Noailles was likewise recalled by his government, and left London forthwith.

One benefit France at once obtained from the rupture. Under the humiliating terms of the last peace, an English representative was stationed at Dunkirk, charged with the duty of seeing that France did not seek to restore the fortifications of that place. This irritating condition was at once ended: by an order sent on the 19th of March, the English commissioner was notified that his errand was closed, and Dunkirk was freed from foreign dictation.[3]

The treaty of alliance with the United States was

[1] Doniol, ii, 823–828.

[2] Letter of Noailles, March 15, 1778; Doniol, ii, 827, 828.

[3] Doniol, ii, 833.

regarded both by France and by England as equivalent to a declaration of war, and yet some little time elapsed before the beginning of hostilities. The action of France excited bitter resentment in England, and quickened the war spirit even among those who had regarded with disapproval the treatment of the colonists by the home government. The dying protest of Chatham against the dismemberment of the British empire was incited by the hostile act of that nation whose pride he had done so much to lower.

Though no collision had as yet occurred, the French prepared actively for a contest that was inevitable. The plan of an invasion of England, so often considered and so seldom attempted, was discussed, and resulted only in talk. But on the 17th of June a frigate and sloop detached from the English fleet opened fire on the French frigate La Belle Poule cruising off Brest. The engagement began about six and, aided by the prolonged light of a June day, the frigates continued firing until nearly midnight. They were at close range and some forty men were killed. At last the firing was stopped by the darkness and the ships parted, not very seriously harmed.[1]

Meanwhile the French government had resolved to send a fleet to America, which might render useful service, both in the United States and in the West Indies. The command of the expedition was intrusted to an officer who had achieved a moderate, though not a brilliant, reputation in the Old World, which he did not enhance by his exploits in the New.

The Comte d'Estaing belonged to an ancient and honorable family. Some of its members sought to trace their pedigree to origins as illustrious as they

[1] Doniol, iii, 163.

were remote, and counted, among other ancestors, the last king of the Visigoths, who died in the eighth century. Without asserting any uncertain claims, the record of the family covered more than five centuries of faithful service and honorable position.[1] The count who took part in our Revolution was born in 1729 at the Château of Ravel, a feudal castle of vast proportions, furnished with much luxury and commanding an extensive view over the surrounding country. The castle had been captured and sacked several times during the internal wars of France, and was again ravaged and many of its treasures were dispersed when it was seized as the property of a suspect in the year IV.

The young d'Estaing entered the army when a lad of nine, and he was a colonel when nineteen. He served with merit in India, and after that he was for two years governor-general of San Domingo. His rule was not acceptable to those he governed. The residents of the island complained of him as headstrong and passionate; they said he had much zeal but little judgment; that he loved pomp and lost his temper; that his plans were vast, but his performance unsatisfactory.[2]

D'Estaing had passed middle life before he transferred his activity from the land to the sea. Such changes were not uncommon in the French service, but it is doubtful if they were often judicious; starting as cabin-boy is usually better training for an admiral than service on land, however long and honorable.

The count was almost fifty years of age when he

[1] Doniol, iii, 197.
[2] *Mém. de la chambre d'agriculture de Port-au-Prince;* Doniol, iii, 179.

was given command of the fleet bound for New York. The generals and admirals whom Louis XVI sent over to America were, for the most part, men of mature years. La Fayette was the only one holding an important command who still retained the enthusiasm of youth and its readiness to take great chances. D'Estaing showed in this expedition a deliberation and a prudence which were in keeping with his years, but were not calculated to secure brilliant results.

On receiving his appointment he at once devoted himself to preparing a fleet for the expedition, and on April 13, 1778, twelve men-of-war and four frigates weighed anchor at Toulon. They encountered adverse weather and the ships were not in the best of order; thirty-five days were spent on the Mediterranean, and not until the 17th of May did they pass the Straits of Gibraltar and enter the Atlantic Ocean.

The fleet had sailed under sealed orders, and on May 20, when they were well out in the Atlantic, these were opened and read by the officers on the various ships. They contained a formal declaration of war against England. The fleet was directed to make prize of English ships wherever found, and, if the vessels should become separated, they were ordered to rendezvous at Boston. Cries of " Vive le roi! " greeted the reading of these instructions; the long-restrained hostility against Great Britain was at last to be gratified, and the prospect of an expedition to a remote part of the world, with the possibility of plunder and the certainty of excitement, was agreeable to all. A solemn mass was said on board the Languedoc, the admiral's flagship; the officers were arrayed in their most splendid raiment, the vessel was covered with flags, the priest blessed their arms and prayed God to send them victory over their enemies.[1] The English, doubtless, were praying God with equal fervor to send victory to them.

The instructions to d'Estaing, while leaving him a large liberty of action, bade him, before sailing to the West Indian islands, to perform "some action advantageous to the Americans, glorious for the arms of the King, and fitted to show the protection which his Majesty extends to his allies." [2] The admiral discussed his plans at great length with Gérard, the minister to the United States, who accompanied him on the journey. He gave utterance to many apothegms, both wise and epigrammatic. "Promptitude is the first quality," he wrote Gérard; "to astonish the enemy is almost to have conquered them; it is this which is desirable, which perhaps will be shown, and to reach which we shall surely do all that is possible. . . . A combination of rapid operations might overcome the ordinary firmness of the British troops. . . . The least act of feebleness or timidity might be very fatal." The count then discussed at much length and with much vivacity the conduct to be pursued in the various contingencies of American warfare.

Unfortunately, his apothegms were not fully carried into effect. As is often the case, the faculty of epigrammatic utterance was not accompanied with efficient execution. Even before the fleet reached America it seemed doubtful whether the desires of the King would be gratified, and any result accomplished that would be advantageous to the Americans or glorious to the French arms. The time occupied by the journey was lamentably long; the vessels were of unequal speed, and the rapid sailers had to delay on account

[1] Journal de campagne du Languedoc; Doniol, iii, 233.
[2] Doniol, iii, 238.

of their slower companions. Moreover, the admiral could not resist making captures, and the pursuit of stray merchantmen occupied much valuable time. D'Estaing also occasionally exercised his fleet in maritime evolutions in mid-ocean. These may have been valuable as practice, but they occupied hours that could have been better employed. As a result of all this, it was not until July 7, eighty-five days after they had left Toulon, that the French fleet anchored at the mouth of the Delaware.[1] It was short of water, short of provisions, and, what was still worse, it was too late for the destined prey. It had been hoped that d'Estaing would surprise and defeat Lord Howe's squadron; but two weeks before his arrival, the English evacuated Philadelphia and Lord Howe sailed tranquilly to New York City.

D'Estaing reported his arrival to Washington in a letter couched in the ardent terms which the French always used in reference to the American commander-in-chief, and which expressed a sincere admiration, that was still further augmented in the years during which they were his companions in arms. Intrusted by his King, said the admiral, with exhibiting his affection for his American allies, the pleasure was increased by the prospect of serving with the American commander. "The talents and great achievements of George Washington," he added, "have secured him in all Europe the truly sublime title of the liberator of America."[2]

As a result of the long cruise the fleet was in great need of provisions. Some officers were sent to Philadelphia to ask for supplies; they received from Congress good words but little else. "It is impossible to

[1] Doniol, iii, 189.   [2] Letter of Aug. 8, 1778; Doniol, iii, 322.

show more good-will," Gérard wrote, " . . . but their resources are almost nothing."[1]

An officer visited Washington at his camp, and reported his reception in favorable terms. " I was weighed down with politeness," he stated. Washington at once wrote, expressing his pleasure that the command of the fleet had been given to one so recommended by talent, by experience, and by reputation as the Comte d'Estaing. The American general was quite the equal of French courtiers and diplomats in the skill with which he bestowed courteous and honeyed phrases.

As Howe had already escaped, nothing remained but to sail to New York in pursuit of him. The French fleet reached Sandy Hook ; at a little distance they could see the Union Jacks floating at the English mast-heads, with some appearance of disorder about the ships, which had made a hasty retreat. It was expected that the fleet under Admiral Byron would soon come to Howe's relief, but the French were unable to pursue him farther and attempt his destruction. At Sandy Hook they encountered insurmountable obstacles. The French ships were large and clumsy, some of them drew twenty-three feet of water, and over the bar at that time such vessels could not pass. D'Estaing offered one hundred and fifty thousand francs to the pilots if they could bring his fleet into the bay, but they either could not or would not.[2] Possibly the pilots were Tories, and had little

[1] Gérard to Vergennes, Aug. 18, 1778; Doniol, iii, 323.

[2] The bay would allow only vessels drawing seventeen feet or less to pass. — Barras to Rochambeau, Aug. 12, 1781 ; Doniol, v, 522.

The reports on file at Washington show that there has always been from 22 to 24 feet of water over the bar at low tide and five feet more at high tide.

heart in the cause; but if they were correct in stating that no vessel could pass drawing more than seventeen feet, it would have been disastrous to make the attempt.

As it was impossible to enter the New York harbor, d'Estaing now sailed on to Rhode Island, in the hope of capturing the English force at Newport. If this enterprise had been successful, it would have been of considerable importance. The garrison consisted of nearly six thousand men, and its capture, following the surrender of Burgoyne, and shedding lustre upon the first appearance of the French in the war, might have hastened the termination. There seemed to be good reason for anticipating a successful result: Washington was to keep the English stationed at New York in check; General Sullivan was placed in command of the forces in Rhode Island, supposed to be ten thousand strong, and it was expected that he would coöperate with the French fleet in capturing the English army.

The arrival of the French fleet filled La Fayette with delight, and his letters to d'Estaing combined youthful enthusiasm with vigorous animosity towards England. "I love to think," he wrote the admiral, "that you will give the first blow to an insolent nation, for I am sure you will appreciate the pleasure of humiliating it and that you know it sufficiently to hate it. . . . May you begin the great work of destruction which will put their nation at the feet of ours. May you do them as much harm as they wish to do us."[1]

Washington showed his appreciation of La Fayette's good work by giving him command of a detach-

[1] Doniol, iii, 324.

ment which was to join Sullivan and coöperate in the capture of Newport. La Fayette's attachment to the Americans did not prevent his observing their peculiarities. "You must find it ridiculous to see me a sort of general officer," he wrote, speaking of his new command. "I confess it makes me laugh myself, and that in a country where there is not as much laughter as in ours." [1] He hoped that some of the French soldiers might also be placed under his orders; to see his compatriots and his brothers of America serving together under his command was, he said, his dearest dream. [2]

On his arrival with his command, he at once reported to the French admiral. The situation in which he met his compatriots was somewhat grotesque. Nominally he was a deserter from the French army, having come to America in defiance of the orders of his government. The order was still in force, directing any French vessel to arrest the fugitive marquis and return him to France. But in the mean time, the nation had followed where the marquis had led ; he was now at the head of a detachment of American troops, ready to coöperate with a French fleet in an attack on the common enemy. When he visited the flagship he was received with due honors, and the order for his arrest was regarded as abrogated by the progress of events.

The movement against Newport which promised so well resulted only in disappointment and recrimination. If the forces on land and sea had been handled with skill, and the attack made at the earliest possible moment, it might have been attended by success ; but the progress of events was very different. For the delays that occurred, the French admiral does not seem

[1] Doniol, iii, 336. [2] Tower, *The Marquis de Lafayette*, etc., i, 429.

to blame; the responsibility rested, perhaps, solely on the lamentable condition of the American army. On the 29th of July the French fleet came to anchor opposite Newport. It was intended that Sullivan with his forces should land on the island, under the protection of the French guns; the French ships would then force their way up the channel and assist in the capture of the town. Unfortunately, the American army, in Sullivan's judgment, was not ready to commence the attack. Washington had sent two thousand Continentals under the command of La Fayette, but the rest of Sullivan's army was to be made up by militia from the New England States, and the militia were not on hand.

"Sullivan's soldiers," said d'Estaing, "are still at home"; and they showed no haste to leave.[1] "Do not trust the figures," a Frenchman already in the United States wrote to the admiral; "the figures have no reality. Three thousand to-day will be three hundred to-morrow. Certainly the number on paper will be double the number in the field."

In fact, Sullivan seems to have displayed the qualities of a Fourth of July orator rather than of an efficient commander. As he had had much experience in politics and little in warfare, this perhaps was not strange. The men under his command, for the most part, were not regular soldiers, and it was difficult to fit them promptly for efficient work. If their commander drilled them but little, he gave them much praise. He expected to have his army ready for the advance on August 12, and on the 11th he issued what was justly called a "patriotic general order." He was happy, so he said, "to find himself at the head of an

[1] Doniol, iii, 449.

army actuated by a sacred regard for the principles of their country, and fired with just resentments against those barbarians who have deluged their country with innocent blood. . . . The prospect before us is now exceeding promising. The several corps have everything to animate and press them on to victory." The general himself did not yield to his soldiers in courage or patriotism, for he adds: "The general assures his brave army that he shares with them every danger and fatigue, and is ready to venture his life in every instance where his country calls for it."

"A noble spirit of patriotism," so ran another general order, "brought numbers of brave men on the ground, whose particular interest loudly called for their presence at home." The general wishes, he continues, "to do everything in his power to forward the return of those brave men to their respective families and business, for which reason he exhorts every one to use their best endeavors to make the siege as short as possible."

Unfortunately, militiamen collected as were the forces under Sullivan, however brave and patriotic, were a very uncertain element. He was unwilling to begin the attack until the troops for which he hoped had assembled, and thus time went by. The days that were consumed, as d'Estaing truthfully said, "were those most favorable ones, the precious moments of the arrival, when all are astonished, and most frequently no one resists."[1] Nine days passed before Sullivan was ready to move, and when he was ready the fateful moment had gone by.

On the 8th of August the French ships forced their

[1] Doniol, iii, 337.

way up the middle passage, and on the next morning
a large force was landed on Conanicut Island. But on
the 9th Howe made his appearance off Newport with
thirteen men-of-war and seven frigates, and the situation at once changed. The French were unwilling to
remain in the harbor with the chance of being taken
at a disadvantage. Accordingly, they started to force
their way past the English batteries and gain the open
sea. In this they succeeded, but the noise of the artillery informed Howe of the movement, and as the
French boats one after another came out from the
inner bay, he forthwith weighed anchor and sailed for
New York.

At a little after eleven o'clock of the morning of
the 10th, d'Estaing's ships were in the open sea and
the signal to give chase was at once raised. There
was little wind at first, but it freshened, and it was
soon evident that the French could overtake the
fugitives. Late in the afternoon they were up with
the rear division; but in the mean time the wind had
been growing stronger, by six it was blowing a gale,
and the weather was so thick that the fleets lost sight
of each other. The misfortunes of the French had
only begun; the gale continued, and at half-past
three in the morning the masts of the Languedoc
went down with a tremendous crash, and the rudder
also gave way. The flagship was now helpless and in
great peril. All the 12th the storm continued, and
not until the 13th did it begin to abate. The French
ships slowly gathered; the Languedoc, though she
had not been shipwrecked, was helpless, and the
Marseillais was in little better shape. The English
had escaped, and with two of their best ships dis-
mantled, the French were now in no condition to meet

them.[1] Some of the officers desired to proceed at once
to Boston, but d'Estaing had promised Sullivan that
he would return, and on the 20th of August the
damaged fleet sailed ingloriously to Newport, severely
battered by the storm and in great need of repairs.

Sullivan was now eager to attempt the capture of
Newport, and demanded the assistance of the French;
but d'Estaing and his officers felt that they could undertake nothing until the ships were put in shape for
service. The English fleet might reappear at any
time and the French ships would be almost helpless
before them. There was nothing to do, so they decided, but to sail forthwith to Boston and have the
needed repairs made. The decision was prudent, but
it was unfortunate. La Fayette told the admiral of the
unfavorable effect such a movement would have, but
d'Estaing said he had no right to risk the destruction
of the King's fleet, and on the 21st he set sail for
Boston.

The wrath of the Americans was even fiercer than
La Fayette had anticipated, and it was expressed with
impolitic frankness. Sullivan had shown little military skill in the campaign, but he manifested much
vigor as a polemic. An order of the day,[2] signed not
only by Sullivan but by many of his subordinates,
declared that the departure of the squadron was injurious to French honor, contrary to the King's intentions and to the interests of the United States, and
harmful to the alliance between the two peoples.
Articles of a similar tone appeared in the news-

[1] Journal de campagne du Languedoc; Doniol, iii, 374. D'Estaing
to Laurens; Doniol, iii, 384–392.
[2] T. C. Amory, *Military Services and Public Life of John Sullivan*,
77.

papers; where officers in the service indulged in such expressions, restraint was not apt to be found among irresponsible journalists. The situation was grave enough at best, and this outburst of vituperation bade fair to make it much worse. La Fayette was summoned to the council at which the resolutions were adopted, but he left in great dudgeon when he discovered the object of the conference. Resolved that their views should be known, Laurens sailed to Boston in pursuit of d'Estaing, and there on his own ship presented him in person with the offensive document.[1]

Naturally, this outburst of ill-will had its effect at Boston. The air was full of abuse of the French, the mob was hostile, and there were some disagreeable scenes. In a riot in the town, two officers of the French fleet were dangerously wounded, and one died from his injuries. The situation was now serious. Such an incident as this might result in an open breach between the United States and the ally of whose assistance they stood in such need. The authorities at Boston, naturally, were much disturbed by the death of the French officer. The City Council proposed to give him a public funeral, but his associates wisely thought that the less publicity given to the matter the better, and he was buried without parade at a private chapel.

There was the possibility that this unfortunate affair might have more serious results than the failure to capture Newport. Not only might the French feel ill affected towards an alliance in which thus far they had gained no glory, but an affront openly offered to the French admiral and his command might

[1] Doniol, iii, 351.

result in a refusal to aid further an ally that repaid assistance by insult. No one realized these possibilities more keenly than Washington. He realized also that the aid of France was indispensable to American success, and he at once exerted himself to restore harmony. He wrote General Heath, exhorting him to see that the French received all proper assistance and courtesy at Boston. To La Fayette he sent an assurance of his appreciation of d'Estaing's services, while to Sullivan, the chief offender, he sent a letter expressed with the courtesy in which he never failed, but calculated to calm Sullivan's wrath and point out the indiscretion of his conduct. Congress acted with equally good judgment. Sullivan had communicated his complaint to that body. Gérard asked that it be not made public, and this was at once agreed to. Steuben was sent to Sullivan to assist in extricating him from the difficulties in which his intemperate speech had involved him.

D'Estaing received this outburst with entire calmness. He answered Sullivan, defending his own conduct and saying it was impossible that the ships should now assist in the attack on Newport; but in order to show his own zeal in the cause, he offered to lead the soldiers under his command by land, to report to Sullivan and serve under his orders. In his report of this transaction to the Secretary of the Navy, he writes: "I desire that there shall not be a single man in America who does not love the French. . . . I have offered to become a colonel of infantry, under the command of one who, three years ago, was a lawyer, and who certainly must have been an uncomfortable person to his clients." [1] To Washington he wrote that

[1] Doniol, iii, 363.

he wished to show the French were not offended by hasty expressions of untimely zeal, and that he himself would always remain one of the most devoted and faithful servants of the United States.

He was not required to serve as a colonel under a general who had been so lately studying Blackstone instead of Vauban. Sullivan had already withdrawn his forces, and the British garrison had been so reinforced that it was now useless to attempt their capture. But harmony was restored; if Sullivan was not placated, he was silenced. Washington wrote d'Estaing thanking him for his services, and regretting that an accident which human wisdom could not avert had prevented the success of sagaciously formed plans.

The restoration of harmony was not followed by any important results. The repairs to the ships were completed, but d'Estaing did not attempt further action. The fleet was needed in the West Indies, and his orders were to proceed there, after having accomplished something in the United States. It must be confessed that he had not accomplished much, except perhaps to divert the attention of the English and keep them from new undertakings. But he was not unwilling to leave a field of action in which he had met with much annoyance and reaped no glory.

On November 4 the French fleet sailed for the West Indies. It encountered bad weather and many of the ships were more or less injured, and not until December 9 did they come to anchor in the bay of Port Royal.

The campaign carried on in the West Indies had no special effect on the progress of the war. D'Estaing was a man of much bravery and of some energy, but he could not handle ships with the skill of one whose life had been spent on the sea. Little was accomplished for some months. D'Estaing certainly did not overestimate his successes, and he was never afraid to tell the truth about himself. He wrote home in January, 1779, that he had gone from one misfortune to another, and the King's squadron had not even been able to retake St. Lucia. "If I do not entirely succumb under the weight of misfortune which has characterized the events of this ruinous campaign, I am none the less filled with extreme regret not to have been more useful in the service of the King."[1]

In the summer of 1779 he was somewhat more fortunate. The French captured Grenada and St. Vincent, and d'Estaing defeated the English under Lord Byron, who was by no means as great an admiral as his nephew was poet. Even then d'Estaing was criticized, and perhaps justly, because he did not utilize his victory to the utmost; apparently, if he had possessed greater talent as a sailor, he might have destroyed the English fleet. "If he had possessed as much sea-craft as bravery," wrote an officer, "we would not have allowed four disabled vessels to make their escape."

He now made a second attempt to coöperate with the American troops, but it was attended with no more success than his luckless expedition to Rhode Island in the preceding year. His assistance was earnestly demanded in the southern states. Georgia was largely in the hands of the English, and South Carolina was in great peril. General Lincoln and the French consul at Charleston wrote to d'Estaing, asking for aid, and to these appeals he decided to yield. "The news which I find at San Domingo," he wrote

[1] Doniol, iv, 130.

the French Minister of Marine, "shows much uncertainty as to the constancy of the Americans. If we only go there and show ourselves, this will produce an effect which I believe will be of the greatest importance."

Before this, Congress had made a request that d'Estaing should send part of his fleet to the Georgia coast.[1] He was then unwilling to do this, and proposed instead an expedition to capture Halifax and Newfoundland. This was submitted to Washington, and he, with his usual good judgment, discouraged the plan, and advised that d'Estaing should act in the South and afterwards turn his attention to New York. The condition in the South was bad and there was sore need of aid. "Never," wrote the Marquis de Brétigny from South Carolina, "was this country in more need of succor. It is necessary to defend it against its enemies and against itself. All is in lamentable confusion, few regular troops, no assistance from the North, a feeble and ill-disciplined militia, and a great lack of harmony among the leaders."[2]

This account of conditions in the South was not overdrawn, and d'Estaing acted with good spirit in endeavoring to aid his allies. But he still clung to his plans of conquering Newfoundland, and he wrote in a manner that indicated somewhat hazy notions of the distances and of the difficulties of the task. "If possible we will enter at Charleston, and then we will sail up as far as Newfoundland."[3]

On the 16th of August, 1779, d'Estaing sailed for

[1] Doniol, iv, 128–129.

[2] Brétigny to d'Estaing, July 17, 1779; Doniol, iv, 297.

[3] *Archives Maritimes*, Aug. 21, 1779; cited by the Vicomte de Noailles, *Marins et soldats français en Amérique, pendant la guerre,* etc.

the United States at the head of a fleet of some forty ships, carrying about four thousand soldiers. On the first of September the expedition came to anchor near the mouth of the River St. John's in Florida, and on the following day it suffered severely from one of the storms which infest that coast. As a result of the losses sustained by the fleet, d'Estaing decided to abandon the thought of an expedition farther north, and to confine his activities to assisting in an attack on Savannah, which was defended by a small garrison of English under the command of General Prevost. "The damage done my ships," he wrote the minister, "has imposed on me the melancholy necessity of acting where I should not and did not wish to act."

Notwithstanding this unfavorable opinion, good results might have been hoped from the coöperation of the French with the American army, but they were not realized. The vessels that were in condition to proceed with the cruise anchored near the mouth of the Savannah on September 8.[1] The French took possession of Tybee Island, but they could make little progress in a maze of creeks and marshes, and after some fruitless efforts the fleet sailed south to the mouth of the Ossabaw. There, during the night of September 11, some fifteen hundred men disembarked. The weather was bad, the soldiers had brought with them rations for only three days, and provisions became scarce; they had little ammunition and no tents, and there for six days they remained, suffering from a never-ending rain, in a position where, if the enemy had known of their plight, they might have been attacked with great advantage. At last the weather cleared and the disembarkment was finished; but

[1] *The Siege of Savannah in 1779* (C. C. Jones, Jr., trans.), 13.

d'Estaing was able to land in all only about thirty-three hundred men, and with these he joined the American army under General Lincoln, some eighteen hundred strong, and advanced toward Savannah.

D'Estaing sent a formal summons to the English commander, asking him to surrender, and giving him twelve hours to consider the proposition.[1] It probably would have been wiser if he had made no demand, but had at once attempted an assault of the town. Prevost had only a few hundred men under his command, but during the delay he received reinforcements to the number of eighteen hundred. He thereupon notified the French commander " that though we cannot look upon our post as absolutely impregnable, yet . . . it may and ought to be defended." [2]

The entire force of the allies taking part in the siege was about six thousand, of whom two thirds were French, and they largely exceeded the numbers of the garrison, even after it was reinforced. But the defence was stout, and the assailants encountered obstacles of every kind. Savannah was encircled by creeks, streams, and marshes, over which any advance was slow and difficult. The French boats attempted to coöperate in the attack, but some of them ran aground and they could accomplish little. An active bombardment was carried on ; many of the houses in the city were burned, but the intrenchments were of earth and suffered little damage. In the mean time provisions were running low, and the time was approaching when the French must rejoin their fleet and sail for home. There was nothing to do but abandon the siege or attempt to carry the city by storm, and d'Estaing decided on the

---

[1] C. C. Jones, Jr., *History of Georgia*, ii, 379.
[2] *Ibid.*, 383.

latter course. At midnight of October 9 the allies
began their march, in the hope of surprising the English garrison; but the English were prepared, while
the eagerness of some of the French to be among the
foremost resulted in considerable disorder. The attack was characterized by much gallantry and no success. The French lost over six hundred in killed and
wounded, a considerable portion of their small army.
The American loss was less than half that of the
French, but among those killed was General Pulaski,
one of the best of the foreign volunteers who came to
assist the cause of American independence. D'Estaing
himself was severely wounded, and upon his assistant,
Colonel Dillon, devolved the melancholy duty of re-
embarking the French troops and sailing ingloriously
away.[1]

During this unsuccessful attempt, those left on board
the ships fared almost as ill as their companions on
land. Food was scanty and good water lacking. The
scurvy raged with such violence that an officer of the
fleet declared that on an average thirty-five men who
had died from disease were committed to the sea each
day. "We could not relieve our poor sailors," he says,
"wanting coats, destitute of linen, without shoes, and
absolutely naked. . . . The bread . . . was so much
decayed and worm-eaten . . . that even the domestic
animals on board would not eat it. . . . Behold," he
adds, "a part of the frightful picture of the cruel and
miserable condition of our crews during . . . the siege
of Savannah."[2]

Even if we allow for exaggeration, the conditions

[1] Journal du Siège de Savannah; Doniol, iv, 303–307. *The Siege
of Savannah in 1779* (C. C. Jones, Jr., trans.), 28–39.
[2] *Ibid.*, 62.

were very bad, and the expedition was a melancholy failure. It is hard to say to what extent this was due to bad judgment, and to what extent it was due to bad luck; the result was the same.

The Americans retreated to Charleston, and on October 28 the French fleet sailed away. "The precautions and sagacious arrangements employed by the officers," says the official report, "are the highest praise of their zeal and their talents." Doubtless this was so; but the second attempt at coöperation between the French and their American allies had resulted, not merely in accomplishing nothing, but in actual defeat. To end this unlucky campaign, a violent storm caused the loss of several of the French ships with all on board.

If the result was unfortunate, at least there was harmony between the allies. D'Estaing had failed in his efforts, but all recognized the zeal and courage with which he had come to the aid of the American cause. No one, wrote General Lincoln, could doubt that the Comte d'Estaing had the interests of America at heart. He had shown it in coming to our aid, by his endeavor to take Savannah by storm, and by the bravery with which he had led his troops to the assault; he could find consolation for his wounds and his reverses in the assurance that America appreciated his efforts, and his merit was not obscured by his misfortune.[1] With the consolation derived from such tributes the unfortunate count was forced to be content; he returned to the West Indies and was shortly succeeded in command by the Comte de Grasse.

D'Estaing took no further part in the war. Like so many others who served in the American Revolution,

[1] Doniol, iv, 265.

he was to meet a sad end in the revolution of his own country. In 1787 he was a member of the Assembly of Notables, and he was afterward a deputy to the States-General. He was a friend of the revolutionary cause, and proved his zeal by enlisting as a grenadier in the Parisian Guards. But his service was found insufficient by those who distrusted all aristocrats. In due time he was imprisoned at Sainte-Pélagie, and brought to trial before the Revolutionary Tribunal. There his rank and early associations were enough to secure his condemnation, and on April 28, 1794, he died upon the scaffold.

CHAPTER XV

THE unfortunate result of the expedition conducted by d'Estaing added to the discouragement which was now widespread in the country. For almost two years the colonists had been allied with a great European power, and yet the situation of affairs seemed worse at the end of that period than at the beginning. England was apparently no nearer acknowledging the independence of the United States in the fall of 1779 than she was in the spring of 1778. Indeed, our alliance with France had inspired the English with a certain amount of new zeal in the war against us. Those who had been reluctant to make war on their own colonists, speaking the same language and allied in blood and race, were stirred to fresh ardor when the war was against France, the ancient and immemorial enemy of England.

The confident hopes excited among the American patriots by the announcement of the French alliance in the spring of 1778 had by no means been fulfilled. The expedition against Newport had accomplished nothing, the endeavor to capture Savannah had ended in defeat, conditions in the South had been so bad as to induce d'Estaing to go to their aid: they were rendered worse by the failure of his efforts. The years 1778 and 1779 were perhaps the most disheartening of the war. France as an ally, instead of bringing speedy victory, seemed less valuable than when she was furnishing secret aid. Such an opinion was indeed unfair. If Newport had not been captured, at least the enemy had been kept from undertakings which might have proved fatal to the American cause. Though the English had made large gains in the South, conditions in the North remained practically unchanged.

In one respect, however, it might be argued that the French alliance worked actual harm. Five years had passed since the first blood was shed at Lexington. With the long continuance of the war had come a weariness of the sacrifices that were required for its vigorous prosecution. The states furnished neither the men nor the money that Congress demanded and Washington needed, and when the French alliance was announced, many were willing to believe that a rich kingdom like France would now supply whatever was wanted; she had great armies and strong fleets and much wealth, with which she could insure the success of her ally, and there was little need for further exertion. Zeal for the cause had been lacking before the French alliance, and it was no more active after it; the duration of the war and increasing disturbances from a disordered currency made it more difficult to furnish pecuniary aid, and it became harder for Congress to obtain the support that was necessary to carry on the struggle. Thus the situation after five years of warfare was far from satisfactory, and patriotic men still doubted what the end would be.

It was a critical period in the history of the war, and the most sanguine patriot might fear that unless efficacious aid were soon furnished, the American Revolution would end as an unsuccessful rebellion. When the surrender of Burgoyne was followed by the French alliance, American patriots hoped that the war would be brought to a speedy and successful termination. These hopes had been by no means realized; though the English had won no notable victories, the ability of the colonists to persist in their resistance seemed more questionable in 1780 than in 1778.

Financial evils were the most serious, and in this respect conditions could hardly have been worse. No other nation has increased in wealth with the rapidity of the United States; no people ever began its national existence with less promise of financial wisdom. In the printing-press our ancestors placed their hopes, and its free use brought the country to a condition of business anarchy. The financial enormities of the French Revolution were as great, and a worthless currency depreciated with the same rapidity, but an extraordinary outburst of popular enthusiasm, controlled by men as full of vigor as they were lacking in scruple, enabled France to carry on war with success.

In America conditions were different: lack of funds and the inability to raise money by taxation threatened to disband the army and disrupt the government; and had it not been for the money advanced by France, it is hard to see how such a disaster could have been averted. At the beginning of 1780 a dollar of Continental money was worth only two cents, and this worthless currency was practically the only asset with which Congress was to carry on the war. The condition seemed the more hopeless because public men still clung to the printing-press as a source of revenue, and charged the state of affairs to the misconduct of those who were unwilling to receive the paper, instead of to the folly of those who issued it.

When a bushel of corn sold for one hundred and fifty dollars and a suit of clothes for two thousand, it was evident that an army could not be supported, nor could business be transacted under such conditions. To some extent, men in their ordinary affairs could resort to the primary usages of barter, but the soldiers had nothing with which to barter. When an army is partially unfed, largely unclothed, and wholly unpaid, its dissolution is imminent. Such was the condition of the force under Washington; the shadow of an army that remained, so he wrote, had no motive save patriotism to continue in the service, and no hope of better things. "If either the temper or the resources of the country will not admit of an alteration, we may expect soon to be reduced to the humiliating condition of seeing the cause of America in America upheld by foreign arms." When Congress could not pay a courier to carry important despatches to the general-in-chief, it was evident that the cause of America in America could be upheld only by foreign money.[1]

In May, 1779, Washington wrote that the rapid depreciation of the currency, the extinction of public spirit, the want of harmony in council, and the declining zeal among the people were symptoms of the most alarming nature, and he added, "If the enemy have it in their power to press us hard this campaign, I know not what may be the consequence. Our army as it now stands is little more than the skeleton of an army."[2] "I have no scruple," he writes a little later, "in declaring to you that I have never yet seen the time in which our affairs in my opinion were at so low an ebb as at the present." And in July he writes that, except four hundred recruits from Massachusetts, he

[1] Report, La Luzerne, April 1, 1780; Doniol, iv, 345.

[2] Letter of May 8, 1779; *Writings of Washington*, Sparks's ed., vi, 251.

had received no reinforcements since the last campaign.[1]

While such was the condition of our army and our treasury, La Fayette did work for his American friends at Versailles quite as valuable as any service which he rendered on American battlefields. In October, 1778, after the failure of the attempt to capture Newport, the marquis asked for a furlough to return to his own land. He hoped to serve again in the American army; but now that his country was at war with England, he wished to see what part might be assigned to him in the struggle. Both Washington and the Congress expressed with entire sincerity their appreciation of the services which La Fayette had rendered. Congress, in extending a leave of absence, gave him a vote of thanks, and directed that a sword should be presented to him by our minister at Versailles.[2] Washington wrote of the many evidences of La Fayette's zeal and ardor, and expressed his own very particular friendship for one who combined the fire of youth with uncommon maturity of judgment. All these words of commendation were well deserved. La Fayette had not only shown himself a brave officer, — of such there is always an abundance, — but he had manifested an extraordinary combination of unselfishness, zeal, and good judgment. Coming a stranger to a strange land, given an important command while still under twenty-one, the French minister could write without exaggeration that La Fayette's conduct had made him the idol of Congress, of the army, and of the people.

In January, 1779, he sailed for home, and escaping

---

[1] *Writings of Washington*, Sparks's ed., vi, 312.

[2] Tower, *The Marquis de Lafayette*, etc., ii, 41, 43.

the dangers of capture by the English and the perils
of an attempted mutiny on his own vessel, on February 12 he reached Brest in safety. He at once made
his way to Paris; but while he returned as a triumphant hero, he returned also as a disobedient officer.
He had left France in defiance of the King's orders,
and of this offence he was still unpurged. There was
indeed no reason to anticipate a severe sentence upon
a youth who came back crowned with laurels, when
his own country had followed his example and enlisted in the cause of American liberty. But he was
forbidden to appear publicly at Versailles, and was to
regard himself as in prison at the residence of his
father-in-law at the Hôtel de Noailles. Imprisonment
in this charming home, adored by his family and flattered by his friends, was not a rigorous ordeal, and
after a week of such punishment he was allowed to
visit Versailles and present himself to the sovereign.[1]

The arrival of La Fayette increased the enthusiasm
for the American cause among the class to which he
belonged. Even Marie Antoinette bade him visit her
and tell her the news about "our good Americans,
our dear republicans." The young marquis enjoyed
the two things most dear to him, assisting a good
cause in which he sincerely believed, and receiving an
unlimited amount of popular applause.

The enthusiasm with which La Fayette was greeted
upon his return to Paris did not make him forget his
American friends; he was constant in season and out
of season in soliciting the ministry to continue with
vigor the war against England. He had left France
two years before, a young man unknown to fame,
owing to his wealth and social position his only claim

[1] Tower, *The Marquis de Lafayette*, etc., ii, 56, 57.

to be listened to in matters of political importance.
He was still very young, but he was now a man of
mark. He had received the public thanks of the American Congress, he had been honored by the closest
confidence of the American general-in-chief. The interest which had been excited by his departure, the
enthusiasm which his conduct had aroused in France,
the courage, the devotion, and the singularly good
judgment which he had displayed in America, made
him on his return a man with whom the minister must
consult in any projects relating to the American colonies. His letters show the zeal with which he utilized
his favorable position. To Washington he wrote, after
lamenting the enormous distance that separated him
from his dearest friend, that he was occupying himself with getting money from the French government.
"I have been so insistent that the superintendent of
finance fears me as he would the devil himself. . . .
To serve America, my dear General, is for me an inexpressible happiness. . . . What would render me
the most happy of men would be to rejoin the American banners, and put under your orders a division of
four or five thousand of my own compatriots." [1]

His letters to the President of Congress also show
the manner in which he utilized his influence at court
for the benefit of his friends. "I shall always regard
the interests of America as my principal affair while I
am in Europe. All the confidence of the King and the
ministers, all my popularity among my compatriots,
all of the means of which I can dispose . . . , will be
employed in a cause so dear to my heart." [2]

[1] La Fayette to Washington, June 12, 1779; Lafayette, *Mémoires,*
etc. (1837), ii, 62, 64.
[2] June 12, 1779: *Ibid.,* 55.

With amiable but unwearied pertinacity, La Fayette continued his labors in behalf of the American cause. He lamented that the cost of a fête at Versailles was enough to equip the American army, and he was accused, justly enough, with being ready to strip the palace in order to buy clothing for American soldiers. " I suppose the expense of this is a million of livres," he writes of a great illumination when home on a visit. " As much as I respect this country, particularly the King and the royal family, I could not help reflecting how many families in another country would this tallow make happy for life ; how many privateers would this tallow fit out for chasing away the Jerseymen and making reprisals on Messieurs les Anglais."

The illuminations were not abandoned, the tallow still continued to light the halls of Versailles and was not used to equip privateers. Marie Antoinette would not give up her balls, nor the King sell his furniture to aid the American cause, and yet the labors of La Fayette were by no means unproductive. He persisted in his demands that more aid should be given the new republic, both by furnishing supplies and money and by preparing for further hostilities. His demands to some extent were answered.

The enterprise to which the attention of the French government was first given resulted indeed in no advantage either to France or her allies. Plans for an invasion of England have allured French statesmen and generals from a remote period, and the fact that from the days of William the Norman no such enterprise has met with any large degree of success has not disturbed the hopefulness of the Gallic mind.

The proposed invasion of England met the decided approval of Spain. Whether Spanish statesmen were naturally inclined to favor this plan because it was unwise, or for whatever reason, they expressed their desire to coöperate with the French in landing an army on British soil. An invasion of England was accordingly planned, and this was not a mere scheme of the Cabinet; troops were gathered, ships equipped, and commanders chosen. La Fayette was promised a command of some importance, and he was filled with delight at the prospect. He wrote Vergennes: " The idea of seeing England humiliated, annihilated, makes me tremble with joy. . . . Judge then if I am eager to know whether I shall be the first to arrive on that coast, the first to plant the French flag in the midst of that insolent nation." [1]

During all the summer of 1779 troops were drilling, ships preparing, and soldiers gathering for the expedition. The chief command was intrusted to the Comte de Vaux ; he was ordered to assemble his forces at Havre and St. Malo, and from there sail to England, land his army, and proceed to the invasion of perfidious Albion.[2] The count came and went from Havre and St. Malo. La Fayette was feverishly active, now at Havre and now at Paris, but still the expedition did not set sail. Though the Spanish had been eager for the invasion, when the time for action came they were not ready. A convoy was sent to meet them at Cape Finisterre, but when, after two months' waiting, the Spanish ships at last arrived, they were in much need of repair and ill fitted for the expedition. But the combined fleet now numbered sixty-six ships of the line, and it sailed up the Channel, exciting a mild alarm at Plymouth and along the English coast.

---

[1] La Fayette to Vergennes, June 10, 1779; Doniol, iv, 291.
[2] Doniol, iv, 294.

La Fayette found the thought that the French flag now floated over English roadsteads a delicious morsel for his pride.[1] It was the only enjoyment he was to obtain from this abortive expedition, and he had no opportunity to plant the French flag in the midst of that insolent nation. The condition of the French ships was better than that of the Spanish, but still the work of preparation had been very imperfect. A violent wind scattered the fleet, many of the ships were out of water and provisions, and they sailed back to Brest with a sick-list of nearly half the men on board. The storms of autumn now began, and the health of the soldiers grew no better. In October it was decided to abandon the expedition. It was justly described by Rochambeau, who was assigned to a command in it, as an exceedingly expensive and an exceedingly ill-arranged enterprise.

Yet the money expended in this foolish project was not altogether wasted, for it led the French to undertake the expedition which resulted in the capture of Yorktown. The decision of the French government to send not only a fleet, but a considerable force of soldiers, to coöperate with the American army was in large degree due to La Fayette. In July, 1779, he submitted a carefully prepared plan for the assistance of their American allies,[2] — for a new expedition, to consist not merely of ships, but of land forces, which should act in coöperation with Washington; the plan contained in substance the project which was put into effect a year later under the command of Rochambeau. This was submitted to the ministers; it received the ap-

[1] Doniol, iv, 243.
[2] *Writings of Washington*, Sparks's ed., vii, 479; Tower, *The Marquis de Lafayette*, etc., ii, 499.

proval of Vergennes, and even of the aged and infirm Maurepas. La Fayette not only asked that these reinforcements should be sent, but he insisted that they should depart, at the latest, by the following spring.

In the summer of 1779 the French were absorbed in their plans of English invasion, but when the failure of that project was admitted, La Fayette's request for a new expedition to America was seriously considered. Such an enterprise was attended by a good deal of embarrassment. It was not only that the cost was large, that there were serious difficulties in sending several thousand men across the Atlantic, exposed both to the perils of the sea and to the vigilance of English men-of-war, but it was not certain that assistance in this form would be agreeable to the Americans, or that French soldiers could coöperate successfully with the American army. The expedition led by d'Estaing in 1778 had not been productive of advantage to the common cause. The French troops finally sailed away from America, having accomplished nothing except to create discontent, the unseemly expression of which was only checked by Washington's prudent counsel. To place several thousand French soldiers on American soil might lead to complications that would destroy the alliance instead of insuring its success.

La Fayette himself, who knew better than any other Frenchman the condition of American feeling, was somewhat apprehensive of the effects that might be produced by the presence of a French army. The Americans had asked for money, for supplies, and for ships, but they had not been zealous in requesting the assistance of French soldiers. When Adams heard of the proposed expedition, he wrote to Vergennes, insisting that a French fleet should remain in American waters, but stating his belief that on land the colonists were quite capable of dealing with the English forces. There was always a possibility of misunderstandings between two armies of different nationalities, differing in speech, faith, and customs.[1] Some of the Americans had complained openly of the conduct of their French allies, and some of the French officers, if they made no open complaint, sent to the French minister unfavorable comments on the American soldiers and the American people.

The unfortunate expedition of 1778 had bred a good deal of discontent on both sides: the French thought that they had done all in their power for helpless allies, and had received as their only reward ingratitude and unfriendly criticism; many of the Americans declared that their French allies might have done much and had done little, and they were more inclined to find fault than to return thanks.

Vergennes's zeal in the cause of the insurgents had perhaps cooled a little. The war in America had not met with the prompt success that had been hoped, and the count felt that the Americans were inclined to rely too much on French aid and did too little for their own salvation; he complained that the burden of the struggle was cast on France, and that her ally's appeals for help were becoming excessive. It was apparent to him, also, as to all, that the average ability in Congress was less than it had been four years before. " There are," Vergennes wrote his representative in Spain, " poor heads and dishonest hearts to be found in Congress."

The quarrels between different factions of Congress were known at Paris, and their importance was

---

[1] *Works of John Adams*, vii, 220–226.

perhaps exaggerated, while the open and unseemly wrangling between the representatives of America in Europe was only too familiar. La Fayette was as much distressed by these bickerings as the most zealous American patriot. "Nothing injures our interests . . . so much," he wrote the President of Congress, " as these stories from which it is supposed that there are disputes and divisions among the Whigs." And he wrote with more frankness to Washington: "There is a very important subject which demands all your influence and all your popularity. For the love of God prevent these clamorous quarrels, the account of which does more harm than anything else to the interests and the reputation of America." [1]

While La Fayette recognized the delicacy of the situation, yet he felt that the assistance of a French army was indispensable to American success, and he was confident that with proper precautions the danger of complications could be avoided. He thought there would be least danger of misunderstanding between the allies if he were himself given the command of the French reinforcements. This aspiring young man was not coy in his demands for important position, but he was quite justified in this request. His service in the United States had displayed considerable military ability; what was of still more importance, he had the entire confidence of Washington, he was by far the most popular of the foreigners who had come to our aid, he had shown tact in dealing with a strange people in a strange land, and by his enthusiasm and his unselfish zeal for the cause had gained the sincere affection of the American people.

[1] Lafayette, *Mémoires*, etc., ii, 62; Tower, *The Marquis de Lafayette*, etc., ii, 73.

"I agree with you," he wrote Vergennes, "as to a certain distrust that can be remarked in our American allies . . . but if to-morrow the King would send me with a French detachment . . . I would wager all most dear to me, not only that the troops would be well received, but that their union with the Continental army would be of great service." [1] And he added that though Franklin was not authorized to ask that troops be sent, he greatly desired it.

In this La Fayette was correct; yet while the American government asked much from France, they did not formally request the aid which was to prove most valuable of all. Franklin had instructions to ask for money but not to ask for troops. There were good patriots, La Fayette said, who feared that such assistance might increase too much their obligations to France. Moreover, the marquis recognized a trait which has always been strong in the people of this country. "It is in the American character," he wrote, "to hope that when three months have passed, they will no longer be in need of anything."

Undiscouraged by such obstacles, La Fayette continued his efforts in behalf of his American friends. The proposition which he submitted in the summer of 1779 had been approved by the ministry, even if not formally sanctioned. Since then, not only had the project of English invasion proved abortive, but news now came of the disastrous failure of d'Estaing's expedition against Savannah. Yet this lack of success did not lead to rejection of La Fayette's requests; it rather impressed upon the French ministry the necessity for some vigorous action.

In January, 1780, La Fayette submitted to Mau-

[1] Doniol, iv, 272.

repas an elaborate paper, in which he declared that the dangerous successes of the English in the South and the unsatisfactory conditions in the North rendered it necessary to send at once a French army to Washington's assistance. There were two objections raised, said the marquis: one, that their American allies lacked the resolution and courage to act with the necessary vigor, and the other, that the presence of French soldiers might breed jealousy and dispute. The first, he declared, his own experience in America enabled him to refute; and as for the second, if the command could be given to him, they would escape even the shadow of jealousy or strife.[1]

There is no doubt that this was true, and the selection of La Fayette as commander of the French expedition seemed the natural course for the French to pursue. But he was still a very young man, with a modest position in the French army; to place him over officers of longer service and higher rank was sure to be distasteful, and it was decided that he should not command the forces to be sent to America. No commander could have brought the expedition to a more successful conclusion than did Rochambeau, yet there is no reason to think it would not have achieved the same success had La Fayette been at its head. But if the French government did not satisfy his ambition, they were ready to gratify his zeal for the cause of his American friends. In February, 1780, the momentous decision was reached, and it was decided to send a French army to the relief of the United States.

Though the command was not given to La Fayette, no mistake was made in the selection of a leader for the forces to be sent to America. The Comte de Ro-

---

[1] La Fayette to Maurepas, Jan. 25, 1780; Doniol, iv, 308.

chambeau had been chosen for an important command in the proposed invasion of England. He had there no opportunity to reap glory, and he expressed his just disapproval of the folly with which the Minister of Marine made his arrangements for that enterprise, and of the prodigality with which he expended money to no avail. Rochambeau had already had a considerable career, though on the expedition on which he was now sent rests his permanent fame. He was born in 1725, a member of a good French family. As he was the second son and his health was delicate, it was decided to make a priest of him. He was first placed in a college of the Oratory, and was there exposed to dangers more serious than threatened him during the years of his service as a soldier. The fathers of the Oratory were strongly suspected of the damnable heresy of Jansenism, and the Bishop of Blois, friend of Rochambeau's family, interfered to save the youth from the spiritual perils to which he was exposed. He carried the lad away from the Oratory, a brand snatched from the burning, and put him in a Jesuit school at Blois. In this pious work he was assisted by the Abbé Beaumont, who afterwards became Archbishop of Paris, and showed his Christian zeal by refusing to allow the sacrament to be administered to dying Jansenists.

But it was not Rochambeau's fate to become a Jesuit priest; when he was about to receive the tonsure, his elder brother died. The good bishop, who had saved him from the Jansenists, now told him that his duty was to serve his country with the same zeal that he would have shown in the service of God. Accordingly young Rochambeau left the college, and when only sixteen, like many another young French noble, he began his career as a soldier. He obtained a commission in the cavalry in December, 1741, and served during the War of the Austrian Succession with credit.

He served throughout the Seven Years' War, always acquitting himself as a good soldier and rising steadily in rank, though he performed no startling feats of arms. After the peace he was made a major-general and received the grand cross of the Order of Saint Louis, an honor bestowed for faithful and gallant service. In 1780 he was made a lieutenant-general, and was given command of the army which the King was to send to the relief of his American allies. He was then a man of past fifty-five. He had less than La Fayette of the fire of youth, but he had the sound judgment which comes as a result of years of active service.

It is proof of La Fayette's loyal zeal that he was more interested in obtaining an army for his allies than in obtaining for himself the position of its commander. If he was disappointed in his hopes, he acquiesced with the cheerfulness that endeared him to his associates. He was not backward in asking, but he always accepted the duty assigned without sulking, and performed his work with diligence. Even if he was not to command the French army, the reputation he had won secured him a prominent part in the future campaign. If the command was not given him, he asked that he should be sent to announce to Washington the assurance of aid, and to resume his position in the American army.

This request was granted. As soon as the expedition was decided upon, La Fayette was ordered to return to America in order to announce the important

news, and to incite the Americans to an active coöperation, that would secure to them the utmost advantage from the assistance France was about to extend.
He was to inform Washington that the French King
would shortly send to him six ships of the line and six
thousand soldiers. They were to be placed under his
command; it would be for him to decide in what manner they could most profitably be used; the King's
only desire, said the instruction, " is that the troops
which he sends to the succor of his allies . . . shall
coöperate effectively to deliver them for all time from
the yoke and tyranny of the English."

While the French soldiers were placed wholly at
Washington's disposal, yet, with a certain pathos he
was asked to watch them with care and to spill no
unnecessary blood. The well-known humanity of General Washington, concluded the instruction, "makes
it certain that he will have specially in care the preservation of a body of brave men, sent more than a
thousand leagues to the rescue of his country. Though
ready to undertake anything for the safety of America, they should not be sacrificed rashly nor lightly." [1]

The progress of the war increased the respect in
which Washington was held in Europe, and lessened
the esteem bestowed upon Congress. The French auxiliaries were to be entirely under Washington's orders,
and to him La Fayette was to report. The French desired that even the pecuniary assistance they were to
render should be placed within Washington's control,
in order that from it the best results might be obtained. It was announced that the money granted by
the French King this year for the purchase of supplies, must be drawn on orders from General Wash-

[1] Instruction and Project, March 5, 1780; Doniol, iv, 314–320.

ington ; only after representations from Franklin that
such a procedure would be contrary to all the usages
of his government, were the officials of Congress
again intrusted with handling the funds.

The Hermione was directed to convey the marquis
on his important mission, and the captain was ordered
to render all the attention due to so distinguished a
passenger. " I shall have for M. le Marquis de La
Fayette," said the polite captain, "all the regard and
respect which are not only directed by your orders,
but dictated by my own heart, for a man whose actions have inspired me with the strongest desire to
know him." [1]

A favorable wind seconded the captain's zeal, and
on March 14, 1780, the Hermione sailed from La
Rochelle carrying La Fayette and his momentous secret. Duplicates of the papers intrusted to him had
been sent to the French ambassador at Philadelphia,
to be used in the contingency, by no means improbable, of the capture of the marquis by some English
cruiser. But the good fortune which deserted La Fayette in his late career still attended his youth. The
voyage of the Hermione was prosperous, and on April
28 she came to anchor in Boston harbor.

There the marquis received new proofs of the affection which the colonists felt for one who had labored
so indefatigably in their behalf. On the 28th he landed
at Hancock's Wharf, where he was met by a procession of soldiers and escorted to the governor's mansion.
He then visited the Legislature, where he was received
with many honors, and in the evening there was general rejoicing in the town. Such a reception, in a foreign city, would be gratifying to any one, and popular

[1] Tower, *The Marquis de Lafayette*, etc., ii, 93.

applause was especially dear to La Fayette. He wrote
Vergennes that the warmth of his reception and the
inexpressible marks of kindness which the American
people bestowed upon him increased, if possible, his
ardor in their cause.[1]

He soon left the enthusiastic Bostonians and made
his way to Washington's headquarters, where he arrived on May 10. He then visited Congress, and that
body passed resolutions, commending the disinterested
zeal and persevering attachment of so gallant and
meritorious an officer. He was at once assigned to the
command of two thousand men, a considerable force,
when the entire army of the general-in-chief did not
exceed six thousand.

La Fayette always displayed an extreme liberality
to his soldiers; he possessed amiable virtues which
made him, if not one of the greatest, yet certainly
one of the most lovable of men. In France he had
purchased with his own money a large stock of clothing and arms which he now distributed among his
command. A good coat and a whole pair of shoes were
usually a mark of distinction for a Continental soldier, and La Fayette's corps were the best-dressed
men in the army.

[1] La Fayette to Vergennes, May 2, 1780; Doniol, iv, 351.

CHAPTER XVI

In the mean time preparations for the expedition that was to go to the relief of Washington's army were carried on in France with vigor. The French government was not a military machine that worked with the efficiency of the administration of Frederick II, and yet, with many delays and disappointments, something was accomplished. At first it had been proposed that an army of four thousand men should be sent out under Rochambeau; but when he accepted the command, he justly remonstrated at the smallness of the force. "I accept with the liveliest gratitude," wrote the count, "the mark of confidence with which his Majesty has honored me, . . . but yet I venture to suggest, . . . that a body of four thousand men is soon reduced." It might well happen, he added, that one third of those engaged should be lost in a single engagement. At the battles of Laufeldt, Crevelt, and Klostercamp, he had lost two thirds of the men under his command, and such a contest in America would leave the remainder of the force in sorry shape. A body of twelve battalions, or six thousand men, he wrote the minister, would allow one third to act in the reserve, and though the Americans had asked for only four thousand men, an increase in the number furnished would naturally fill them with the liveliest gratitude.[1]

These suggestions were favorably received, and it

---

[1] Rochambeau to the King; Doniol, v, 313.

was decided to increase the force to eight thousand; but this wise resolution was not entirely carried into effect. In fitting out the expedition for America, as with the proposed invasion of England, the inefficiency of the naval department was manifest. "The watch of M. de Sartine is always slow," said Choiseul of the Minister of the Marine. The required number of soldiers gathered at Brest with commendable despatch, but though the men were ready, the boats on which they should sail were lacking.

The Spanish might have furnished some aid, but they were not inclined to do so. When the resolution to send an army to America was communicated to Madrid, the Spanish ministers manifested a strong desire to have the expedition sent to the southern states, where it might assist Spain in her designs on Florida. Vergennes did not receive this suggestion kindly. The war against England in Europe was conducted on lines by which Spain hoped to gain some advantage, and a large force was occupied in the siege of Gibraltar; but in America the French minister resolved to furnish aid where it would be most advantageous to their American allies. The Spanish, therefore, viewed the expedition with indifference, and the French naval department found it impossible to get together a sufficient number of transports. Seventy-six hundred soldiers were at Brest ready to depart for America, but only five thousand five hundred actually sailed under Rochambeau, and this was entirely due, wrote one of those who took part in the expedition, "to the negligence and incompetency which attend everything in this country." [1]

---

[1] April 4, 1780; *Diary and Correspondence of Count Fersen, relating to the Court of France* (translated by Miss Wormeley), 22.

The situation was urgent: America needed aid, and delay would increase the danger of an attack from the English fleet. Instead of waiting indefinitely for boats for all the men, it was decided to sail promptly with as many as could be carried. Rochambeau had intended taking horses enough to mount a small body of cavalry, but this plan had to be abandoned; even his own horses he left behind. Not a horse shall be taken, he wrote: "It is with the greatest regret that I separate from two war-horses that I can never replace, but I do not wish to reproach myself that they are occupying the room of twenty men, who otherwise might have embarked." [1]

The supplies occupied a large amount of space; there was little certainty of obtaining on the other side the articles necessary for the comfort and the efficiency of the men; munitions of war, clothes, tents, supplies of every sort had to be carried with them. The soldiers en route for our country were provided with everything necessary for their sustenance and comfort, with the same care that would now be shown in an expedition about to start for Central Africa. Especial attention had to be given to a sufficient provision of money; this required as careful attention as if the army were to embark for a land whose only currency was beads and cotton cloths, and indeed the currency system of our forefathers was not far superior to that which now prevails in Uganda. American paper money, wrote Rochambeau, had fallen into such disrepute that they must carry French coin to pay the men and to purchase supplies. Everything which the French army needed they must buy; and the count added, with just prevision, that for all they

[1] Rochambeau to Montbarey, March 27, 1780; Doniol, v, 331.

bought in America they would be obliged to pay good prices.[1] The expedition was a costly one, and nearly eight million livres were at once advanced for its needs.

While Rochambeau desired to sail as soon as possible with the men who could embark in the transports, he fully expected that a second detachment would speedily follow and furnish him with the number of soldiers that he had asked and had been promised. In this expectation he was doomed to be disappointed, and the second detachment of his army never crossed the Atlantic.

In all about fifty-five hundred soldiers sailed, whose fortune it was to coöperate in the capture of Yorktown and assist in the establishment of American independence. They were divided into four regiments: Bourbonnais, Soissonnais, Saintonge, and Royal Deux-Ponts. The names of the commanding officers show that members of the most ancient and illustrious French families took part in the struggle of American backwoodsmen for independence. Of the first regiment the colonel was the Marquis de Laval-Montmorency, and the Vicomte de Rochambeau lieutenant-colonel; the Comte de Saint-Maime was colonel of the Soissonnais regiment, and the Vicomte de Noailles lieutenant-colonel; the Saintonge was commanded by the Comte de Custine and the Comte de Charlus; of the Royal Deux-Ponts the Comte Christian Deux-Ponts was colonel and the Vicomte Guillaume Deux-Ponts was lieutenant-colonel. In addition to this was the Legion of Lauzun, consisting of six hundred men, under the Duc de Lauzun, a member of one of the greatest French families, and a man whose reputation for

[1] Rochambeau to Montbarey; Doniol, v, 315.

gallantry in love affairs gave him preëminence among the beaux and libertines of the time. Such follies did not prevent his being a brave and efficient soldier, and during two years in America he not only acquitted himself as a good officer, but conducted himself with as much discretion as if he had been a descendant of a governor of Massachusetts instead of a favorite of Louis XIV. The Vicomte d'Arrot and the Comte Dillon served under him, and the fleet was commanded by Admiral Ternay, an officer of long and honorable service.[1]

There was much complaint from those assigned to the second division, when at the last moment they found that they were to be left behind. The young French officers were eager for an opportunity for distinction, and those who could not embark were bitterly disappointed. Many efforts were made to obtain an assignment which would secure passage with the first division, but for the most part they were in vain. "These poor young men," wrote Rochambeau, "are very much interested and they are in despair, but the Chevalier Ternay literally does not know where he can put them."

In April the men were on board and ten ships of war and thirty convoys were ready to sail, bearing the soldiers, equipment, and provisions. On the 12th, Rochambeau wrote that as soon as the weather cleared and the north wind blew they would be under way. But there was tedious delay waiting for fair weather. Not until the first of May was the wind favorable, and in the mean time the soldiers wearied of their long detention on board ship and the number of sick was considerable. At last a start was made from

[1] *Les Combattants Français*, etc., edited by H. Mérou, *passim*.

Brest, and on May 3 Rochambeau wrote from his ship: " We are sailing by a fair northeast wind . . . and traversing the gulf in the very weather we could desire."

This favorable condition did not long continue. A violent storm scattered the fleet, but they gathered without loss, while the same storm drove into port the English fleet under Admiral Graves, which was intended to check the expedition. Graves was unable to sail again for two weeks, and in the mean time, favored at last by fair winds and undisturbed by the English fleet, the French ships made their way slowly but safely, sailing well to the south and by the Azores, in the hope that the good weather would remain with them, — a hope that was not disappointed.

On June 5, five English ships were in sight, but Ternay did not wish to delay his progress by seeking any adventures on the way. " This occasion showed how little taste the commander had for chasing and pursuing vessels one might meet," a disappointed officer entered on his log; " it is a great misfortune." In this the officer was probably mistaken ; the voyage was long and perilous at best, and Ternay was resolved it should not be made longer by any pursuit of prizes. On June 11 a sloop was taken, sailing from Halifax, and by this capture they got a cargo of codfish. On the 18th they took a cutter, with no cod, but with the unwelcome news that the English had captured Charleston and taken four thousand prisoners. On the 20th the fleet was south of Bermuda, and there they fell in with some English men-of-war and had a mild engagement. If Ternay had been more adventurous he might have captured one of the English ships, but he allowed her to escape and proceeded on

his way.[1] On the 4th of July the French were opposite
Chesapeake Bay and saw a fleet of eleven sail, mer-
chant-ships under convoy. Greatly to the disgust of
some of his followers, Ternay declined to pursue them,
and on July 11, after a voyage of seventy days, the
entire French fleet anchored safely off Rhode Island.
Admiral Ternay had performed his duty with vigilance and ability and with commendable caution; a
few days later it would have been possible for the
English fleet to interpose a stout resistance; as it
was, the French soldiers disembarked at Rhode Island
as peacefully as if they had been landing at Brest.

As soon as the French troops were safely landed,
Rochambeau reported their arrival to the commander-
in-chief. "My master's orders," he wrote Washington
on July 12, "place me at the disposal of your excellency. I am arrived full of submission and zeal, and
of veneration for yourself and for the talents you
have shown in sustaining a war that will be forever
memorable." [2]

On the whole, the French troops reached this side
in good condition, though the tedious waiting at Brest
and ten weeks spent on the Atlantic had resulted in a
long sick-roll. But no serious malady had shown itself,
and Rochambeau reported that a three weeks' rest in
their comfortable quarters at Rhode Island would put
the army in condition for service. General Heath met
the French with a thousand men, to insure them a safe
landing; as there was no opposition the American contingent was soon allowed to return, but in the mean
time the officers met in what General Heath affably
called "happy fraternity." The friendly intercourse

[1] Doniol, v, 342.
[2] Rochambeau to Washington, July 12, 1780; Doniol, v, 348.

of soldiers and citizens and the social functions which greeted the new arrivals afforded, so a newspaper declared in the sounding periods in which journals of that day indulged, " a pleasing prospect of the future felicity and grandeur of this country, in alliance with the most polite, powerful and generous nation in the world."

Both the officers and men of Rochambeau's command conducted themselves with a discretion which healed old grievances and prepared the way for effective coöperation. " The French officers of every rank," says a correspondent, " have made themselves agreeable by that politeness which characterizes the French nation." Polite our guests certainly were, and yet, by a most judicious respect for American social usages, they did not attempt to be too polite. This was the peril most to be apprehended, but the officers recognized how broad a gulf at that period divided the social life of Paris and Newport. The Duc de Lauzun, if we may credit current reports or unauthentic autobiography, had in France made love to almost every woman he met. In Newport he was quartered for the winter with Mrs. Deborah Hunter. He was keen enough to recognize the difference between Mrs. Hunter and Madame du Barry.

The citizens of Newport celebrated the arrival of the French fleet with proper festivities. On July 11 all the houses in certain streets were directed to be illuminated, and such other homes as the abilities of the inhabitants would permit, and these illuminations were to be continued until ten of the evening, which was then a late hour for the residents. With laudable prudence, Job Easton, Rob Taylor, and some others, were appointed a committee to prevent damage from fire and to preserve the peace of the town. Newspapers had a small circulation, and therefore this resolution of the council was made known to the citizens by beat of drum. To assist those who were ordered to illuminate, but were too poor to furnish lights, the council directed that in such case the lighting should be at the public expense; but, with a judicious thrift characteristic of our forefathers and little practised in modern city governments, the treasurer was ordered to buy one box of candles which must answer the needs of all.[1] If the celebration was economical, it was acceptable to our guests, and many social entertainments and balls were given by the French officers and their American hosts. The Duc de Lauzun gave a great ball, and so did the officers of the Royal Deux-Ponts, and dinners were a frequent mode of entertainment.

The appearance of the French regiments was sufficiently gay to furnish pleasure to the Newport of to-day, and was a rare spectacle for the Newport of the eighteenth century. The dress of officers and men bore little resemblance to the ragged regimentals of the American army. The uniform of the Deux-Ponts was white; Saintonge white and green; Bourbonnais black and red. All wore cocked hats and their hair was carefully done up in pigtails. The regiment of Soissonnais was especially picturesque, with rose-colored facings to their coats, and grenadier caps adorned with white and rose-colored plumes. The artillery were dressed in blue with red facings.

These well-equipped and well-drilled regiments excited confident hopes of victory in the hearts of American patriots, while the officers, as charming in manners as they were in dress, the representatives of

[1] *Magazine of American History*, iii, 433.

ancient names and historic titles, excited admiration, or even stronger feelings, among the American ladies. There were no multi-millionaires at Newport, few Americans had visited France, and French counts, dukes, and princes were new elements in American society. The French nobility of to-day has lost its ancient power, much of its social prominence, and almost all of its ancient wealth, yet its members are often attractive to young ladies far more experienced in society than the Newport belles of 1778.

Variety was furnished by the visit of a band of Indians. The French were always adroit in dealing with the Indians, and these warriors, mostly Oneidas and Tuscaroras, were much pleased by their reception. General Heath also entertained them, and he says with satisfaction that he gave them a "sumptuous feast"; the Indians showed their appreciation by performing a war dance, which perhaps pleased the French officers as much as the general's dinner.[1]

Some of the Indians who had visited Rochambeau at Newport went to West Point, and Dr. Thacher describes them in terms which expressed the views of nine tenths of the New England men of that period. "The army was paraded to be reviewed by General Washington accompanied by a number of Indian chiefs. His Excellency, mounted on his noble bay charger, rode in front. . . . Six Indian chiefs followed in his train, appearing as the most disgusting and contemptible of the human race ; . . . dressed in a miserable Indian habit; some with a dirty blanket over the shoulders, and others almost naked. . . . These bipeds could not refrain from the indulgence

[1] *Memoirs of Gen. William Heath*, written by himself; Aug. 29, 1780.

of their appetites for rum on this occasion, and some of them fell from their horses on their return to head-quarters." [1] Admiration for the noble red man is modern.

The social intercourse between the Americans and their new allies was agreeable, but it was not for dinners and balls, nor to enjoy the smiles of Newport belles, that an army of over five thousand men had been sent across the Atlantic. As soon as the soldiers had fairly recovered from the fatigues and discomforts of their journey, the question of the action to be taken against the English occupied the attention of their leaders. Another French fleet had come to America, but had sailed away, having accomplished no important work, sowing discontent rather than gratitude among those it came to aid. Such a result for the second expedition was as much dreaded by Rochambeau as by Washington, and yet almost a year elapsed before the French army took any active part in the war.

It seemed possible at first that some slight shadow of pique and misunderstanding — the evil which the French ministers had feared when considering the expedition — might hinder its usefulness. Washington reposed the fullest confidence in La Fayette, and it was natural that he should especially rely upon the marquis in dealing with his own countrymen, but La Fayette's eagerness led him to manifest a zeal that, if not undue, was perhaps unfortunate.

A movement against New York naturally suggested itself as the most desirable that could be undertaken. "It seems to me," La Fayette wrote to Rochambeau and Ternay, "that New York is in every respect an

---

[1] James Thacher, *A Military Journal, during the Revolutionary War;* Sept. 13, 1780.

object preferable to any other. This city is the pivot
on which turn the operations of the enemy, and upon
which rest any hopes which the King of England can
still entertain. . . . In a word, it is clear that an
expedition against New York would be the most
glorious and the most advantageous to France and
America, the most desired by the two nations, and, in
a certain sense, the only one that is practicable." [1]

In this and following letters the marquis demonstrated to his own satisfaction the feasibility of such
an attack and pressed the measure upon Rochambeau
with increasing urgency. After stating Washington's
views, he added: "I assure you . . . in my own name
that it is important to act in this campaign, that all
the troops you hope to receive from France the coming year, as well as all the projects with which you
flatter yourself, will not repair the fatal injury resulting from our inaction." [2]

Rochambeau was not persuaded by these reasonings, and while he recognized the importance of the
capture of New York, he asserted with positiveness
that the success of such an attempt was impossible
unless the French possessed a decided superiority on
the sea. This certainly they did not have, and furthermore the forces under his command, even when united
with the small army under Washington, he regarded
as entirely unequal to the capture of New York.

Rochambeau confidently expected that he would
soon receive additional troops from France. He had
been promised that eight thousand men should follow
him to America. Nearly eight thousand soldiers gathered at Brest, ready to sail, but a third of the army

[1] Doniol, v, 356.
[2] Aug. 9, 1780; Lafayette, *Mémoires*, etc. (1837 ed.), ii, 125.

had been left behind on account of the insufficient number of convoys. Rochambeau sailed with the assurance that the twenty-five hundred men composing the second division of his command would soon follow. For some months their arrival was constantly anticipated; when rumors came of ships seen at sea, the count flattered himself that the long-expected reinforcements would soon be at hand. But the twenty-five hundred men who had gathered at Brest to form part of Rochambeau's army, never sailed to America. For a while there was talk of their departure, and preparations for the expedition were carried languidly along, but it was at last announced that the plan of sending them had been for the present abandoned. Apparently the explanation of this failure was the inefficiency of the French naval department, of which the war furnished so many illustrations. It was difficult to procure transports, it required energy to secure provisions to equip the fleet for the long journey, and at last the undertaking was abandoned.

Not only did Rochambeau desire to await the arrival of the second division, but he was somewhat nettled at the peremptory zeal with which a youth like La Fayette assumed to direct his movements. The relations of the two men were friendly, but after all Rochambeau was a much older officer, and he was the commander of the expedition; he was subject to Washington's orders, but not to those of La Fayette. The marquis, so Rochambeau wrote the French minister, had sent him a despatch twelve pages long, in which, "at the instigation of some foolish heads, he proposes extravagant things, such as taking Long Island and New York without a fleet."[1] He would in

[1] Rochambeau to La Luzerne, Aug. 14, 1780; Doniol, v, 364.

the future, so the count continued, write directly to Washington, whose letters were always judicious, and thus avoid correspondence "with young and ardent persons."

La Fayette's amiability was proof against any rebuff, and secured him the affection of those who were annoyed by an eagerness which sometimes savored of impertinence. Rochambeau remained the sincere friend of the young marquis, who was as ardent in affection as in advice. These feelings are shown in letters that bear little resemblance to the ordinary correspondence between generals in the field. " Permit, my dear marquis," wrote Rochambeau, " an old father to answer you as a son whom he loves and esteems infinitely." After arguing against an attack on New York, he adds : " It is well to believe the French invincible, but I confess to you in secret, after the experience of forty years, there are few soldiers easier to beat when they have lost confidence in their leaders, and this they lose when they are put in perilous positions to please some personal ambition. . . . I have spoken of some things that displease me in your last letter; I judge that the warmth of your soul has a little affected the correctness of your judgment. . . . But it is always the old father Rochambeau who talks to his dear son whom he loves and will love and esteem to his last breath." [1]

Washington had been inclined to allow La Fayette an active part in the negotiations with his countrymen, but, with his usual tact, he felt that his associate wished to receive orders directly from the general-in-chief, and that it was judicious to accede to his request

[1] Rochambeau to La Fayette, Aug. 27, 1780 ; Tower, *The Marquis de Lafayette*, etc., ii, 154.

for a personal interview. Rochambeau had been insistent for this, and hostilities were not so active that Washington could not find time for a conference.

It was accordingly agreed that the commanders should meet at Hartford. This town was about equidistant between Newport and Washington's headquarters, and both French and Americans occupied some three days in riding to the rendezvous. Washington was accompanied by La Fayette, Knox, and six aides, of whom Hamilton was one. Rochambeau and Ternay left Newport September 18, accompanied by four French officers, and reached Hartford on the 21st. The French and American commanders met for the first time and each created a favorable impression on the other. If the interview produced no important result, it was valuable because the generals of the two nations conferred in harmony and parted with increased respect for one another. The courtesy and dignity of Washington's bearing corresponded to the idea which the French already entertained of the American commander. "I had time to see this man, illustrious, if not unique, in our century," writes one of the French aides. "He looks a hero. He is very cold, speaks little, but is courteous and frank. A shade of sadness overshadows his countenance, which is not unbecoming and gives him an interesting air." [1]

Washington and his suite arrived first at Hartford and were received with imposing ceremonies. The governor with his guards and his artillery came out to meet the commander-in-chief, and the crowd was enthusiastic. The French officers arrived soon after and they were received with the same formalities. Every-

[1] Fersen to his father, Oct. 16, 1780; *Diary and Correspondence of Count Fersen*, etc. (translated by Miss Wormeley), 30.

body was civil. " The highest marks of polite respect
and attention were mutual," says the Hartford "Cou-
rant." Even the bills of the members of the conference
were paid by the state, as they found when they came
to leave. Judging from the complaints of many officers as to the unconscionable sums they were obliged
to pay in their travels, this experience must have been
both rare and agreeable.

La Fayette acted as interpreter, as Washington
could neither speak nor understand French and Rochambeau was unable to speak English. This difficulty
did not interfere with the freedom of the interview,
nor with its agreeable character for the participants.
The results of the conference illustrated the extreme
caution of Washington's character. He was inclined
to make an attack upon New York, but when he found
the French generals regarded such a movement as
premature and ill-advised, he at once acceded to their
views. To some extent he may have been convinced
by their arguments, but he realized, also, that, although
the French contingent was subject to his orders,
his authority must be exercised with great discretion. The interview at Hartford, he wrote La Fayette, showed how nominal was the authority which he
exercised over the French auxiliaries.[1] This was not
strictly correct, for Rochambeau was ordered, not only
to coöperate with Washington, but to act under his
command. He was, however, expected to exercise his
own judgment as to the plans of the campaign, and
Washington was far too cautious to insist upon the
adoption of any course of action which would not receive the hearty coöperation of his associates.

[1] Washington to La Fayette, Dec. 14, 1780; *Writings of Washington*, Sparks's ed., vii, 322.

The French government was informed of the difference of opinion between the two generals, and approved the decision of its own officer. "The King approves of your conduct at the conference at Hartford," wrote Ségur, "and especially the care you showed not to allow your own views to be controlled by those Washington might hold." [1] Owing to the tact and consideration shown by Washington, the conference was entirely harmonious, and the French officers expressed the utmost admiration of the American commander-in-chief.

As a result of their deliberation Washington, Rochambeau, and Ternay joined in a despatch, asking the French government for further assistance, both in men and money. A memorandum, signed by them, declared that the capture of New York would be the most advantageous operation that could be undertaken; but that for the success of any movement the French must have a superior naval force, while, if they were to undertake the capture of New York City, the allied armies ought to be thirty thousand strong. All, therefore, joined in a memorial to the French government, asking that a naval force might be sent sufficient to insure the success of future operations, that a liberal supply of money be furnished for the necessities of the French army, and that, if possible, their force might be increased to fifteen thousand men. [2]

While the generals were in conference at Hartford, alarming intelligence hastened their return to their commands. News came that Admiral Rodney, with a fleet of thirty-one ships, had arrived at New York, and in view of this great increase in strength, an im-

[1] Ségur to Rochambeau, Feb. 25, 1781.
[2] Hartford Conference; Doniol, vi, 404–407.

mediate attack on the French fleet seemed probable.
Washington rode back to the Hudson, to make discoveries more alarming than the arrival of Rodney.
On his way from Hartford he held a conference with
La Luzerne; from there he went to West Point and
was met with the news of Arnold's treachery. Both
the American and the French armies were shocked by
this blow to the common confidence.

In the mean time the army under Rochambeau rested
comfortably at Newport. The troops landed in July,
1780, and there still remained four months of pleasant
weather before winter set in, but these were passed in
tranquillity. Yet the presence of the army at Newport
was by no means without value. La Fayette, when he
was arguing for an attack on New York, wrote that a
French army at Rhode Island was of no use to America, to which Rochambeau replied, rather tartly, that
he had yet to hear that the French at Rhode Island
had done the Americans any harm. If they took part
in no important movement, at least they rendered
valuable service in fostering hearty good-will between
the Americans and the allies, and preparing the way
for harmonious coöperation in the future.

If the French gained no victories, they escaped any
disaster, though with a more enterprising general opposed to them a different result might have ensued.
The American army was scattered along the Hudson
and in New Jersey. The English had some thirteen
thousand men at New York, and their fleet was superior to that of the French, but Rochambeau and his
command were left undisturbed.[1] Owing to the prudent

[1] B. F. Stevens, *Facsimiles of Manuscripts in European Archives relating to America*, no. 730, p. 8.

celerity with which Ternay conducted the expedition, the landing at Rhode Island had been unopposed. The fleet which sailed from England under Admiral Graves was driven back to Plymouth by a storm and remained there two weeks. At last they started in pursuit of the French convoy, but they could not recover the time lost; on July 11 the French were at Newport and on the 13th Graves reached Sandy Hook.

The English ships stationed at New York made no endeavor to hinder the French landing, but, upon Graves's arrival, the combined forces at once set sail for Rhode Island. On the 21st of July the English appeared off Newport with a fleet of nineteen men-of-war. In the mean time, the French had been actively engaged in fortifying their position, and the English admiral decided that it would not be prudent to attack by water, but that he would await the arrival of the land forces under Clinton. Clinton was reported to have ten thousand men, with which to begin hostilities, and the allies continued with vigor the work of fortification. The Continental soldiers under Heath and the militia from Rhode Island and Massachusetts engaged in the work with much zeal. Redoubts were built and cannon were put in position; the allied forces numbered some eight thousand men and were ready to give the English a warm reception.

Clinton proceeded with his customary procrastination and vacillation. Six thousand of his soldiers were embarked on transports ; they sailed across the Sound, and on July 31 they disembarked at Whitestone. But, in the mean time, their commander had changed his mind. He was informed that the French were strongly intrenched and that Washington was preparing to move against New York; to attack the

French successfully and then return to meet the American army, required decision, celerity, and boldness. Clinton possessed none of those qualities, and the idea of an attack on Newport was abandoned.

The English fleet lay outside the harbor ready to intercept any expedition the French might attempt; it did not venture an attack, but, as it was superior in numbers to the French, they could undertake nothing in behalf of their allies. On September 16 Rodney, with thirty-one ships, arrived at New York, and thus reinforced it was thought the English would enter Newport harbor and destroy the French fleet. The English had a large preponderance in force; if the attempt had been made and had proved successful, it would greatly have altered the future of the war. The daring that takes great risks and accomplishes great results had been common in the officers who were inspired by Chatham, but it was not found in the generals and admirals whom George III sent out to fight with his rebellious subjects. In September the English vessels arrived off Newport. Later Rodney won important victories in the West Indies, but he now decided against an attack; presently he returned to New York, and in November sailed back to the Antilles, leaving twelve vessels to strengthen the fleet under Arbuthnot, which continued, from Gardiner's Bay, its watch upon the French. Thus the autumn ended with nothing of importance undertaken by the French and their American allies.

During the winter Washington thought it might be possible to attempt some action jointly with the Spanish. Spain was not indeed an ally of the United States, but she was an ally of France and engaged with her in war with England. The Spanish at this time contemplated sending an expedition from Havana to Florida, and Washington thought this might furnish an opportunity for achieving results important to all combatants. If they would unite with the French and Americans, he wrote Rochambeau, in an attack on Georgia and the Carolinas, this would not only be invaluable to the Americans, but the defeat of the English in the southern states would procure for the Spanish the tranquil possession of Florida. If the scheme met Rochambeau's approval, he desired that a vessel should at once be despatched with the proposition. If you approve, he wrote, there is no time to lose in making your reply.[1]

Washington's judgment was rarely at fault, but he anticipated from Spanish aid advantages that were never realized. Rochambeau knew the Spanish better than the American general. He knew that it was useless to expect coöperation from them; that they would take part in no movement, unless the advantages were to be reaped solely by Spain, and that it was impossible for them to realize that Florida could be conquered in Georgia or Carolina. The Spanish commander, he assured Washington, having received orders from his own court, would not disturb them for a single moment in order to coöperate with the allies.[2] The plan was, therefore, abandoned, and Rochambeau fared no better in an endeavor to get assistance from the French fleet in the West Indies.

Thus the year 1781 arrived, and as the winter wore away the Americans and French began to prepare themselves for what it was hoped might prove a de-

[1] Washington to Rochambeau, Dec. 15, 1780; *Writings of Washington*, Sparks's ed., vii, 325.

[2] Rochambeau to Washington, Dec. 22, 1780; Doniol, v, 398.

cisive campaign. That this could not long be postponed Washington thoroughly realized. The mutinies
of the Pennsylvania and New Jersey soldiers had been
quelled; but it was impossible that an army should
much longer be kept together without money, and,
with the best of will, they could not serve indefinitely
without food and clothes. Nor was it certain how
long Washington could rely upon French assistance.
These auxiliaries were not sent here for any definite
period; pestilence, defeat, or other discouragement,
might induce a speedy return to their own land, and
if this expedition failed, it was most unlikely that the
French King would send another army to assist in an
unlucky war waged three thousand miles away.

The French were equally desirous for an active
campaign. The responsibility of the result of the war
did not rest upon them; but they sighed for activity,
they were weary of inaction, and eager to be led
against the English. The first movement was made by
the French fleet. The English ships in Gardiner's
Bay, and between Block Island and Point Judith,
kept vigilant watch, but their position was much exposed to bad weather, and a January gale disabled
several of Arbuthnot's ships. Encouraged by this,
Des Touches, who, owing to Ternay's sudden death, was
temporarily in command, resolved to break the mo-
notony of inaction. On March 8 the French fleet, carrying twelve hundred troops, set sail for Chesapeake
Bay, to coöperate with La Fayette in his campaign
against Arnold. Washington came to Newport in order to view the embarkment, and was received with
the formalities of which the French were masters. In
the instructions issued at Versailles it was directed
that the American general-in-chief should receive the

honors of a French marshal, and these were not denied him. Salutes were fired, and the ships and the city were illuminated. Not only did the French show their enthusiasm, but the town council voted to buy candles for the occasion. Thirty boys bearing lighted candles marched before the father of his country. The illumination was not dazzling, but it showed patriotic hearts.[1]

In the mean time the fleet had sailed away, but it did not accomplish any important results. The French had been slow in getting off; Arbuthnot had time to repair the injuries to his ships, and he sailed in pursuit after an interval of only twenty-four hours. At the mouth of Chesapeake Bay an engagement took place, each side having eight men-of-war. The victory was doubtful. Both sides fought with resolution, and neither gained any marked advantage. But the French vessels had been roughly handled, and Des Touches decided to return to Rhode Island. Twenty days after the French ships had sailed away they were back in port, having gained nothing but experience by their expedition.

Letters were so frequently intercepted that one needed to be discreet in his correspondence, and Washington now became involved in an annoying experience. He wrote Lund Washington, after the return of the Des Touches expedition, that it was unfortunate the French fleet had not undertaken the enterprise when he advised; Arnold's forces would then have been destroyed, while, by reason of the delay, the little squadron sent out had been unable to accomplish anything. The reproach cast upon his associates was not severe, yet it is strange that even this should

[1] Thomas Balch, *The French in America*, etc., i, 137.

have been indited by Washington's cautious pen. The penalty for a rare offence was prompt and disagreeable. The letter was intercepted, the English published it in "Rivington's Royal Gazette," and Rochambeau at once sent a communication to Washington, expressing his doubts as to whether such remarks could have been made by him, and sharply criticizing the criticism.[1]

Washington surely told the truth when he replied that Rochambeau's letter had caused him great pain. Naturally the man who as a boy could not lie about a cherry tree would not tell a lie in mature years; besides there would have been no advantage in doing so. He had no copy of the letter, so he wrote; he could not say whether it was correctly published, and probably it was not. But still he must admit that the report was substantially correct; the letter was addressed to a private person in whose discretion he could rely; only by an unlucky accident had the contents become public, and he added, in soothing words, that at that time the causes for the delay in sailing were not known to him; with these explanations, he said in closing, " I leave the matter to your candor." [2]

Rochambeau was too sensible to cherish any rancor; it was certainly indiscreet for the American general to criticize his French associates, and the consciousness of such indiscretion, to a man as rigid as Washington in the scrupulous observance of every propriety, was probably the most disagreeable feature of the episode. It bore no evil fruit, and it is certain that all his subsequent letters could have been inter-

[1] Rochambeau to Washington, April 26, 1781; *Writings of Washington*, Sparks's ed., viii, 27–28.

[2] Washington to Rochambeau, April 30, 1781 ; *Ibidem.*

cepted and published in the "Gazette" without danger of wounding the susceptibilities of his allies.

This unsuccessful enterprise was succeeded by movements of far greater importance. The arrival of intelligence from the other side enabled Washington and Rochambeau to form their plans for the campaign of 1781.

CHAPTER XVII

"THE SINEWS OF WAR"

ROCHAMBEAU'S son had been chosen to convey to the French government the result of the deliberations at Hartford. He did not sail at once, for there was still hope that the second detachment might appear, and the arrival of these new recruits would render unnecessary any appeal for assistance. But neither French soldiers nor word of any sort from the French government arrived at Newport. Communications between distant parts were slow at best, and because the delivery of letters was so uncertain, it often seemed simpler not to send any at all. The representatives of governments were left uninstructed and uninformed to an extent that seems amazing, and was often embarrassing. Silas Deane wrote to his employers in Congress, in November, 1776, that he had received no letter from them for five months; and in the following year reported that in the twelve months since he had left Philadelphia on a diplomatic errand he had received from his principals three letters in all.[1] Franklin was left equally unadvised as to the progress of events or the desires of Congress; for long months his only communications from Congress were the drafts they drew upon him, without informing him of their dates, or taking steps to provide the funds with which they could be honored. Generals were in as bad a plight as diplomats. For months Rochambeau expected

[1] *Deane Papers*, i, 340; ii, 18.

the arrival of recruits, who were never sent, and he was not even notified that it had been resolved not to send them.

It had been agreed that if no soldiers arrived by October 15, Rochambeau's son, a colonel in the French army, should sail for France with a full report of the Hartford conference, and ask in person for the relief, which was unlikely to be granted in answer to any written application. The envoy was in some respects specially well fitted for his task. In case of capture all his papers and instructions were to be thrown into the sea; but the son had so good a memory that he could deliver to the minister, word for word, the contents of his despatches.[1] His memory was not put to so severe a test. Not until October 28 was there a favorable wind, but on that day the French frigate Amazon went to sea, starting in a violent gale that she might better avoid the vigilance of the British squadron. She was discovered and chased, but made her escape, and reached the French coast without further peril and after an unusually fast voyage. On the 26th of November the Vicomte de Rochambeau made his bow to Louis XVI at Versailles.

If the voyage had been auspicious, the time of the arrival was less so. During the three years since the treaty of alliance was signed, little but discouraging news had come from France's ally across the water, and Rochambeau had to bring still more unfavorable reports: to tell of small armies, of soldiers who were receiving poor food, poorer clothing, and no pay at all, and to ask further aid from France to buy for them muskets and uniforms and rations.

France had just gotten through the third campaign

[1] *Mém. de Rochambeau*, i, 256, in Doniol, iv, 384.

of the alliance at an outlay of one hundred and fifty million livres, and the fourth campaign bade fair to cost much more. At this era of discouragement, the Spanish were strenuous in their advice that France should get such terms as she could for her American allies and make peace without more delay. The Spanish were engaged in negotiations with England, from which they hoped to get the utmost for themselves, by conceding to England the best possible terms with the United States. The Spanish ministers looked forward with Christian resignation to sacrifices to be made by the American colonies, in order to secure the blessings of peace for Spain. The French, said the Spanish prime minister, would become the victims of their own folly, and would find that the Americans, when once independent, would be zealous allies of England.[1] So if a treaty could now be made which would leave the contesting parties where they were, France and the colonies ought to be content.

But the English were in possession of New York and Charleston, and practically of three of the thirteen states; a truce for ten or twenty years on such terms would have left the colonies in evil plight. Yet Louis XVI, in the autumn of 1780, was in so despondent a mood that he was ready to authorize Spain to act as a mediator to secure peace between France and Great Britain.

At this crisis, as during all the war, Vergennes showed himself not only a friend to our country, but a statesman of no inferior rank. He was no international philanthropist, he considered first the interests of France, but he knew that a cowardly and unsatisfactory peace was neither for the interest nor for the

[1] Doniol, iv, 509.

fair fame of his own land. " If we impose on Spain
the duty of obtaining peace for us," he wrote the
King, "no one can answer for the results, nor assure
your Majesty that your reputation and your honor
will not be compromised." [1]

It was easy for a strong will to control the vacillat-
ing purposes of Louis XVI, but requests at this time
for still greater exertions in the war naturally received a somewhat languid reception. Rochambeau
transmitted to the ministry the messages of the Hartford conference, but any response was long delayed.

The French treasury was in need ; it was rarely in
any other condition, but the cost of the war aggravated its chronic distress. Yet Vergennes was not
discouraged, and the French government was not remiss in its responses to calls for aid. " It would be
a misfortune," Vergennes wrote, in February, 1781,
" if this campaign should pass like the preceding one,
without any important result. . . . We must occupy
ourselves in ending the war, and this we cannot do
without striking some great blow. If we succeed, that
will bring an honorable peace ; if we fail, we shall
not suffer the shame of having neglected anything in
our power to procure it." [2]

Not until March 9 was the answer to the propositions of the generals at Hartford formally announced. [3]
Their demands were not agreed to, and yet the aid
promised was of still greater importance. Rochambeau's request for ten thousand more men was refused,
and he was informed that the second detachment,

---

[1] Vergennes to King, Sept. 27, 1780; Doniol, iv, 488.

[2] Doniol, iv, 544.

[3] Réponse aux conclusions arrêtées à Hartford, le 9 Mars, 1781;
Doniol, iv, 584, 548.

which he had so long expected, would never be despatched. If more troops were required, the French government thought it best to supply Washington with money, so that he could strengthen his command with American volunteers. Accordingly, six million livres were promised, not as a loan but as a free gift, to be placed at Washington's disposal.[1] The most important decision was imparted in secret, for the information of Washington and Rochambeau. The Comte de Grasse was to depart with a powerful fleet for the Antilles, with instructions later in the year to sail to the coast of North America and there coöperate with the French and American armies in some joint movement against the English. "Provided we strike a great blow at the common enemy, and the result is fortunate, . . . the place of action is of no importance."

While the French ministers were ready to extend aid liberally, both in men and money, they felt very doubtful about the result. They had been discouraged by years of ill-success, and still more so by the difficulties under which their American allies now labored in obtaining recruits and keeping an army in the field. News of the mutiny of the Pennsylvania regiments had reached Paris, and it was feared that Washington's entire army might dissolve. Should this calamity ensue, said the instructions to Rochambeau, he must abandon the lost cause and sail away with his army to San Domingo or the Antilles.

The Vicomte de Rochambeau departed with these promises of aid, but the colonists were to receive from their French ally during this eventful year a still larger measure of assistance. Not only had Washing-

[1] Doniol, iv, 587.

ton and Rochambeau sent requests for help, but Congress had resolved on a special mission, to ask for money with which to pay the expenses of a war that could no longer be defrayed from American resources. In December, 1780, a resolution was passed that a special envoy repair to Versailles, and ask a loan of twenty-five million livres, in order that an army of thirty-two thousand American soldiers might be kept under arms until the end of the war. The demand was large, but the need was great.

This action was accompanied by parliamentary manœuvres, which, if they had proved successful, would have been most harmful. The most enthusiastic admirer of the Continental Congress cannot feel that it always showed wisdom in the selection of its agents. Intrigues in the halls of Congress resulted in the incompetent Gates being sent to replace the competent Schuyler, and were often directed against Washington himself. By similar processes it was now sought to displace the minister who, next to Washington, did most to secure success in the war of independence. Lee and Izard had returned from their unproductive errands abroad, and were doing all the harm they could at home. Of Franklin their denunciations were as persistent as they were virulent. If, said Lee in one of his jealous attacks, "the total disorder and neglect which prevails in the public affairs committed to him will not satisfy gentlemen that the continuance of him in office is incompatible with the public honor and interest," there is no use of my making further charges. [1]

If Franklin had enemies at home, he had firm friends in the government to which he was accredited. "His conduct leaves nothing for Congress to de-

[1] Wharton, iv, 184.

sire," wrote Vergennes. " It is as zealous and patriotic
as it is wise and circumspect. . . . The method he
pursues is much more efficacious than . . . if he were
to assume a tone of importunity in multiplying his
demands, and . . . in supporting them by menaces,
. . . which would only tend to render him personally
disagreeable." [1]

That Franklin made himself agreeable to the French
minister was a cause of offence in the minds of some
of his enemies. They believed that the way to get the
most help from France was to complain of the past
and threaten for the future, and that some patriot who
would bluster to Vergennes, with bad manners, and
in worse French, would obtain more than the smiling
plenipotentiary. No idea could have been more mistaken. No man could have obtained so much from
France as the minister who during long years combined unfailing tact and unbroken courtesy with unwearied zeal for the land he served.

The effort to remove Franklin failed, but it was
resolved to send a special envoy to urge the demand
for a loan of twenty-five million livres which Congress
now made. The choice lay between two of Washington's aides, Alexander Hamilton and John Laurens.
There was no one better fitted for such a task than
Hamilton, but the Congress preferred Laurens and he
was selected. The mission was regarded as of much
importance. No reply had yet come to the requests
sent from Hartford, and the need of immediate aid
was great. Washington, most of all, realized how
critical was the situation. A little before this he had
written Mason : " We are without money, and have

[1] Vergennes to La Luzerne, Dec., 1780; *Writings of Washington,*
Sparks's ed., vii, 379.

been so for a great length of time; without provision and forage except what is taken by impress; without cloathing, and shortly shall be (in a manner) without men. In a word, we have lived upon expedients till we can live no longer." [1]

He wrote Sullivan, who was now in Congress, to the same effect: "I will take the liberty in this place to give it as my opinion that a foreign loan is indispensably necessary to the continuance of the war. Congress will deceive themselves if they imagine that the army, or a state that is the theatre of war can rub through a second campaign as the last. . . . To depend, under these circumstances, upon the resources of the country, unassisted by foreign loans, will, I am confident, be to lean on a broken reed." [2]

With still more emphasis did he seek to impress upon the envoy who was to visit the French court in search of aid the importance of success in his mission. "Be assured, my dear Laurens, day does not follow night more certainly than it brings with it some additional proof of the impracticability of carrying on the war without the aids you were directed to solicit. As an honest and candid man, as a man whose all depends on the final and happy termination of the present contest, I assert this, while I give it decisively as my opinion, that without a foreign loan, our present force, which is but the remnant of an army, cannot be kept together this campaign, much less will it be increased and in readiness for another." [3]

A little earlier Washington had written Laurens:

[1] Washington to Mason, Oct. 22, 1780; *Writings of Washington,* Ford's ed., ix, 13.

[2] Washington to Sullivan, Nov. 20, 1780; *Writings of Washington,* Sparks's ed., vii, 297.

[3] Washington to Laurens, at Paris, April 9, 1781; *Ibid.,* viii, 5.

Without efficacious succor in money " we may make a feeble and expiring effort the next campaign, in all probability the period to our opposition." [1] " We are at the end of our tether," he writes again, " and now or never deliverance must come."

The words of Washington had their full weight at the French court; all recognized him as the bulwark of the American cause, they knew he would send no request for aid that was not justified, and that he would utilize to the utmost whatever assistance in men or money was granted. There were others who also sought to impress on the French minister the gravity of the crisis. The last campaign, La Fayette wrote in January, had been conducted by the Americans, without having a shilling, but that miracle could not be repeated.[2] Rochambeau told the American envoy to speak the absolute truth, and state the condition of distress in which his unhappy country would be unless she received prompt support.[3] The Americans were at the end of their resources, Rochambeau wrote his government, and if aid were not given, the dissolution of their army was not only possible, but probable.

Thus fortified, Laurens sailed for France, and he arrived there in March, 1781. The French had just transmitted, by Rochambeau's son, a promise to furnish six million livres to the colonies as a gift, besides sending a fleet under de Grasse, to assist in the cause. Naturally, still further demands were not agreeable when made upon a benefactor which was itself very hard up. Vergennes complained that he was beset

[1] Washington to Laurens, Jan. 15, 1781; *Writings of Washington*, Sparks's ed., vii, 371.

[2] La Fayette to Vergennes, Jan. 30, 1781; Tower, *The Marquis de Lafayette*, etc., ii, 194.

[3] Rochambeau to Washington, Feb. 2, 1781.

from every side, and that of requests for money there was no end. France was, unluckily for herself, the only country where the United States could get money. Nothing could be obtained from Spain; no other European country was willing to risk a penny in aid of the American colonies or to discount their promises to pay at any price. Frederick the Great wished them well, but not a groschen could be extracted from his firm grasp.

Holland was friendly with the states, and at war with England, but she would not lend a guilder unless the French King would guarantee the debt. Our country was ready to send ministers to Tuscany, to Russia, to any country that would receive them; rarely did they obtain a courteous reception, and never a dollar in hard money. An American envoy was looked upon as we regard an acquaintance who, if he obtains an interview, is sure to ask for a loan, and whose ability to repay is very doubtful. A few months before, Jay, unable to raise a dollar at Madrid on the credit of the United States, had written to see if the French King would not guarantee a loan of one hundred and fifty thousand dollars. "I experienced the sad sensation," he said in his letter, "of those, who already weighed down by benefits, are forced by cruel necessity to ask for more."[1]

Vergennes, with many apologies, had been obliged to decline this request; but when Franklin a little later asked for money with which to meet drafts for a million livres, drawn upon him by Congress with no provisions for payment, the French minister saved the American ambassador from bankruptcy. Those at home who declared that Franklin was an aged trifler,

[1] Doniol, iv, 388.

too absorbed in social pleasures to attend to his political duties, should have been comforted with the unbroken success with which their representative found
means to open the French treasury, and extract money
of which the French government itself had great need.

Laurens was far from an ideal envoy. He had little
experience and much impetuosity, he desired to storm
the French ministry, as, at the head of his regiment,
he would have stormed a barricade; he did not ask
aid but demanded it; he uttered few thanks and many
threats. Such conduct was little to Vergennes's taste,
and in his letters to La Luzerne he complained bitterly of Laurens's procedure. This officer "is little
familiar with the usages and consideration which are
due the ministers of a great power; he has made his
demands, not only with unfit importunity, but even
employing threats." [1]

But if the young officer was often indiscreet, and
sometimes impolite, he was assisted by the unfailing
adroitness of Franklin, and moreover the situation
spoke for itself. In a pathetic letter Franklin pressed
the claims of his country. " I am becoming old, I am
weakened by my last illness, and it is not probable
that I shall be long occupied with these matters.
Therefore I seize this occasion to let you know my
opinion on the subject. The present conjuncture is
critical. Congress is in danger of losing its influence
with the people; if it cannot obtain the aid it needs,
the whole system of a new government in America
may be overthrown." [2]

The Dutch would not lend to the United States,
but it was decided that Louis XVI should borrow of

[1] Vergennes to La Luzerne, May 11, 1781; Doniol, iv, 560.
[2] Cited by Doniol, iv, 540.

them ten million livres and let his allies have the money. This was added to the six millions already furnished, to the cost of the French troops at Newport, and of the expedition to be despatched under de Grasse.

Laurens sailed for home in May well satisfied with the result of his mission. "This court," wrote Franklin in a letter he sent with Laurens, "continues firm and steady in its friendship, and does everything it can for us. Cannot we do a little more for ourselves?"[1]

A little later Laurens arrived in Boston, bringing with him the money that had been raised in answer to the supplications of the American representatives. Louis had promised to assist the Americans in all to the amount of six million livres. A considerable part of this was spent in the purchase of arms, clothing, and ammunition for the American troops, but two million and a half Laurens brought with him in cash. It was a most seasonable gift; for it is hard to say how, without it, it would have been possible for Washington to conduct successfully his expedition to the South. It should not detract from the gratification which an American feels in the capture of Yorktown that it could not have been accomplished without the coöperation of French troops, and without the assistance of French money.

Not only did France increase her military strength in America in preparation for the campaign in 1781, but changes in administration relieved somewhat the scandalous inefficiency of late years. The average of administrative efficiency under the old régime was poor. There were indeed illustrious exceptions: Colbert devoted to the finances of the kingdom not only

[1] Doniol, iv, 562.

a disinterested zeal, but great ability; Louvois made
the army of Louis XIV the best-equipped military
machine in Europe; but the average of executive ability was very moderate. Of corruption there was much;
of inefficiency there was more; of indolence and neglect of duty there was most of all. By court intrigues
and personal preferences, most of the great positions
in the state were filled. The traditions of public life
were low. No man was thought the worse of because
he became rich through the opportunities of office, while
for the zealous reformer there was no room. Turgot
and Malesherbes and Necker were ministers of Louis
XVI, but none of them had a long tenure of power.
An ancient trifler like Maurepas was selected as chief
minister when Louis XVI became king, and held his
place for seventeen years, until death released his
grasp upon it. Sartine had been minister of the marine and Montbarey of war. Both were nobles, men
of the court and of the world, agreeable to Maurepas,
amiable and inefficient. Ships were not ready when
expeditions should sail; provisions were unfit for use,
or were not supplied at all; money flowed freely, but
the results were not to be seen. "The expenses of the
marine," wrote Vergennes in 1779, "are really frightful, and I was far from having a true idea of them."[1]
The Minister of War was no better. His private conduct, wrote the Queen, as well as the pillage which he
tolerated in his department, made it impossible for him
to accomplish any good.

These positions were now filled by men who were at
least far superior to their predecessors. Castries succeeded to the marine, and the Comte de Ségur to the
bureau of war. It was a son of the Minister of War

[1] Doniol, iv, 491.

who served in America in the patriot cause, and has left agreeable memoirs in which he has described the impressions produced on an habitué of Versailles by the modes of life he found in the remote west. They excited in him only enthusiasm. Ségur was one of the most zealous of the patrician youths who sighed for a new society and new modes of government, and who saw only felicity in a future which was to overthrow the class to which he belonged and bring to the block many of his associates.

The Ségur family displayed the contrasts so common in this period of unrest. If Ségur's views seem out of due season when France was assisting at the birth of a republic, and was herself on the verge of a revolution, he was an efficient administrator, and under him the condition of the army steadily improved.

Another change in the French administration had little effect on the fortunes of the American war, but was of evil omen for France herself. Necker, unlike his predecessor Turgot, was neither a great statesman nor a great man. He was, however, a person of financial ability and honest purpose.

The conditions of the French treasury grew steadily worse; the unfair imposition of its burdens and the repudiation of its obligations were potent causes of the impending cataclysm. If the French government would have paid its debts regularly, spent its money wisely, and imposed its taxes justly, the revolution, if not arrested, might have had a different history. Necker was honest and wise, he endeavored to strengthen credit, to prevent waste, and to check fraud. In one year five hundred sinecures were swept away. Internal duties which obstructed trade were abolished, the government received more money from its taxes and

made better terms for its loans. By his most famous
act, Necker published the "Compte Rendu" and gave
to the public some account of the use of the money
which was taken from it.[1]

If such acts pleased the public which paid the
taxes, and encouraged the bankers who bid on the
government loans, they aroused a spirit of discontent
among those who had favor at court. Every courtier
who had lost a position or feared to lose a pension
was ready to intrigue against the man who questioned
his right to live from the public purse. Necker was
harassed at every turn. The King was weak in his
support, Maurepas was active for his overthrow. The
minister was denounced as a foreigner and a Protest-
ant by those who hated him as a reformer and an econ-
omist, and in 1781 he fell from power. A successor
was found in Joly de Fleury, who fostered every abuse
and opposed every reform. As a result of his management the court was content and the treasury was
empty.

[1] Charles Gomel, *Les Derniers Controleurs*, chaps. 1 and 2.

CHAPTER XVIII

THE FRENCH TROOPS IN AMERICA

On May 10, 1781, the Concorde reached Newport, bringing Rochambeau's son and the Comte de Barras, who was to succeed Ternay in command of the French fleet. The intelligence conveyed was of the highest moment, for it brought a reply to the requests which Washington and Rochambeau had sent to France after their conference at Hartford. In some respects the answer was not wholly satisfactory; the ten thousand French troops that had been asked for were not to be sent, and it was announced that the second division, which Rochambeau had so long expected, would never set sail. These were discouraging announcements; but the aid now given, and the still more valuable assistance that was promised, atoned for any disappointments. Six million livres were brought Washington, that he might sustain his troops in the field; and such were their needs that, without this assistance, it is doubtful if even the small army which Washington then commanded could have been kept under arms.

But the most important intelligence was contained in Ségur's letter to Rochambeau.[1] The Comte de Grasse, so he was informed, had already sailed for the West Indies with a powerful fleet, and at some time during the summer he would coöperate in any expedition upon which Washington and Rochambeau

[1] Ségur to Rochambeau, March 9, 1781; Doniol, v, 466.

might agree. In view of this information, it was decided that the commanders of the two armies should
meet and discuss the campaign for the ensuing year.

On May 21 Washington and Rochambeau met at
Wethersfield. Rochambeau was accompanied by the
Marquis de Chastellux, while Washington was accompanied by Knox and Duportail. The generals
were not altogether in accord. Washington had long
felt that the capture of New York would be the
most serious blow that could be inflicted on the
enemy, and with the coöperation of the two armies
and the assistance of the French fleet, he thought
this was not impossible. Rochambeau was inclined
to think that operations in Virginia, in coöperation
with de Grasse's fleet, might be more efficacious.
The ships of one French fleet had been unable to get
over the bar at New York City, and this might prove
to be the case with the present expedition, while the
place was defended by an army equal in strength to
that which could be led to the attack. It was finally
decided that a movement against New York was the
only practical one at present. The French ships at
Newport were not equal to transporting the armies
by sea, and the march to Virginia by land was long
and arduous.[1] Intercepted despatches indicated that
Clinton would probably send some of his forces to
Virginia; either the English at New York might be
taken at a disadvantage if he did so, or the threat of
an attack might prevent his sending reinforcements
to complete the ruin of the American cause in the
South. It was therefore decided that the French
should march to the Hudson, and there join their
American allies in the hope of a successful movement

[1] *Writings of Washington*, Sparks's ed., viii, 53.

against New York. In the mean time a frigate was despatched to de Grasse to ascertain when and where his arrival could be expected. When the answer came, the commanders could then decide upon their future plans, so as to coöperate most efficiently with the fleet that the French admiral would bring to their aid.

If the arrival of a French fleet secured a naval superiority to the allies and made it possible to transport an army by sea, Washington contemplated the possibility of changing his plans and transferring the campaign southward; but the difficulties of the long march by land, the danger of disease in the southern climate, and the disinclination of the troops for such an undertaking, decided him to concentrate his forces upon New York.[1]

He was not without hope of success. Unless New York were reinforced from the south, he thought, the city would fall; while to compel Cornwallis to send troops to Clinton's relief would be a godsend to the struggling patriots in Virginia and the Carolinas. Accordingly he wrote Sullivan that at the Wethersfield conference it had been decided that both armies should take the field and advance upon New York City.[2] This letter, by some good luck, fell into the hands of the English, and Clinton's delusions as to Washington's plans proved so valuable later in the campaign that some have imagined the despatch was prepared in order to be intercepted. Nothing was further from Washington's thoughts; the letter stated the decision which had actually been reached, and it

[1] Diary, May 22, 1781; *Magazine of American History*, vi, 112.
[2] Washington to Sullivan, May 29, 1781; *Writings of Washington*, Sparks's ed., viii, 58.

was not until months later that the movement against
Cornwallis was decided upon.

Curiously enough, a similar letter from a French
officer fell into Clinton's hands and strengthened his
conviction that New York was to be the objective
point of the allies in this campaign. Chastellux wrote
the French minister at Philadelphia, stating that at
last he had induced Rochambeau to agree with Washington, and the siege of New York had been decided
upon. This letter was also intercepted; and as it
contained some caustic and unseemly criticisms by
Chastellux on his commander, it was forwarded to
Rochambeau, — "certainly not," writes the count,
"with the purpose of fostering peace in my military
family." [1]

It was debated whether Newport should not now be
abandoned, and the French fleet that was gathered
there take refuge at Boston. Such a change was approved by the French admiral, who desired to undertake a separate expedition in the North, and was little
inclined to a course of action that would result in his
serving as a subordinate in the South, with de Grasse
as his commander. After much discussion it was decided that the French ships should remain at Newport, from which point they could more readily reach
de Grasse should his fleet arrive at New York or the
Chesapeake, but that the army should join the American forces under Washington.

The eventful campaign of 1781 now really began.
It was the only year in which American and French
armies fought effectively side by side; and through
their successful coöperation the independence of the
colonies was forever assured. Not even Rochambeau's

[1] *Mém. de Rochambeau,* i, 274.

judicious course had prevented discontent from spring-
ing up among the French during the long months of
inactivity. His army was vegetating in sight of the
enemy, so said the grumblers; plunged in idleness,
with its only employment the monotonous toil of watching defences, it was a burden to its allies, consuming
supplies and rendering no service. The generals dis-
puted and the soldiers grumbled, the commander was
reserved and distrustful, the officers were dissatisfied
and querulous.[1]

Such discontents evaporated when the order for action was at last given. The soldiers had been comfortably lodged, and had suffered little from sickness;
their number was not much less than when they had
landed at Newport almost a year before. At five in the
morning of June 10, the French broke up the camp
in which for eleven months they had been stationed;
they were taken on boats to Providence, and there at
nine in the evening the first brigade arrived. At Providence they halted for a week, making their camp
on land adjoining the burying-ground. Washington
wrote, desiring that the armies should unite for joint
action as soon as circumstances would admit, and
thereupon the French began their march toward the
Hudson. On the 18th the regiment of Bourbonnais,
and on successive days the Royal Deux-Ponts, Soissonnais and Saintonge started on their way, keeping
a day's march apart.[2] Crowds of friendly onlookers
cheered them as they went. If the French had as yet
won no victories for the American cause, they had
made fast friends of the American people among whom
they had been stationed.

[1] Count Fersen, *Magazine of American History*, iii, 304, 375.
[2] Baron Cromot-Dubourg's Journal; *Ibid.*, iv, 293.

On the 23d the van reached Hartford, and the other detachments followed in turn. A local paper expresses the approval excited by their conduct and their appearance: "A finer body of men was never in arms. . . . The exact discipline of the troops and the attention of the officers to prevent injury to individuals, has made the march of this army through the country very agreeable to the inhabitants." This good conduct was rewarded by a good reception, and they met with friendly greetings; the farmers harnessed up their oxen to help the baggage trains at a pinch; at the cider-mills new cider was freely furnished to the thirsty soldiers.

Rochambeau decided that he must stop two days at Hartford, in order to mend the broken carriages and give a rest to the artillery horses and oxen. The movement of an army was attended with many difficulties in those days, yet the French proceeded, not only in good order, but with considerable celerity. The officers set an excellent example to the men; the Vicomte de Noailles and the Comte de Custine made the entire distance from Providence to the North River on foot, at the head of their regiments. The French aristocrats, who came over to aid the embattled farmers of America, had many faults and foibles, but they were good soldiers. In eleven days the army marched two hundred and twenty miles; the weather was at times very hot, but they bore it well, and their commander boasted, with good cause, of the fact that perfect order prevailed; more than half the officers marched on foot with the men; there was no waste and no confusion.[1]

On the 30th the French encamped at Newtown. There a courier arrived from Washington, stating that

[1] Rochambeau to Ségur, July 8, 1781; Doniol, v, 511.

he had planned a surprise of one of the enemy's posts, and urging Rochambeau to send on a portion of his force with all possible haste.[1] In compliance with this the Duc de Lauzun, with two regiments under his command, left Newtown at early dawn on July 4, in order to coöperate with the Americans under General Lincoln. Washington hoped to surprise a body of refugees under Delancey, then encamped at Morrisania, but the endeavor proved a failure. The English had received some intimation of the plan, and they were not taken by surprise. There was a little skirmishing with a trifling loss. The refugee corps made its escape and nothing of importance was accomplished. Lauzun mildly criticized Lincoln's movements;[2] some of the Americans suggested that Lauzun, with all his zeal, did not reach the appointed place quite on time. But Washington was prompt to recognize the celerity with which his allies had come at his request, and he never forgot to express an ample though judicious commendation. He now issued a general order thanking Lauzun, his officers and men, for the extraordinary zeal they had displayed in their rapid march and prompt action.[3] The commendation was well deserved; it was no one's fault that the English succeeded in escaping. To Rochambeau he wrote that, while he had not been so fortunate as to succeed according to his wish, yet from the opportunity to reconnoitre the enemy's position he hoped some benefit would result.

On July 5 Rochambeau met Washington at White Plains, and the two armies were at last united. Wash-

[1] Washington to Rochambeau, June 30, 1781; *Writings of Washington*, Ford's ed., ix, 288.

[2] Balch, *The French in America*, etc., i, 155.

[3] General Order, July 3, 1781; *Writings of Washington*, Ford's ed., ix, 295.

ington gave fitting recognition of this important event. In a general order he expressed his thanks to the Comte de Rochambeau for the unremitting zeal with which he had prosecuted his march, in order to form the long-wished-for junction between the French and the American forces. It was, as he truly said, an event from which the happiest consequences were to be expected; the future was to show that such expectations would be more than realized.

The impression produced was favorable on both sides. The fatigue of a long and hot march did not injure the brilliant appearance of the French regiments. The contrasts of white and pink, of blue and green, the well-setting long coats, the three-cornered hats, all had a pleasing aspect, and the manœuvres of the men were as precise as their dress. The French were well impressed, if not by the clothes, at least by the soldierly qualities of their new associates. The American regiments had no regular uniform, but their clothes were kept clean, their discipline was good, they supported heat and fatigue with ease. Their table equipments were the simple ones to which they had become accustomed by years of simple fare, varied at times by no fare at all. "Their cooking gives them little trouble," writes the Abbé Robin,[1] "they are satisfied to broil their meat and cook their corn-cake in the ashes."

The army now numbered about ten thousand men, composed equally of French and Americans. The American forces rested on the Hudson, while the French were at their left, their line reaching to the

---

[1] Abbé Claude Robin, *Nouveau Voyage dans l'Amérique Septentrionale dans l'année 1781, et campagne de l'armée du Comte de Rochambeau.*

Bronx. Rochambeau's headquarters were at Hart's Corners, near where the line of the Harlem Railroad was subsequently built.

Dinners to the officers were frequently given, and the difference in customs furnished the opportunity for some criticism. The French commissary, naturally critical in such matters, writes of a dinner given by Washington, that it was served in the American fashion and abundantly provided, but vegetables, beef, lamb, chickens, salad dressed with only vinegar, peas, pudding, and pie were all put on the table at the same time.[1] "They gave," he says, "on the same plate, meat, vegetables, and salad." The dinner was served in Washington's tent, and this, in part, may excuse serving many viands together; but after more than a century of development, the Americans are still inferior to the French in the judicious division of courses.

If the order of the dinner was faulty, the manners of the host made amends. Critical French officers recognized the distinction of Washington's bearing and felt the dignity of his presence. "He received us," writes one of Rochambeau's aides on July 5, "with the affability which is natural to him and depicted on his countenance. . . . His physiognomy is noble in the highest degree, and his manners are those of one perfectly accustomed to society, a rare thing certainly in America."[2] "In his private conduct," says de Broglie, "he preserves that polite and attentive good breeding which satisfies every one and offends nobody. He is a foe to ostentation and vainglory." "Brave without temerity, . . . generous without prodigality,

[1] *Catholic World*, xi, 797.
[2] Dubourg's Journal, July 5, 1781; *Magazine of American History*, iv, 296.

. . . virtuous without severity," says the academician, Chastellux.[1]

The manners of our ancestors seemed provincial to the habitués of Versailles, and doubtless they were so; but the French admitted that if few of our officers had the tone of polite society, and none of the men could compare in appearance with the regiments of Bourbonnais and Royal Deux-Ponts, they had the essential qualities of good soldiers. "The American army . . ." writes the same observer, " seemed to me to be in as good order as possible for an army composed of men without uniforms and with narrow resources. The Rhode Island regiment, among others, is extremely fine." And he adds a few days later : " I was astonished at the manner in which they march; perfect silence and order reigned, to which they added the greatest possible celerity. . . . An American regiment was sent forward to capture a Redoubt and marched under the fire of the cannon in the best style possible." [2]

The two armies were now united, but no movement of importance was attempted. Washington and Rochambeau frequently conferred, occasional skirmishes furnished some slight excitement, but this was all. On July 18 the generals, with an escort of one hundred and fifty men, crossed the Hudson at Dobbs Ferry, and from the Palisades observed the island on which stood the little town that has since become the greatest commercial city of the world. But no opportunity for a successful assault revealed itself.

[1] Marquis de Chastellux, *Travels in North America in the Years 1780, 1781, 1782*, i, 137 (ed. 1787).

[2] Dubourg's Journal, June 7 and July 22; *Magazine of American History*, iv, 299, 302.

On the night of the 21st, a reconnoissance in force was attempted. At eight in the evening five thousand French and Americans were under marching orders and slowly advanced during the night. At five in the morning they met at Valentine's Hill, four miles from King's Bridge. The Connecticut militia and the regiment of Soissonnais, Lincoln and Waterbury, the Duc de Lauzun and the Marquis de Chastellux, farmers' sons and the descendants of a feudal aristocracy, moved side by side, scouring the country around Morrisania and beyond. A few of the French soldiers forgot that the territory which they passed through was not a hostile land and indulged in plundering, but they were severely punished by their own officers. At Harlem Creek Rochambeau met with an experience new to him in his forty years of service. The reconnoissance was pushed on to Frog's Neck, and on the return the tide had risen and the bridge was down. The officers crossed in boats, while the horses were driven in a crowd and, following one or two leaders, swam across. The sight was a novel one to Rochambeau, who likened it to the movement of a great herd of wild horses.[1]

The wildness of the country and the novelty of the modes of warfare gave to these western campaigns an indescribable charm for many of the French soldiers. They were familiar with military movements in Flanders and by the Rhine, in a thickly populated country, and with great cities scattered about; with marches over well-built highways, some of which had been first constructed for the use of Roman legions; they were accustomed to the evolutions that were

[1] Mém. de Rochambeau; Balch, *The French in America*, etc., i, 162. Washington's Diary; *Writings of Washington*, Ford's ed., ix, 311.

possible where means of communication were perfect, where well-drilled soldiers could march in order over a finished country. They now found themselves amid very different surroundings. The people and their customs bore little resemblance to the peasantry of France or Germany, to the burghers of the Low Countries or the dwellers in sunny Italy. There was small chance for the tactics of Turenne or Vauban, where armies had to labor over almost impassable roads or make their way through primeval forests. It was necessary to learn lessons from the craft of the Indian, to avail one's self of the resourcefulness of the pioneer. Those who endeavored to carry on war in America on the model of a European campaign met with the disastrous overthrow of Braddock and Burgoyne. New phases of nature had to be encountered, new problems in warfare solved, new privations borne, new difficulties overcome.

Our French allies met these novel conditions with cheerfulness and skill. Occasionally some officer grumbled because the roads were impassable and his food was uneatable, but most of them found a relish in privations and enjoyed the campaigning. The men were equally philosophical in their trials and zealous in their service. To have served in the American war furnished a richer food for memory than to have fought by the Rhine and been defeated under Soubise. The abundant journals and memoirs in which our visitors told of their adventures disclose not only the enjoyment which they found in fighting anywhere, but the special pleasure they found in fighting by the swamps of the James and the banks of the Hudson.

The reconnoissance led to no important action, and the allies and the English continued to watch each other without daring to hazard a battle. Some of the French officers complained because no definite plan was formed, because the movements of the army were slow and Washington seemed fluctuating in his purposes. He could be nothing else. It was impossible, he said to Rochambeau, in the uncertainty in which they were, to fix on a definite plan of campaign; their measures must depend on circumstances, and on the situation of the enemy at the time of de Grasse's arrival.

He wrote in his diary on July 19: "I could not but acknowledge that the uncertainties under which we labour, — the few men who have joined, . . . and the ignorance in which I am kept by some of the states on whom I mostly depend, — especially Massachusetts, from whose governor I have not received a line since I addressed him from Weathersfield on the 23rd of May last, — rendered it impracticable for me to do more than to prepare, first, for the enterprise against New York as agreed to at Weathersfield, — and, secondly, for the relief of the southern states, if, after all my efforts and earnest application . . . it should be found at the arrival of Count de Grasse that I had neither men nor means adequate to the first object." [1]

The anticipations of any successful operation against New York were fast disappearing. Washington had been more hopeful of capturing the city than his French allies, and his disappointment was correspondingly greater. "We would have been in readiness to commence operations against New York," he wrote on August 1, "if the states had furnished their quo-

[1] Washington's Diary, July 20; *Magazine of American History*, vi, 122.

tas, agreeable to my requisitions." Unfortunately, they had been far from complying with the requests of the commander-in-chief, and not one half the men needed and asked for had joined the army.

He wrote the governors of the four New England states, calling on them in vigorous terms to complete their battalions, and to adopt effective means for furnishing supplies to their troops during the campaign. Unless they filled their battalions, he said, the result would be an inactive and inglorious campaign, and at that critical moment such a thing would be ruinous.[1] But these appeals met with very insufficient response. There was indeed little encouragement to enter the service; more as a result of vicious legislation than from any exhaustion of the national resources, the finances of the country were in a condition of collapse, the absence of any central authority left the army dependent upon the exertions of the states, and these were either slack in performance or unsuccessful in accomplishment.

"In view of this," Washington writes, "I turned my thoughts more seriously than before to southward." He had long contemplated transferring the seat of war to the South, and on August 2 he wrote to Morris, the superintendent of finance, suggesting the possibility of a movement to Virginia, and asking that vessels and supplies might be prepared for that contingency.[2]

The English, meanwhile, wishing to gather their army where the allies were to make a serious attack, executed various manœuvres, and each side was mys-

[1] *Writings of Washington*, Sparks's ed., viii, 124.
[2] *Ibid.*, 122.

tified as to the purposes of the other. A plentiful crop of deserters furnished either army with information more or less accurate. On July 30 news was brought to the American camp that Cornwallis, with a strong detachment from the forces in Virginia, had arrived at New York. This was important, but it proved not to be true. The arrivals were the garrison from Pensacola, captured by the Spanish and sent to New York on parole. But on August 11 the long-expected reinforcements from Europe reached their destination. Three thousand Hessians, thirteen weeks out from Bremen, landed at New York and were added to Sir Henry Clinton's army. He now had eleven thousand men, and the defenders of New York were more numerous than the forces that hoped to capture the city.

On August 13 news of this arrival reached Washington, but still more important information was to settle his plans and bring on the crisis of the war. It had been uncertain as to when, and where, de Grasse would make his appearance. Rochambeau had advised him to sail to Chesapeake Bay, but it was possible he might proceed directly to New York, and lookouts watched from the Jersey Heights, expecting any day that the French fleet might be seen sailing up the New York harbor. On the 14th of August information reached Washington that the fleet under the Comte de Grasse had sailed for Chesapeake Bay, and it shortly after arrived there.

CHAPTER XIX

THE EXPEDITION OF DE GRASSE

WE must now follow the fortunes of the expedition which had sailed from France under the command of the Comte de Grasse, and which was to exercise a decisive influence on the fortunes of the American Revolution.

The count was a member of one of the oldest French families. They traced their line back to a Prince of Antibes in the tenth century, and boasted that members of their family had intermarried with many royal houses. They had, at all events, a long and honorable ancestry, and their forefathers had for centuries acquitted themselves with valor in the wars in which France took part. François Joseph de Grasse was born in 1723, in the château of Bar, on a property that had belonged to his ancestors for five hundred years. His father was a captain in the army, but the son sought his fortune in the marine. In that service he worked his way with success, though without special distinction, and he was a captain when war was declared between France and England. He served under d'Estaing in the West Indies, and in 1781 was selected as commander of the expedition to be sent to America. His enemies asserted that he owed this command to court intrigues rather than to past service; his friends declared that he assumed it unwillingly and only by the express order of Louis

XVI.[1] However this may be, the expedition was to bring him permanent fame, and yet to involve the remainder of his life in unhappiness and disgrace.

Active preparations were made to equip the new fleet, and it was a more formidable reinforcement than any of those which the French had thus far sent to the assistance of their American allies.

The fleet sailed from Brest on Thursday, March 22, 1781. Privateers were so numerous that merchant ships delayed long for an opportunity to proceed under convoy; no less than two hundred and fifty sail, with cargoes valued in all at thirty million livres, accompanied the expedition. On the 29th of March, forty of them parted from the rest and proceeded to the East Indies under the guard of five men-of-war. Later, on April 5, the Sagittaire, with a convoy of forty sail, steered for Boston and reached there in safety. But the rest of the merchant ships were bound for the West Indies, and they proved a serious impediment to any rapid movement of the fleet. Before they reached their destination, each of the men-of-war had a merchantman in tow.[2]

The fleet proceeded without interference from storm or the enemy, and on April 28 the mountains of Martinique were sighted. The chronicler of the expedition expresses a relief which was probably felt by many of his companions: " What a vast desert does not the

---

[1] See *The Operations of the French Fleet under the Count de Grasse in 1781-2, as described in Two Contemporaneous Journals* (New York, 1864), 27, 28, 139. The author of the first Journal, the Chevalier de Goussencourt, asserts that de Grasse "obtained the command by his intrigues at court; the second diarist," an officer in the Naval Army in America, says that the count accepted the command reluctantly. The volume cited is number 3 of the publications of the "Bradford Club."

[2] *Operations of the French Fleet*, etc., 30, 32, 34.

solitude of the sea then present! . . . What a secret pain does not a man then experience who, accustomed to live with his fellowmen, lives but with the fish!"[1]

These gloomy reflections were dispelled by the sight of land, and, to increase the pleasure of the young Frenchmen, who were spoiling for a fight, they found themselves at once engaged off Martinique, with the English fleet under Hood. The combat was of short duration, and it was not followed by any action of importance.[2] The West Indies were the chief object of de Grasse's cruise, and any expedition to the United States was regarded as of secondary interest. But as matter of fact, the fleet accomplished little during its first stay among the islands, and met with serious disaster in the year following, while the expedition to the Chesapeake ended a long and momentous contest.

The future importance of the West Indies was then much overestimated. These fertile tropical islands were more considered than the colder and less alluring mainland, and both France and Spain attached great weight to their possession. Moreover, the French West Indies were enjoying an unprecedented season of prosperity, which naturally encouraged great hopes for the future. San Domingo was then an important possession of France. It has since come under colored rule, and from the accounts given by members of the French fleet of its former condition, we can see how lamentable a decline the island has suffered as a result.

At Cap François the fleet had their headquarters. It was then regarded as the most agreeable town of the West Indies, the Paris of the islands. It was the handsomest and, next to Havana, the richest city;

[1] *Operations of the French Fleet*, etc., 39, 40, 41, 140.
[2] *Ibid.*, 42–45, 141–147.

regularly laid out, built largely of stone, and enjoying lucrative trade. In the French portion of San Domingo there were excellent roads over which an active commerce was carried on, and the island aspired to become a rival of Jamaica in its products. Luxury under a hot sun had indeed brought its frequent result in a low morality. Some of the rich planters paid six and seven thousand francs for handsome mulatto girls, a great price for that period. The prosperity of this region has departed, without, it is to be feared, any improvement in its morality. Cape Haytien, to use its present name, has now hardly a quarter of the population of a century ago, and the whole island has sunk into anarchy and barbarism.

The English were not anxious for an engagement, and the French could not compel one, because the English ships were the better sailers. The French captured the unimportant island of Tobago, and the months passed uneventfully until the Comte de Grasse was ready to unite his forces with Rochambeau and the American army.

The count had not been unmindful of his instructions to attempt some enterprise for the relief of the American colonies; even before he reached the West Indies he wrote Rochambeau, saying that by the end of June he wished to be fully informed as to the strength and position of the English armies in North America, as a guide for his future action. Not before the middle of July could he leave the West Indies, and as the time for his stay on the American coast must be short, it was important for him to have full information at the earliest possible moment.[1] The time required for communication between these widely sep-

[1] De Grasse to Rochambeau, March 29, 1781; Doniol, v, 488.

arated forces added to the difficulty of the situation.
De Grasse wrote on March 29. Not until the 10th
of June did the convoy by which the letter was sent
reach Boston, after many vicissitudes and much bad
weather.

Immediately after the conference at Wethersfield,
Rochambeau communicated to de Grasse the views
held by Washington and himself. On May 28 he wrote
saying that, as it was impossible for the fleet under
the Comte de Barras to transport the French army to
Chesapeake Bay, a movement against New York had
been decided upon, in the hope of capturing the city
or at least of relieving the situation in the southern
states. After dwelling on the insufficiency of the army
for any important movement, he added : " Such is the
crisis in which America, and especially the southern
states, are now involved. The arrival of the Comte de
Grasse may save the situation. The resources which we
have can accomplish nothing without his assistance,
and the naval superiority which he can furnish us.
There are two points where the enemy can be attacked :
the Chesapeake, and New York. . . . You will probably prefer Chesapeake Bay, and it is there we think
you can render the greatest service." To this he added
a request that de Grasse would bring with him soldiers
as well as ships. The American and French armies
united would not exceed twelve thousand men, and if
de Grasse could bring five or six thousand soldiers and
a million livres, of which the need was almost as great,
he would render invaluable assistance.[1]

On the receipt of de Grasse's letter of March, Rochambeau at once despatched another communication,

[1] Rochambeau to de Grasse, May 28 and 31, June 6, 1781; Doniol,
v, 475.

in which he portrayed the needs of the situation in gloomy but truthful colors. He sought to impress on de Grasse the necessity for prompt relief in men and money. He informed the admiral of the contemplated advance on New York, and then added : " I ought not to conceal from you that these people are at the end of their resources ; Washington will not have half the troops he counted upon, and I believe, although he conceals the fact, that he has not now six thousand men. . . . Such is an actual picture of the lamentable condition of the forces in this country. . . . It is, therefore, of the greatest importance that you take in your ships the largest number of soldiers possible ; four or five thousand will be none too many. . . . I am certain you will assure us maritime superiority, but I cannot tell you too often to bring us also soldiers and money." [1] " You can see," he wrote again, "how necessary it is that you bring troops with you. This country is in extremity; all its resources have failed at once; Continental paper has become worthless."

Rochambeau had advised that the French fleet should proceed to Chesapeake Bay, but in a postscript he said that a letter of La Luzerne's indicated that Washington preferred that de Grasse should first make land at the Hook before New York, in order, if possible, to cut off the squadron under Arbuthnot. " I yield, therefore," he added, " as is proper, my opinion to his ; although the latest information tells us that the enemy's squadron, after anchoring a few days off the Hook, has sailed for the South."

While Washington regarded the capture of New York as the most serious blow that could be inflicted on the English, he recognized its difficulty and was

[1] Rochambeau to de Grasse, June 11, 1781 ; Doniol, v, 489.

ready to adopt other plans which his associates favored and which promised good results. Two days later he wrote Rochambeau saying that, while New York had been considered the only practicable object, other opportunities might present themselves. He then suggested that it might be well to leave de Grasse, in view of all the information he had, to decide for himself where he should first make land.[1]

This letter was forwarded, and the French admiral was left to govern his own conduct as he deemed most judicious. He decided on the Chesapeake, and there can be no doubt that he decided wisely. No one, indeed, could foresee that Cornwallis would allow himself to be captured with such ease; it might well have been expected that Clinton and the English fleet would make vigorous efforts to furnish him succor; but in any event the chance of important success was much better in Virginia than in New York. It is unlikely that the forces under Clinton could have been forced to surrender, even by the junction of an army and fleet as large as that which beleaguered Yorktown. An attempt to capture New York in the short time that de Grasse could be absent from the West Indies would probably have failed, and the campaign of 1781 have ended in disaster. The French might have wearied of an inglorious war, and the history of the American Revolution have been different.

An additional difficulty in a movement against New York was the uncertainty whether de Grasse's boats could get into the harbor. The passage was intricate and the bar would not allow the entrance of the great ships which now sail past Sandy Hook. The French boats were heavier than the English and drew more

[1] Washington to Rochambeau, June 13, 1781; Doniol, v, 491.

water. When d'Estaing made his luckless cruise, he was stopped at Sandy Hook, and not by any promise of money could he hire pilots who would undertake to guide his ships over the bar. Clinton was confident that de Grasse would be stopped by the same obstacles as was d'Estaing; those long-legged French ships, he said, could never get over the bar.

But de Grasse followed Rochambeau's suggestion and decided to proceed to the Chesapeake, there to take part in whatever enterprise might be decided upon. On the 28th of July he wrote Rochambeau a letter in which, referring to the appeals made upon him for help, he said: " I see with regret the distress in which the American continent is involved, and the necessity for the prompt succor which you ask." He then announced the steps which he had taken, and that on August 13 his fleet would sail for Chesapeake Bay, and in addition would carry three thousand French soldiers from San Domingo, under the command of the Marquis de Saint-Simon. "This destination," he added, " seems to be indicated to me by you and by Washington, Luzerne, and Barras as the best fitted to secure the advantages which you wish to obtain." When they arrived at Chesapeake Bay they would await further orders, but their assistance must necessarily be brief; the soldiers were borrowed and must be returned; his own fleet must soon sail back to southern waters. By the 15th of October they must all start on their return. " Employ me promptly and usefully that time may be turned to profit. . . . You will appreciate the necessity of employing well time that is precious." [1]

[1] De Grasse to Rochambeau, July 18, 1781; Doniol, v, 520.

CHAPTER XX

On the 14th of August the momentous letter of the Comte de Grasse reached Washington's headquarters. The situation required immediate decision, upon which might depend, and in fact did depend, the result of the war. When the letter arrived de Grasse's fleet was already under sail, and in two months they would start on their return. But during that brief period the allies would have an army of considerable strength, supported by a preponderance on the sea which they had not before enjoyed during the war. The possibilities were great and the time was exceedingly brief.

There was no delay in deciding on the course to pursue. For de Grasse to reach New York would consume some of the brief space of time he had at his disposal; there might be trouble at the bar, and there was a certainty of meeting an English army, hardly inferior to that of the allies even after the arrival of de Grasse's troops. In the mean time, Cornwallis, proceeding in his injudicious campaign in Virginia, and relying on the naval superiority of the English, was placing himself in a position that might be fatal when he should be attacked by a superior army on land, assisted by a powerful fleet at sea. When the critical hour came the decision was quickly made. On the day the letter was received, Washington entered in his diary that the shortness of de Grasse's stay, the disinclination of the French officers to force the harbor of New York, and the feeble compliance of the states with his demands for men, had compelled him to abandon his idea of taking New York, and he should coöperate with the French in a campaign in Virginia. On the next day a messenger was despatched to La Fayette, urging him to do all in his power to prevent Cornwallis from retreating into the Carolinas.[1]

The utmost celerity was required. The soldiers must march or be transported over three hundred and fifty miles, capture a hostile army, and all within two months. Such a march was a formidable undertaking in days when there were no means of rapid communication, and yet, if modern inventions would have rendered the enterprise easier, they would also have prevented its success. It took a long time to go from the Hudson to the James, but the news of Washington's approach could be kept from the victim in a way that would now be impossible. No telegraph wires informed Cornwallis of the dangers by which he was threatened, and such information as could have been given was delayed by the masterly way in which Washington concealed his purpose from Sir Henry Clinton.

Clinton had long been convinced that New York was the objective point of Washington's campaign, and in this he was perfectly correct; if he was slow to discover that changed circumstances had caused a change in the plan, every effort was made to conceal the truth from him. The soldiers were actively engaged in repairing roads that might be required in an advance on New York; at Chatham, near Staten

[1] *Writings of Washington*, Sparks's ed., viii, 134, 127.

Island, the French were busy erecting large bakeries, apparently to be used in the siege of the city.[1]

All, except those favored with Washington's confidence, were uncertain as to what the next movement would be. In a letter of one of the French officers, on August 15, it is noted: "Those who hoped we were going to Virginia begin to fear they have been deceived; the roads below here have been repaired towards New York; orders have also been given to repair those on the other side towards Staten Island, and even to build ovens there. . . . What to believe! This resembles the scenes at a theatre; the interest and uncertainty of the spectators constantly increase." [2]

The first movement was entirely consistent with an attack upon New York, and did not enlighten Clinton as to Washington's plans. The allied army was encamped round Dobbs Ferry and White Plains. A change to the other side of the river might well indicate an intention to move toward Staten Island and coöperate with de Grasse when his fleet reached New York from the South. On August 19 the entire French army, about five thousand men, and two thousand American troops marched to King's Ferry and prepared to cross the Hudson. The remainder of the American forces, some three thousand men, were left under General Heath. His duty was important and difficult; he was, so long as possible, to keep up the illusion that a strong force was before New York, and when that was removed, he must guard against a possible attack from an army much larger than his own.[3]

---

[1] Washington's Journal, Aug. 18; Henry P. Johnston, *The Yorktown Campaign and the Surrender of Cornwallis*, 88.

[2] Abbé Claude Robin, *Nouveau Voyage*, etc., 75.

[3] *Memoirs of William Heath*, Wilson's ed., 314, 315.

King's Ferry was about eight miles below Peeks-
kill, and Washington declared it to be the best and
only passage of the river for his army below the
Highlands. At two o'clock in the morning of August
20 the American forces began to cross, and by the
night of the 21st they were safely over. It was a more
serious undertaking to transport the French army.
They were more numerous, they had more baggage,
and they had heavy siege-trains. On the 19th rain
fell in torrents, and when the French halted for the
night half of their wagons were in the rear, stuck in
the mud. Not until the 22d were they encamped on
the brow of the hill at King's Ferry overlooking the
river.[1] All the ferry-boats that could be impressed in
the cause were kept busy. The weather was fine and
the sight was an imposing one. A large number of
boats were constantly crossing, bearing French soldiers arrayed in full military attire. They were commanded by the flower of the ancient French nobility,
the reading of whose names, as has been said, sounds
like a page from the chronicles of Froissart.

Not until the 26th was the entire army on the west
side of the river. Washington superintended the crossing, watching the operation from Verplanck's Point.
He was, wrote one of the officers, " manifestly elated
at the spectacle ; he seemed to see a better destiny
arising as he watched the French army embarking on
this expedition." [2] Weakened as his own army was, and
destitute of resources, this joint enterprise promised
the great success which was sorely needed.

Washington's headquarters were at a stately man-

---

[1] Dubourg's Journal, Aug. 19–22; *Magazine of American History*,
iv, 306–307.

[2] Blanchard's Journal; Johnston, *The Yorktown Campaign*, etc., 89.

sion, which had been the scene of Arnold's plot for the surrender of West Point, and had gained the opprobrious title of Treason House. It stood on a table-land, overlooking the Hudson for many miles. There he invited Rochambeau to breakfast when the French commander had crossed the Hudson, and on the high land about the house the French troops made their camps as they arrived on the west side of the river.

No sooner was the crossing completed than the allied armies resumed the march, but their movements were consistent with an advance upon New York. On the 27th the French officers were still debating whether the object was Staten Island or Paulus Hook, opposite New York, where Jersey City now stands. By the 29th the pretence could be sustained no longer, and, turning its back on New York, the army marched with all possible despatch to Philadelphia. From King's Ferry to Philadelphia was one hundred and thirty miles, and on September 2 the army entered that city.

The French occupied the right of the position and marched through Somerset Court House, Princeton, and Trenton, moving with rapidity and making about fifteen miles a day. The visitors expressed their approval of the country through which they passed. The roads were good, the foliage rich, the climate exhilarating, existence was a delight on those bracing plains ; the farms were large, cattle plentiful, and fruit, especially peaches, were abundant. The land needed manure, but apparently little else was required to make of Jersey an earthly paradise. The country was chiefly inhabited by Dutch, nearly all of whom were rich. The women who brought provisions to camp were adorned with jewelry, and their wagons, driven by themselves, were generally drawn by two or three spirited horses.[1] Princeton they found a well-built town, pleasantly situated, with a fine college, attended by fifty students. Trenton, though not as pleasant, was a larger place; it contained one hundred houses, while Princeton had only about sixty.

The level plains of New Jersey seem to have been more agreeable to our visitors than scenery which tourists now come from all the world to view. The taste for the picturesque, and certainly the taste for wild scenery, was little developed in the last century. One of the visitors praises the banks of the Delaware and says, by way of commendation, that they presented nothing of the sombre and savage aspect of the banks of the Hudson.[2]

The commanding officers had ridden ahead, and on August 30 Washington, accompanied by Rochambeau and Chastellux, entered Philadelphia. They were received with fitting honors. The object of the march had ceased to be a mystery, and the city was excited to an unusual degree of enthusiasm. On Thursday, says the "Packet," the commander-in-chief, Rochambeau, and their suites, were received by the militia light horse and escorted into the town. They dined with the Superintendent of Finance, and the ships lying in port fired salutes as the toasts were drunk, to the United States and His August Majesty, to the allied armies, and the speedy arrival of the Comte de Grasse.[3]

On September 3 the first division of the French

[1] Dubourg's Journal, Aug., 1781; *Magazine of American History,* iv, 376.

[2] Robin, *Nouveau Voyage,* etc., 84.

[3] Diary of Morris, Aug. 30; *Diplomatic Correspondence,* Sparks's ed., xi, 462; Frank Moore's *Diary of the American Revolution,* 1002.

army marched through the city, and the second division entered on the following day. It was an inspiring sight; the veteran regiment of Soissonnais, brilliant in pink trimmings and grenadier hats with white plumes floating in the air, astonished, so we are told, and doubtless also delighted the beauties of the town. The soldiers paraded in the presence of Congress, and the President of that body, not versed in the etiquette of the great world, asked if he should return their salute. Being informed that the French King was accustomed to salute his troops with kindness, the President profited by the royal example, for the "Packet" tells us that he took off his hat and bowed in return for every salute of officers and standards. The soldiers, so the paper continues, presented a most martial and grand appearance, and it adds with the fervor of the period, that the spectators were filled with gratitude to that noble prince, the soldier's king. "Angels," wrote the enthusiastic editor, "envy him his acquired glory." [1]

On the 5th of September there was a review of the French soldiers that was attended by a great crowd. Twenty thousand people watched the evolutions, which were performed with the utmost precision. The President of Congress was there; but he had not advised with the French about his dress, as he did in regard to the salutes, and he was arrayed in a long black velvet coat, which they found very extraordinary.

In the evening a great banquet was given by La Luzerne, the French minister. He entertained in princely fashion; covers were laid for eighty guests, and at the dinner there was a diversion that could be

[1] Dubourg's Journal; *Magazine of American History*, iv, 383 and v, 15; *Packet*, Sept., 1781.

provided at few banquets. " Hardly were we seated," writes one of the guests, " when a courier arrived. An unquiet silence prevailed among all the guests. All eyes were fixed on the Chevalier de La Luzerne, each one sought to divine in advance what the news might be. 'Thirty-six ships of the line,' he said, 'commanded by the Comte de Grasse, are in Chesapeake Bay, and three thousand troops have disembarked and are now in communication with the Marquis de La Fayette." [1]

The toasts were drunk with renewed vigor when the great news was announced, every one was filled with delight, our impatient warriors counted the time when they should be face to face with the enemy.

Philadelphia was then the largest city in America, and even those accustomed to European capitals found in it much to admire. The population was about forty thousand, the buildings were good, the streets broad and straight, and they were even provided with sidewalks. The shops were numerous and richly supplied. Some of the brick buildings on Market Street were of such proportions that the visitors called them immense. [2]

The town was seen at its best. The citizens had been fairly cordial in their treatment of the English army; the intense patriotism which at Boston scowled at invaders, was less pronounced in the City of Brotherly Love. Still, the prevailing spirit was loyal to the American cause, and the allied army was now greeted with genuine enthusiasm; even those who were not stirred by patriotic fervor were pleased at

[1] Robin, *Nouveau Voyage*, etc., 90; also in *Granite Monthly*, iv, 425.
[2] Dubourg's Journal, Sept. 1, 1781; *Magazine of American History*, iv, 380.

the good order, the good discipline, and the good clothes of the French allies.[1] The interest was greater because the object of the march was generally understood, and even the boys in the streets knew that Washington and the French soldiers had started to capture Cornwallis. Secrecy was no longer enjoined, as there was no danger of information being transmitted to Yorktown. The news of the arrival of de Grasse's fleet soon spread through the town; it aroused enthusiasm among the patriotic, and furnished excitement to all.

Washington and Rochambeau did not wait for all these reviews and dinners, but pushed on, eager to reach the Head of Elk and embark the army for its destination. On September 5 the first division of the French army arrived at Chester. Rochambeau took a boat down the Delaware, and, as he approached, Washington was on the bank waving his hand. The news of de Grasse's arrival had reached him, and he was aroused to a degree of elation very rare in him. All were impressed by an excitement so unlike his habitual reserve. "He threw off his character as arbiter of his country," writes the Comte de Deux-Ponts; "a child whose wishes had been satisfied could not have expressed a more lively sensation of pleasure." The good news was soon known by all, the prospect of capturing Cornwallis excited both officers and privates, and all were sanguine of the result.

Even at this critical time the need of money threatened to check effective operations, and only from the French could it be obtained. The American treasury was bare of anything except debts and paper currency.

[1] *Magazine of American History*, v, 13–18; Thacher, *A Military Journal*, etc. (1827 ed.), 264.

The small army which Washington still had under his command was eager for the southern expedition, and well qualified for the work, but it was in serious need both of supplies and money. On the 17th of August Washington wrote Morris, saying it would be necessary to give the American troops destined for southern service a month's pay in specie. To this Morris replied that he had none to give, and though he would make every exertion, he was not sanguine of success.[1]

On the 27th Washington wrote again asking that deposits of flour, salt, meat, and rum might be made at the Head of Elk, and entreating that the troops under his command might receive one month's pay in specie. Part of them, he added, had not been paid anything for a long time, they were going on a disagreeable service, and a little hard money would put them in a proper temper. As was so often the case, the money which the states failed to raise was furnished by their good ally the King of France.

"I made application to the Count de Rochambeau for a loan of twenty thousand hard dollars," says Robert Morris. "General Washington was extremely desirous that the troops should receive their month's pay, as great symptoms of discontent had appeared on their passing through the city without it. This affair being considered of great importance, I desired Mr. Gouverneur Morris, my assistant, to accompany me on account of his speaking fluently the French language."

The interview was had at Chester, and apparently Gouverneur's fluency was efficacious, for Rochambeau agreed to supply twenty thousand hard dollars, that

[1] *Writings of Washington*, Sparks's ed., viii, 134; *Diplomatic Correspondence*, Sparks's ed., xi, 431.

were to be repaid by October 1.[1] The necessity of the case had stirred Washington to a poetry of expression unusual with him. I cannot leave, he wrote, "without entreating you in the warmest terms to send on a month's pay at least, with all the expedition possible. I wish it to come on the wings of speed." [2]

The march thus far had been rapid and successful, but difficulties were encountered at the Head of Elk. It was at the mouth of this little river, running into Chesapeake Bay, that Washington expected to put his army on transports and have them carried to Yorktown. This would save a long and severe march through Maryland and Virginia, and with the French fleet in control of Chesapeake Bay, transportation by water would be both easy and safe. Before the expedition was decided on, Washington had written to see what boats could be obtained in case of need, and he had made every effort to have facilities ready. But when the army reached its destination, the means of transportation were lamentably deficient. Washington wrote to persons of influence in the neighborhood, beseeching them to furnish any sort of vessel that would serve the purpose, but few responded. There was nothing to do but to use what could be found; a thousand American soldiers and portions of some of the French regiments were embarked, and the rest of the army proceeded on foot. They pressed on, crossing the Susquehanna and averaging twenty miles a day over a woody country and indifferent roads, and by September 12 were at Baltimore. This city also impressed the French officers very favorably as a com-

[1] Diary of Morris, Sept. 5; *Diplomatic Correspondence*, Sparks's ed., xi, 464, 465.

[2] Washington to Robert Morris, Sept. 6, 1781; *Ibid.*, 467.

mercial town, well built, with straight streets, a feature which drew the attention of those accustomed to the intricate and devious highways of Paris and continental cities. They also noticed here the existence of sidewalks.[1]

Some of the French officers were too impatient to wait for the ships, and made their way overland from Baltimore to Williamsburg. They found the country monotonous. Indian corn and tobacco were the only crops, and the corn-bread, which was nearly all they had to eat, they unjustly denounced as " the meanest and worst thing in the world." [2]

The bulk of the army was transported by water. The first detachment, which sailed from the Head of Elk, made its way down Chesapeake Bay without molestation and landed safely on the peninsula. The troubles which the others encountered were relieved at Baltimore. The defeat of the English fleet by de Grasse enabled the French to provide the necessary transportation, and after the withdrawal of Graves, Chesapeake Bay was free from hostile ships and could be traversed with safety. Five frigates with nine transports sailed to Annapolis, and on them most of the army which had marched to Baltimore was speedily embarked. They had a prosperous journey, sailed peaceably into the James River, and landed without opposition. By September 28 the troops had taken their places under Washington's command, and all was ready for a vigorous siege.

Washington and Rochambeau did not wait for the embarkment of the army, but pressed on to reach the

[1] Dubourg's Journal, Sept. 11, 1781; *Magazine of American History*, iv, 441.

[2] Id., Sept., 1781 ; *Ibid.*, 443.

scene of action. On September 8 they left the Head of Elk, and on the same day reached Baltimore. There Washington received addresses from his admiring fellow citizens; but he did not tarry long.

They left Baltimore and rode through Virginia, making sixty miles a day, and on the 9th they arrived at Mount Vernon. Washington visited his home for the first time since he had left it on May 4, 1775, to enter the Continental Congress. There he made a brief stay, and entertained the French officers in his stately mansion overlooking the Potomac. His plantation had not suffered from the ravages of war, having been spared by the English. Fond as he was of his estate and the care of it, there was no time to tarry now. On the 12th he and his associates were again on horseback. They rode at top speed, and on the 14th they reached Williamsburg. There Washington assumed command of the allied armies encamped before Yorktown.

The accuracy with which the different sections of the army and navy formed their union was unusual, and reflected high credit on both the French and the American commanders. It was this which makes the capture of Yorktown a notable military achievement, as well as a momentous political event. The distances which separated the different forces of the expedition would be considerable now, and they were prodigious then. In July de Grasse's fleet was in the West Indies, anchored off Cape Haytien; the French troops under Saint-Simon were stationed on the island of San Domingo; while the army under Rochambeau and Washington was by the Hudson, and the fleet under Barras was still stationed at Newport. By land and sea these different detachments made their way to the scene of their common action. On August 3 de Grasse sailed from San Domingo, and a month later the French troops of Saint-Simon were landed at Jamestown. On August 25 Barras sailed from Newport, and on September 10 he made his junction in safety with the fleet from the West Indies. On the 19th of August the allied army before New York broke camp, they marched over two hundred miles by land, sailed down the Chesapeake, and on September 23 entered the James River. Not a serious mishap had attended the union of two fleets and two armies, which had been separated by sixteen hundred miles of land and water. The fleet under de Grasse had to come from the West Indies by a sea prolific in storm. The troops made a journey of over three hundred and fifty miles, a large part of it through virgin forests and over primitive highways. The extraordinary accuracy with which the forces from either section assembled at Yorktown assured the success of the enterprise.

The Comte de Grasse performed his part with great exactitude, and is entitled to a large share of the credit for the capture of Yorktown. He brought an important reinforcement to the forces on land, he prevented the English from relieving Cornwallis; the capture of Yorktown would have been impossible if his fleet had not arrived promptly and remained until the work was done.

Rochambeau had written in the spring and early summer, describing the needs of the American army and asking for prompt coöperation against the common foe, and de Grasse proceeded with vigor and boldness in the steps he took in answer to these pressing calls for help. No plan of coöperation had been marked out for him; in transporting a body of soldiers from the West Indies to Virginia he acted upon his own responsibility: he had to negotiate with Spaniards who felt no interest in the American allies of France; he had to incur the risk of disapproval from his own government.

On July 16 he arrived at Cape Haytien and found the letters of Rochambeau and the French minister, stating the importance of prompt aid to the American cause. He at once endeavored to meet these requests to the utmost of his ability. A considerable force of French troops was stationed in San Domingo, but the French government had agreed that they should be at the disposition of Spain and might be utilized for an expedition to Florida. Fortunately, the Spanish admiral was not ready for his Florida campaign and wished to postpone it until winter. De Grasse availed himself of this opportunity, and asked the French governor to lend him these troops for the interim. This was not an altogether simple operation. The French were careful to carry out their agreements with Spain, for the Spanish were rancorous in their outcry over aught left undone, and torrents of vituperation were poured out over the slightest delay or hesitation in the performance of any promise. People who complain constantly and acrimoniously are usually promptly served; the fear of reproach secures advantages to the termagant which are not always obtained by the more amiable. De Grasse had therefore to incur the risk of severe censure by his own government, if the troops he borrowed were not returned to San Domingo in readiness to embark for Florida whenever the Spanish asked for them. He was, however, able to persuade the governor that these troops could be spared for two or three months.

He could not obtain the five thousand men that Rochambeau had suggested, but it was decided that thirty-four hundred could be spared from San Domingo until November. They were borrowed from the governor upon the express promise that they should be returned by that time. In the mean time, Spanish ships were to keep guard of the island, and so indirectly the Spanish rendered some assistance to the colonists whose allies they had refused to become.

It was impossible also to obtain the amount of money which Rochambeau had asked for, and it was not easy to obtain any. De Grasse sought, without success, to borrow from some of the merchants at San Domingo, though he offered to pledge his own estate as security for repayment. He then proceeded to Havana to see if he would have any better fortune in raising money there. Seventeen Spanish men-of-war were then lying peaceably at that port, with the inactivity that was habitual in Spanish warfare. "Is it not a shame for these vessels to lie rotting two years in port?" exclaims our chronicler. "It is only a nation as cowardly as the Spanish that can wallow so in inaction, leaving its allies to bear all the brunt of the war." [1]

But if their fleet remained inert, the Spanish furnished de Grasse four million livres in cash, which was probably more useful than the coöperation of their ships. It supplied the necessities of his fleet and also left a considerable surplus which he gave to his associates in America. The necessary money being provided and the fleet now being off Havana, its destination was at last publicly announced.

[1] *Operations of the French Fleet*, etc. (Bradford Club Publications, no. 3), 63.

On August 28, after a voyage of twenty-three days, de Grasse's fleet anchored off the roadstead of Chesapeake Bay, and on September 4 and 5 the troops were landed at Jamestown Island. Cornwallis made no effort to prevent the landing; an enterprising general might have attacked the French in the confusion of disembarking, but the British left them undisturbed, and they joined the forces under La Fayette, who now had an army of seven thousand men.

La Fayette had been sent in the spring to take charge of the defence of Virginia, and early in May, when Cornwallis came there after his unfortunate campaign against Greene in the Carolinas, he found La Fayette stationed at Richmond with an army of some three thousand men, of whom the majority were raw militia; Cornwallis had high hopes that with his five thousand veterans he could soon trap the young Frenchman. He begged Clinton to send aid from New York, but declared, " The boy cannot escape me." As Cornwallis advanced, however, the French Fabius retreated and wrote to Washington, "I am not strong enough even to be beaten." Finally he reached a safe position across the Rapidan, and though Tarleton meanwhile made a very destructive raid, La Fayette was able, by uniting with one thousand troops under General Wayne, to prevent the British from seizing the military stores at Albemarle. Then La Fayette's force was augmented to some four thousand men and Cornwallis began retreating down the James toward Richmond. Though La Fayette was not strong enough to press him, the earl was anxious to make sure of his supplies and continued his retreat down into York peninsula. Cornwallis placed himself on Malvern Hill to keep watch, and meanwhile French and American allies were hastening to his overthrow.

Neither on land nor on sea did the French at first meet with any opposition, but on September 5 the English fleet under Graves at last made its appearance. It was too late to prevent the landing of the troops; however, if Graves could defeat the French fleet Cornwallis would be saved and Washington's expedition would come to naught; a decisive victory at sea would have rendered the capture of Yorktown impossible.

But while Washington's army was hastening from the Hudson to meet the French fleet coming from the West Indies, the success of his enterprise was assured and the fate of Cornwallis was settled. Earlier it would have been possible for Cornwallis to retire into the Carolinas, but after the arrival of the French reinforcements, to attempt this would have been a desperate chance. Unless, however, the allies could keep control on the water, relief was sure to come to him, and on the superiority which had so long attended the English navy Cornwallis relied to his ruin.

Whether Clinton did all he could to assist Cornwallis in his danger was acrimoniously debated between those generals in their life-time, and has been a theme for discussion ever since. Clinton had shown little energy or capacity in the campaign about New York. Cornwallis proceeded on his own judgment in Virginia, and between the two commanders there was abundant jealousy and distrust. Clinton was long deceived by Washington's manœuvres, but at last the truth was apparent even to him, and the fleet at New York was at once despatched to the Chesapeake.

The management of the English fleets in America

was as unfortunate as the leadership of the English armies. Rodney was the only admiral who displayed the qualities that had been so common twenty years before, and he at the critical moment was obliged to return to England. Hood took command of the fleet in the West Indies ; he was informed of de Grasse's movements and started in pursuit. His vessels sailed well, perhaps too well, for they lost track of the French squadron and reached Chesapeake Bay three days before de Grasse's arrival. Not finding the French there, Hood decided that they must have sailed to New York, and thither he accordingly proceeded.

In the mean time, Admiral Graves had done what he could to render the English fleet stationed in North America useless to the English cause. Guided by motives which no one can comprehend, he took the summer months, when the French and Americans were planning for an expedition in the South, to sail north to Boston. Having reconnoitred Boston to his satisfaction, he then proceeded to Rhode Island and set a watch upon the French ships stationed there under Barras, in order to prevent their escape. This would have been of some service if it had been accomplished; but apparently the watch was not diligent, for Barras and his little fleet made their way out without being noticed, and sailed off to meet de Grasse at Chesapeake Bay.

Finding that the bird had flown unseen, Graves returned to New York, after some weeks of idle sailing. By this time Clinton had discovered Washington's plans, and he realized the danger in which Cornwallis would soon be placed. Hood's vessels had arrived at New York, having missed de Grasse, as Graves had missed Barras; it was evident that the situation was critical and no time could be lost. Graves took command of the united fleets and at once (August 31) sailed south, and on September 5 they made their appearance at the mouth of Chesapeake Bay.

There they found the French fleet under de Grasse, and upon its defeat depended the possibility of rescuing the army under Cornwallis. The hostile fleets at once prepared for an engagement. In strength the French had some advantage, having twenty-four ships of the line, carrying seventeen hundred guns and about nineteen thousand seamen, while Graves had nineteen ships of the line and five frigates with about fourteen hundred guns.

The ships manœuvred for position, and as the wind finally brought them nearer together, about four o'clock in the afternoon the engagement began, and it lasted with considerable briskness until sunset. The French won no decisive victory, but they reaped the fruits of victory. On neither side did the losses exceed a few hundred men, but several of the English ships were seriously damaged. The French also suffered somewhat; the Diademe, which had been especially exposed, lost one hundred and twenty men, her rigging and sails were shot away, she received one hundred and twenty-five balls in her hull and twelve below the water-line.

For five days the fleets remained in sight of each other without attempting any further engagement. But the English fleet was seriously crippled and its position did not improve. The Terrible was so injured that the English blew her up; the Irish and the Richmond, separated from the others, were captured, and on the 9th the squadron from Newport under Barras sailed into the Bay. The English were now decidedly inferior in force, and Graves insisted that he could attempt nothing further until his ships had been repaired, and so with his damaged fleet he sailed away to New York.[1] Perhaps he could have done no more, but his failure sealed the fate of Cornwallis, who was now left without hope of relief, surrounded both on land and sea.

In order to bring together the armies and fleets which should coöperate in the capture of Yorktown, it was necessary, not only to overcome physical obstacles, but to sacrifice individual ambitions and quiet many heart-burnings. Unless the fleet under de Grasse had been strengthened by the arrival of the fleet commanded by Barras, which had been stationed at Newport, it is not certain that the French could have kept control of Chesapeake Bay and rendered it impossible for any relief to reach Yorktown. Yet it was with much difficulty, and only by the repeated solicitations of Washington and Rochambeau, that Barras at last consented to join an expedition of which, as he justly foresaw, the credit would belong to another, and there would be small opportunity for gaining glory for himself.

Rochambeau left the French fleet at Newport, under Barras's command, and there they remained quietly in the harbor until the letter arrived in which de Grasse announced that he was to leave the West Indies and sail for Chesapeake Bay. Perhaps de Grasse hesitated to summon Barras to take part in an expedition of which de Grasse himself would be the commander, and the glory of which would redound chiefly to him. At all events, he wrote Barras that it was for him to decide whether he would join the expedition at Ches-

[1] *Operations of the French Fleet*, etc. (Bradford Club Publications, no. 3), 66–75, 154–158; Report of Admiral Graves.

apeake Bay, or act on his own account, as might be most advantageous to the common cause.

Barras was eager to avail himself of the permission thus vaguely given. He had little desire to participate in this expedition as a subordinate; he was now in an independent command, and he sighed for some enterprise the glory of which would be his. It was easy for him to persuade himself that good military judgment coincided with his own desires. On the 12th of August he wrote Rochambeau that de Grasse did not count on him for assistance, and he thought, therefore, that he would sail to Newfoundland. He asked Rochambeau to send a speedy reply, and he would embark as soon as it reached him.[1]

This letter came as a thunderbolt to Washington and Rochambeau, who were about to begin their march southward. Each of them felt that the expedition to Virginia might decide the fate of the war, and its success could only be insured if the French maintained a superiority on the sea. Yet here was Barras, with a considerable fleet, instead of taking his ships where their assistance might be of vital importance, contemplating a voyage to Newfoundland that would probably be without any result, and by no possibility could have an important result. Nor had Rochambeau the right to give a peremptory order; he commanded the forces on land, Barras commanded the fleet; neither was dependent on the other; joint action could only be secured by the agreement of both commanders.

Rochambeau sent a letter forthwith, dealing very delicately with his associate, though stating with energy his own opinion and that of Washington. "I confess, my dear Admiral," he said, "that the project of

[1] Barras to Rochambeau, Aug. 12, 1781; Doniol, v, 522.

Newfoundland has a little surprised General Washington and myself." He then begged Barras to abandon his project. " I beseech you," he said, " come and join us." [1] Washington added a memorandum in his own hand, stating the probability that the English fleet might prove the stronger, if Barras persisted in his purpose not to join de Grasse.

Barras yielded to these appeals, but very reluctantly. He described the advantages of the Newfoundland expedition, and dwelt on the perils of proceeding to Chesapeake Bay, where de Grasse did not need him.[2] But if his acquiescence was sulky, his performance was prompt. He at once sailed from Newport, escaped Graves, who was watching for him with the dull inefficiency that seemed characteristic of the operations of the English in America, and reached the Chesapeake in safety. His union with de Grasse secured the superiority of the French fleet and was another link in the chain which held Cornwallis firmly bound. His action deserves the more commendation because the fate which doubtless Barras anticipated in fact befell him. De Grasse commanded the united fleet; it was engaged in a great historic undertaking which brought honor to the participants at the time, and to the chief actors a prodigious amount of permanent fame. But Barras was not a chief actor; he did his duty faithfully, got small reward at the time, and of the fame for which he longed, absolutely none at all. The names of Rochambeau and de Grasse are familiar to all Americans; even those who know little else of history, can tell who captured Cornwallis. But Barras is not on the list, and his name is unknown; he performed his

---

[1] Rochambeau to Barras, Aug. 15, 1781; Doniol, v, 523.

[2] Barras to Rochambeau, Aug. 17; Doniol, v, 524.

duty reluctantly but conscientiously, and reaped small reward except from the consciousness of virtue.

After the arrival of the French recruits, La Fayette had under his command an army of seven thousand men. The French fleet was unopposed, and it could furnish from the marines considerable assistance for a land attack. At that time a man-of-war carried a small army on board, and the entire strength of the fleet was over twenty thousand men.

The time for utilizing this formidable force was brief, for on the 15th of October de Grasse felt he must start on his return. It was now September, and there was as yet no sign of the troops under Washington or Rochambeau. There was a strong feeling in favor of an immediate attack upon the English under Cornwallis; if this seemed an attempt to gain the glory before their companions in arms could arrive, they had been warned how short was the time, and a great opportunity should not be allowed to escape on a question of etiquette. It was certain that under any circumstances there would not be time for the leisurely movements of a regular siege, and it seemed highly probable that Yorktown could be captured by assault. If the advice of some of the officers had been heeded, the attempt would have been made, and it is by no means certain that it would have failed. The resistance made by Cornwallis when the siege was undertaken was not so determined as to make it clear that he would have repulsed a vigorous assault. Considering the ordinary impetuosity of French tactics, the self-control now exhibited deserves much commendation. De Grasse had written on the day of his arrival at Chesapeake Bay that he hoped to find everything ready for the undertaking they had on hand. Five days passed, and yet there was no sign of the northern army. "Come quickly, my general, come quickly," one of the officers wrote Rochambeau; "the 15th of October is near. . . . I remember that a certain officer, being ordered to reconnoitre a fort, found occasion to capture it. If such a thing should happen to us, I hope you will pardon it." [1]

But it was finally decided that no assault should be attempted, and this decision was due to the calm and mature judgment which La Fayette displayed in every phase of our Revolutionary War. There was the chance of brilliant success, but there was the possibility of disastrous failure. Even more than by this consideration, La Fayette was controlled by a feeling of loyalty to Washington. He had the opportunity to snatch the glory that afterwards fell to Rochambeau and Washington; but with all his desire for fame, he never tried to obtain it unfairly. His orders were to hold Cornwallis in check until the general-in-chief could arrive. He had no desire to snatch the glory of victory from the one to whom it justly belonged, no wish to hazard the success of his plans by hasty action. "I hope with my own eyes," he had written Washington in August, "to see you at the head of the combined armies." [2] "Thanks to you," he wrote again on September 1, "I am in a charming position, at the head of a superior body of men; but I am not in such haste as the Comte de Grasse and, having a sure game to play, it would be folly by risking an attack to expose anything to chance." "Our young

---

[1] Doniol, v, 535–536.

[2] La Fayette to Washington, Aug. 21; Lafayette, *Mémoires,* etc. (ed. 1837), ii, 237–247.

General," wrote Duportail, " has a mature head, and with all his ardor he is able to wait the proper moment and will not gather the fruit until it is ripe." [1]

The French officers yielded to La Fayette's arguments; indeed, he was at the head of the army until Washington's arrival, and an attack upon Yorktown could only be made by his order; but he convinced his associates that delay was the part of wisdom.

On the 14th of September the commander-in-chief arrived at Williamsburg. At four o'clock in the afternoon the guns fired a royal salute as the generals approached. Washington and Rochambeau, accompanied by La Fayette, the commander of the American forces, and the Marquis de Saint-Simon, commanding the French, reviewed the two armies drawn up in battalion parade. The French officers then gathered at Saint-Simon's headquarters and were presented to the American commander-in-chief. An elegant supper was served, attended by all the principal officers; American colonels and French marquises mingled together in good fellowship; the French band played selections from French operas, and at the seemly hour of ten the feast was ended.[2] La Fayette's dream was at last realized, and he saw the united armies of France and America joined in a common enterprise under the command of Washington.

Washington recognized that success was only possible if the French fleet could hold its ascendancy on the sea; if Cornwallis were reinforced it would be useless to attempt the capture of Yorktown; on the maintenance of de Grasse's position in Chesapeake Bay rested the hope of victory. As soon, therefore, as

[1] Duportail to Rochambeau; Doniol, v, 535.
[2] Butler's Journal; *Historical Magazine*, March, 1864, 106.

Washington had reached Williamsburg, he prepared to visit the French admiral, and arrange with him plans for the capture of Cornwallis's army. The Comte de Grasse was stationed at Cape Henry, and on September 17 Washington set out with Rochambeau, Chastellux, and Knox, and by noon on the following day they reached de Grasse's flagship, the Ville de Paris. Washington was received with due honors, and the meeting was in all respects cordial. Not only his achievements, but his stately courtesy and perfect tact, peculiarly fitted him to deal with our French allies. The natural brusqueness of some of the American officers was distasteful to those drilled in the elaborate etiquette of the French court and French society, but Washington was as well fitted for it as if he had been to the manner born.

CHAPTER XXI

YORKTOWN AND DE GRASSE

WHEN compliments had been exchanged with due formality, plans for the campaign were discussed, and de Grasse agreed to furnish assistance as Washington desired except in one respect. Washington was anxious that ships should be sent up the James River above Yorktown to cut off the possibility of Cornwallis's retreat, but to this plan the admiral would not agree.[1] As Cornwallis made no effort to escape, the failure to guard this avenue of retreat was unimportant.

It had been announced that the French fleet must leave the American coast by October 15, and this was now less than a month off; but de Grasse agreed that the period should be extended to the first of November. Even then the time for the reduction of a well-defended town was brief, and the siege had to be pushed with vigor if it was to be successful. No matter what progress had been made on land, so soon as the French fleet sailed away, Yorktown could be relieved by water and the chance of capturing Cornwallis's army would be lost.

The return of the generals was delayed by the bad weather which is common on this roadstead. A violent and contrary wind came up, and not until the 22d were Washington and his associates able to get back to Williamsburg.

[1] Doniol, v, 554.

Cornwallis, meanwhile, hoped for relief, and the allies feared that a new English fleet might appear and destroy de Grasse's ascendancy. Admiral Digby had not yet been heard from, and the size of his fleet was multiplied by the fears of his opponents. De Grasse felt that he must prepare for the arrival of the English admiral, and the preparations that he desired to make brought dismay to the generals at Yorktown.

On September 24 he wrote them that he must sail out of the bay in order to meet Digby, but he would leave behind the forces under Saint-Simon. "If I am forced by the winds, or as the result of a contest, not to come back, have the goodness to send the regiments to Martinique on the boats left in the river."[1] This sudden announcement brought consternation. If de Grasse's fleet were driven to the West Indies by foul weather or ill fortune, it would be the end of the great plan for the capture of Cornwallis's army. Washington and Rochambeau were appalled at the possibility,[2] and yet they could not interfere in movements which de Grasse thought were required for the safety of his fleet. Fortunately, the matter was not brought to a decision. The fleet under Digby did not appear at all, and de Grasse remained quietly in the bay, shutting off all relief from the besieged city.

During the time that the armies were assembling it was possible for Cornwallis to avoid his fate, if he had broken through La Fayette's forces and made his escape southward; but either because he did not realize his peril or deemed the effort dangerous, he did not attempt it.

[1] De Grasse to Rochambeau, Sept. 24, 1781; Doniol, v, 544.

[2] Doniol, v, 545; *Writings of Washington*, Sparks's ed., viii, 163–165.

The only hope of escape after the siege began lay in its prolongation. The Comte de Grasse had extended his stay somewhat and doubtless would have been reluctant to sail away when success seemed near at hand; but the operations in the West Indies, really so much less important, he regarded as his chief mission, and he was certain to sail from Chesapeake Bay before the winter began.

The allies pressed their work with vigor, and the besieged made a feeble defence. On the 30th the exterior fortifications were abandoned, and for a week the French and Americans labored zealously in preparing fascines and trenches. On the 6th of October the trenches were sufficiently completed to cover the men, and on the 9th the batteries opened fire on the English forces before Yorktown.

On October 12 the second parallel was begun. The work was carried on vigorously under officers familiar with siege operations, and it progressed the more rapidly because the English made little attempt to check it. On the 14th Washington made a note of the casualties down to that day, which showed how slight had been the resistance, and also showed the preponderant part taken by our allies in what Cromwell would have called the " Great Deliverance." The Americans had lost twenty-three killed and sixty-five wounded. The French loss also was small, but it was more than twice that of the American army, and consisted of fifty-two killed and one hundred and thirty-four wounded.[1]

Each army praised the conduct of its associates and with good cause. The Americans, said Rochambeau, showed a courage and an emulation which never

[1] *Writings of Washington*, Sparks's ed., viii, 181.

allowed them to lag behind their allies, though these were more familiar with the operations of a siege. The French had the advantage of more experience in such matters, and exhibited equal courage and zeal. The operations were singularly free from bickerings and heart-burnings. All coöperated amicably, and there was no wrangling over the praise to be awarded. Washington and Rochambeau displayed moderation and judgment, and their example furnished a model for others to follow. The joint operations against Newport in 1778 had been attended with disputes and ended in reproach; the fact that Sullivan commanded the Americans at Newport and Washington at Yorktown accounted for the difference in the spirit displayed as well as in the result accomplished.

On October 9 the allies were ready to begin an active bombardment, and on the 17th Cornwallis sent a flag of truce to consider terms of surrender. Two weeks remained of the time de Grasse had agreed to stay when the English general began to parley; only seventeen days had passed since the siege formally began. The importance of the victory was only exceeded by its ease; the English army was mild in resistance and prompt in surrender, and yet the disparity in numbers was less than in many a siege which has been long and stubbornly contested. The allied army contained about 15,000 men, and 7157 laid down their arms.[1]

The ease of the victory seems to have been regretted by some who loved war for the fighting there was in it. " I have wrott to you twice during the siege," says an ally whose zeal for our liberty surpassed his mastery of our grammar. " I hope my letters are arrived safe into your hands. Our successes have not, indeed,

[1] H. P. Johnston, *The Yorktown Campaign*, etc., 165, 195.

costed very dear to us. However, we must not measure our glory by the dangers we run to obtain it, but by their utility. Cornwallys, the Southern Lyon, has been very tame to us." [1]

It was for Washington to fix the terms of the surrender; those which he imposed were not severe, but they were humiliating. The English were forced to march in solemn parade before their victors and stack their arms; the bands were instructed to play " The World Turned Upside Down." The English had insisted on similar terms when Lincoln surrendered at Charleston. They could not now complain, but they did not relish the requirements. It was undoubtedly a relief to British sensibilities that a large portion of the army to which they surrendered was composed of French. The French were hereditary enemies, they were the regular troops of an ancient monarchy, and they could be regarded as professionals in the art of war; it was less humiliating to yield to them than to American soldiers whom they stigmatized as rebels and despised as irregulars.

Washington signed the articles of capitulation for the Americans, Rochambeau and Barras for their French allies, and Cornwallis and Thomas Symonds for the English. On October 19 the momentous ceremony took place. The English desired to surrender to their French opponents and not to their rebellious subjects; but no desire for spectacular triumph induced Rochambeau to disregard the strictest observance of the proprieties. One of the French visitors has described the scene at the surrender. The lines of the allied army extended for more than a mile; the Americans holding the right. The youth of many of the American

[1] Marquis de Fleury, Oct. 31, 1781.

troops, their lack of uniforms, their dirty and torn clothes, made the French appear to advantage ; for they, notwithstanding their long march and the fatigue of the siege, preserved a neat and warlike aspect. All were surprised by the good condition of the English troops. They had not suffered sufficiently from the siege to injure their health or their looks. The English soldiers were all smartly dressed in new clothes, but this, says our writer, seemed to humiliate them the more, as they contrasted themselves with their American opponents. They dared not lift their eyes upon their conquerors, he declares. The English officers were polite enough to salute the least important French officer, but they would not condescend to salute Americans even of the highest rank.[1]

Notwithstanding the completeness of the victory, it was not supposed that the English would abandon their endeavors to reduce the colonists to subjection. " It is not in the character of the English to yield so easily," Vergennes wrote La Fayette ; " you must expect great efforts on their part to recover what they have lost " ; and he bade the marquis to excite the Americans to greater exertions, in order that they might retain the advantage which had been gained.[2]

Washington had the same expectations, and he was, therefore, the more anxious to utilize still further the assistance which had already secured so great a victory. De Grasse had originally written that by October 15 he must sail for the West Indies, but he agreed to remain until November in order that the capture of Yorktown might be assured. On the 19th day of October, the English army surrendered, and Washington, stim-

[1] Abbé Robin, *Nouveau Voyage*, etc. (1782 ed.), 140, 141.
[2] Vergennes to La Fayette, Dec. 1, 1781 ; Doniol, iv, 688.

ulated by the success of this joint action of army and navy, wished to make new endeavors. On the day Cornwallis surrendered he wrote de Grasse, suggesting a further expedition for the capture of Charleston. The capture of that city, he said, would be certain, and would destroy the enemy's last hope of continuing the war. The proposition was gilded with alluring suggestions. "It will depend upon your excellency, therefore," wrote Washington, "to terminate the war, and enable the allies to dictate the law in a treaty. A campaign so glorious and so fertile in consequences could be reserved only for the Count de Grasse."[1]

These compliments, however adroit, did not accomplish their aim. The date had already passed at which de Grasse intended to sail for the West Indies, and he would not further delay his return. Washington had contemplated the possibility of this, and he suggested another and less ambitious scheme. If de Grasse did not find the expedition against Charleston practicable, he might convey a body of soldiers to Wilmington, who would capture that town and thus render valuable assistance to General Greene in his campaign in the Carolinas. To this plan de Grasse at first gave his consent. The orders of his court and his engagements with the Spanish, so he wrote, rendered it impossible for him to remain for the expedition against Charleston, but he would transport two thousand troops to Wilmington, provided they sailed by November 1, or as soon as possible thereafter.[2]

But before the expedition could be prepared, de Grasse withdrew his offer. The matter of his return

---

[1] Washington to Count de Grasse, Oct. 20, 1781; *Writings of Washington*, Sparks's ed., viii, 186.

[2] Doniol, iv, 694.

to the West Indies might be too much delayed. The undertaking was abandoned, and the troops sent to reinforce Greene had to make their way by land. Though disappointed in his hopes of further aid at present, Washington fully expected the coöperation of de Grasse in the following campaign.

On November 4 the French fleet sailed out of Chesapeake Bay.[1] De Grasse left the scene of triumph behind him and sailed away to defeat and disgrace.

The vicissitudes of the war in the West Indies did not affect the interests of the American colonists, but they deserve some brief mention. As a result of the assistance given the United States, France found herself involved in hostilities in Europe, the East Indies, and the Western Main; the sun never set on the contest which had grown out of the protest of American colonists against illegal taxation.

Exultant over the great success of the Virginia campaign, de Grasse set sail for the West Indies. There was the field to which he was specially bidden to devote his energies; his interference in North America had been regarded as an interlude, and he now returned to the contest with Great Britain for the West Indian islands. After a stormy passage of three weeks, the fleet reached Martinique, and during the winter months it achieved some small successes. There were a few unimportant engagements, but not until the spring did the decisive action take place. On April 12, 1782, near some West Indian islands known as "The Saints," the fleet under de Grasse engaged the English under Rodney in what one of

[1] *Operations of the French Fleet*, etc. (Bradford Club Publications, no. 3), 88, 164.

the French officers pronounced the hottest and most terrible, and also the most disastrous, of sea-fights since the invention of gunpowder.

The English had the advantage in numbers: they had about forty ships of the line and over twenty-six hundred cannon, while the French mustered thirty-three ships of the line and about two thousand cannon. More important to the English than this preponderance of ships and cannon was their superiority in the officers who commanded them. In the weary investigations which followed this disastrous day, it was decided that de Grasse was not deserving of censure, and also, on the other hand, despite his accusations, that his commands were not disobeyed by disloyal subordinates. If he was guilty of no grave mistake, he showed no military genius; but it is without question that some of his officers were disaffected and viewed with pleasure the defeat of their commander. Possibly the desire for personal distinction was stronger with the French than with the English; certainly disappointment in this respect seemed to bring more harmful results; some of de Grasse's captains were discontented and they managed their ships with an inefficiency that came perilously close to disloyalty.

Doubtless there were heart-burnings among the English also, — they are found in every army and every fleet; but they did not show themselves in the day of battle; the English captain who believed Rodney had not treated him fairly did not think Rodney's defeat would be a consolation to his lacerated feelings; but in this disastrous battle, and in many an encounter on land and sea, some French officer, rankling over a real or supposed injustice, forgot his duty to his country in his enmity toward his commander or his associates.

The battle of the 12th was brought on because an ill-managed vessel, after running into several other ships, was at last left unmasted at the mercy of the enemy. Some English boats started to capture the luckless Zélé, the French fleet formed for action to protect her, and the engagement began. The manœuvres of the French have been severely criticized, and of every blunder Rodney took advantage. The Comte de Grasse showed abundant courage but little skill; his ship was in the thickest of the fight until her ammunition was exhausted and she was forced to surrender; the flagship of the admiral fell into the hands of the enemy, — a disgrace which had attended few French defeats. The crew fought with desperation, if not with judgment; rigging was gone as well as rudder, the masts were ready to fall and the ship to sink, when the flag was at last pulled down. Critics at Paris said it would have been more glorious to blow up the flagship than to allow her to be taken. But de Grasse's friends justly replied that even an admiral had no right to blow up his crew in order to save his own honor. Before he surrendered, the admiral signalled the other ships to save themselves as best they could; at half-past seven the battle was over.

The French had lost three thousand men and five ships. To add to the horrors of the fight, the sharks that abound in those waters followed its progress, in search of food; over a thousand of them, it is said, were close by the ships, watching for the bodies that were constantly thrown over. What was left of the French fleet found refuge at Cap François, and their last degradation was in seeing ten Spanish ships come out to protect their entrance into the harbor.[1]

The credit which de Grasse won at Yorktown was wholly obscured by the defeat of his fleet at "The Saints." The capture of Yorktown assured the independence of the United States; but its importance was hardly appreciated at the time; no one realized how great a power the United States was to become, or what weight attached to the victory by which its existence was assured. While the French had taken an important part in the capture of Cornwallis's army, after all they acted as auxiliaries, and it seemed an American rather than a French victory.

On the other hand, the defeat which de Grasse had sustained at "The Saints" was one of the most disastrous in the disastrous history of the French navy. His fleet was practically destroyed; the admiral's ship was sunk and the admiral himself captured. Nothing could be more irretrievable. It is not strange, therefore, that, when de Grasse was finally released from captivity and returned to Paris, he met with a chilly reception from King and court. He insisted upon a court-martial, and it was accorded to him. After long and tedious investigation he was exonerated from blame, but he remained a disgraced man, and he was never again assigned to active service. He married for a third time and married unwisely. His wife brought him social reproach and domestic infelicity. Honors were heaped upon Rochambeau, who had taken part in the Yorktown expedition; but though de Grasse's coöperation had assured the suc-

[1] *Operations of the French Fleet*, etc. (Bradford Club Publications, no. 3), 120–126, 176–178. Capt. A. T. Mahan, *The Influence of Sea Power upon History* (1889), 481–504.

cess of the enterprise, he received no marks of royal approval; subsequent disasters had obscured the recollection of prior service. In January, 1788, he died. Washington wrote to Rochambeau regretting his death, but he added: "Yet his death is not, perhaps, so much to be deplored as his latter days were to be pitied. It seemed as if an unfortunate and unrelenting destiny pursued him, to destroy the enjoyment of all earthly comfort. The disastrous battle of the 12th of April, the loss of favor with his King, and the subsequent connection in marriage with an unworthy woman, were sufficient to have made him weary of the burden of life."[1]

[1] *Writings of Washington*, Ford's ed., xi, 259.

CHAPTER XXII

THE surrender of Yorktown proved to be the end of the Revolutionary War, but its importance was not at first realized, even by the victors. The French army remained for a year longer in America, and at the close of 1781 all looked forward to an active campaign in the following year.

After the surrender, Washington and the northern army returned to the Hudson. The Continentals under La Fayette were transferred to Greene, the militiamen went home. Rochambeau and his command went into winter-quarters near Williamsburg in Virginia. They were looked on askance by the people among whom they were quartered; the Virginians were anxious to believe that the war was over, and they did not wish to see either friendly or hostile troops. An army is usually a poor neighbor, but Rochambeau's soldiers, both in New York and Virginia, were kept in extraordinarily good order. Among a strange people, whose language they could not understand, the French soldiers maintained a strict discipline. Rochambeau endeavored to quiet the burghers of Williamsburg by telling of the good record his troops had made during a march of seven hundred miles. They were little comforted by this, but when Rochambeau proceeded to repair, at his own expense, any injuries done, the fears of the townspeople were somewhat quieted. The French during the winter were treated with reasonable cordiality by those whose liberties they came to establish.

While Rochambeau was endeavoring to get from France instructions as to the coming campaign, he desired himself to be relieved from duty. He had asked for his recall some time before, and only by fortunate circumstances was he kept in command and enabled to share in the glory of Yorktown. His statue would not stand in front of the White House at Washington had his first request for a release been granted.

In June, 1781, four months before the siege of Yorktown, he asked for his recall. His health had long been poor, the campaign in America thus far had not been productive of glory, and he was anxious to return to France. Fortunately for his fame, this request experienced the delays of the period. Not until the 24th of August did it receive attention in Paris. The demand was a reasonable one and was promptly granted, and on that day Ségur, the minister of war, wrote Rochambeau that he had communicated to the King his wish to return to France to reëstablish his health; and that the King had approved the request, leaving the count to fix the time of his return whenever he thought that his presence was no longer necessary and that no injury would result to the good of the service. He was directed to turn over the command of the army to the Baron de Vioménil. The despatch reached Boston on the 6th of November, but not until the 6th of December did it reach Rochambeau at his headquarters.

The campaign of Yorktown was now over, the war was ended, and there was no reason why he should not return to France. " The air of Virginia," he writes,

" while healthy in winter, is laden with fever in the summer, and I have never failed to catch a fever wherever I have found it epidemic." In the mean time Vioménil had been obliged to go back to France on account of his health, but he returned, and when Rochambeau left, the remaining French troops were placed under his command.

Ségur congratulated Rochambeau on these fortunate delays. " I am persuaded," he writes him on the 7th of December, " that, notwithstanding your poor condition of health on the 20th of October, you are well pleased that you had not received consent for the leave of absence which you had asked."

Not until June, 1782, did the French army start on its march northward. No plans were made for the campaign, because it now became evident that with the surrender of Yorktown the war had practically ceased. Parliament had voted to acknowledge the independence of the colonies, and negotiators were already engaged in agreeing on terms of peace. The war had become a picnic, and the anxieties and hardships of the past were succeeded by a year of leisure and comfort. At Baltimore the detachments united, and from there they marched north until, on September 14, they reached the Hudson.

Social diversions replaced military activity during this peaceful summer. A son was born to Louis XVI, who was not destined to inherit his throne, but the event was celebrated in a manner befitting its supposed importance. Washington had proper demonstrations in his army: the soldiers paraded, a great dinner was given, and a ball closed the day. The French minister at Philadelphia celebrated the event with special splendor. Eleven hundred tickets were issued for the entertainment. "The ladies," so read the card, "will be so obliging as to provide them-selves with partners before the evening." There was abundant opportunity for the dancing that was so carefully regulated. A dancing-room was erected, forty feet by sixty, and when the guests were weary of this they could walk into a garden, arranged in the highest style of eighteenth-century art.

Hairdressing for men and women was then an elaborate process, and the artists of Philadelphia were hardly equal to the demand. At six in the morn-ing of the great day many ladies were found in the hands of their coiffeurs. Ten thousand outsiders were given an opportunity to watch the eleven hundred elect, and some Quaker ladies, who were unwilling to adapt their dresses to the occasion, looked at their more worldly sisters through a gauze curtain pre-pared for their use. Even the eleven hundred were truly republican: there were found among them repre-sentatives of the army and the professions, of mer-chants and tradesmen, of families old and new, as we are told by a Philadelphian who himself belonged to one of the old families. The gayeties of our ancestors were not carried to excess; by three o'clock in the morning all the guests had retired and the house of the minister was dark.

In September the French army marched to King's Ferry, where it was received with due honors by the Continental forces under Washington. The American soldiers were drawn up in a double line, and through this the allies passed, the drums beating a French march.[1] Rochambeau had commended highly the good

[1] *Mémoires de Rochambeau*, i, 309; James Thacher, *A Military Journal*, etc., 312.

bearing of the American troops, and declared that Steuben had made of them soldiers worthy of the King of Prussia. Their appearance was certainly more pleasing now than in the trying years of the war. Large supplies of clothing had been sent from France, and large amounts had been captured at Yorktown. All of the latter the French had abandoned to their allies, who certainly stood in need of them, and for almost the first time, the American soldiers had stout clothing to cover their stout hearts.

There was no more fighting for them, and the French troops began their march to Boston in order to be ready for the homeward journey. As they were leaving, an incident occurred which showed that seven years of conflict had not accustomed our people to the usages of war. As Rochambeau was about to start at the head of his staff, a sheriff appeared with a summons in his hand, and, tapping the general on the shoulder, said, "You are my prisoner." Some of the young officers wished to resent such conduct, but Rochambeau more sensibly contented himself with telling the sheriff to take his prisoner away if he could. The sheriff replied that he had done his duty, and if the general decided to set justice at defiance, he only asked for himself a safe retreat.[1]

The writ was issued for the value of some trees, which one of the French regiments had cut down for firewood. The owner seems to have been more enterprising than patriotic. Rochambeau amiably submitted the matter to the court, which awarded two thousand francs instead of fifteen thousand, the amount of the demand; and as the award was less than the French

[1] *Mémoires de Ségur* (1825 ed.), i, 414.

had offered to pay, the owner was condemned to pay the costs.

Perhaps as a precaution against similar attempts, Governor Trumbull issued a proclamation to the good people of Connecticut, telling them that they must not charge the French soldiers more than current prices for provisions. The warning was heeded, and the French bore testimony to the moderation in price of all they bought during their last march through that state.

When they reached Rhode Island in November, after their victorious campaign in the South, they were received with ardent felicitations. The Council and representatives adopted resolutions, expressing their appreciation of the services rendered by the French; they asked Heaven to reward these exertions in the cause of humanity and the regard which the French had shown for the rights of citizens, and they expressed the hope that these laurels might be crowned with the smiles of the best of kings, and the gratitude of the most generous of peoples.[1] To this Rochambeau made fitting reply, and his army again camped at their old winter-quarters in North Providence.

The citizens were ready to welcome them, and the newspapers sought to excite their zeal by the stilted appeals to ancient history which suited the somewhat crude literary taste of that day. Let us consider, said the " Providence Gazette," "the great toils and hardships they have cheerfully undergone in America. Let our ladies be persuaded cheerfully to suffer a part of their houses and furniture to be used a few days by those who have rendered their country such essential services. This will be but a small sacrifice compared

[1] *Rhode Island Colonial Records*, ix, 619–620.

with the Roman ladies, who repeatedly, in the exigen-
cies of the state, cheerfully gave up their rings, dia-
monds, and personal ornaments. They will thus raise
their characters for patriotism and hospitality, to be
carried on the wings of applause across the Atlantic." [1]

Fortunately, our French friends demanded neither
jewels nor furniture. The officers were given a dinner, and in return Rochambeau gave several balls.
The amiable and enthusiastic Broglie found new objects of admiration at these entertainments. "It was
at the first of these balls that I saw for the first time
the Misses Brown, sisters of the Governor of the city.
I do not give their portraits here because I do not
wish to turn all the men crazy, and render all the
women jealous." But he does add a fervent description of the manner in which Betsey's long eyelashes
hid her great black eyes, "a thing," he says, "both
rare and lovely." She told the prince that she had
never imagined that this was a beauty, and he adds:
"It is quite certain that it was for her a discovery."
It is quite certain that this young beauty fooled the
prince, that the charms of those eyelashes had been
told by other admirers and were not unknown to
Betsey.

The army found comfortable quarters for the winter. Lauzun's legion of cavalry was to be quartered
at Providence; but Rochambeau was a prudent general,
and he discovered that the dealers in forage in the
town had raised their prices to an extravagant figure,
considering that the French paid in louis d'or instead
of Continental currency. Accordingly he declined the
kind invitations and sent the cavalry to seek cheaper
quarters near Lebanon, in Connecticut. At Hartford

[1] *Providence Gazette*, Nov. 2, 1782.

Lauzun found the taverns full of legislators, so he and Chastellux stopped with Colonel Wadsworth, whom they declared to be "tall, well made, and of a noble and agreeable countenance." [1]

The larger part of the infantry remained in New-port; the rest were sent to North Providence and camped on the Dexter Farm, open land that now forms part of the city. Camp Street perpetuates the memory of their stay, in the nomenclature of the town. The officers were quartered with various citizens, all of whom, from Governor Cook down, seemed to have opened their doors to receive our allies. Those who paid rent for their rooms had no reason to complain of high prices. For seven weeks' use of Major Robin-son's great room, Comte Dumas paid but ten dollars. Penelope Peck received from Dr. Fersen, principal marine physician of the navy of France, for the rooms he occupied, the modest rental of six shillings per week. But the payments were all made in lawful sil-ver money, and not in Continental currency.

An army quartered on a city is usually an unwel-come guest, but the French made no disturbance and paid cash for what they got. They were, therefore, popular among the people, while the presence of the French officers furnished an interest to Newport and Providence society which those staid towns had not before known.

Rochambeau now turned over his command to Baron de Vioménil, and on January 11, 1783, he sailed for France.[2] In a farewell letter to him Washington stated, with his usual accuracy, the value of Rochambeau's

[1] Chastellux, *Travels*, etc. (1787), i, 30.
[2] 59th Cong. 1st Session Sen. Doc., vol. 32, no. 537 (Count de Ro-chambeau Commemoration), p. 500.

services. "I cannot permit you to depart from this country," he wrote, "without repeating to you the high sense I entertain of the services you have rendered to America, by the constant attention which you have paid to the interest of it, by the exact order and discipline of the corps under your command, and by your readiness at all times to give facility to every measure which the force of the combined armies were competent to." [1]

After a stormy passage Rochambeau reached France, and at once presented himself at Versailles. It is melancholy to consider how many French gentlemen who risked their lives in the cause of American independence ended honorable careers on the scaffold in their own country. Rochambeau was more fortunate. He received from the King the commendation to which he was justly entitled, and he was afterwards made a marshal of France. Like many of his old comrades in America, he was brought before the Revolutionary Tribunal and condemned to death. It is said that on the day appointed for his execution the cart which transported prisoners was so full that there was no place for him, and before his turn came again Robespierre had been sent to the block and the prisoners were liberated. He was an old man when Napoleon's great career began, but he was held by him in high esteem, and was made a grand officer of the Legion of Honor. He died in 1807, full of years and honors.

After the departure of Rochambeau, the French army remained for a while at Rhode Island waiting for the fleet, which was to convey them home, to be put in readiness. A final ball was given at Newport on the 16th of November, at Mrs. Crowley's assembly-room,

[1] *Writings of Washington*, Sparks's ed., viii, 368.

by some of the young noblemen of Rochambeau's army.
The "Mercury" informs us that the rooms "exhibited
a sight beautiful beyond expression, . . . and the whole
transactions of the evening were conducted with so
much propriety and elegance that it gave the highest
satisfaction to all who had the honor of being present."

The Prince de Broglie described the matter in somewhat different terms. The young people declared that
since the French had been away there had been no
more amusements at Newport, and accordingly he and
a few others decided to give a ball to those disconso-
late fair ones. " We met with neither reluctance nor
refusal when we spoke of dancing. Our company was
composed of some twenty young ladies, some of them
married, all of them beautifully dressed, and all appearing to be pleased. . . . We quitted Newport with
great regret, but not without having first kissed the
hand of Polly Leiton." [1]

The weather during the march to Boston was cold
and disagreeable. Quite a number of the common soldiers were ready to leave their colors and stay in America, where the chance of a prosperous existence seemed
as good as in France. There were, therefore, some
desertions, but on the 7th of December the army
reached Boston and made its triumphal entry. The officers and soldiers were dressed in their best. " A great
part of the population of the town," says the Comte
de Ségur, "came out to meet us; ladies stood at their
windows and welcomed us with the liveliest applause;
our stay was marked by continued rejoicings, by feasts
and balls which succeeded each other day by day." [2]

If the Bostonians were sorry to have their guests

[1] Journal du Voyage du Prince de Broglie, Colonel, etc. ; in *Société
des bibliophiles françois:* Mélanges, 2d part.

[2] *Mém. de Ségur* (1825 ed.), i, 418.

leave them, many of the French shared their regret. "I leave," says Ségur, " with infinite regret a country where men are, as they ought to be everywhere, sincere and free. Private interests are there confounded in the general interests. . . . Each man dresses according to his means and not according to the fashion. Each thinks, says, and does what he wishes. . . . Nothing drives one to be false, to be base, or to flatter." [1]

On the 24th the fleet under Vaudreuil sailed from Boston, carrying with it the French army. The legion of Lauzun remained south and did not sail until May 12, when it embarked at the Capes of Delaware.

The French government was liberal in the bestowal of rewards upon those who had reflected honor upon their country by their service in the United States. Vioménil was made a lieutenant-general, La Fayette and Lauzun were made maréchaux de camp, Deux-Ponts was made a brigadier, and the Vicomte de Rochambeau, the son of the Comte de Rochambeau, was made a Knight of St. Louis.

We feel a natural interest in the fortunes of those gallant volunteers in the cause of American liberty. It is impossible to trace the fate of all, but among the officers were members of great French families, who, from their rank as well as from their ability, were certain to hold prominent position when they returned to the land of their birth. A direful fate awaited many. Apparently most of them had everything to hope from life, but while they had been fighting on American battlefields they had been preparing a more portentous and sinister upheaval in their own land. Many bore back laurels won in the American Revolution only to meet death in the French Revolution.

[1] *Mém. de Ségur* (1825 ed.), i, 422.

The officers of the army under Louis XVI were recruited almost entirely from the nobility, and these well-born volunteers were involved in the ruin of the class to which they belonged. The young men who fought for liberty on our side of the Atlantic were, for the most part, ready to welcome liberty in their own land; but that did not protect them from the violent hands of those who guided the fortunes of the French Revolution; they came under the ban, not because their patriotism was weak, but because their pedigree was good.

La Fayette was the most conspicuous volunteer in our cause, and the fame he won in America made him a leading figure in the political upheaval in his own country. Here his career had been one of unusual success. His good judgment never failed, his military achievements, if not extraordinary, were meritorious and at times brilliant. But the orderly progress of our Revolution was well adapted to the manner of man that La Fayette was. His unselfish zeal endeared him to those in whose behalf he came to fight. The purity of his motives and his patriotism received full appreciation when he served under a leader like Washington. For the dark passions, the stormy tumults in which France became involved, La Fayette was not the man; he exerted little influence over the Revolution in his own country. If he did not tarnish his former fame, he did not gain any new glory. He preserved the lofty elevation of his character through all the trying ordeals of a long and eventful life. But it must be confessed that he was unequal intellectually to the great crisis into which he was thrown. Indeed, to many students of French history he appears only, as Mirabeau declared him, a Cromwell-Grandison.

The Prince de Broglie was among the most distinguished in birth of the French noblemen who came to our aid. His father was a duke and marshal of France, and a prince of the Holy Roman Empire, who had commanded an army during the Seven Years' War. The son came over to America in 1782, and had no opportunity for active service; but his memoirs show him to have been sincere in his devotion to our cause, and singularly acute, for a young man a little over twenty, in his judgments upon the new and strange people among whom he was thrown. Unlike some of his associates, his zeal for political liberty was not confined to this country; after his return he was active in advocating reforms in France, and was sent as a deputy to the States-General. There he acted with the liberal element, and after his term had expired, he served in the army of the Rhine. But the overthrow of the monarchy went beyond his desires. He resigned from the army, and, instead of taking refuge abroad, sought peace in his country-seat. He did not find it there, for he was arrested as a suspect, and on June 27, 1794, was executed on the guillotine. He met his fate when safety was just at hand; a few days later Robespierre was overthrown, and the Reign of Terror ceased.

A similar fate awaited an officer who played a more important part both in America and in France. The Comte de Custine came here in 1781. After his return to France, he became maréchal de camp and governor of Toulon. In 1789 he was elected to the National Assembly, and in 1792 he commanded an army on the lower Rhine. He was popular with the soldiers, but his conduct did not suit the Jacobins; he was arrested at the head of his army, taken to Paris, and brought to trial. It was still in the early days of the Committee of Public Safety, and Custine's friends thought the condemnation of the general impossible, as it could be based only on perverted slanders. They soon discovered their mistake. The general defended himself in a way that would have convinced any ordinary tribunal, and indeed there was nothing he had done which required defence. The crime charged was treason. The crime he had committed was the giving offence to the Jacobins, who were resolved to show that no man, either in the army or in private life, was strong enough or popular enough to withstand their hostility. Custine was one of the first notable victims of the Terror; he was condemned and executed with the promptitude that added consternation to such downfalls.

The Duc de Lauzun was one of the most amiable, as well as one of the most gallant of the French volunteers, and if he was a leader of the *roués* in France, he was a model of the proprieties in America. He, too, met the common fate of a trial before the Revolutionary Tribune and death upon the scaffold. Vioménil, who was second in command to Rochambeau, fell mortally wounded when defending the royal family in the Tuileries against the attack of the mob on August 10, 1792. The Chevalier Duportail, another brilliant French officer, early enlisted in the American service (1777), and at Yorktown commanded the engineer corps. He was received with honor on his return, and in 1790 was made minister of war. It was a perilous dignity at such a time, and neither the minister's patriotism nor his capacity saved him from accusation when accusation often meant death. He also came before the Revolutionary Tribunal and met the usual condemnation, but he made his escape and found safety in the land for whose liberties he had fought.

The list of those who thus met death or ruin in the Revolution in their own land could be long extended.

While many of the officers who took part in our war met an early and evil fate, for some of them a very different fortune was reserved. The three Lameths served in America with credit, and one of them was severely wounded at Yorktown. Two of them were for a while prominent figures in the French Revolution, and were fortunate enough to live through it and occupy positions of prominence afterwards. Theodore Lameth, who served in this country when a little over twenty, died in 1854, at the extreme age of ninety-eight. Had he lived a few years longer, he would have seen the country in whose formation he had assisted on the verge of dissolution from internal dissensions.

With the exception of La Fayette, Alexandre Berthier was destined to the most conspicuous lot. He served with great credit in this country with La Fayette and under Rochambeau, and he took part in the final victory of Yorktown. He passed through the French Revolution with honor and with safety, and at last became a follower of Napoleon. He was one of those whose extraordinary fortunes corresponded with that of their extraordinary leader. Berthier accumulated an enormous fortune; he was made a marshal of the empire; he was created Prince of Wagram; he married the niece of the King of Bavaria; he was loaded with life's honors, only at last, as was believed, to take his own life in the agony of conflicting emotions excited by Napoleon's return from Elba.

Dumas, who so often expressed unfavorable views as to his American associates, helped to organize the National Guard, escorted the King, and protected him during his return from Varennes. Later he became a general under Napoleon and was minister of war to Joseph Bonaparte when he was king of Naples.

The Comte de Ségur, whose memoirs contain one of the most interesting accounts of the condition of French society when he was a youth, and of the conditions of our own country when he was here, also found fortune under Napoleon, and became a member of the Imperial Senate.

CHAPTER XXIII

AT the beginning of the Revolution the colonists knew little of the French, and what they did know was not reckoned in their favor. French Canadians had been objects of immemorial dislike, strengthened during occasional periods of acute apprehension. To the American colonist a Frenchman was a papist, which was bad, and much given to using Indian allies in war, which was worse; he had neither political traditions nor political rights, and his views on questions of government were not worthy of consideration.

In social and domestic life he was still less to be copied. The American colonists shared the belief of their English cousins, that the French, for the most part, starved on bad food, that they believed in a bad religion, and were addicted to bad morals. A Frenchman did not eat roast beef, nor read the Scriptures, nor keep the Sabbath, nor regard other men's wives with puritanical rigor.

By French literature the colonists were unaffected, because, with few exceptions, they knew nothing about it. The number who could read French was small, the number who did read French to any extent was smaller. The teachings of the physiocrats had no effect upon American economic thought, except as some trace of them may have been distilled through English writers; the political theories of Montesquieu and of Rousseau, the wit of Voltaire, the infidelity of the encyclopædists, had no influence upon men, the most of whom did not know these writers even by name. Our ancestors' modes of thought were essentially English; the political traditions which they inherited, the political institutions which they founded, were unaffected by French thought.

These conditions were not largely modified in the years during which French and American soldiers stood shoulder to shoulder in the War of Independence. The influence upon the French soldiers, and especially upon the officers, of what they saw in the country they came to assist, was very considerable. But their own modes of thought had little effect on American society or American politics. In the sentiments of our ancestors towards the French people a very great change was, indeed, produced by the war. This was natural; however much the French had interfered with the comfort and happiness of the American colonists in the past, they now came as their friends and benefactors. The value of the French alliance was recognized by all intelligent Americans.

Furthermore, the French soldiers made themselves personally popular. The first arrivals were indeed little relished. For the most part they consisted of adventurers who came here with exaggerated views of their own importance, who offended their associates by their overbearing manners, and wearied them by their incapacity. But this was no longer the case after the French government espoused the American cause, and sent over officers and soldiers from the regular army to coöperate with their American allies. Considering the character of the average Frenchman, especially when campaigning in foreign lands, and how strange to them seemed many of the customs of the colonists, the uniform propriety of their conduct is deserving of all praise. During the four years that French soldiers were on our soil, there was a universal chorus of laudation over their conduct. It seemed the more meritorious when contrasted with the brutalities of the Hessians. The Hessians came, indeed, as enemies of the American government, but they were nominally the friends of the large body of Tories whose sympathies were still with England. Yet the Hessian soldiers, and indeed the English soldiers, plundered friend and foe with impartiality. The loyalist found that his crops were stolen, his house pillaged, and his family maltreated, quite as much as if he were the most ardent of patriots.

But the French soldiers were models of propriety. They paid for what they got, they respected the chicken-roosts, they were polite to the women. In the latter years of the war, most of the gold in circulation was French gold, sent over by the French government, and paid out by the French army. The farmer and the storekeeper who substituted louis d'or for American Continental currency naturally entertained a kindly feeling for France. When the Marquis de Chastellux was travelling in Virginia in 1782, he recorded his satisfaction at observing that most of the money staked at the cock-fights was French gold. It was found in equal abundance in other channels of trade, and our ancestors viewed it with quite as much satisfaction as the marquis.

Rochambeau says that when the Indians visited his camp at Newport, they manifested no emotion as they gazed at the cannon, or watched the French troops at their exercises, but they could not overcome their astonishment when they saw ripe apples hanging upon the trees under which the soldiers had long been camped. In all his three campaigns, the count says, there was never a disturbance between a soldier of the French and of the American army.[1]

The credit for such a result was largely given to Rochambeau by an officer who seems to have doubted whether the allies were really as fond of each other as they professed to be. He was, says Count Fersen, "the only man capable of commanding us here, and of maintaining that perfect harmony which has reigned between two nations so different in manners, morals, and language, and who, at heart, do not like each other." Such a statement was perhaps modified by the writer's own feelings, for he adds : " Our allies have not always behaved well to us, and the time that we have spent among them has not taught us to like or esteem them."[2]

The good order maintained by the French soldiers was chiefly due to the discipline enforced by the French officers. It is perhaps more surprising that the officers themselves, who were brought in contact with American society, should have conducted themselves in a manner in which even our Puritan ancestors found nothing to criticize. Some of the officers appreciated the delicacy of the situation and were surprised, as well as pleased, at the result. One of them writes his father: "You know Frenchmen, and what are called courtiers, enough to judge of the despair of our young men of that class who find themselves obliged to pass the winter tranquilly in Newport. . . . No suppers, no theatres, no balls. Yet they acquit themselves creditably amid such privations." [3] Another praises the good example set by

---

[1] *Mémoires de Rochambeau*, i, 254, 314.

[2] Fersen, *Diary*, etc. (translated by Miss Wormeley), 63.

[3] *Ibid.*, 26.

Vaudreuil, the commander of the squadron at Boston, and says that such conduct, " followed beyond all hope and belief by the officers of his squadron," captivated the hearts of a people which had not hitherto been friendly to the French. " The officers of our navy," he adds, " were everywhere received, not only as allies, but brothers ; and though they were admitted by the ladies of Boston to the greatest familiarity, not a single indiscretion, not even the most distant attempt at impertinence ever disturbed the confidence or innocent harmony of this pleasing intercourse." [1] Their record at Newport and Philadelphia, and wherever they went, was equally blameless.

To-day the Frenchman of the better class finds many of our social usages strange to him, and the difference was even more marked at the time of the Revolution. French customs have changed somewhat, and American customs, with the growth of wealth and fashion, have changed still more. But in the days of 1776 the simplicity of life to which our colonial fathers were bred had been little modified.

The widespread well-being, the rarity of poverty, made its impression upon our allies. It was, indeed, a favorable time for French gentlemen to investigate the ways of a simpler and more wholesome society. The artificiality of life in the upper circles had begun to pall on those who mingled in it. The Queen sought to gratify her desire for change by playing dairy-maid at her miniature farm at the Trianon ; philosophers praised the primitive man ; courtiers and fine ladies babbled of green fields and running brooks. Somewhat of this was artificial, but much was genuine. There was also a more active interest in the condition

[1] Chastellux, *Travels*, etc., ii, 291, 292.

of the masses of the people than France had before witnessed. Both officers and men came from many a sad sight of poverty and distress, from peasants living in huts, on black bread, pinched by hunger because so great a share of their scanty crops was absorbed by the tax-gatherer.

It is from the officers that we must take our record, but the privates were quite as much impressed by a country where every man had his fowl in the pot, where hunger was rare, and extreme poverty unknown.

"In America," wrote La Fayette, "there are no poor, nor even what we call peasantry. Each individual has his own honest property." "Such is the present happiness," writes another, "that the country has no poor, and every man enjoys a certain ease and independence." "This little establishment," writes the Marquis de Chastellux, of the house of an American colonel, where he visited, "in which comfort and simplicity reign, gave an idea of that sweet and serene state of happiness which appears to have taken refuge in the new world." Speaking again of a gathering of ladies that he attended, he says: "This assembly recalled to my mind in every respect those of Holland and Geneva, where one meets gayety without indecency and the wish to please without coquetry." [1]

Gayety without indecency can still be found in American society, but with the growth of wealth it is doubtful whether any one would now find close resemblance between social life at New York and Geneva. Change has been more rapid in the great republic than in the small republic. Even Fersen, who did not love us, found the inhabitants of the country prosperous without luxury or display. "They content themselves,"

[1] Chastellux, *Travels*, etc., i, 286.

he writes, " with mere necessaries. . . . Their clothes
are simple but good, and their morals have not yet
been spoiled by the luxury of Europeans. It is a
country which surely will be very happy if it can enjoy a long peace, and if the two political parties which
now divide it, do not make it suffer the fate of Poland
and so many other republics." [1]

In the residence of the wealthy simplicity was still
found. A party of officers visited the country house
of Mr. Tracy, the most considerable merchant at
Newbury, which was then an important port. They
found a terraced garden, a hothouse, the residence
handsome and well furnished, and, says the narrator,
" everything breathes that air of magnificence, accompanied with simplicity, which is only to be found
among merchants." Here indeed the guests, after an
excellent supper, drank good wine, and continued
drinking Madeira until bearers of the names of Talleyrand and Montesquieu became intoxicated. It
should be said that this was attributed to the fact that
the host offered them pipes to smoke, and they were
overcome by the tobacco. A similar result has been
attributed to the same cause by others besides French
officers.[2]

While our allies found our modes of life simple,
they pronounced our drinks both good and potent. At
General Heath's, the guest says the dinner was plain
but good, and adds, " It was true that there was not
a drop of wine, but with excellent cider and toddy one
may very well dispense with it." [3] As they got farther south they found both wine and whiskey were to
be had, and usually both were acceptable. One, in-

[1] Fersen, *Diary*, etc., 26.   [2] Chastellux, *Travels*, etc., ii, 245.
[3] *Ibid.*, i, 82.

deed, writes from Virginia: "The whiskey or corn spirits we had in the evening, mixed with water, was very bad." But this may have been owing to the mixture.

On the whole, the meals were satisfactory. The French became accustomed to the American custom of drinking coffee with meat and vegetables, and learned to appreciate an American breakfast. Prairie chicken they found to their taste, and declared its black meat was more delicate and higher flavored than that of the heath-cock.

At some places trials were experienced. In Virginia, wrote an officer, the people ate nothing but cakes made of Indian corn and baked before a fire. The outside was hard, and the inside was dough, and the only drink was rum mixed with water, and called grog, which the officers did not like. But as they themselves on this excursion were well provided with pâtés, hams, wine, and bread, this, says the writer, "prevented our feeling the misery that reigns in inns where nothing is found but salt pork and no bread."[1]

Some customs were distasteful to the visitors. The Marquis de Chastellux lamented the feather-beds, from which many of them suffered greatly. A usage equally disagreeable sometimes prevailed at dinner. The practice of asking a friend at table to drink a glass of wine with one, our ancestors were charged with carrying to excess. " I find it an absurd and truly barbarous practice," writes one of the victims. . . . "They call to you from one end of the table to the other, 'Sir, will you permit me to drink a glass of wine with you?' . . . The bottle is then passed to you, and you must look your enemy in the face. . . .

[1] Fersen, *Diary*, etc., 54.

You wait till he likewise has poured out his wine and taken his glass. You then drink mournfully with him, as a recruit imitates the corporal in his exercise." [1]

Meat, when paid for in French gold, was cheap; but the foreign officers who were in the American service and were paid in Continental currency found a very different condition of affairs. Kalb, who was a major-general in our army, was full of just laments. His pay as a general was nominally two thousand dollars, but he tells us that this represented little more than fifty dollars in gold. "My journey," he writes a friend in 1780, "costs me immense sums. I cannot have my equipage follcw me, I have to live in the taverns, or in private houses, where I pay at the same rate. My pay for six months is hardly enough for the necessary expenses of one day. . . . I was once directed to take up quarters in a private house for the night. They gave me some bad soup and grog for drink. Yet the next morning, without breakfast, my account for four men and three servants was eight hundred and fifty dollars. The mistress of the house told me politely that she had put in nothing for lodging and left it to my discretion, but three or four hundred dollars would not be too much for the trouble she had had with my servants." It is not strange that the baron adds : "These people pretend that they are sacrificing everything for . . . liberty. . . . An ordinary horse costs twenty thousand dollars; I say twenty thousand dollars"; and he sighs. "Would that I were at my own home, and had never embarked in this galère." [2]

[1] Chastellux, *Travels*, etc., 185–186.

[2] Kalb to Baron Holtzendorff, from Petersburg in Virginia, May 29, 1780; Kapp, *Life of Kalb*, 325.

The character and conduct of our women were of great interest to the young beaux and dandies who came over from France, and who, at home, showed as much recklessness in making love as they displayed on the field of battle. Their judgments were almost uniformly favorable, and were creditable to their intelligence. They were surprised at the freedom with which women met them, yet they had sense enough to realize that the women were not in love with them, but that such were the usages of a society in which intrigues were unknown. The contrast between the freedom of our young girls and the strictness with which the French *jeune fille* is guarded constantly impressed our visitors. One of them was a little shocked when he found even so staid a personage as Samuel Adams tête-à-tête with a young girl of fifteen, who was preparing his tea. "But," he adds, "we should not be scandalized at this, considering that he is at least sixty." The strictness of the married women surprised them as much as the freedom of the unmarried. "I went to see Mrs. Bingham," writes one, "a young and handsome woman only seventeen. Her husband was there, according to American custom." When the young women discovered that a man was married, lamented Rochambeau, forthwith they regarded him as a person possessing no possible interest, and would have nothing to say to him.

Either the women were graver than their descendants or they appeared sedate to those accustomed to French vivacity. In one place Chastellux speaks of meeting Mrs. Spencer, and says she was gay and even given to laughter, a rare thing among American women.[1] Certainly this remark would not be made

[1] Chastellux, *Travels*, etc., ii, 130.

now. Another criticism made by our allies in the Revolution is still made by foreigners, for it was declared that all American children were spoiled.

In some respects the women of the Revolution seemed less attractive than would their descendants of to-day. In dress, indeed, they were reasonably satisfactory. "Be assured," writes a French officer in a formal letter to the father of James Madison, "that during a three years' residence in America the progress in women's dress has not escaped me." But in music, drawing, and indeed in all the arts, they were found sadly lacking. Musical taste was undoubtedly little developed. Yet though there was little of musical education, it was not unknown. In Philadelphia one of our guests made the round of the churches, and at last found satisfaction at the English church. It appeared to him a sort of opera. A handsome minister in the pulpit, reading, speaking, and singing with a grace entirely theatrical; a number of young women answering melodiously from the galleries; a soft and agreeable vocal music well accompanied on the organ; "all this," he adds, "compared to the Quakers, the Anabaptists, Presbyterians, etc., appeared to me rather like a little paradise itself than as the road to it." [1]

On the whole, American women, if we may believe our visitors, had not yet attained to that degree of social charm which is now accorded to them even by foreigners who criticize the manners of our men. One of the officers wrote that they were little accustomed to giving themselves trouble either of body or mind. " Making tea and seeing that the house is kept clean," he complains, " constitute the whole of their domestic

[1] Chastellux, *Travels*, etc., i, 289.

province." This did not apply to all; he found many of them agreeable, but still, when compared with their French sisters, lacking in accomplishments. This was undoubtedly true. Men who moved in the best society in Paris could find in the ladies of their acquaintance a familiarity with art in all its forms, and a degree of skill in many of them, a knowledge of literature, a brilliancy of conversation, which to say the least was much less common among the women of the Revolution. It may gratify our patriotic pride to feel that if such an inferiority existed then, it does not exist now.

In other respects the French also asserted their superiority. When the Marquis de Chastellux went to a ball in Boston with his acquaintance Mr. Breck, the agent of the French navy, he speaks of various French gentlemen who danced the minuet and did honor to the French nation by their noble and easy manner. But I am sorry to say that the contrast was considerable between them and the Americans, " who are in general very awkward, particularly in the minuet. . . . The ladies," he adds, "were all well dressed, but with less elegance and refinement than in Philadelphia." But when he dined at Mr. Breck's he reports : "There reigned in this society a tone of ease and freedom which is pretty general at Boston, and cannot fail of being pleasing to the French." [1]

The dancing of the Boston ladies seems to have been decidedly unsatisfactory. Another officer tells us that before leaving that city he wished to make acquaintance with the fair sex. " Twice a week," he writes, "there is a ladies' hall or school where the young ladies meet to dance, from noon until two o'clock. I spent some moments there . . . I found nearly all

[1] Chastellux, *Travels*, etc., ii, 259, 262.

the women extremely handsome, at the same time extremely awkward. It would be impossible to dance with less grace, or to be worse dressed, although with a certain extravagance." [1] It is pleasant to reflect that the progress made by American women in the arts since the days of the Revolution has extended to dancing, and that even at Boston a French officer would now find nothing to criticize.

At this time social life in Philadelphia was probably more agreeable than in any other American city, and the Prince de Broglie is one of many who bear witness to its charms. He speaks first of his visit to a small town of which the social requirements were apparently simple. " I only knew a few English words," he writes, " but I knew enough to drink excellent tea made with the best of cream, and to say to a young lady that she was pretty. . . . As a result I had the necessary elements for success." It is doubtful if at Philadelphia compliments so direct in their form would have been relished, though they might have been excused on account of the prince's scanty knowledge of English. He writes of his journey to that city: "It was very warm, but the beauty of the roads, the attractiveness of the country, the imposing majesty of the forests, the air of abundance that everywhere appeared, the fairness and courtesy of the women, all contributed to atone for any sensations of fatigue." [2] In Philadelphia he took tea with Mrs. Morris. He found the furniture elegant, the table handsomely arranged, the mistress of the house fair and pleasing; everything was charming. The tea was still excellent, and the

[1] Dubourg's Journal, June 14, 1781 ; *Magazine of American History*, iv, 214.

[2] Narrative of the Prince de Broglie, in Balch's *Les Français en Amérique*, tr. by E. S. Balch, vol. i.

prince seems to have rivalled Dr. Johnson in his fondness for it, for the French minister checked him at his
twelfth cup. Even at Philadelphia the dancing did
not correspond to the high ideals of the French. "The
ladies of Philadelphia," writes the prince, "though
sufficiently magnificent in their clothes, are not generally dressed with much taste; alike in their head-
dress and their heads, they have less of vivacity and
charm than our Frenchwomen. Although they are well
shaped, they are lacking in grace, they do not courtesy
well, nor do they excel in dancing. But," he adds,
"they know how to make tea well, they educate their
children with care, they are scrupulously faithful to
their husbands, and many of them have natural wit." [1]

Lack of grace in dancing was excusable in a country where this amusement was sometimes forbidden
by law. Gérard, the French minister, speaks of the
complications in which he was involved in this respect.
He desired to acknowledge the civilities which he had
received by a banquet, which was to be followed by a
ball. To this some objected, and Gérard says : "They
allege a law of Congress which forbids public entertainments. This law originated with the northern
Presbyterians at the time when Congress fervently be-
sought the aid of Heaven. Things have taken another
turn, and now quite a number of senators dance every
week." With diplomatic reserve Gérard expressed no
opinion as to whether the senators danced well or ill.[2]

Social differences were observed, not only between
Boston and Philadelphia, but between the North and
the South. Of the southern women our marquis speaks
less favorably, though it was in Virginia that he made

[1] *Journal du Prince de Broglie*, 46, 47.
[2] Correspondence of Gérard; in Durand, *New Materials*, etc., 166.

his observations. He found them poorly educated and indolent, as a result of being served by slaves. "The consequence of this is," he writes, "that they are often pert and coquettish before, and sorrowful helpmates after marriage." [1]

The young nobles who went to America were in fit condition to be affected by what they saw; they came well prepared to absorb the teachings of American life and American institutions, and the simplicity that was found among some of the American women produced a strong impression upon them. A certain weariness of elaborate dress and conventional modes of life had already manifested itself in Paris. The ardent youths of the period were ready to be favorably affected by different ideals. It was not only the natural ardor of youth for a pretty woman, but a reaction from the life to which he had been accustomed, that excited the Prince de Broglie's enthusiasm when he met Polly Leiton, the Quakeress. "The simplicity of her dress gave to Polly," he tells us, "the air of a Holy Virgin, and to this the modesty of her speech and the grace of her bearing corresponded. I confess," he adds, "this beguiling Polly seemed to be the chef-d'œuvre of nature, and whenever her image presents itself to me, I form the plan of writing a large book against the attire, . . . the coquetry, and factitious charms of various women that are admired in the world." [2]

The charming Polly excited equal admiration in the Comte de Ségur. He says: "So much beauty, so much simplicity, so much elegance, so much modesty, were perhaps never before combined in the same person"; and adds: "Had I not been married and happy, I should,

---

[1] Chastellux, *Travels*, etc., ii, 203.
[2] *Journal du Prince de Broglie*, 68.

while coming to defend the liberty of Americans, have
lost my own at the feet of Polly Leiton." [1] He also
expresses his admiration of the country in much the
same terms as de Broglie. He was charmed alike by
the beauties of virgin forests, and fields that had not
yet known the plough, and by the spectacle of prosperity and thrift where civilization had already
found its way. Wherever he stopped, he tells us, he
was received with simplicity of manner, courtesy, and
urbanity. He met neither poverty nor vice, but everywhere ease and contentment, with neither the prejudices nor the servility of European society. To such
blessings, he added, that if the fare was simple, it was
everywhere abundant; that if the rum was too strong
and the coffee too weak, the tea was excellent. [2]

The French officers were equally ready to criticize
their American allies. This insolent conduct, one of
them wrote, deserved to be severely reprimanded, but
how could one punish those in office in a country
where the people were governed by caprice rather than
by reason. "The Americans," he adds a little later,
"are easy to deceive, indolent by nature, suspicious;
they always think they see what they fear; they won't
take the trouble to examine the reasons for their belief." They were so indolent, he declared, that they
allowed the English to destroy Bedford without even
sending notice of what was going on. [3]

That the Americans should have appeared to the
French reserved or even phlegmatic, is not strange,
but often they are accused of indolence and lack of
business habits. It is hard to believe that the energy
so noticeable in their descendants could have been

---

[1] *Mém. de Ségur* (1825 ed.), i, 396.   [2] *Ibid.*, 569.

[3] *Extrait du Journal d'un officier de la marine de l'escadre de M. le
comte d'Estaing* (1782), 39, 41.

lacking in any large proportion of our ancestors. Yet the Prince de Broglie, who, for the most part, judged us favorably, declared that our people were irresolute, as well as phlegmatic and greedy for money.[1]

The Abbé Robin, who was an intelligent observer, makes somewhat similar criticisms. "Their character," he says, writing of our ancestors, "is cold, slow, and mild. They are not very industrious. . . . Their softness of character is due to the climate as much as to their customs; one finds it even in domestic animals. The horses are docile, one does not meet with those that are restive or high-strung; even the dogs are caressing and timid; strangers have nothing to fear from their violence."[2]

The cultivators of the soil seemed to him more simple than French peasants, though without their rusticity or their roughness; more intelligent, with less dissimulation, but less industrious. In this judgment perhaps the abbé was not altogether wrong; the French peasant then and now is willing to undergo continuous labor to an extent distasteful to the American farmer. The distinction between the two classes was the same as it is now; the abbé found our farmers less attached to ancient usages and more ready for improved methods of cultivation.[3]

He thought that the American women regarded church as a paradise, though not always from the highest motives. "Piety is not the only thing," he says, "that brings American women in crowds to church. Without theatres, without public promenades, it is there they go in the desire to show their increas-

---

[1] *Journal du Prince de Broglie*, 48.
[2] Robin, *Nouveau Voyage*, etc., 41, 42.
[3] *Ibid.*, 43.

ing luxury. They appear dressed in silks and shadowed sometimes by superb feathers. Their head-dresses imitate those which our French ladies wore a few years ago. They do not use powder, but the most fashionable begin to adopt European customs." [1]

An associate of the Prince de Broglie, the Comte de Ségur, one of the young aristocrats who was especially fascinated by the hopes of a better future for humanity that seemed opening to the world, writes, when leaving Boston in December, 1782: " I leave a country where one follows a simple code of simple laws, and respecting good morals, one is happy and tranquil. It is in outraging morals that one becomes the fashion in Paris. I was treated as a brother everywhere in America. I saw only public confidence, hospitality, and cordiality. The girls are coquettes in order to find husbands, the women are discreet in order to hold them. I know that this country cannot long preserve morals as pure as this, but if it keeps them for only a century, is a century of happiness nothing?" [2]

All were not arrayed with the simplicity of Broglie's Polly Leiton. " I was surprised," writes another, "to find the traces of French fashions in the forests of America. The head-dresses of all the women except the Quakers are high and complicated. One is lost in reflection, when he finds in the province of Connecticut so strong a taste for dress and so much luxury, combined with customs that are so simple and pure that they resemble those of the ancient patriarchs." [3]

Another writer described the women as tall and well proportioned, generally with regular features,

---

[1] Robin, *Nouveau Voyage*, etc., 14.

[2] *Mém. de Ségur* (1825 ed.), i, 423.

[3] Robin, *Nouveau Voyage*, etc., 38.

with a pale complexion and little color. They have less charm and less ease, he writes, than Frenchwomen, but more nobility of bearing. The men, he said, were usually well made, and few were fat, but they also, for the most part, had pale complexions.

Another comment was truer then than it would be now, for on the whole life was then harder, and the progressive ease of civilization, amid many other beneficial effects, tends to preserve the good looks of women to a greater age. " At twenty-five years," writes the abbé, " the women have no longer the freshness of youth, at thirty-five or forty they are wrinkled and decrepit." [1]

The immoderate use of tea is constantly criticized. " They take a great deal of tea, the use of this insipid drink is their chief pleasure. There is not an inhabitant who does not take it, and the greatest mark of politeness they can show is to offer it to you." To the tea, he adds, the loss of their teeth was attributed. The women were ordinarily pretty, but at eighteen or twenty they had often lost this precious ornament. But he himself attributed this rather to hot bread, because the English and Dutch preserved their teeth, though they also were tea-drinkers.[2]

La Fayette viewed everything in this country with the eyes of youthful enthusiasm. He found the women of the South pretty in appearance, simple in manners, and neat in dress, and he was no less pleased in the North. When travelling from Washington's camp to Albany, to take command of the army which was to conquer Canada, but which never started on the ex-

---

[1] Robin, *Nouveau Voyage*, etc., 14, 15. See also *Granite Monthly*, iv, 424.

[2] Robin, *Nouveau Voyage*, etc., 39.

pedition, he was greatly charmed by his journey of
four hundred miles. Travelling leisurely on horseback, so he writes, he had the opportunity of observing the customs of the people and their patriarchal
life. The women were devoted to their own homes;
there they found happiness and there they gave happiness. It was only to unmarried girls one talked of
love, and coquetry of this sort was amiable and decent.
La Fayette goes on to complain of his own country,
though certainly his own marriage was an exception
to those of which he speaks. "In the marriages of
chance one makes in Paris, the faithfulness of the
women is often contrary to nature, to reason, and, one
could almost say, to justice. In America one marries
her lover. To accept another would be to break a
valid treaty, because both parties know to what they
are engaging themselves." [1]

The Comte de Deux-Ponts was among the officers
who came over with Rochambeau, and he noted down
his impressions of our people. They were always com-
plimentary. "The Anglo-American," he says, "is
fleshier than the Frenchman, without being taller."
This certainly is not true unless Frenchmen have
diminished in height and increased in breadth. Then
he adds: "He is quite strong, of a robust constitution,
his phlegmatic temperament renders him patient, de-
liberate, and consistent in all his undertakings."
He gave the preference to those who lived north of
the Delaware. They possessed, so he wrote, more
courage and energy, and a rigid Presbyterianism had
strengthened their character, while the people south
were less energetic and less capable of enduring
the fatigues of war. Neither the war of the Revolu-

[1] Lafayette, *Mémoires*, etc., 40.

tion nor the Civil War justified this depreciation of
southern men.

Naturally enough, American manners seemed cold
to those accustomed to French exuberance. One of
the followers of Rochambeau complains of the reserve
of the Americans, and the coldness with which they
received those who came to their assistance.[1] " We
did not meet with that reception on landing which we
expected, and which we ought to have had. A coldness and a reserve appear to me to be characteristic
of the American nation. They seem to have little of
that enthusiasm which one supposes would belong to
a people fighting for its liberties, and to be little
suited to inspire it in others."

The gloom of the New England Sabbath also impressed itself upon our visitors. " What a gloomy
silence reigns in all your towns on Sunday," writes
one. "A stranger would imagine that some epidemic or
plague had obliged every one to confine himself at
home." The women are at a loss what to do with their
fine dresses that have shone only at the meeting, and
can only divert themselves by scandal, while the men,
wearied with reading the Bible to their children, assemble round the bowl. "Make happy days then of
Sundays," he continues, " and you will confer on them
an inestimable present." [2]

This advice was sent to Mr. Madison. It is quite
certain that if it had been sent to John Adams it
would have strengthened the poor opinion he entertained of the French.

[1] Comte de Deux-Ponts, *My Campaigns in America* (translated by
S. A. Green), 91.

[2] Chastellux, *Travels*, etc., ii, 383-387.

CHAPTER XXIV

AFTER the capture of Yorktown the time had at last arrived when there was a possibility of closing the long contest for American independence. Nearly two years elapsed before a treaty was agreed upon, and the negotiations were attended with much distrust and recrimination among those charged with them. Not only at the time, but ever since, they have been a fertile theme for controversy; the representatives of America were not sparing in their criticisms of one another, and they founded schools of partisans who dispute the credit or the blame which should be attributed to each. Among the allies, also, the harmony that had prevailed during the prosecution of the war was not found in equal measure in the negotiations for peace. Some Americans declared that France proved an unfaithful friend at the end. Some Frenchmen asserted that the United States considered only their own interests, and deserted the cause of their benefactress. It is possible now to study the diplomacy of both nations, and see whether either can be justly accused of bad faith toward its ally.

Suggestions of reconciliation between England and the United States had often been advanced during the progress of the war, and, naturally, they were made to the representative of the colonies in France. Dr. Franklin was by far the most conspicuous American in Europe, and it was probable that any negotiations for peace would be in his hands. In 1778 one Pulteney, a member of Parliament, visited France, under an assumed name, and sought to open a conference with Franklin.[1] He seems to have proceeded without authority, and his action bore no fruit. The English still clung to the hope of retaining some control over the colonies, while both France and the thirteen states had agreed that absolute independence must be the first condition of peace.

A few months later Pulteney was followed by a still more mysterious intriguer. A letter signed Charles de Weissenstein, a name savoring of many nationalities, was thrown over the gateway of the house occupied by the American minister. It suggested a plan of reconciliation, as a part of which Adams, Hancock, Washington, Franklin, and others should receive either valuable offices or pensions for life, for amounts to be inserted in blanks left opposite their names; and it further promised that if American peers were ever created, these leaders should be included in the first promotion. The letter closed with the statement that the writer would be at Notre-Dame at a certain hour, with a rose in his hat, ready to receive a reply.

The American minister did not attempt to meet this extraordinary negotiator, but some French police officers were on hand and reported that a man corresponding to the description wandered about the cathedral at the appointed hour, and at last returned to his hotel and was heard of no more.[2] Franklin was convinced that the Weissenstein letter was George III's own conception, and he prepared a fiery answer to it. It is not impossible that the English King

[1] Wharton, ii, 523, 527.   [2] Bigelow, *Franklin*, ii, 435–436.

thought that the American colonies could be led back
to loyalty by making Washington a peer, and Franklin and John Adams pensioners. His treatment of the
colonists in the past showed no better understanding
of their character.

In 1779 Vergennes suggested to Congress that it
might be well to select an envoy empowered to treat,
in case England should at any time manifest a desire
for peace. There was little prospect of such overtures
at this stage of the war, but even the suggestion of
peace was grateful, and Congress at once took action.

The selection of a commissioner was not free from
intrigue and state jealousies. The choice lay between
Adams and Jay. Franklin's name was not suggested;
he was already at Paris as the American minister,
and possibly it was thought that his services could be
secured without a formal appointment as peace commissioner. Moreover, the persistent slanders which
Lee and Izard poured out against him had their effect
on members of Congress, who, for the most part, were
ignorant of the condition of foreign courts and of the
position held by our representatives abroad. Adams
was the choice of the New England states, who desired some one to press with unwearied zeal for the
recognition of the rights of New England fishermen
in the Newfoundland fisheries, and in Adams they
selected a man who certainly was faithful to their
trust. His name was naturally suggested for the
position: he had been for nearly a year and a half at
Paris as one of the representatives of the United
States, and had lately returned; the experience which
he had gained would surely be of much value. Jay
had the support of New York and the South, and
was agreeable to the French minister.

At first Adams received the votes of five states and Jay of four, and there was no choice; but a compromise was reached: Adams was selected as commissioner for the peace negotiations, while Jay was sent as minister to Madrid, where he spent two years of discomfort, obtaining few promises of aid and still less performance.

Having chosen a commissioner, Congress next proceeded to frame his instructions. There had already been much and fervent discussion of the terms to be demanded: the New England states regarded the question of the fisheries as all important, the southern states were equally interested in the extension of the western frontier, and in securing the free navigation of the Mississippi. In all these matters, Gérard, the French minister, took an active part; and that his counsel should be much heeded was not unnatural, when we consider the importance of the French alliance to the young republic. There were in Congress factions largely under the influence of the French minister, and factions that were not influenced by him at all, on whom he naturally looked with ill-favor. Partly to simplify the issues, and partly because he regarded himself as bound to protect the interests of Spain and of all the Bourbon family, he had been anxious that Congress should take no decided stand on any question except the recognition of independence.

Both Gérard and his successor were instructed by Vergennes to moderate the demands of Congress, not only lest these should hinder the attainment of peace, but still more from regard for the Spanish allies of France. It was desired by many members that the right to the fisheries, a proper western boundary, and the free navigation of the Mississippi should be included in the ultimata to be presented by the representatives of the United States. But Spain wanted the American colonists to be kept as far as possible from her possessions, and the free navigation of a river was to the Spanish as distasteful an idea as freedom of commerce.

In the negotiations for peace at Philadelphia, as at Paris and London, the demands made by Spain constantly embarrassed the representatives of France. Gérard was able to secure the adoption of instructions in a form agreeable to him. It was decided that an acknowledgment of the absolute independence of the United States must be a condition of peace, but all other matters were left to the fortune of negotiation.

Adams arrived at Paris in February, 1780, but his presence in the French capital did not foster cordial relations between the young republic and her powerful ally. The selection of Adams by Congress as commissioner to treat of peace was not agreeable to Vergennes. In his first foreign mission Adams had not created a favorable impression on the French minister. Vergennes had probably assumed that Franklin would be designated as commissioner, and Adams, when he reached the French court, was *persona non grata*. Naturally complications soon arose between the American commissioner and the French minister. Adams suggested that he should at once formally notify the English that he was an envoy sent from the United States, and empowered to agree on terms of peace. As the English King and his prime minister had no thought of making peace, unless the colonists were ready to return to their former allegiance, it was not important that they should be informed that Adams was at Paris, ready to sign a treaty which should recognize American independence. At all events, Vergennes advised against announcing Adams's official character. He may have thought it was premature, he may have wished that there should be no suggestion of readiness for negotiations, until France and the United States could coöperate. But Adams was annoyed at the failure to make solemn announcement of his official position, and he saw in this action manifest proof of the bad, faith of France, and of the ill-will of her minister. He soon decided in his own mind that the colonies were to be used as an aid to French ambition, and were to have no opportunity to act as their own interests might require, but this belief does not seem to have been well founded.

There is no doubt that Vergennes feared that the Americans might abandon the French alliance, make their own peace with England, and leave France to carry on alone the war she had begun to secure independence for the colonies. Apprehensions of this sort led him to discourage negotiations with England until France could join in them. His fears appeared in a letter written to La Luzerne soon after Adams arrived at Paris. " My opinion has been, and still is, that there is a party which desires Congress to make peace without any attention to our alliance. In other words, to obtain an assurance of American independence directly from England, without our participation." [1] In this suspicion he was wrong, and no one would deny that such action would have been in the highest degree dishonorable. Washington, Franklin, the Congress, all declared, that under no circumstances could the United States make terms with England unless France was included in the treaty.

[1] Doniol, iv, 414.

Other causes of disagreement soon arose and increased Vergennes's distaste for the American plenipotentiary. It was disagreeable for Adams to acknowledge obligations to any one, either for his country or for himself. The assistance given by France, he thought, should be credited, not to the kindness of the donor, but to the unusual merit of the recipient. This was an unfortunate frame of mind. There is nothing ignoble in sincere gratitude ; a man or a nation may gladly admit that others have acted as friends. " I think," Franklin wrote to the President of Congress, " an expression of gratitude is not only our duty, but our interest. A different conduct seems to me what is not only improper and unbecoming, but what may be hurtful to us. Mr. Adams, on the other hand, who at the same time means our welfare and interest as much as I or any man can do, seems to think a little apparent stoutness and a greater air of independence and boldness in our demands will procure us more ample assistance. It is for the Congress to judge and regulate their affairs accordingly." [1]

Adams was convinced that Franklin's way to secure aid from France was not the right way, and he adopted a course of his own with such success that Vergennes at last refused to have any further communication with him. Adams informed the French minister that the colonies were under no distressing burden of obligation to their ally. " On the other hand, the French could not acknowledge too much obligation to America," he said, " for, without their coöperation, England was too powerful for the House of Bourbon, . . . and France should not grow weary of a policy that had secured for her an amount of con-

[1] Aug. 9, 1780; Wharton, iv, 23.

sideration in Europe such as she had never received before." [1]

A further controversy was excited over the repudiation by Congress of its paper money. Apart from the aid furnished by the government, French merchants had sent large quantities of supplies to the Americans, and they held large amounts of the Continental paper currency. In March, 1780, Congress recommended that this should be redeemed at the rate of forty to one, and Adams informed Vergennes of this action. Not unnaturally, the minister was greatly disturbed. This, he wrote, will be a most severe blow to the French, who have been ready to furnish the Americans with articles necessary for them, and who will be ruined as a return for their aid. Little of this currency had come into the hands of other foreigners, and now those were to suffer who had been willing to assist the Americans in their distress. [2]

When Franklin was constantly asking for new loans, it was hardly the part of wisdom to insist that the colonies had the moral right to settle with their creditors at two and a half cents on the dollar, but Adams did not hesitate. He sent Vergennes an elaborate argument, showing that Congress had the right to adopt this measure, and there could be no exception in favor of foreigners. " I flatter myself," he wrote, " that I am so much a master of the principles as to demonstrate that the plan of Congress is not only wise but just." [3]

He flattered himself without cause. Doubtless the demonstration convinced Adams, but it produced in Vergennes an indignation that was not unnatural. He

[1] Relation, June 17, 1780; Doniol, iv, 416.
[2] Despatch, June 3, 1780; Doniol, iv, 415.
[3] Doniol, iv, 418.

wrote La Luzerne asking that Congress should modify the resolution so far as it concerned French subjects, and added, " His Majesty flatters himself that
this assembly, actuated by other principles than those
Mr. Adams has shown, will think the French worthy
of some consideration, and that it appreciates the
marks of interest which the King has incessantly manifested towards the United States." [1]

Refusing to be convinced by the arguments of
Adams, Vergennes carried his woes to Franklin. "Mr.
Adams . . . has sent me," he wrote, "a long disserta-
tion, . . . but it contains only abstract reasonings, hy-
potheses, and calculations, . . . principles than which
nothing can be less analogous to the alliance subsisting
between his Majesty and the United States." [2]

It is not strange that Franklin should have regretted the unwise activity of his associate, and he
endeavored to sooth Vergennes's irritation. " When
we are asking aid," he wrote Arthur Lee, " it is necessary to gratify the desires, and, in some sort, comply
with the humors of those we apply to." This sentiment would have been approved by Adams as little as
it was by Lee. At all events, on July 10, Franklin
wrote Vergennes that it was just that foreign merchants, and especially the French, should not suffer
from this action, and he agreed to lay the whole question before Congress for its consideration. This he
did, much to Adams's annoyance, and the incident
helped to increase the latter's irritation against both
Vergennes and Franklin. [3]

This episode was followed by another, in which
Adams could only have volunteered his advice because

[1] Doniol, iv, 419.   [2] Translated in Wharton, iii, 827.
[3] Wharton, iii, 844.

he felt that Franklin was not capable of attending to
the interests of the country he represented. In July,
1780, Adams sent Vergennes a letter in regard to
directions to be given Rochambeau and Ternay, who
were about to sail to America with an army to assist
Washington. Adams informed the French minister
that, while he did not know to what part of America
Ternay and Rochambeau were destined, he had no
hopes of anything decisive from their operations,
even though they were instructed to coöperate with
General Washington. Having indulged in this prophecy, which the result did not verify, he stated that
what America desired was the presence of French
ships cruising along the coast and giving an opportunity for American privateers to levy contributions
upon English commerce. He added, in somewhat
questionable taste, that many Americans thought the
court of France did not mean to give any effectual
aid to America; and while he deprecated such an opinion, he suggested that the action he recommended
would prove the sincerity of the French in their alliance. Of a French army he saw less need, because
he said that the English troops in North America
for the last two years had been absolutely in the
power of their enemies, so nothing was wanted but a
little attention to accomplish the entire reduction of
their power.[1]

If Adams thought the American troops were able
to overcome the English forces unassisted, he certainly
did not share Washington's opinion. A little earlier
Washington had written: " Unless a system very
different from that which has for a long time prevailed be immediately adopted throughout the states,

[1] *Works of John Adams*, vii, 219–227.

our affairs must soon become desperate, beyond the possibility of recovery. . . . Indeed, I have almost ceased to hope."

Whether Adams's suggestions were marked by more or less wisdom, Vergennes might properly have replied that his advice would be considered when it was asked. He sent, however, a civil answer, saying that the troops were directed to act under Washington's orders. This drew a further reply, in which Adams criticized the manner in which the French had furnished military assistance, and this he accompanied by the announcement that advice might be expected frequently from him in future. " I am determined," he wrote, " to omit no opportunity of communicating my sentiments to your Excellency upon everything that appears to me of importance to the common cause, in which I can do it with any propriety." [1]

He might well have omitted the last clause. Franklin was the minister by whom such communications could properly be made, but Adams was convinced of his own superior wisdom, and felt that his counsels must fill the gaps left by the indolent voluptuary who was neglecting his country's interests.

This criticism exceeded the limitations of Vergennes's endurance, and the prospect of endless communications from this self-appointed counsellor doubtless filled him with dismay. He forwarded the entire correspondence with Adams to Franklin, with the request that it should be sent to Congress, in order that that body might know how its representative was discharging a duty equally important and delicate. To Adams himself he replied that Franklin was the only person accredited from the United States to the French

[1] Doniol, iv, 422 ; *Works of John Adams*, vii, 241.

King, and with him alone such matters must be treated. And he added, as a farewell shot, that his Majesty did not require Mr. Adams's solicitations in order to interest him in the welfare of the United States.[1]

To La Luzerne Vergennes laid bare his heart. " This plenipotentiary will only cause embarrassment and mischief. He possesses a rigidity, a pedantry, an arrogance and a vanity which render him unfit to treat political questions." [2]

Adams's relations with the French minister were now so strained that even he realized that he could not be of service in Paris. On July 27, 1780, he left for Holland and endeavored to obtain assistance for the United States from the States-General. He insisted that the French representative hindered his progress in Holland, but in this he seems to have been mistaken. Vergennes did not allow any petty annoyance to interfere with his exertions for the success of the allied cause, and as the Dutch were unwilling to lend on the credit of the United States, the French King borrowed ten million livres and turned them over to his allies.

Patriotism does not require us to say that in these controversies the American was always right, and the Frenchman always wrong. Vergennes disliked Adams and believed him more friendly to England than to France. The belief was not correct, but the dislike was natural. The qualities which Adams manifested in a still more striking way when he was president, were displayed in his career as a diplomat. He not only suspected of wickedness those who differed from him, but he was sure they were wicked. The man who

---

[1] July 29, 1780; Doniol, iv, 423.
[2] Letter of Aug. 7, 1780; Doniol, iv, 423.

believes every one else a thief and a liar is usually a rogue himself, but Adams's frame of mind was exceptional. He was a man of the utmost uprightness and veracity, and yet he found it hard to believe that others possessed any of the honesty of which he had so much. To conciliate, to use the wise arts of a Franklin, he regarded as unworthy conduct, to which he would not stoop.

During all the late years of the war it was necessary for the states to obtain large sums of money from an ally whose own financial condition was constantly becoming worse. The French people were ardent in the American cause, and Vergennes was sincerely anxious for the independence of the colonies. But the most zealous friend can be chilled, and Adams was peculiarly fitted to make the French minister button up his pockets and leave the American colonies to carry on the war, unaided by French gold, and with a paper currency of which five hundred dollars would not buy as much as one louis. Adams was patriotic and upright, but these qualities alone could not make an adroit negotiator for a struggling state demanding aid. If Franklin had been recalled, as Lee and Izard and his other enemies desired that he should be, and Adams alone had represented the United States at the court of Versailles during these closing years, when our success was assured by French aid, it is entirely possible that the aid would have been refused and the alliance would have come to naught. The sympathy of the French people for our cause had much to do in keeping the French nation constant to our alliance, but it is impossible to overestimate the value of the aid which Franklin rendered.

It was unfortunate that Adams excited the animosity of the French minister, and his usefulness was also diminished by the morbid jealousy with which he regarded Franklin's position. Even if Franklin had not been at the zenith of popularity and fame, his character would have been distasteful to this exact and rigorous Puritan. There was, apparently, something to criticize in the conduct of the American minister. He was old, rather infirm, fond of pleasure, and by no means an accurate man of business. He sent few letters to Congress, and went to a great many dinners with entertaining Frenchmen and charming Frenchwomen. There is no doubt he found the latter occupation more agreeable, and, considering the conditions of French society, it is by no means certain that he was not serving his country quite as well when delighting diplomats and philosophers with his conversation, as when writing letters that would reach Philadelphia six months after the events they narrated.

Very improperly, important financial duties were added to Franklin's diplomatic responsibilities. He asked to be relieved from them, but he asked in vain. Whenever Congress was in need of money, and it was always in need, a bill of exchange was drawn on Franklin, and he was expected to get the French minister to advance the funds with which to honor it. He succeeded in doing this for years with marvellous success, and it was largely owing to the qualities which Adams condemned, that Franklin was rarely sent away empty-handed from a begging trip to the chamber of Vergennes. It is certain that if Adams had been minister, the French treasury would have been soon closed to such requests, and dishonored Congressional drafts would have been as plentiful as discredited Continental currency.

It must be said also that when it came to the accounts of the moneys disbursed by Franklin upon innumerable requests and demands, they were carelessly and imperfectly kept. Franklin had little clerical assistance; he was not systematic, he disliked detail work, and the accounts of the American treasury in Paris were in great confusion. Not even Franklin's enemies ever questioned his absolute integrity, but integrity is not all that is required in public finance.

From the nature of his being, Adams was jealous of Franklin's popularity, and he found abundant grounds for criticisms, which he honestly believed to be just. He wrote his cousin in 1778 of his views on Franklin. " The other you know personally, and that he loves his Ease, hates to offend, and seldom gives any opinion till obliged to do it. I know also, and it is necessary that you should be informed, that he is overwhelmed with a correspondence from all quarters, most of them upon trifling subjects and in a more trifling style, with unmeaning visits from Multitudes of People, chiefly from the Vanity of having it to say that they have seen him. There is another thing that I am obliged to mention. There are so many private families, Ladies and gentlemen, that he visits so often, — and they are so fond of him, that he cannot well avoid it, — and so much intercourse with Academicians, that all these things together keep his mind in a constant state of dissipation. . . . But if he is left here alone, . . . and all maritime and Commercial as well as political affairs and money matters are left in his Hands, I am persuaded that France and America will both have Reason to repent it. He is not only so indolent that Business will be neglected, but you know that, although he has as determined a soul as any man, yet it is his constant Policy never to say 'yes' or 'no' decidedly, but when he cannot avoid it."[1]

Adams's animosity toward Franklin grew no less with time. In 1811, when Franklin had been dead for twenty-one years, and Adams had long retired from public life, he accused Franklin and Vergennes of conspiring to crush him, of indulging in low intrigues and base tricks; he charged the philosopher with extreme indolence and dissipation, and denounced the turpitude of his conduct when he entered into partnership with the Comte de Vergennes, the most powerful minister of state in Europe, to destroy the character and power of a poor man, almost without a name, born and educated in the American wilderness and unknown in the European world.[2]

Franklin's position in France was too brilliant to be disturbed by any jealousy of Adams, though doubtless he was annoyed by the latter's ill-timed activity. To plot and intrigue, as Adams charged him with doing, would have been as foreign to Franklin's character as to Washington's. In the intensity of his atrabilious character, Adams's judgment went far astray, and his conviction of Vergennes's furtive and wicked hostility toward America seems as groundless as his belief that Franklin was guilty of tricks and low intrigues.

Vergennes was an astute and experienced diplomat, yet if it be the test of diplomacy to get the utmost possible for the country one represents, Franklin was his superior. Personal liking had much to do with

---

[1] To Samuel Adams, Dec. 7, 1778; Hale, *Franklin in France*, i, 229.

[2] *Works of John Adams*, i, 664.

the fact that the French minister was loath to say no to any request of the American envoy; but no man realized more thoroughly than Franklin how valuable is personal popularity in such negotiations, and no one used it more unsparingly, — Vergennes might have said, more unmercifully. Even Adams admitted that the French court put its confidence in Franklin alone, but still he felt that the vigor and intellect of an Adams ought to be more effectual than the affability and adroitness of a Franklin.

A new endeavor for peace led to some change in Adams's position and increased his irritation against the French court. In the early part of 1781 there seemed little reason to expect a speedy and favorable termination of the war. The year 1780 was one of disaster: Charleston had been captured, Gates had been defeated at Camden, and much of the South had fallen into the possession of the English. In the North the treachery of Arnold had threatened the country with ruin. The finances of the colonies were at their lowest ebb, Continental currency had become practically worthless, a suit of clothes cost two thousand dollars, a barrel of flour sold for fifteen hundred dollars. The results of the alliance between France and the United States had not, thus far, corresponded to the hopes which had been entertained; the cost of the war was constantly increasing, while the expectation of a successful termination grew less. It was at this juncture that Russia and Austria offered to act as mediators and close this protracted and unfortunate contest.

Vergennes was unwilling to repel the offer, lest he should give offence to those countries, and, moreover, he was quite ready for peace. The English, so it was said, would accept the mediation, but France could take no step without the consent of her allies. In his desire for peace, the terms to which Vergennes wished Congress to agree seem singularly unsatisfactory, and differ widely from those that were obtained a few years later. But although the French minister was eager that the ultimatum should be so moderate as to insure its acceptance, his subsequent conduct showed that he was willing his allies should get as much more as they could. The proposition of mediation was made at almost the lowest era of depression during the war. It was not strange that Vergennes advised his allies to be satisfied with moderate terms, when victory seemed so remote, and in writing to the French minister at Philadelphia, he even suggested that it might be necessary to consent to the loss of some of the thirteen states.

"It is certain," he said, "that the United States . . . would suffer a sensible loss by the separation of some of the provinces. . . . In this the King entirely agrees with Congress, and his Majesty, guided by an intelligent policy and by his engagements, will do all he can that the thirteen colonies may preserve their union without alteration. But only too often circumstances furnish the law to the most powerful sovereigns. . . . The King will not change his resolution, unless he sees the absolute impossibility of obtaining a reasonable peace without some sacrifice. But . . . a sacrifice is among the possibilities, and if it becomes unavoidable, it is necessary to be resigned. Most of the Belgian provinces threw off the Spanish yoke, but only seven preserved their independence. . . . It is well that we should make the Americans realize that the war cannot be eternal, and there is a time at which one must needs stop. . . . His Majesty will suggest no sacrifice to them. This unpleasant task he will leave to the two mediating powers if ever it becomes necessary." [1]

This suggestion was not made to Congress, but the possibility that it might be necessary to accept a long truce, instead of a formal recognition of independence, was not only suggested to Congress but was acknowledged by that body. In advising Congress to obtain the good-will of the mediators, by exercising the utmost moderation in their demands, Vergennes added the judicious counsel, that whether treating for a permanent peace or for a truce, the war should be carried on with the utmost vigor, for this was the true way to bring the English to reason and secure honorable terms. [2]

In June, 1781, Congress authorized the commissioners to accept the mediation of the Emperor of Russia and the Emperor of Germany (as he was inaccurately styled), insisting only that no peace should be made without an acknowledgment of the independence of the thirteen states. As to all other matters, they were left to the suggestions already given Adams, in which they could see the desires and expectations of Congress, but they were bound by no fixed instructions: they were to secure the interests of the United States in such manner as circumstances might direct. So far as their relations with France were concerned, the instructions were couched in language which the French minister might well have dictated, and which was probably due to his inspiration, in substance if not in form. "You are to make the most candid and confidential communications upon all subjects to the ministers of our generous ally, the King of France;

[1] Vergennes to La Luzerne, June 30, 1781; Doniol, iv, 601-602.
[2] Doniol, iv, 553-556.

to undertake nothing in the negotiations for peace or truce without their knowledge and concurrence, and ultimately to govern yourselves by their advice and opinion." [1]

If these instructions were followed literally, the American commissioners must adopt whatever conditions of peace the French minister should decide to recommend. Probably so extraordinary an abrogation of independent action was not intended to be taken literally; the commissioners were to pay to the opinion of a valued ally the deference to which it was justly entitled, and to sign no treaty unless France joined. As a matter of fact, the instructions did not prove of any importance. They were drawn in view of the mediation offered by Russia and Austria, and this came to nothing; when peace was made, the representatives of England and America conferred with one another and agreed on terms, and the American commissioners decided that it was not advisable to have Vergennes join in their deliberations. The instructions of Congress, to obtain which La Luzerne had spent so many anxious hours, proved of no more value than so much blank paper.

The action taken by Congress in another direction was of more practical importance. Adams had become distasteful to Vergennes, and the French minister would have been pleased if some one else had replaced the belligerent New Englander, but to this his friends would in no way consent. The people of New England felt that Adams would be to them a tower of strength in the great question of the fisheries, and a large party in Congress was loath to inflict upon him the affront of a recall, even if he had not always been

[1] Wharton, iv, 505.

judicious in his diplomatic career. It was decided therefore to create a commission to treat of peace, instead of leaving Adams alone. Jay was unanimously chosen as his associate, and Laurens, who was then a prisoner in the Tower of London, and Jefferson were selected as other associates. The French minister was anxious that Franklin should be one of the commissioners, and Franklin was manifestly a fit man for the work. But there was strong opposition to him in Congress. Arthur Lee and Izard had returned home filled with anger, and had followed him with unwearying animosity. The Lees had an important following in Congress, and they were all hostile to Franklin. Only by the active manipulation of Sullivan was it possible to elect Benjamin Franklin as one of five commissioners.

It is sad to find that the influence of the French minister rested in part on the arts of corruption. Tom Paine had used his ready pen in a manner distasteful to the minister, and the latter adopted a simple remedy. He saw Paine and suggested that he should employ his pen in inspiring his people with proper feelings in reference to France and the alliance, and with hatred toward the English. "He informed me, that he would accept this task with pleasure. I promised him an allowance of a thousand dollars a year." [1] The same simple appliance obtained the support of General Sullivan when he became a member of Congress, and his action secured Franklin's selection as one of the peace commissioners. "This delegate," writes La Luzerne, "has shown in this affair equal patriotism and attachment for the alliance." [2]

[1] Gérard to Vergennes, Jan. 17, 1779; Doniol, iv, 60.
[2] La Luzerne to Vergennes, May 13, 1781; Doniol, iv, 608.

The selection of additional commissioners to treat for peace was naturally distasteful to Adams, and he was offended also by the form of the instructions. In this, as in many other things, he saw sure proof of the duplicity and bad faith of the French government. The action of Congress excited him to an outburst which seems somewhat frothy. " Congress surrendered their own sovereignty into the hands of a French minister. Blush, blush, ye guilty records, blush and perish. It is a glory to have broken such infamous orders. Infamous, I say, for so they will be to all posterity. How can such a stain be washed out!" In declaring that his country had prostituted its own honor Adams was sincere, as he always was; but there seems no reason that the records of which he complains should stain their yellow parchment by a blush, or that posterity should be disturbed by their infamy.

Congress insisted on less than its commissioners obtained, but the instructions were given when the fortunes of the colonies were almost at their lowest ebb; the commissioners undertook the negotiations when the victory at Yorktown had brought the war to a successful termination. When the instructions were adopted, it was asking much to insist on American independence. When the representatives of America and England began their formal conferences American independence had been recognized, and they had only to deal with the other questions arising between the two countries. To Vergennes's firmness as much as to any other single fact, the commissioners were indebted for this advantage.

CHAPTER XXV

NEGOTIATIONS FOR PEACE

In the conduct of Vergennes during the negotiations there was little of which a reasonable man could complain. Adams's belief, that France nearly bankrupted herself in a Machiavellian scheme to save the colonies from utter overthrow, and yet keep them from becoming powerful or rich, might almost seem the product of a diseased imagination. Vergennes wrote La Luzerne, his representative in America, that the King would use his influence for the advantage of the United States, and if he did not succeed in procuring for them all that they desired, the fault would be not his, but that of the circumstances which controlled him.[1] There was nothing in Vergennes's conduct which did not correspond to this profession, and nothing to show that he was displeased at the success of the American plenipotentiaries in their demands ; even when they agreed on terms with the English without consultation with him, he manifested only transient and not very strong annoyance. The diabolical ingenuity which Adams and Jay detected in the conduct of the French minister appears neither in his acts nor in his correspondence.

On the other hand, Vergennes was anxious, and, from the standpoint of French interests, justly anxious, that peace should be made. Prudent men like Turgot had advised the King that in the financial

[1] Doniol, v, 42.

condition of the country it was perilous to incur the expense of a new war. But the desire to avenge past defeats and humiliate England, together with a sincere sympathy with the efforts of the colonists to achieve freedom, united in overcoming these prudent counsels. In 1775 the debt of France had reached over two milliards and the expenses exceeded the income by twenty million livres.[1] The cost of the war had been great.[2] Vergennes felt that it was important that France should have peace, and have it speedily. He had undertaken war to obtain the independence of the colonies, and that result was now secured. It was neither strange nor reprehensible that he did not desire to continue the war in order to secure advantages for his allies in which France felt no special interest.

Except so far as they might conflict with the desires of Spain, to which France was bound by closer bonds than to the colonies, Vergennes was willing that the Americans should make the best terms they could. He neither said nor did anything to interfere with the success of their negotiations, but he was exceedingly anxious that they should not protract the war over the question of their fisheries and their western boundaries, and thus involve France in further contest. Therefore it was that he desired that Congress should not put forward these demands as an ultimatum, but should so leave it that peace might be made, even if all the advantages desired were not obtained. And, therefore, he wished that, so far as possible, the American commissioners should consult with the French King; not that he might betray them, but that negotiations might be so guided that peace should be the sure result.

[1] Doniol, i, 282.   [2] Gomel, *Les Derniers Contrôleurs*, i, 36.

It is evident that Vergennes would have cared little about the form of the instructions adopted by Congress if the negotiations had been entirely in Franklin's hands. In his sagacity and fairness Vergennes had the utmost confidence, but he felt, and not unjustly, that Adams was hostile to France and himself. He wrote La Luzerne, expressing his pleasure at the action of Congress because, otherwise, Adams would have been free to follow or reject the advice of France. "It is sufficient to know the character and principles of Mr. John Adams to realize how dangerous such power would have been in his hands, and how we might have been exposed to scenes that would have been disagreeable and even scandalous." But now that "the ardor, the stubbornness and the roughness of Mr. Adams will be tempered by the calmness, the wisdom and the experience of Franklin," Vergennes thought that all would be well.[1]

Throughout the war France dealt liberally with the colonies. She had driven no hard bargain, when she promised them her aid; if it had not been for French assistance, the army of Washington would have disbanded because the states were unable or unwilling to raise the money to supply the needs of the soldiers; had it not been for the assistance of the French army and fleet, Yorktown would not have been taken. So when Adams called on the guilty records to blush and perish, because they instructed him and his associates to consult with the French King as to terms of peace, his emotions as well as his metaphors were somewhat exaggerated; and when he accused the French of acting from a malicious purpose to cripple the country they had befriended, the

[1] Doniol, v, 43.

fact that he entertained such a belief is not creditable to his intelligence.

Such was the condition of affairs when the news of the surrender of Yorktown reached Paris. It was apparent that the war was practically ended, and the long endeavor of England to reduce the colonies to subjection must now be abandoned. George III indeed refused to recognize the situation; his indomitable stubbornness, if it had been attended by intelligence, would have made him almost a great man. " The getting a peace at the expense of separation from America," he wrote after the fatal news, ". . . is a step to which no difficulties shall ever get me to be, in the smallest degree, an instrument." [1]

But even North would no longer heed the royal commands, and in the brief interval before his overthrow, he made some overtures for peace. Apparently his hope was to divide the allies, and by making terms with one, to gain the chance of obtaining better terms from, or of continuing the war against, the other. Secret emissaries visited both Franklin and Vergennes to see if either would consider separate action, but they met a similar rebuff from both.

In the choice of the agent sent to Franklin a stupidity was shown worthy of George III in his best days. A man named Digges, a Maryland merchant and a protégé of Arthur Lee, had some dealings in relation to the American prisoners in England. Franklin, at various times, furnished money to relieve the needs of these unfortunate men, and a portion of this Digges received for distribution. Some four hundred pounds of it he misapplied to his own use. Such a

[1] William B. Donne, *The Correspondence of George III and Lord North*, ii, 398.

dastardly theft, practised upon these unfortunates, excited the wrath of the benevolent philosopher. " What is he," he wrote, " who can break his sacred trust by robbing a poor man and a prisoner of eighteen pence given in charity for his relief, and repeat that crime as often as there are weeks in a winter. . . . If such a fellow is not damned, it is not worth while to keep a devil." [1]

Yet Digges was sent to visit Franklin, and see if he would enter upon secret negotiations for peace between England and the colonies. Suggestions for a separate peace had been made before, but had received no encouragement from Franklin. " There is not a man in America, a few English tories excepted," he wrote his friend Hartley, a member of Parliament, who often suggested the desirability of a reconciliation, " that would not spurn at the thought of deserting a noble and generous friend for the sake of a truce with an unjust and cruel enemy. . . . The Congress will never instruct their commissioners to obtain a peace on such ignominious terms, and though there can be but few things in which I should venture to disobey their orders, yet if it were possible for them to give me such an order as this, I should certainly refuse to act." [2] Digges was now informed that the American commissioners were ready to treat, but there could be no peace with America unless France were included.

Another emissary named Forth visited Vergennes and suggested the possibility of peace between France and England on terms favorable to the former country; but throughout all negotiations and suggestions

[1] Franklin to Hodgson, April 1, 1781; *Writings of Franklin,* Smyth's ed., viii, 231.

[2] Franklin to Hartley, Jan. 15, 1782 ; *Ibid.,* 358.

for negotiations, Vergennes had one answer: that France would agree to nothing unless peace were made also with her allies on terms satisfactory to them.[1]

The situation was a complicated one. England had begun war with her revolted colonies alone, but there were now four nations in arms against her, and the field of hostilities extended from the banks of the James to the mouths of the Ganges. Hostile fleets met on the Atlantic, the Mediterranean, and the Pacific; while Washington was besieging Yorktown, the Spanish were besieging Gibraltar, and Dutch crews were infesting the British Channel and the North Sea. England's enemies were actuated by different purposes, and not all of them were even bound together by any formal alliance. France had made a treaty with the United States, in which she agreed to carry on war until their independence was secured. Spain had entered the contest somewhat later as the ally of France, but she was in no way an ally of the United States. Her action had been welcome, because it increased the difficulties England had to meet, and Spain and the colonies had, to a certain extent, acted harmoniously. Jay had been received as the American minister at Madrid, and the Spanish had furnished some money to the Americans, though very much less than had been asked.

But Spain was making war for her own hand: she had succeeded to the rights of France in the vague and vast possession which went by the name of Louisiana, and looked with jealousy on the desire of the United States to extend their western boundaries and share in the navigation of the Mississippi. Spain had taken part in the war, not from any desire to assist in

[1] Doniol, ii, *passim* (see Index, under Forth).

procuring American independence, but because she hoped, as a result of the struggle, to extort advantages for herself. France and Spain were closely united by the Family Compact, and the French minister felt bound to obtain satisfactory terms for France's ally, the Spanish King, no less than for her other ally, the American colonies. From this came many of his embarrassments: neither wished to be sacrificed to the other, and their desires in some respects were likely to become antagonistic.

The French had not asked at any time any important advantages for their own country. It was believed that the independence of the American colonies would be a fatal blow to the mercantile supremacy of England, and the French anticipated sharing in the trade with the young and growing nation, which, in the past, had been monopolized by the English. Vergennes hoped also to secure for France some minor advantages in India, and some modifications in the ignominious treaty which had closed the Seven Years' War.

The States-General of the Netherlands had recently been forced into the war by the overbearing conduct of England, but they were not allies of any of the other three combatants, and only friendly feelings required them to be included in the negotiations for peace.

Such was the condition of the various belligerents when the prospect of peace began to assume practical shape. The efforts to induce either France or the colonies to desert their alliance, so that England might make terms with one and continue war against the other, had been made and had failed. The English ministry now proceeded in good faith to bring to an end a disastrous war, which had continued for seven years without advantage or glory. On March 20, 1782, Lord North resigned, and the negotiations passed into the hands of the Rockingham ministry.

In the new administration Lord Shelburne was secretary of state for the colonies, and with him Franklin had been on friendly relations when in England years before. Franklin found an opportunity to send a note of congratulation, in which he expressed the hope that Lord Shelburne's return to power might lead to a general peace. In answer to this, informal negotiations soon began, which at last resulted in a formal treaty.

The first suggestion of the English was that the independence of the United States should be accorded, and that, in return for this concession, peace should be made between France and England on the terms of the Treaty of Paris in 1763. But this involved the surrender of all the advantages France had gained in the war, in return for an acknowledgment of independence, which had been actually won. As Franklin said, "This seems to me a proposition of selling to us a thing that is already our own, and making France pay the price they are pleased to ask for it." [1]

In April, one Oswald, an amiable but not especially astute old gentleman, visited Paris, and received from Franklin a rough statement of the demands that would be made by the United States, and Fox, the secretary of foreign affairs, sent Mr. Grenville on a similar errand to Vergennes. In one of Grenville's interviews with Franklin he suggested that France might insist on conditions that were not provided for in the original alliance, and if so the Americans were

[1] Franklin to Adams, May 8, 1782; *Writings of Franklin*, Smyth's ed., viii, 487.

not bound to continue the war in order to obtain them. But Franklin, during his years of residence at Paris, had learned the value of the assistance which France rendered the colonies, and was distressed by a suggestion that savored of scanty gratitude. "I told him," he writes, "I was so strongly impressed with the kind assistance afforded us by France in our distress, and the generous and noble manner in which it was granted, without exacting or stipulating for a single privilege or particular advantage to herself in our commerce or otherwise, that I could never suffer myself to think of such reasonings for lessening the obligation; and I hoped, and, indeed, did not doubt, but my countrymen were all of the same sentiments." [1]

The attitude of France was the same. The credentials of Grenville authorized him to treat with the French; but either from accident or design their allies were omitted. But Vergennes repeated what he had so often said, — that France would enter into no negotiations unless her allies were included in them. [2]

Shelburne and Fox were distrustful of each other, and played at cross-purposes. Fox desired that the independence of the United States should be at once acknowledged. Perhaps his desire was the stronger, because negotiations with the United States as a foreign power would come within his province, and Shelburne, as secretary for the colonies, could then have no pretence for interfering in them. Shelburne, on the other hand, thought that the acknowledgment of independence should be left for the treaty, and that he should remain in charge of the matter. The quarrels of the ministers in London found their echo in the

[1] Franklin's Journal; *Writings of Franklin*, Smyth's ed., viii, 499.
[2] Conference, May 26, 1782; Doniol, v, 113.

reports of the envoys at Paris. Grenville complained to Fox that Oswald seemed the favorite channel of communication, and that when he sought to learn from Franklin the views of the American commissioners, he encountered an impenetrable reserve.

Fox soon quarrelled with Shelburne and resigned, and the negotiations were left entirely in the hands of the latter. In April, 1782, the Comte de Grasse suffered a crushing defeat in the West Indies, and both Vergennes and Franklin feared that this disaster might check the anxiety of the English to end the war. Apparently it had no such effect; the English minister was still ready and anxious to make peace, if it could be obtained on reasonable terms. So far as the United States were concerned, the defeat of de Grasse proved in no way prejudicial to their interests. The war in North America had practically ceased, and, as a result of this disaster, France and Spain were less apt to delay peace by demanding advantages which the English would not grant.

Accordingly Oswald was selected to treat with the American commissioners, while Grenville was replaced by Fitzherbert in the negotiations with Vergennes. The choice of Oswald to continue the work he had begun must have been satisfactory to Lord Shelburne, and it was certainly very agreeable to Franklin. The Scotsman seems to have been one of the most amiable of men, and one of the poorest of diplomats. He was, as Shelburne truly said, "a pacifical man," while Franklin styled him "a very honest, sensible man." The American commissioner might well have thought Oswald sensible, for whatever Franklin advanced Oswald regarded as worthy of serious, if not of favorable, consideration ; and by his plaintive eagerness to obtain

peace at any price, he encouraged the American representatives to insist upon their demands, when their
antagonist was plainly ready to concede everything.
Oswald said, indeed, that the English were ready to
carry on war, if France demanded humiliating terms
of peace. But as a means of raising supplies, he could
only suggest they might follow the example of Charles
II, shut up the exchequer, and default on the payment
of interest on the public debt.

If only in this way could England raise money to
carry on the war, Franklin felt that her enemies need
not be afraid. Accordingly he suggested to Oswald
that if England wished to make reparation for the
harm she had done, and avoid future trouble, she
had best cede Canada to the United States. This he
said would really be a reconciliation, which, he added,
" is a sweet word." To obtain Canada was a favorite
scheme of Franklin's, and if it had been insisted upon
as strenuously as the American right to the fisheries,
possibly it might have been granted. " Her chief advantage from that possession," said Franklin, " consists in the trade for peltry"; and this was not seriously
contested.[1]

The complacent Oswald, if we can trust Franklin,
liked the idea, and said that, while England was too
much straitened to make reparation in money, he
would try to persuade the minister to offer it in this
form. But Shelburne did not view the proposition
with favor, and New England and its representatives
were more interested in the banks of Newfoundland
than in the farms of Canada. So Franklin's favorite
scheme came to naught, though the acquisition of

[1] Lord Edward Fitzmaurice, *Life of William Earl of Shelburne*,
iii, 180–182.

Canada would have been worth more to our country than all the cod in the sea.

The United States were a small and poor people dealing with a rich and powerful monarchy, yet they had an advantage of position in these negotiations which their representatives used to the utmost. As it was certain that the independence of the colonies must be recognized, Shelburne now desired to restore, so far as possible, friendly relations. If the Americans were to be no longer English colonists, there was no reason why they should not remain England's customers and furnish an important outlet for English trade. The long war had embittered their feelings, and Shelburne feared lest this might divert from hostile England to friendly France a great portion of their valuable commerce; therefore he wished to make peace promptly, and was willing to concede liberal terms.

There was, however, delay over the preliminaries. The powers granted Oswald authorized him to treat with the thirteen colonies or plantations. As it was understood on all sides that recognition of the absolute independence of the United States would be the first article of any treaty, any preliminary acknowledgment was a matter of form rather than of substance. So at least it seemed to Franklin, who was anxious to proceed, so that terms might be agreed upon before Parliament met on the 26th of November. The condition of Shelburne's ministry was one of unstable equilibrium, and both the minister and Franklin desired that an agreement between England and the United States should be presented to Parliament at its opening as an accomplished transaction, and beyond the power of parliamentary interference.

But John Jay arrived in Paris in June, and he soon became the leading actor in these negotiations. Franklin was not well and much of the time was confined to his bed. Jay was young, ambitious, and vigorous, and, after two years of uselessness at Madrid, he naturally yearned for a field where something could be accomplished. He at once declared that he would not proceed with the conferences unless the independence of the United States was first formally acknowledged.

If the English had desired delay, this furnished them with abundant pretext for it; but Shelburne wanted peace, and was ready to please the Americans in every respect. He had cherished the dream of a federation between the mother country and the American colonies, a vision which, applied to other colonies of England, still allures the English statesman. In his instructions to Oswald he suggested the possibility of some plan of federal union, and wished Franklin to consider the suggestion; but he was soon convinced that the day for this had gone by. For political reasons of his own he did not desire delay, and he was willing to grant favorable terms in the hope of preserving for the mother country a liberal share in the trade with the new nation. These considerations made him ready to yield on debated questions, and accordingly the instructions were modified to meet Jay's requirements. Oswald was authorized to treat with the commissioners of the thirteen United States, and their existence as a nation was formally acknowledged at the beginning of the negotiations.

In October Adams arrived from Holland and assumed his duties as one of the commissioners. In his diary he expressed his opinion of his associates.

"Between two as subtle spirits as any in this world, the one malicious, the other I think honest, I shall have a delicate, a nice, a critical part to act. Franklin's cunning will be to divide us; to that end he will provoke, he will insinuate, he will intrigue, he will maneuver. My curiosity will at least be employed in observing his invention and his artifice." [1]

Such was Adams's judgment upon one who had done as much to secure the success of the colonies in Europe as Washington had done in America. It is sad that a man who was honest, able, and patriotic could view no one who obtained a larger degree of popular favor than himself except with a malevolent jealousy that blinded his judgment and lessened his usefulness.

Whatever lack of harmony existed among themselves, the American plenipotentiaries were now ready to proceed, and the question arose as to how far they should confer with their French allies. Jay, as well as Adams, had little love for France. " Mr. Jay likes Frenchmen as little as Mr. Lee and Mr. Izard did," writes Adams; " he says they are not a moral people; they know not what it is; he don't like any Frenchmen. The Marquis de La Fayette is clever, but he is a Frenchman." [2] Jay's dislike of the French prepared him to distrust their policy, and he soon formed the opinion that Vergennes was secretly manœuvring against the interests of the United States. These suspicions became certainties in his mind when he discovered that one Rayneval had been sent on a secret mission to London. His object, so Jay was convinced, was to tell Shelburne that France disapproved of the American demands in reference to

[1] *Works of John Adams*, iii, 300.　　　　[2] *Ibid.*, 303.

the fisheries and the boundaries, and would not support them.

Both Americans and Frenchmen may feel some interest as to the justness of this suspicion. The French did so much for our ancestors that it is unpleasant to believe that at the last they acted in bad faith, and looked with ill-favor upon demands that were important to the young republic. The entire record is before the world; we can read the instructions of Vergennes to La Luzerne, the reports of Rayneval, all that was said and done in the negotiations carried on between France and England, and nothing can be found which shows any endeavor on the part of the French to prevent the entire success of their American allies. Even if Vergennes was not anxious that all their demands should be granted, he did nothing and said nothing which could be criticized as in any way showing bad faith.

It is indeed certain that Vergennes did not wish to continue an expensive war in order to secure for the United States either fisheries or enlarged boundaries; in the matter of the Mississippi Valley he probably would have been glad to see an agreement reached that might be satisfactory to Spain. But in this there was no ground for complaint, and when it came to the actual negotiations, Vergennes's course was consistent and upright. He repeatedly informed the English that France had no authority to treat for the United States, and in no way did he interfere with the success of their negotiations. The history of the Rayneval mission can be studied in the records of the French foreign office; it is honorable both to Shelburne and to Vergennes.[1] It was on account of this mission that Jay and Adams

[1] Doniol, v, chap. 4.

decided that the French were acting in bad faith, and it is worth while, therefore, to give a brief account of the transaction.

In April, 1782, the unfortunate Comte de Grasse was defeated by Rodney, and he was made a prisoner and carried to England. In August, he was released, and Lord Shelburne availed himself of this opportunity and sent by de Grasse a secret message assuring Vergennes of his sincere desire for peace, and suggesting that the French despatch a special envoy to London. Accordingly, early in September, Rayneval was sent to confer with the English minister; but if Adams and Jay could have read his instructions and reports, they would have found in them no guilty secrets. There was, indeed, very little said about the United States. The instructions given Rayneval contained but one article on the subject, and in this it was stated that absolute and unconditional independence must be accorded to the colonists, while the envoy was to inform the English minister that it was the unalterable resolution of France to make peace only in connection with her allies. In the treaty between France and the United States it had been agreed that war should be continued until their independence was recognized. This demand and this alone, in behalf of the United States, France presented; this only was she bound by her treaty to obtain for her ally. All other questions that might arise were left for the English and the Americans to settle between themselves. On the other hand, the demands to be made in behalf of France and Spain were practically in the hands of the French. On these points Rayneval had full instructions; these and these alone he was sent to discuss; these and these alone he did discuss. The restoration of some of the West India islands to France, her rights in the Newfoundland fisheries, and advantages to be secured for her trade in the East Indies were matters he was to debate, while, on behalf of Spain, he was to insist upon acquisitions for her in the Gulf of Mexico, and the restoration of Gibraltar.[1]

The interviews between Shelburne and Rayneval were satisfactory; on both sides there was a desire for peace, and a readiness to agree on terms that should be just and honorable. The articles concerning France and Spain were debated at length and on most points with a reasonable prospect of agreement. Shelburne met the question of peace with France in a spirit far different from that which actuated Chatham at the close of the Seven Years' War, and he seems honestly to have desired unity of action between the two great powers in the affairs of Europe. " Let us change our mistaken principles," he said ; " let us act in accord, and we can furnish the law for the rest of Europe." [2]

Like a true disciple of Adam Smith, Shelburne was ready to consider propositions of commercial freedom that would have been regarded as ruinous by most Englishmen. "I regard a commercial monopoly," he said, " as an odious thing, and a device to which the English nation is especially inclined. . . . My ideas are exactly opposed to the catechism of the English merchants." [3]

The suspicion that Rayneval was sent to assert the claims of Spain on the Mississippi Valley, which also haunted Jay, proved to be entirely without foundation. Indeed, only once were the affairs of America

---

[1] Doniol, v, 104–105, 143.

[2] Conference of Sept. 18; Doniol, v, 128.

[3] Report, Nov. 11; Doniol, v, 128.

discussed at all, and then in a very cursory manner. Shelburne said that he anticipated much trouble with the Americans on the subject of the fisheries, and he hoped the French would not support their demands. But the cautious emissary replied in diplomatic language that doubtless the French King would desire the Americans to restrain their demands within the bounds of justice and reason. And when his own opinion was asked on the question of the fisheries, he said that he was not familiar with the subject. An inquiry on the subject of the western boundaries was no more successful: the envoy neither supported nor denied the American demands, although Shelburne declared that the pretended charts, on which they were based, were mere folly. Shelburne closed the interview by saying that the revolt in America was really the work of France; but Rayneval justly replied that the English should charge this lamentable result to the folly of their own ministers.[1]

The report of Rayneval convinced Vergennes that the English were ready to make peace on fair terms, while the interviews persuaded Shelburne that the requests of France and Spain would contain nothing on which an agreement could not be reached except, possibly, the demand for Gibraltar. " Gibraltar," said the English minister, "will be as formidable a rock in these negotiations as it is in the sea." [2]

Shelburne's inquiries as to the support France would give the American demands were apparently intended to gratify an idle curiosity, for the English had already practically decided to grant them. Possibly the English minister thought he could assume a more determined air with the American commissioners if the French

[1] Doniol, v, 133.   [2] Doniol, v, 126.

intimated any ill-will towards the attitude of their allies; but if he entertained any such purpose he got no encouragement, and the negotiations with the United States continued their placid course.

But Jay's suspicions of the Rayneval mission led him to a step which might be justly criticized. Convinced that Rayneval was occupied in evil devices, he himself sent an emissary to London, whose instructions could not have been made public without injury. He selected one Vaughan, whose commission was to suggest to Shelburne that now was the time for England to choose between France and the United States, and by granting the demands of America, to secure the future good-will of their country. It is hard to say what effect this message had on the English minister. Certainly if Vergennes had adopted a similar measure, he would be denounced as a false ally by every American writer.

Another incident led Jay and Adams to distrust Vergennes, and with somewhat better reason. One Marbois was secretary of the French legation at Philadelphia, and in March, 1782, he sent a letter to Vergennes criticizing the position taken by the Americans in reference to the fisheries, and suggesting that the French King should declare that their contention was ill founded and would receive no support from him. This letter was intercepted by the English, and they sent a translation of part of it to the American commissioners, with the laudable desire of exciting irritation between the allies.[1]

Assuming that the letter was correctly translated, which Franklin seemed to question, it was a stupid, injudicious, and unfriendly message, which showed that Marbois was a very poor man for his place. Apparently

[1] Wharton, v, 238.

the letter never reached Vergennes, and certainly the advice was not heeded; for the French King never intimated that he would not support the Americans in their demand for participation in the Newfoundland fisheries. The English minister, Vergennes wrote some months later, sent the American commissioners a letter from Marbois, "in order to make them suspicious of our attitude on the fisheries. . . . There is a brief reply to this; the opinion of the Sieur du Marbois is not that of the King and his Council, and Congress knows well that the steps indicated in that despatch were never taken." [1]

In view of all this, the American commissioners had to decide how far they would confer with Vergennes in their negotiations with England for peace. Their decision created much ill-feeling at the time, and is still a subject for complaint by French historical writers. Upon this point the instructions of Congress were specific: the commissioners were to undertake nothing without the knowledge of the French King, and were to govern themselves by his opinion and advice. But the commissioners were reluctant to comply with these instructions, specific as they were. Jay distrusted Vergennes and wished to proceed with the negotiations without conferring with him. If the French minister was hostile to the demands made in behalf of the United States, the less he knew about them the better; and if he should advise against pressing them, their position would become embarrassing. On the other hand, Franklin had confidence in the friendliness of their allies, and probably had still more confidence in his own ability to induce Vergennes to agree to whatever he recommended. The question was

[1] Doniol, v, 297.

settled by Adams, who arrived in October and at once cast his vote with Jay. Franklin acquiesced in the view of his associates without further debate, and the commissioners proceeded with the negotiations, asking Vergennes neither for assistance nor for counsel.

The importance of this action has been exaggerated both by those who approved and by those who condemned it. If the commissioners had obeyed their instructions, consulted regularly with Vergennes, and yielded entire respect to his opinions, the final treaty would have been the same. Doubtless, if the English had been obstinate in refusing any of the American demands, and there had been danger that the negotiations would fail, Vergennes would have been anxious that his allies should yield and peace be insured. But no such contingency arose; and considering the pacific mood of the English minister and the pacific character of the English negotiators, there was little danger of a breach. The conduct of the English would not have been different had full reports of the conferences been daily transmitted from Franklin's house in Passy to Vergennes's apartment in the Louvre. Nor would Vergennes have been so obtuse as to advise the Americans to yield what it was evident the English were ready to grant. No one knew better than he that such advice would not be followed, and that it would prejudice France with the country whose gratitude and whose trade he greatly desired to obtain.

On the other hand, there was no special reason why the French should have complained of the conduct of their American allies, nor did they complain very strenuously. As to any violation of the instructions of Congress, that was for the commissioners to settle with their own government. Jay said he would

break them as readily as his pipe, which he forthwith
proceeded to smash. In the outcome, while the action
of the Americans possibly interfered with some of the
aspirations of Spain, a country to which we were
bound neither by treaty nor by gratitude, it was indirectly of service to France, as the history of the
negotiations will disclose.

Vergennes had repeatedly said that the conditions
of peace between the English and the Americans
must be settled between them, and he had no concern
in the matter, except that none of the allies should
conclude a treaty until all had obtained satisfactory
terms.[1] He knew of the progress of the negotiations,
and if he was not informed of the details, he made no
complaint. The commissioners were daily conferring
in Paris, and it was easy for him to get whatever
information he desired as to their progress. Even to
his representative at Philadelphia he expressed his
discontent at the conduct of the American commissioners in very mild and guarded terms. He wrote, in
October, that Jay and Franklin preserved a strict
reserve, and suggested that Livingston, if he thought
proper, might write reminding them of their instructions; but he added, "you will be very careful not to
present this 'as a complaint, and ask Mr. Livingston
not in any way to reprove Mr. Franklin and Mr. Jay.
. . . It is enough that he will excite them to show us
the confidence which they have been directed to give."[2]
Nor, when terms had been agreed upon without consultation, did Vergennes manifest anything more than
a little not unnatural pique, except when, for a brief
period, he feared that this action might result in the
failure of his own negotiations, and prolong the war.

[1] Doniol, v, 86, and *passim*.   [2] Doniol, v, 139.

Vergennes repeatedly notified the English that he had no authority to treat with the United States, and it was agreed on all hands that the negotiations for each country should proceed separately. Doubtless, Vergennes expected that the American commissioners would confer with him as the matter progressed, but at no time did he show any desire to interfere in their negotiations. The statement he sent to La Luzerne was entirely correct. " If the American commissioners are exact in the reports they send, they will not complain that we seek to influence them or to hinder their negotiations. I receive what they see fit to tell me. They know 'that when needed, I would render them all the good offices in my power, but I do not put myself in the way of knowing more than they are disposed to disclose." [1]

Doubtless, Vergennes feared that some of the requests made by the Americans might be stubbornly refused by England, and hostilities be indefinitely continued for this reason. He had repeatedly sought to moderate the demands of his allies, not because he was hostile to their success, but because he feared they would be unsuccessful, and peace be postponed. He was far from realizing the willingness of the English to yield all that was asked, and he did not foresee the easy victory which awaited the American representatives. In the same letter to La Luzerne, he adds : " Despite all the cajoleries which the English ministers shower upon the Americans, I do not think they will be facile upon the fisheries nor upon the boundaries as the American commissioners understand them." And he foresaw yet more difficulty in the matter of the loyalists, whose claims, he said, the

[1] Doniol, v, 177.

English could not decently abandon and the Americans were resolved not to concede.[1]

Having determined to act without Vergennes's counsel, the American commissioners proceeded resolutely and successfully in their work. Practically all that the Americans asked, the English conceded, and naturally this facilitated the progress of the negotiations. There had been associated with the amiable Oswald a Mr. Strachey, who was supposed to be deeply versed in the matter of the fisheries. He was a man of little diplomatic experience and very moderate ability. It is strange that when the United States were represented by diplomats such as Franklin, Adams, and Jay, the interests of England should have been intrusted to men who were alike mediocre and obscure. But Shelburne wished for peace, and as apparently he was willing to grant whatever was asked, it made little difference what manner of men were chosen as negotiators.

The first question that arose was as to the fisheries, and Adams presented the American case with great ability, fully justifying the confidence placed in him by his New England constituents, to whom the question of the fisheries seemed of the highest importance. Jay was equally successful in the far more important question of the western boundaries, and the Mississippi Valley east of the river was ceded to the United States. Apparently the desire of Franklin for Canada was not shared by his associates. Probably it would not have been agreed to, and still it is possible that Canada might have been obtained, as Franklin suggested, by satisfying the demands made in behalf of the American Tories. At this price it would

[1] Doniol, v, 177.

have been as good an investment as the purchase of Louisiana.

The English commissioners yielded easily on the right of fishing and the western boundaries, but they were strenuous in their demands in behalf of the American loyalists. This was regarded as a point of honor, and on this Shelburne said they could not yield. Vergennes seems, also, to have felt that some satisfaction might properly be given the loyalists, though it is hard to see that it was any business of his. But Franklin was strenuous in his opposition, and at last the English yielded on this also. As a solace to their pride it was agreed that Congress should recommend legislation by the states for the restoration of the confiscated property of British subjects; but both sides knew that this meant nothing. On November 30, 1782, the articles were signed, with an agreement that they should not go into effect until peace was made between France and England.

Certainly it would have been courteous to notify Vergennes of the agreement before the American commissioners set their hands to it. The two nations had been allies in a great war, and the law, as well as good manners, forbade either partner making a secret bargain for his own advantage. But the breach was one of manners rather than of substance. It had been left to the American commissioners to make their own bargain with England, and they had done so. It would have been absurd for Vergennes to object to the terms that had been agreed upon, when they in no way affected the interests of France. If he had objected, he would have put himself in so false a position that the American commissioners would have signed without his approval, and the French minister made no blunders of that sort. He might, indeed, have asked them to withhold their signatures until the French had made terms with England, and they might properly have acceded to his request; but their agreement did provide that it should only become operative when France also had made peace. So far as the moral effect was concerned, it would have been the same whether the document was formally signed or was merely waiting for signature.

Franklin informed Vergennes that the articles had been signed, and that experienced diplomat evidently realized that if the Americans were new to diplomacy they understood the art of attending to their own interests. But he received the information calmly, and on December 4 he wrote Rayneval, who was then at London: "You did not suppose when you left us that the negotiations of the Americans were almost concluded. Yesterday I received a letter from Franklin announcing that everything was agreed upon and about to be signed. . . . The translation of the preliminaries which I enclose saves my entering on any detail. You will remark that the English buy a peace rather than make one. Their concessions on the boundaries, the fisheries and the loyalists, exceed all that I believed possible. . . . I said to Mr. Franklin that notwithstanding the provision that these articles should not take effect until peace was agreed upon between France and England, their signature was none the less premature."[1]

Vergennes also wrote La Luzerne, enclosing a copy of the preliminaries: "You, as well as I, will surely applaud the extensive advantages which our allies, the Americans, have obtained by the peace, but certainly

[1] Doniol, v, 188.

you will not be less surprised than I was at the action of the commissioners. According to the instructions of Congress, they were to do nothing without our participation. I informed you that the King would not seek to influence the negotiations, except so far as his good offices were necessary for his friends. The American commissioners will not say that I have sought to interfere, and still less that I have wearied them with my curiosity. They held themselves carefully aloof from me. . . . You can judge of my surprise when on November 30 Mr. Franklin informed me that the articles were signed. The reservation made in regard to us does not prevent this being an infraction of the promise to sign jointly. I owe Mr. Franklin the justice to say that he sent a copy of the articles on the next day. He will not complain because I received them without any demonstrations of sensibility. It was not until he came to see me a few days later that I showed him how hastening their signatures was not an obliging proceeding towards the King. He appeared to see this and excused himself and his colleagues as best he could. Our conversation was amicable. . . . I accuse no one; I do not blame even Mr. Franklin. He yielded perhaps too easily to the impulses of his colleagues, who affect to ignore the rules of courtesy. . . . If we can judge the future by what we have just seen, we shall be poorly repaid for what we have done for the United States of America." [1]

Though Adams and Jay regarded France as a poor friend, Congress still turned to that country for the money which could not be obtained at home. Upon Franklin the duty of making requests for money was always imposed, and certainly no one else could have

[1] Doniol, v, 192.

been so successful in obtaining it. "Dr. Franklin," so Adams wrote, " who has been pliant and submissive in everything, has been constantly cried up to the stars, without doing anything to deserve it." Only the extraordinary combination of tact, courtesy, and social charm which Franklin possessed could have procured, year after year, from a bankrupt treasury, the money necessary for the success of the American cause. If Adams had been our minister at Paris, France would probably have left us to our fate long before Yorktown was captured.

And now, by an unhappy combination, hardly had Franklin performed the disagreeable duty of notifying Vergennes that the American commissioners had signed articles of peace without the coöperation of France, than he was required to follow this errand with a request for more money. The necessity of obtaining financial aid from France and the frequency of the calls might properly have modified the severity of Adams and Jay towards our ally. It is not altogether in place to assume the dignity of a hidalgo towards a man from whom you have just borrowed five dollars, and of whom you are about to ask ten more. The applicant who receives a loan with a haughty expression and refuses to degrade himself by saying thank you, may save his face, in Chinese phraseology, but after all his attitude is not heroic. Such was never the position which Franklin assumed. He asked many favors from the French, but he always insisted that it was both good policy and good manners to be thankful for them.

On November 30, Franklin notified Vergennes of the signature of the articles. A very few days later the doctor again visited the minister and asked him to lend

the states twenty million francs. Certainly it was an
unfortunate time for such a request. Even the mildest
of men, when still smarting from a snub, does not receive with enthusiasm a request for a loan, and this
demand came when it seemed that the snub might do
serious injury. When the Americans signed the articles with England, though Vergennes was annoyed,
he evidently regarded their act as an offence against
manners rather than a serious political blow. But at
that time the terms of peace between England, France,
and Spain seemed to be agreed upon by the apparent
willingness of England to restore Gibraltar. Now the
English said they would not surrender Gibraltar, and
the Spanish said they would make no peace unless it
was restored to them; as a result there seemed a possibility of the continuance of the war, and Vergennes
naturally attributed the change in the English position
to the fact that they had agreed with the United
States and regarded that country as practically off
their hands.

Another incident increased the irritation of the
French minister. Franklin told him that he was about
to send the preliminaries to the United States in a
ship under English safe conduct. This was natural
enough, but Vergennes was alarmed at the condition of
negotiations in London, and feared that when Congress
and the American people found that terms satisfactory
to them had been agreed upon, they would drop out
of the contest, and France might be left to carry on
the war with only Spain as an ally. And now on top
of all this, came a request for a further loan of twenty
million francs!

On December 15 Vergennes sent Franklin a note
expressed with unusual acerbity. "I am embarrassed,"

he wrote, " to explain your conduct and that of your associates. . . . You agreed on preliminaries without conferring with us, though Congress instructed you to take no step without the participation of the King. You are going to excite in America the belief that peace is assured, without even informing yourself what progress we are making in our negotiations. You are wise and discreet, you know what is fitting, you have performed your duty all your life ; do you think you satisfy the obligations which bind you to the King? . . . When you can solve my doubts on this subject, I will ask his Majesty to satisfy your demands." [1]

Such a letter would have discouraged most applicants for money, but nothing discouraged Franklin. He at once presented his apologies in the best form in which they could be put. "Nothing," he wrote, " has been agreed in the preliminaries contrary to the interests of France, and no peace is to take place between us and England until you have concluded yours. Your observation is, however, apparently just, that, in not consulting you before they were signed, we have been guilty of neglecting a point of *bienséance*. But, as this was not from want of respect for the King, whom we all love and honor, we hope it will be excused, and that the great work, which has hitherto been so happily conducted, is so nearly brought to perfection, and is so glorious to his reign, will not be ruined by a single indiscretion of ours. And certainly the whole edifice sinks to the ground immediately, if you refuse on that account to give us any further assistance." [2]

[1] Doniol, v, 191.

[2] Franklin to Vergennes, Dec. 17, 1782; *Writings of Franklin*, Smyth's ed., viii, 642.

It illustrates the uniform generosity shown by France to her American allies that, notwithstanding Vergennes's temporary irritation, he soon acceded to Franklin's request for more money. "I will add nothing," he wrote La Luzerne, after referring to this action of the American commissioners, "in respect to the demand for money which has been made upon us. You can judge if conduct like this encourages us to new demonstrations of liberality." But he did not execute the threat which he made in his irritation. The United States needed money, as they always did, and Vergennes was ready to assist them, as he always was. To furnish the entire amount of twenty millions was indeed impossible. The French treasury was in sore need, and Vergennes could truthfully have said that her own financial distress left France in no condition to be generous. But if the King did not supply the twenty millions, he did what he could, and lent the United States six millions at five per cent, when he was himself paying seven per cent on borrowed money.

Such proof of honest friendship cannot be overthrown by the jealous suspicions of Adams or the unfounded apprehensions of Jay. "I pressed hard, therefore," said the indefatigable Franklin, "for the whole sum demanded, but was told it was impossible, the great efforts to be made . . . and the enormous expense engaged in, having much embarrassed the finances."[1] And he adds the just reflection: "Our people certainly ought to do more for themselves. It is absurd, this pretending to be lovers of liberty while they grudge paying for the defence of it."

Similar complaints are often found in Washington's

[1] Franklin to Morris, Dec. 23, 1782; Wharton, vi, 159.

and Franklin's correspondence, and they suggest some reflections on American character and patriotism as they were displayed at the time of the Revolution and in the Civil War of the following century. Certainly it does not reflect unfavorably on the men of the Revolution if we find progress in succeeding generations. It would be a poor commentary on the liberty they established and the government they founded, unless their fruits were shown, not merely in growth of population and increase of wealth, but in the development of national and individual character. The patriotism and devotion displayed by many in the Revolution must not blind us to the fact that many others showed little desire to devote themselves, and still less willingness to devote their money, to their country's cause.

It was the remissness of the states in furnishing money, as well as the difficulty in raising troops, which rendered the aid of France so indispensable to success. Doubtless there were many reasons which explained in part the scanty pecuniary assistance which the people of the thirteen states were willing to give to the cause of their independence.

The inability of Congress to impose taxes aggravated the situation ; a strong central government could have adopted some system of taxation, and to this most would have submitted, peacefully if not cheerfully. The states themselves, if their legislators and their people had been actuated by a generous patriotism, could have done much to remedy the condition. But not only was each state unwilling to contribute more than its share ; few showed any strong desire to contribute even so much. Undoubtedly, a large part of the population were not eager for separation from England, and if they acquiesced in the revolutionary movement, it was more from the fear of offending others than from any zeal in the cause. Naturally they did as little as they could without incurring the ill-will of their neighbors, and those most indifferent to the success of the revolutionary cause were found largely among the prosperous members of the community. The well-to-do are rarely eager for radical political change, and many were bound by religious, pecuniary, and social ties to the old country.

It is sometimes said that the poverty of the colonists rendered it impossible for them to raise the funds necessary to carry on the war, but this apology does not seem well founded. The financial needs of the Revolution were insignificant when compared with the wars of to-day. The English had no more than thirty thousand soldiers in America at any one time. It did not require a great army to contend successfully with such a force, and the colonists, though their wealth was insignificant compared with our present standards, were a prosperous and not a poor people. Issuing paper money that soon depreciated was an act of folly that brought ruin to many honest people and aggravated the difficulties of the situation. But to some extent Congress was driven to this measure because it was impossible to raise money in any way except by the printing-press; and while paper money brought ruin to some, it furnished to others an opportunity for the rapid accumulation of wealth. The prosperity which had prevailed in America prior to the Revolution did not entirely vanish after the war began. On the other hand, there were displays of wealth and luxury which had formerly been infrequent.

It is impossible not to contrast the niggardliness shown, not by all, but by a considerable proportion of the population, with the extraordinary liberality with which the entire community met the calls of the government when our national existence was in peril during the Civil War. There are abundant explanations of the contrast, and an undue reverence for the past should not lead us to overlook them. It would be sad, indeed, if a century of liberty and prosperity had not developed a broader and deeper patriotism. At the time of the Revolution there was no country with great traditions to which patriotism could strongly cling ; the new Confederacy was an experiment, whose workings at the beginning were far from satisfactory. The United States of 1861 had a stronger hold on the love of its citizens than the Confederacy of 1776.

Moreover, the traditions of American life during two generations, the activity of business, the opportunities for the rapid accumulation of wealth, had fostered the willingness, which is so strong an element in American character, to spend money without limit, when the end is worthy of the expenditure. No people has acquired wealth with such success, no people expends it with such readiness. The energy with which Americans accumulate money has led to the erroneous belief that they are, above other peoples, worshippers of the almighty dollar. The worshipper of the dollar is the man who will not spend it for a good cause, and no people deserve so little to be reproached for that offence. Our ancestors had not yet developed that liberality of expenditure which is now an element of American character. They had not learned that the value of money consists in the ability to do something with it. But if these qualities were not largely developed in the thirteen colonies in 1775, they can claim the glory of founding a nation whose people have shown their willingness to give their money freely for a good cause and to sacrifice their lives to save the republic.

CHAPTER XXVI

CONCLUSION

It is now time to trace the history of the negotiations between France, Spain, and England, and see the effect produced on them by the agreement made between England and the United States. If the signature of preliminaries by the American commissioners had any influence on the treaty finally made by England with France and Spain, it is impossible to see where it worked any injury to French interests.

The visits of Rayneval to London, which Jay viewed with such distrust, had, as we have seen, nothing to do with questions affecting the United States. His only mission was to ascertain if the English were ready to grant France and Spain terms that would be fairly satisfactory to these countries. As soon as the French were satisfied that Shelburne in good faith desired peace and was willing to agree to reasonable conditions, the negotiations took formal shape. While the American commissioners remained at Paris, the questions affecting France and Spain were for the most part considered at London.

So far as France was concerned, terms were agreed upon with the utmost ease. The French were singularly modest in their demands; they had begun the war to assist the United States, and they asked little for themselves at its close. Fitzherbert, the English commissioner at Paris, and Vergennes soon reached an agreement, and there was little need of applying to the ministers at London for instructions.

On one question, not of large importance except as it affected the national dignity, Vergennes was inexorable. The Treaty of Paris in 1763 contained a provision that the fortifications of Dunkirk should be destroyed. This provision was a constant irritation to France, and was not without its effect in making the French people eager for a new war with England whenever opportunity offered. At the beginning of the negotiations it was now suggested that all clauses in former treaties relating to Dunkirk should be abrogated, and to that proposal Shelburne offered no objection except that he hoped France would not exercise the right of restoring the fortifications of Dunkirk, as English pride would not suffer " a pistol to be pointed at the mouth of the Thames." [1]

The matter was of small practical importance, but the French felt their honor was involved in the abolition of a humiliating condition. England was in no position to insist on it at the end of a disastrous war, and it was therefore agreed that in the future France might fortify and reëstablish the Port of Dunkirk as she saw fit.

In India, where the French might fairly have claimed large advantages, they obtained little save some unimportant acquisitions in territory and some slight ameliorations in trade conditions. The rights of the French to fish in Newfoundland were left substantially as they had been fixed by the Treaty of Utrecht seventy years before. In the West Indies the islands captured by either party were restored.

France secured the independence of her American

[1] Fitzmaurice, *Life of Shelburne*, iii, 260; Doniol, v, 144.

allies, but the material advantages she obtained were
small recompense for a war which had cost her seven
hundred and seventy-two millions.

In 1783, as in 1763, her embarrassment grew
chiefly out of the demands made by her Spanish ally.
Few political combinations were more extolled, and
with less reason, than the family alliances of the
Bourbon kings. What everybody believes to be a
source of strength is not infrequently a source of
weakness, and of this truth in politics there is no
better illustration than the relations between France
and Spain in the eighteenth century. For centuries
before, the nations had been on terms of chronic
hostility. Frequent intermarriages had not checked
national animosities nor interfered with national ambitions. Louis XIV, having a Spanish woman for his
mother and another Spanish woman for his wife,
devoted himself with pertinacity and success to filch-
ing the possessions of Spain for the aggrandizement
of France. His policy was wise if not chivalric, and
France profited largely by these acquisitions, while
Spanish power continued the long decline which began under Philip II.

In an evil day Louis abandoned a national policy
for dynastic ambition : he resolved to place his grandson on the Spanish throne, and at once the European
nations banded themselves together to oppose this
action. The most sagacious statesmen saw in it grave
danger to the balance of power and the liberties of
Europe. William III declared that if a French prince
should reign at Madrid, England and Holland were
in great danger of total ruin. Louis himself believed
that with the elevation of his grandson to the Spanish
throne the Pyrenees would cease to exist. Both were

mistaken. At the end of a long contest a French prince was recognized as king of Spain, but the influence of France in Europe was less after the War of the Spanish Succession than before it. Nor was this merely the result of the long and disastrous conflict; closer relations between the two countries proved an element of weakness to France, the assistance she obtained from Spain was of little value, the Spanish ships were usually rotten, their soldiers were ill equipped and ill disciplined. The alliance between France and Spain was regarded by the latter as existing solely for the benefit of Spain; the Spanish would do little to assist France, they expected the French to do everything to assist Spain.

Three "Family Compacts" were signed by the Bourbon monarchs during the eighteenth century. As each was announced, statesmen grew pale and neighboring peoples anticipated calamity from the alliance of two great nations. But each of these compacts made France less dangerous to the rest of Europe, and procured little advantage for Spain.

In 1733 the Treaty of the Escurial, the first of the Family Compacts, was signed between Louis XV and Philip V. It resulted in the establishment of the Bourbons as kings of Naples, where they reigned for over a century and a quarter, to the infinite harm of their subjects, and established one of the most retrograde and corrupt of European monarchies.

In 1743, during the War of the Austrian Succession, a second Family Compact was entered into between Louis XV and Philip V. By it great possessions were to be obtained in Italy for the younger son of Philip, Gibraltar was to be captured from England, and the colony of Georgia was to be destroyed because it might be injurious to Florida. The endeavor to obtain for Spain what this treaty demanded prolonged the war for years, and cost France an infinite amount of blood and money. France won great victories during the war, but as a sagacious French minister said, her zeal for the welfare of Spain extended to the sacrifice of her own interests. "The Spanish alliance," he laments, "is like a ball attached to the leg of a criminal. If the Spanish would only desert us, we might keep our acquisitions for ourselves." All that France gained from the war was the recognition of a Spanish prince as Duke of Parma, where he and his posterity ruled for fifty years, without advantage to the people or glory to themselves, until the soldiers of the Revolution sent them adrift.

In 1761 the third family alliance was formed, and this was still in force when the American Revolution began. Like the treaties which preceded it, it was fraught with disaster to both parties. Spain was too infirm to be of any assistance to France, and her scattered possessions afforded rich plunder for the English during the Seven Years' War. When peace was made in 1763, the French King treated his Spanish relatives with a generosity that would have been admirable in a kinsman but was criminal in a ruler. Spain was forced to surrender to England Florida and her possessions in North America east of the Mississippi. As a compensation for this, France ceded to Spain the province of Louisiana, which included not only New Orleans and the mouth of the Mississippi, but a vague claim to territories which now contain more people and more wealth than the Kingdom of Spain.[1]

[1] See the author's *France under Louis XV*, i, 131–137, for an extended discussion of the effect upon France of her family relations with Spain.

The possible value of these possessions was realized by no one, but their ownership made Spain look with jealousy upon the growth of the English colonies in America, and no European nation was less inclined to assist the colonists in their struggle for independence. Most of the European powers regarded the question with entire indifference. A few desired the success of the colonists, not because it might help them, but because it would harm England. The English were not popular on the Continent; the growth and power of Great Britain excited the jealousies of less fortunate lands, and most of the European nations were quite willing that the United States should achieve their independence if they were able to do so. The feeling in Spain was different. No nation had so much reason to fear colonial revolts; if the English colonists were successful in throwing off the authority of the mother-land, this would be a dangerous example for Spanish colonies, which suffered from more unwise regulations than were ever devised by George III.

There were other reasons why the cause of American independence aroused no sympathy in Spain. Not only did French statesmen see in the American war an opportunity to injure England and extend the influence of France, but popular sentiment was strong in compelling intervention. The sympathy of French society and French philosophy for the American patriots, the enthusiasm for the young republic, which pervaded the nation, compelled the interference of France in their behalf and helped to make it successful. Of such feeling there was in Spain absolutely none. The teachings of French philosophers found no entrance into the kingdom of Philip II. The enthusiasm of

Parisian society for liberty and progress found no echo in the palaces of Madrid. There were no young Spanish noblemen eager to follow La Fayette and assist in securing the liberty of the young republic. The new wine of hope and progress which was making France drunk did not pass the Spanish frontier. When we compare the political beliefs and aspirations of the French under Louis XVI with those which found utterance under Louis XIV, we seem to have entered a new world. Doubtless the rule of Charles III, the best of the Spanish Bourbons, improved somewhat the condition of his country, but in religious or political or social beliefs and sympathies, it is hard to find any difference between Spain under Charles III and Spain under Philip II. Of the great literary activity in France there was no trace in Spain. There was no Encyclopædia, and no Social Contract; neither disciples of Voltaire nor disciples of Rousseau. The influence of French thought seems to have been absolutely null upon the subjects of Bourbon kings who lived beyond the Pyrenees. In this also it was shown how unimportant was the result of the great war which placed a French prince on a Spanish throne.

It was not, therefore, any interest in the cause of the thirteen colonies which led Spain to enter into the war against Great Britain. After the surrender of Burgoyne, Vergennes believed that the time had come to recognize American independence, and to promise the assistance of France. But the Spanish King was not ready for action, and was unwilling that France should take the decisive step. His counsels were disregarded, and in 1778 the treaty of alliance between France and the United States was signed. Though Vergennes had disregarded the advice of Charles III, he sought to induce him to accept the decision and assist in the war which was certain to ensue. His overtures were received with little favor. The Spanish King, so said Florida Blanca, his prime minister, was offended at the disregard with which France received his counsels. Regarding himself as the head of the Bourbon family, he was quick to resent any imaginary slight, and he now declared that he was treated like a viceroy of a French province, who must take up and lay down arms as he received orders.[1]

But apart from Spanish irresolution and Spanish pride, there were deeper reasons for his unwillingness to act, and in view of subsequent history, we can hardly complain of them. The founding of a republic in America was necessarily repugnant to an illiberal and unprogressive monarchy. Moreover, even Spanish pride could not wholly disregard the growing weakness of a fossilized government, and to that effete power the establishment of a new and vigorous republic in the West seemed fraught with peril. Timidity gave the Spanish rulers a more intelligent foresight than they usually displayed; their apprehension of the future position of the American Republic was more correct than Vergennes's prophecies. Undoubtedly Vergennes sought to minimize the dangers to be apprehended, in order to dispel the fears of a desired ally; but the United States has proved to Spain as dangerous an enemy as Charles III and his ministers feared. Its example influenced the colonies of Spain in South America to throw off her yoke, and in the last few years the American Republic by force of arms has stripped the ancient monarchy of all that was left of its colonial empire either in the Atlantic or the Pacific.

[1] Montmorin to Vergennes, Aug. 18, 1778; Doniol, iii, 545.

The apprehensions of the Spanish were therefore well justified. "They do not view without inquietude," writes the French ambassador, "the prosperity of the colonies, and fear they will prove to Spain an enemy far more dangerous than the English. They desire them to be so enfeebled by the war that they must accept the terms which Spain might dictate. These conditions would have kept them in anarchy, like Germany, and it is for this reason that the Spanish feel aggrieved towards us for treating with them." Repeatedly the French ambassador wrote that an entire lack of sympathy with the American cause was the obstacle he met in his efforts to induce Spain to join in the war against England.[1]

Vergennes sought to allay these fears by reflections on the probable future of the new republic, which do not disclose any prophetic ken. Will not England be a more formidable neighbor, he writes, "than the United States for a long time and probably forever; left to themselves, and subject to the inertia which is the essence of all democratic institutions, it would be a mistake to be apprehensive of their future prosperity. I fear, rather, the anarchy into which the states may fall, when they enjoy the sweets of peace. It is enough to consider the extent of territory they occupy, the differences in climate, in industry, in soil, . . . to understand that their union will never be perfect even if they are not actually divided."[2] "If we can believe Gérard," he writes again, "it will be a long time, even centuries off, before this republic will have sufficient consistency to take any part in foreign politics."[3]

---

[1] Montmorin to Vergennes; Doniol, iii, 20.

[2] Vergennes to Montmorin, April 3, 1778 ; Doniol, iii, 51.

[3] Same to Same, Oct. 30, 1778; Doniol, iii, 561.

Thus the French minister sought to allay Spanish apprehensions of the influence of the new republic, but Vergennes's arguments did not excite in the Spanish court any sympathy with the American colonists or any desire for their independence. Neither among Spanish politicians, nor in Spanish society, nor in Spanish literature, did the struggle of the American people for independence arouse any sympathy. Vergennes realized that the widespread enthusiasm for the insurgents which existed in France was not to be found in Spain, and therefore he appealed, not to sympathy, but to greed; not to any desire to help the Americans, but to the hope of gaining advantages for herself, as a means of inducing Spain to join in the war against England. Here he struck the only chord to which the Spanish court would respond, and by such means he at last brought Spain into the contest.

But we may wonder why a sagacious statesman should have thought it worth while to offer so great inducements in order to get such scanty assistance. He was not ignorant of the weakness of the Spanish navy, nor of the dilatory and inefficient manner in which Spain would furnish aid. He knew, or might have known, that she would be slack in supplying her quota, and only vigorous in demanding the advantages that had been promised. Her energy would be displayed, not in the prosecution of the war, but in the negotiations for peace. The French ambassador at Madrid truthfully described the hopeless and helpless condition of that effete monarchy. Her treasury was controlled by a minister who was true only to dishonest subordinates ; the Minister of War had neither industry nor credit ; in the navy one could trust neither officers nor soldiers. The magazines were poorly furnished and the navy yards were ill equipped.[1]

These gloomy pictures were verified when war was at last declared, and yet so strong was the glamour that clung about the Family Compact, that Vergennes thought it necessary to obtain the coöperation of Spain on almost any terms. He lived to see his mistake : the alliance with Spain was a detriment to the progress of the war, and her demands very nearly destroyed the possibility of making peace.

It was at first suggested that the Family Compact bound Spain to come to the assistance of France. By the terms of that compact, Spain was to furnish France with ships when she was attacked, but it could not justly be said that this provision now applied. France had not, indeed, declared war on England when she recognized the independence of the United States and by a secret treaty agreed to go to their aid, but she deliberately placed herself in a position that made war certain. When the first encounter took place, Vergennes tried to show that the English had been the aggressors, that the war was made upon France and not by her, so that she was entitled to aid under the express terms of the treaty. But the Spanish King had no thought of risking his fleet in response to the demands of the Family Compact, unless he was promised some reward for his efforts.

For months war between France and England was practically waging, and still the Spanish King sent neither arms nor fleets to assist his nephew of France. Instead of this, he assumed the rôle of arbitrator, and wished England and France to submit to his judgment the settlement of their differences. This proposed arbi-

[1] Report, Dec. 24, 1777 ; Doniol, iii, 35.

tration bade fair to put the French in a most embarrassing position. For them to decline the proffered mediation would be highly offensive, and might destroy any hope of retaining Spain as an ally if the endeavor for peace came to naught. Yet any suggestion of mediation would excite in America the suspicion that France was ready to abandon her ally, and such a fear would be increased by the knowledge that Spain was wholly indifferent to the fate of the thirteen states. In these negotiations Vergennes displayed that just regard for the obligations France had assumed which he always manifested down to the final treaty of peace. He said that the first and indispensable article in any treaty must be the absolute acknowledgment by England of the independence of the United States.[1]

But the Spanish King was not inclined to accept this as a basis for negotiations, and he suggested that instead of a recognition of American independence, there might be a long truce such as Spain had made with the United Netherlands in 1609. Such an expedient was sure to be unacceptable to the Americans, and Vergennes explained how different was their situation from that of the Dutch, who, two centuries before, had revolted against the authority of Spain. Charles brought the matter to a conclusion by notifying the English minister that he was ready to act as mediator upon the understanding that there should be an immediate suspension of arms, and that terms of peace should then be agreed upon at Madrid.

Vergennes was appalled at this announcement ; it

---

[1] Vergennes to Montmorin, May 1 and Oct. 17, 1778 ; Doniol, iii, 63, 523. " Bien entendu, que la reconnaisance de l'indépendance des États Unis sera la base de toute négociation." " L'entière indépendance politique et territoriale des États Unis en le premier article."

was not only that Spain declared with how little interest she viewed the interests of the colonies, — of this there had long been no concealment, — but either France must offend Charles by refusing to accede to such terms, or she must stand convicted of manifest bad faith. Such a truce would have left Rhode Island, New York, and many other places in the possession of England. " America will justly believe that she is abandoned by us," he wrote, " and believe that she is free from all obligations. I fear she will return to the leading strings of England." [1]

From this embarrassment the French were saved by the stubbornness of their opponents. George III refused to proceed, even on the terms suggested by the Spanish King. England, he replied, would accept Charles as a mediator, if France would first withdraw her fleet from America and cease furnishing aid to the American colonies.

Such an answer closed all efforts at mediation, and the Spanish now began to consider how large a bid for their assistance could be obtained from France. The peculiarities of the monarch, said his minister, rendered it important that the bid should be high. "It is necessary," he writes, " to calm the scruples of a conscience that is so delicate and so timid." [2] It could only be quieted, like many another delicate and timid conscience, by the prospect of large and substantial advantages. "To ask everything and grant nothing is their desire with us," wrote the French ambassador. Spain was playing with an eager suitor, and could safely practise the arts of a greedy mistress. " The King is no longer young," said his minister ; " he has been pious all his life and his scruples beset him." The

[1] Doniol, iii, 768.   [2] Doniol, iii, 643.

recollection of past defeats had made him timid; all
these things concurred to make him wish to avoid war.
" But," he added, " I know him: though devout, the
love of glory will affect him "; and therefore he asked
the French ambassador to put in writing the advantages that Spain would gain if she became the ally of
France. " In order to get Spain to declare herself,"
wrote Montmorin," we must agree not to make peace
until she has received Gibraltar, Florida, and Jamaica."

It was not precisely in this form that France made
her bid, but it was suggested that for Spain should be
procured Mobile and Pensacola, the expulsion of the
English from the Bay of Honduras, and the revocation
of their right to cut wood in the Bay of Campeachy,
and, lastly, the restitution of Gibraltar. The Spanish
meditated long on these propositions, and when they
appeared in the form of a proposed treaty, they had
gained in vigor and dimensions.

First and most clearly, was it declared that his Catholic Majesty should obtain by the future treaty of peace
the restoration of Gibraltar. The possession of the
famous fortress touched Spanish pride, and pride, more
than policy, controlled their councils. For seventy
years they had sought to recover this fortress, with
a tenacity of purpose that would be entitled to respect
if it had been accompanied by any display of ability
in the effort. But to wrest this impregnable rock from
England was an enterprise the hopelessness of which
soon became evident, and over the agreement so lightly
given to procure Gibraltar for Spain the negotiations
for peace at the end of the war nearly came to shipwreck. In addition to this Spain was to have, as fruits
of the victory, Mobile and all Florida; the English
were to be expelled from the Bay of Honduras, and

should no longer cut wood on the Bay of Campeachy. Last of all, the island of Minorca was also to be recovered for Spain.[1]

While the Spanish demanded more than Vergennes had offered, they would not agree to furnish the American colonies even the moderate assistance which the French minister had asked. His draft of the proposed treaty read : "The independence of the United States of North America being the basis of the engagements which his Majesty has contracted with them, the two powers agree that they will not lay down arms until this independence has been recognized by the English King." It was a very different condition to which the Spanish were willing to agree. After reciting this article as proposed by France, the treaty prepared by them proceeded to say that the Catholic King wished to please his nephew and procure for the United States the advantages they desired, but as he had as yet made no treaty with them, he reserved this question for the future. In other words, Spain would not promise any aid to the United States ; she would not wage war to insure their independence, and to that decision she religiously adhered.

Such was the treaty proposed by Spain. By its terms France assumed serious obligations, some of which she was finally unable to perform. She incurred the possibility of unpleasant complications growing out of the conflicting demands of her American allies and her Spanish allies ; having begun war to secure the independence of the United States, she involved herself in further obligations to continue it until Spanish ambition should be satisfied. And for all this she received nothing but promises of assistance,

<hr>

[1] Convention of April 12, 1779 ; Doniol, iii, 760.

the small value of which had been proven by the experience of half a century. But alliance with Spain was deemed the corner-stone of French policy; the French had a wholesome fear of the power of England on the seas, but with the aid of the Spanish navy they believed that victory could be assured. It was only a few years since the alliance of Spain in the Seven Years' War, instead of securing victory to the French, had resulted in more disastrous defeats than they had suffered when they were carrying on a naval war with England alone. But the teachings of experience are as little heeded by nations as by men. In the seventeenth century France grew great by the spoils of Spain. It might have been some consolation to a vindictive Spaniard that in the eighteenth century France exposed herself to constant defeat by allying herself with Spain. Spain was to France a valuable enemy and a costly friend.

In April, 1779, the convention between France and Spain, which had been the constant object of Vergennes's diplomacy for more than a year, was at last signed.[1] The terms of the treaty were kept secret, but the fact of the alliance was at once proclaimed. Though the United States had not gained a new ally, the English had another enemy, and the action of Spain excited much enthusiasm in America as well as in France. Washington hoped soon to have the pleasure of sending thanks to the King of Spain and the Two Sicilies, as the ally of the United States, but this hope was not realized.

It was not strange that the Spanish King was unwilling to bind himself to the American colonies, for nothing would have been more agreeable to him than

---

[1] Found in Doniol, iii, 803–810.

their return to their former allegiance. The arguments of Vergennes did not overcome the just apprehensions of the Spanish as to the outcome of the establishment of a free and independent government on American soil, whose political and religious traditions would be at variance with the principles of government dear to Spain, and would be fraught with danger to the vast possessions of that country in America. While Charles and his ministers did not venture to oppose the fixed resolution of France to secure independence for the American colonies, they were full of projects that might cripple the growth and power of the new republic.

The treaty made by France with America, so Florida Blanca declared, was worthy of Don Quixote; certainly his countrymen did not resemble that hero in their dealings with the thirteen colonies. Canada, they insisted, must be left to England, that the seeds of division and jealousy might remain between the United States and the mother country. The Americans, so Florida Blanca declared, were in sore need of France, and they must agree to such terms as France and Spain should dictate. Only thus, he continued, could the colonies be kept in a sort of dependence which would leave them in constant need of the assistance of the two crowns.

These ungenerous suggestions found no response from French diplomats. If Adams and Jay could have had access to the Spanish State Papers, they would have found in them no proofs of that jealousy of American growth which they erroneously attributed to Vergennes. Neither he nor his associates received with favor suggestions of that character. "I observe with some pain," writes the French ambassador at

Madrid, "that the Spanish are in singular dread of
the prosperity and progress of the Americans . . .
To me it appears that the danger which may some
day result from the prosperity of the United States is
very distant." [1]

However, it was almost certain that the independence of the United States would be acknowledged,
and the Spanish were ready to make terms with the
new republic if they could obtain much and give
little. These endeavors were not successful. Family
affection and political traditions induced the French
to accede to almost all that Spain demanded; but
while the colonists were eager to obtain a new ally,
they did not propose to check the future development
of their country. The Spanish desired Florida, and for
this the people of the United States had then no special longing, but the question of western boundaries
was more difficult. Louisiana was now the property
of Spain, the free navigation of the Mississippi was
contrary to the precepts of Spanish colonial government, and the extension of the American Republic
westward was abhorrent to Spanish prejudice.

The vast territories that were covered by the name
of Louisiana were not indeed growing in wealth and
population; they added little, if at all, to the resources of Spain; but the Spanish were jealous of
any interference with their possessions, even if these
were inhabited only by Indians and wild beasts; they
wished no boat to float down the Mississippi bearing

[1] Montmorin to Vergennes, Oct. 19, 1778; Doniol, iii, 558–559. "It
is plain that Spain regards the United States as soon to become her
enemy and . . . will spare nothing to keep them remote from her
possessions and especially from the Banks of the Mississippi"
(Doniol, iii, 576). "They wish to render access to their colonies forever
impossible to the Americans" (Doniol, iii, 585).

the American flag, even if the Spanish flag was rarely seen upon its waters.

But the extension of her western boundaries and the right to the navigation of the Mississippi were indispensable to the development of the United States, and no one was inclined to barter such advantages for the uncertain aid that could be expected from Spain. Little progress, therefore, was made towards a treaty between the two nations, and in truth the Spanish had no desire for such a treaty. They took part in the war, allured by the hope of important gains from England; they had no thought of assisting the American colonies; their troops and fleets they wished to use exclusively in quarters where Spain could gain advantages for herself. And they wished also to be free from any embarrassing alliance with the United States, so that when the time of peace-making came, they could endeavor to keep the English colonists as far removed as possible from their own possessions.

Feeble as was the Spanish rule, it extended over larger portions of North and South America than in the days of Charles V or Philip II. In addition to the South American territory, Mexico, Cuba, and large portions of the West Indies were still subject to the Spanish crown, and to these had been added Louisiana, with vague claims over the Valley of the Mississippi and the Pacific slope of North America. Spain's foreign empire was probably a source of weakness rather than of strength. Her rule bore so hardly upon the inhabitants of scattered lands and islands, that the home government could derive small profit from them; they were so rigorously excluded from dealing with other nations, that they could not increase in wealth, and there was little to be gained, even by the Spanish who held the monopoly of their trade.

But these vast possessions gratified national pride, and the thought of losing them was bitter. Moreover, if they did not add materially to the national wealth, they furnished an opportunity for many favored individuals to acquire riches. If the natives were overtaxed and the merchants so burdened by restrictions that they could make no profit, the viceroys, the governors, the host of lesser officials, often reaped gains as liberal as they were illegitimate. Many an impoverished nobleman replenished the family coffers as president or corregidor in Peru or Mexico or Cuba. Many a needy adventurer purchased official protection, and returned to Spain having accumulated in a few years more than he could gain in a lifetime in Madrid or Cordova. At all events, the Spanish regarded as of vast importance the preservation and extension of their foreign empire, though it was a curse to the subject peoples and of no real advantage to the governing state.

Such were the relations between France and Spain when the question of peace with England became a practical one. The demands made by France for herself were simple and were soon disposed of. She had begun the war largely influenced by a desire to weaken the power of England, and largely influenced also by a sincere sympathy for the colonists in their struggle for independence; there had been no expectation of reaping great advantages for herself. But she had bound herself to obtain much for her ally, and the bond was held by a creditor that would yield nothing from its terms. Some of the requests advanced by Spain were agreed to, but the demand for Gibraltar seemed, as Shelburne had prophesied, the rock upon which the negotiations might suffer shipwreck. For years the forces of France and Spain had been engaged in the siege of the fortress; the soldiers and ships which Spain promised the alliance had been used almost exclusively in the effort to capture Gibraltar for her own use.

There was now no hope of recovering the fortress except by negotiation, and the Spanish court declared that the restoration of Gibraltar was their ultimatum. To Spain the French were so bound by treaty and by family ties, that Vergennes felt that he must support this demand, even if it resulted in a continuation of the war. But to surrender Gibraltar by treaty, after the heroic defence of it by English soldiers and sailors, was sure to be in the highest degree unpopular, and the Cabinet was divided on the question. Shelburne apparently contemplated the possibility of granting the request if it were necessary for peace, but he insisted that England must have compensation in territory elsewhere.

The Spanish King proposed that the French cede Corsica to England; but devotion to the Family Compact had not prepared the French King to surrender this great island in order to buy a fortress for another country.[1] Shelburne then suggested, as a compromise, Guadeloupe and Dominica, or Martinique and Sainte-Lucie, and Vergennes felt that, if necessary, France, though at the end of a successful war, must sacrifice her own possessions in order to satisfy her ally. It was decided that the French would cede Dominica and Guadeloupe, if England would restore Gibraltar to Spain. " France will suffer a substantial

[1] Doniol, v, 210.

loss," said Vergennes, "but this consideration . . .
will not prevent the King from contributing a reasonable proportion towards the establishment of peace.
. . . He will make a sacrifice worthy of his magnanimity." [1]

Rayneval thought that the English had decided to
accept this proposition, but it is by no means certain
that they would have done so. The possessions to be
ceded by France were indeed valuable and important.
But, as Shelburne said, Gibraltar was dear to the
English nation, and it had been further endeared by
a heroic and successful defence. Even if an advantageous exchange had been offered, it is doubtful if
Shelburne would have faced the English Parliament
with the announcement that the Union Jack was no
longer to float over the rock of Gibraltar. At all
events, when Vergennes thought that peace was about
to be made with the surrender of the fortress as one
of its conditions, the news reached London that preliminary articles with the United States had actually
been signed. Whether this was the cause or the pretext, the proposed agreement as to Gibraltar was rejected. Five members of the Cabinet, so Shelburne
told Rayneval, now wished to break off negotiations
with France, and only by incredible effort, so he said,
did he check this newly excited enthusiasm for a continuation of the war. [2] If the question of Gibraltar
were to be further considered, Shelburne declared
that they must have more in exchange, and he now
suggested la Trinité or Sainte-Lucie. " See the result
of the secret signature by the Americans," says a
French historian, speaking of the relations between

[1] Fitzmaurice, *Life of Shelburne*, iii, 302–315 ; Doniol, v, 219.
[2] Doniol, v, 229.

our country and France. "It saved Gibraltar to England by allowing her to raise the price and making it impossible for us to reduce it. . . . Jay and John Adams unknowingly made a gift of Gibraltar to the enemy of their country. . . . And they prevented our paying the debt contracted to Spain." [1]

It is by no means certain that this is correct, or that the English would have brought themselves to the point of surrendering Gibraltar, no matter what they got in exchange; but if it were correct, the French had every reason to feel grateful to the American commissioners for their action. The possession of Gibraltar by Spain was of no advantage to France, and yet to obtain this for her ally France was asked to surrender valuable islands in the West Indies. Her obligation was a foolish one to assume, and she was fortunate to be relieved of it. If Jay and Adams saved Guadeloupe and Dominica for France, they did her a friendly turn, and certainly there was no reason that the Americans should have sacrificed anything to assist Spain. Spain had no claims on the United States; she had wished ill to the cause of American independence and had done nothing to further it; her policy had been selfish and she could not ask for generosity; there was no reason that the people of the United States should sacrifice one cod on the Newfoundland Banks or one acre of land in the Western Reserve to obtain Gibraltar for Spain. It was more fitting that this fortress should remain the possession of a power that was able to protect it, and certainly its ownership by England could do America no harm.

But no such considerations lessened Vergennes's

[1] Doniol, v, 230.

anxiety when Rayneval forwarded the last demand of the English Cabinet. It was manifest that the English were resolved to ask a price for Gibraltar to which the French could not agree, while on the other hand, the Spanish King kept himself aloof in sulky state, declaring that Spanish honor could accept no peace without Gibraltar. " I dropped my arms when I read your despatch," Vergennes wrote Rayneval; "Porto Rico, Sainte-Lucie, la Trinité, do they think we do not know the value and importance of those possessions? . . . The King desires peace, . . . but this desire is a virtue and not a weakness. They are mistaken in England if they believe it is only necessary to inflate their demands in order to obtain them. . . . If it is necessary to prolong the calamities of war, his Majesty will submit with resignation." [1]

The negotiations for peace could not be conducted with entire secrecy, and from every side came voices of disapproval. There was a party in France eager to continue the war, and still more eager to discredit Vergennes. They declaimed in all the antechambers of Versailles against a policy that at the end of a successful war would sacrifice valuable possessions — the fair islands of Guadeloupe and Dominica and la Trinité — in order to gratify Spanish pride.

There was also a strong party in England eager to continue the war and overthrow Shelburne, and they could make their sentiments known in Parliament and in the press. They declaimed against the ignominy of surrendering Gibraltar, which had been won and held by the expenditure of so much British blood, the possession of which was part of the heritage of British glory. ".There is a great deal of bitterness and a great

[1] Doniol, v, 234–235.

deal of indecency in the House of Commons," wrote Rayneval,[1] to whom, naturally, the usages of a free government and criticisms of the ministers of the crown seemed very insolent. Nor were the opponents of the proposition consoled by the islands that were to be received in exchange. Spain might compensate France for her generosity by ceding to her the Spanish portion of San Domingo, and then France, said the English merchants and planters, as the owner of San Domingo would furnish sugar to all the markets of the world.

So the French decided to continue the war, if England refused to cede Gibraltar, and Spain would not make peace without it. Such a decision showed the fidelity with which France kept her agreements with her allies, but it was not creditable to the wisdom of her rulers. If they had made an agreement which would involve the country in the evils of further warfare, for an object in which France had no interest, their only course was to break the agreement. Their highest duty was to their own country, they had no right to sacrifice the welfare of their people in an attempt to execute unwise compacts. Fortunately, they were saved the necessity of having to carry on a costly war, or to break a foolish bargain.

The English now proposed that Florida and Minorca should be ceded to Spain instead of Gibraltar. Vergennes submitted the proposition to the Spanish minister at Paris, expecting the usual response, that the surrender of Gibraltar was the ultimatum of Spain. To his amazement, he was told that the Spanish King would accept the offer. Even now it is difficult to see what led to this change of heart. Possibly the am-

[1] Rayneval to Vergennes, Dec. 4, 1782; Doniol, v, 251.

bassador's instructions bade him say that Spain would never abandon Gibraltar so long as there was a chance of getting it; but when he saw that this determination would result in a continuation of the war, he was to admit that he had used the expression in a diplomatic sense.

The decision was as grateful as it was unexpected. Vergennes was filled with joy that France had saved for herself the valuable islands which she had been ready to sacrifice in order to satisfy the demands of her ally. With Gibraltar still English, Shelburne believed he could present the treaty to Parliament without fear of disaster.

There was now no obstacle to an agreement, and in January, 1783, the preliminaries between France and Spain were signed. " It is with the sweetest satisfaction," writes Rayneval to Vergennes on January 20, " that after the trials of four months of negotiation, I inform you that the preliminaries of peace have been this day signed."

On September 3, 1783, the formal treaty of peace was signed by the representatives of the four nations which had been at war. In view of all that had gone before, the American commissioners, at Vergennes's request, executed a declaration that in signing the preliminary articles they had no object but to facilitate the progress of the negotiation, and that their act was in no wise to be regarded as an abandonment of their engagements with France. " We hope this treaty will dispel suspicion and show that the young republic places above all else fidelity and constancy in its engagements." [1]

---

[1] Doniol, v, 277. Jay was absent, but Franklin and Adams executed the paper.

I have endeavored to give some account of the aid furnished by France to our ancestors in the war for national existence. It is difficult to surmise what might have been, but apparently it would have been impossible to bring the war to a successful termination if France had not interfered in our behalf. Possibly, if the states had been forced to rely entirely on their own resources, assistance would have been given more freely to the general government, taxes would have been voted, money raised, troops enrolled, clothed and fed. But if the colonies unaided had done no more for themselves than they did when they had France as an ally, the Continental Army sooner or later would have disbanded. Resistance could only have been carried on by guerilla warfare, and inasmuch as a considerable proportion of the population were not zealous in the cause, it is doubtful if guerilla warfare could have been continued indefinitely.

At all events, the new nation owed a heavy debt of gratitude to France for assistance in the hour of need. The obligation was fully recognized, and a strong feeling of affection for our allies long prevailed in this country; it was sufficiently active to be an important factor in our politics when the French Revolution threatened to involve us in dangerous complications.

Yet the union between the two countries proved less durable and less important than was anticipated in the first fervor of their alliance. Gratitude does not often continue indefinitely as an active force, and untoward events hastened the chilling process which the years in due time would have produced. France as a republic was less agreeable to deal with than France under the old régime. However much our ancestors sympathized with efforts to establish political freedom, it was more difficult to agree with the citizens of the new republic than with the servants of an absolute king. The French Republic treated America with the same inattention to established usage that it showed towards European governments, and the antics of such representatives as Genet caused our ancestors to regard the Frenchman with a very chastened affection.

The Napoleons discarded many of the traditions of the old régime, and certainly they did not inherit its friendship for America. The first Napoleon, in his dealings with this country, showed his customary disregard for the rights of others; as a result of his arbitrary action, we found ourselves in war with England and narrowly escaped war with France. After the Napoleonic era France was regarded by the average American in the same light as any other nation; our relations were friendly but there was no pretence of effusive affection. Louis Napoleon increased the ill-feeling which his uncle had aroused. If Napoleon III could have had his way at the time of our Civil War, France would have done what she could to destroy the nation which she had helped to create. It is doubtful whether the Emperor in his intrigues represented the French people, whom he governed so poorly and injured so greatly. But as a result of the ill-feeling which his policy created, most Americans sympathized with Germany rather than with France when their final struggle came.

While the War of the Revolution decided the fate of the American colonies, it was only an incident in the long record of French warfare. France had the satisfaction of humiliating an ancient rival, but the expectation of materially weakening England's power was disappointed. England was as important a factor in European politics after the loss of her American colonies as she had been before.

The influence of the American alliance upon France was of a character that no one had anticipated. The power of England was not broken, France gained no monopoly of the trade with America and not even any important part in it; if the irritation caused by the disasters of the Seven Years' War was somewhat allayed by England's defeat, yet the position of France on the Continent was not materially strengthened by the American Revolution. The important effect was on the French people themselves: the success of the American colonists in establishing a free government had a great influence upon the French mind during the years before their own Revolution.

INDEX

INDEX

In this index, for convenience, the first commission sent to France, consisting of Deane, Franklin, and Lee, is indexed as "American Commissioners," and the Commission of 1782, as "Peace Commissioners." In the text, the action of the various governments concerned is sometimes attributed to the king, sometimes to the ministry, and sometimes to the country; therefore it will be well, for instance, in seeking references to the action of France on any subject, to consult entries under France, Louis XVI, French government, and Vergennes.

---

[1] Mr. Thomas Balch, in his work *The French in America*, gives Kalb's name thus : Henry-Jules-Alexandre von Robaii.

Reprisal, sloop-of-war, carries Franklin
to France, 131, 154 ; prizes taken by,
154 ; escapes English ship, 155 ; 157,
160.
Revolution, American, would it have
been successful without French aid ?
5, 7, 9, 10, 11, 522 ; and the French
Revolution, 11, 524.
Revolution, French, and the American
Revolution, 11, 524.
Richelieu, Duc de, and Beaumarchais's
accounts, 116.
Rivière, Mlle. de La, mother of La Fayette, 170.
Rivière, Marquis de La, La Fayette's
maternal grandfather, 170.
Rivington's Royal Gazette, prints intercepted letter from Washington, 323.
Robin, Abbé Claude, his *Nouveau Voyage*, quoted, 347, 365, 368, 394, 395,
434, 435, 436.
Robinson, Major, 409.
Rochambeau, Donatien-Marie-Joseph de
Vimeure, Vicomte de, in his father's
army, 303 ; sent to Paris with resolutions of Hartford Conference, 325, 326,
328 ; returns with reply of ministry,
329 ; 333, 340, 412.
Rochambeau, Jean-Baptiste-Donatien de
Vimeure, Comte de, on the proposed
invasion of England, 289 ; chosen
to command French troops in U. S.,
294, 295 ; his birth and history, 295,
296 ; secures increase of proposed
force, but sails with only 5000 men and
no horses, 300, 301 seqq. ; composition
of his army, 303, 304 ; his voyage, May
3 to July 11, 1780, 304–306 ; lands at
Newport, 306 ; decides against attack
on N. Y., 311, 315 ; his hope of reinforcements never fulfilled, 312 ; and
La Fayette, 312, 313 ; first interview
with Washington, at Hartford, 314
seqq. ; in quarters at Newport, 317 ;
hopeless of Spanish coöperation, 320 ;
and the intercepted letter of Washington, 323 ; his instructions, 329 ; con-
fers with Washington at Wethersfield,
Conn., 341 ; their views not altogether
in accord, 341 ; and Chastellux's letter, 343 ; his force joins Washington's
at White Plains, 346 ; at Frog's Neck,
350 ; correspondence with de Grasse as
to destination of fleet, 358 seqq. ; at
Phila., 368 ; starts south, 371 ; advances $20,000, 372 ; at Williamsburg,
375 ; his appeal to Barras, 383–386 ;
praises conduct of Americans at Yorktown, 392, 393, 405, 406 ; refuses to
accept surrender, 394 ; in winter-
quarters at Williamsburg, 402 ; had requested to be recalled in spring of 1781,
403 ; his request granted after the fall of
Yorktown, 403 ; arrested on civil process, 406 ; sails for France, Jan. 1783,
409 ; Washington's farewell letter to,
409, 410 ; sentenced to death during

the " Terror," but escaped, 410 ; his
death, 410 ; good conduct of French
troops in U. S. attributed to him, 421 ;
310, 316, 325, 330, 333, 345, 347, 348,
352, 376, 377, 378, 387, 389, 391, 400,
401, 407, 408, 420, 427, 448.
Rockingham, Charles Wentworth, Marquis of, succeeds Lord North, 468.
Rodney, Cæsar A., attorney-general of
U. S., 117.
Rodney, George B., Baron, admiral, at
N. Y., 316, 317 ; off Newport, 319 ; goes
to West Indies, 319 ; defeats de Grasse
at "The Saints," April, 1782, 397–400 ;
381, 476.
Roman names, fondness of Americans
for, 219.
Rousseau, Jean-Jacques, and his *Con-
trat Social*, 214 ; 217, 418.
Royal Deux-Ponts regiment, 303, 308,
344.
Russia, possible interference of, 43 ;
proffered mediation of, 455, 457, 458.

Sabbath, the, in New England, 438.
Sagittaire, man-of-war, 356.
Saint-Germain, Claude-Louis, Comte
de, minister of war, 55, 121, 337.
St. Jean-de-Luz, 183.
St. John's River, 275.
St. Lucia (Lucie), 273, 516, 517, 519.
Saint-Maime, Comte de, in Rocham-
beau's army, 303.
St. Malo, 288.
Saint-Simon, Claude-Anne Montbléru,
Marquis de, in command of troops on
de Grasse's fleet, 362, 375, 376, 388, 391.
St. Vincent, 273.
Saintonge regiment, 303, 308, 344.
" Saints, The " (Les Saintes), islands
near which Rodney defeated de
Grasse, 397–400.
San Domingo, d'Estaing governor of,
259 ; 357, 520.
Sandy Hook, depth of water on bar, 263
and note.
Saratoga, battle of, 230 ; decisive of
French intervention, 230, 231.
Sartine, Antoine-R-J-G-G. de, minister
of marine, 55, 121, 181, 301, 337.
Savannah, siege of, 10, 275–278.
Schuyler, Gen. Philip, 330.
Scientific research in the 18th century,
effect of, in France, 215, 216.
Secret Committee of Congress. See Committee of Foreign Correspondence.
Ségur, Philippe, Comte de, minister of
war, 337, 338, 340, 403, 404.
Ségur, Louis Philippe, Comte de, son of
above, his *Mémoires* quoted, 133, 173,
217, 316, 411, 412, 432, 433, 435 ; offers
his services to Deane, 173 ; balked by
ministry, 173 ; 337, 338, 417.
Seven Years' War, contrast between,
and the American Revolution, 4 ; an
almost unbroken record of defeat and
disgrace for France, 12 ; effect of, to